Middle English Literature

A HISTORICAL SOURCEBOOK

Matthew Boyd Goldie

Blackwell
Publishing

D0275905

© 2003 by Matthew Boyd Goldie

350 Main Street, Malden, MA 02148-5018, USA
108 Cowley Road, Oxford OX4 1JF, UK
550 Swanston Street, Carlton South, Melbourne, Victoria 3053, Australia
Kurfürstendamm 57, 10707 Berlin, Germany

First published 2003 by Blackwell Publishing Ltd

Library of Congress Cataloging-in-Publication Data has been applied for.

ISBN 0-631-23147-1 (hardback); ISBN 0-631-23148-X (paperback)

A catalogue record for this title is available from the British Library.

Set in 10/12.5pt Galliard
by Graphicraft Limited, Hong Kong
Printed and bound in the United Kingdom
by MPG Books Ltd, Bodmin, Cornwall

For further information on
Blackwell Publishing, visit our website:
http://www.blackwellpublishing.com

Contents

Literary Works and Related Topics

Table of Dates, 1325–1500

Historical events

1396	Richard II marries Isabelle of France.
1397	Revenge Parliament.
1398	Exile of Bolingbroke and Mowbray.
1399	Deposition of Richard II. Accession of Henry IV. Death of John of Gaunt.
1400–9	Welsh rising of Owain Glyndwr.
1401	Statute De heretico comburendo, One the burning of heretics.
1403	Henry IV marries Joan of Navarre.
1406	James I of Scotland taken prisoner.
1409	Publication of Arundel's Constitutions. Death of Isabelle of France.

Literature

1398	John Trevisa translates Batholomeus Anglicus' De proprietatibus rerum (On the Properties of Things).
1400	Death of Geoffrey Chaucer.
1400	John Gower, Chronica Tripartita. Alliterative Morte Arthure.
ca. 1400	John Mirk, Instructions for Parish Priests.
ca. 1400–10	Nicholas Love, Mirror of the Blessed Life of Jesus Christ.
ca. 1400–25	Dives and Pauper.
ca. 1400–25	Castle of Perseverance.
1401–21	Adam of Usk, Chronicon.
ca. 1405	Hengwrt and Ellesmere manuscripts of Canterbury Tales.
1405–10	Dives and Pauper.
1406	Thomas Hoccleve, La Male Regle.
1406–13	Edward, second duke of York, The Master of Game.
1407	William Thorpe examined before Archbishop Arundel.
1408	Death of John Gower.
ca. 1408	Lovell Lectionary.

Historical events		Literature	
ca. 1410	Lollard Disendowment Bill.	ca. 1410	Bodleian MS Digby 102 (political and other poems)
		ca. 1410	*Mum and the Sothsegger.*
		ca. 1410–15	Julian of Norwich, *Shewings.*
		ca. 1410–ca. 1420	*The Tale of Beryn.*
		ca. 1411	Thomas Hoccleve, *Regiment of Princes.*
1413	Death of Henry IV. Accession of Henry V. Richard's body reinterred in Westminster Abbey.	1412–20	John Lydgate, *Troy Book.*
1414–18	Council of Constance.		
1415	Battle of Agincourt.		
1415–40	Charles d'Orléans prisoner in England.	1416	John Lydgate, *Life of Our Lady.*
1417	End of Great Papal Schism.	1416–17	*Gesta Henrici Quinti.*
		ca. 1419–22	Thomas Hoccleve, *Series.*
1420	Treaty of Troyes: Henry V ruler of England and France, marries Catherine of Valois.	ca. 1420	Corpus Christi College manuscript of *Troilus and Criseyde.*
		ca. 1420	Translation of Catherine of Sienna's *Orchard of Syon.*
		ca. 1420	*Tretise of Miraclis Pleyinge.*
1422	Death of Henry V. Accession of Henry VI (9 months old).	1421–2	John Lydgate, *Siege of Thebes.*
		ca. 1423	Bedford Hours.
		1424–37	James I of Scotland, *The Kingis Quair.*
		1425–ca. 1500	Paston letters.
		1426	Death of Thomas Hoccleve.
1431	Burning of Joan of Arc.	1431–8	John Lydgate, *Fall of Princes.*
1436	Henry VI assumes full royal power.	1436, 1438	Margery Kempe, *Book.*

Historical events	Literature
1437 Death of Joan of Navarre. Death of Catherine of Valois. Henry VI assumes the throne.	
	1440 First English–Latin dictionary.
	1443-7 Osbern Bokenham, *Legends of Holy Women.*
1445 Henry VI marries Margaret of Anjou.	1448-9 John Metham, *Amoryus and Cleopes.*
1447 Death of Humphrey, Duke of Gloucester.	1449 Death of John Lydgate.
	1449-55 Reginald Pecock, *The Repressor of Overmuch Blaming of the Clergy.*
	ca. 1450–1500 Robert Henryson, *Fables, Testament of Cresseid.*
1453 Fall of Constantinople to the Turks. End of Hundred Years' War.	ca. 1450–1500 Wakefield pageants in Towneley cycle.
1455 Beginning of the Wars of the Roses.	
1461 Deposition of Henry VI. Accession of Edward IV.	ca. 1460 Findern manuscript
	ca. 1460 Inner Temple Library illuminations.
1464 Edward IV marries Elizabeth Woodville.	1463-77 Compilation of York Corpus Christi pageant.
	ca. 1465 Oxford, New College MS C.288.
1470 Deposition of Edward IV. Accession of Henry VI.	ca. 1465–70 *Wisdom, Mankind.*
	ca. 1468 N-Town plays.
1471 Deposition and murder of Henry VI. Accession of Edward IV.	1471 Death of Sir Thomas Malory.
	ca. 1475 *Floure and the Leafe, Assembly of Ladies.*
	ca. 1475 Manuscript of N-Town plays.
	1476 William Caxton introduces printing to England.
	1478 William Caxton first prints *Canterbury Tales, Parliament of Fowls.*
1479 Outbreak of pestilence.	
1481 War with Scotland.	

Historical events		Literature	
1482	Death of Margaret of Anjou.	1482	William Caxton prints *Troilus and Criseyde*.
1483	Death of Edward IV. Accession of Edward V. Deposition of Edward V. Accession of Richard III.	1483–4	William Caxton translates Geoffrey de la Tour-Landry's *Book of the Knight of La Tour-Landry*.
1485	Death of Richard III. Accession of Henry VII.	1485	William Caxton prints Sir Thomas Malory's *Morte Darthur*.
1486	Henry VII marries Elizabeth, daughter of Edward IV.		
1492	Christopher Columbus arrives in the West Indies. Death of Elizabeth Woodville.	ca. 1490	William Caxton translates "The Caxton Abstract of the Rule of St. Benet."
1495	Treaty of Drogheda.		
1497	Cabot arrives in North America.		
1498	Erasmus at Oxford.	1499	John Skelton, *Bowge of Court*.
		ca. 1500	Composition of Digby *Mary Magdalen* and *St. Paul*.

Plates

Acknowledgments

I would like to thank colleagues and other people, institutions, and students for helping me develop this collection. For hearing and promptly responding to my earlier ideas and then judging astutely along the way, as well as their encouragement, I would like to express gratitude to the National Endowment for the Humanities Seminar "Chaucer, Ancient and Modern" held at Pennsylvania State University, and particularly the organizer Robert R. Edwards, and Brian Gastle and Dan Kline. For his generous assistance and assurance, Steve Kruger also deserves warm thanks. Anne Hudson, Norman Tanner, and Derek Pearsall quickly and helpfully responded to my queries and requests. I am also grateful to have received assistance with the Latin texts from Jim Mulkin. Among institutions, Rider University very kindly provided me with support in the form of two Summer Research Fellowship and Reimbursement awards, assistance greatly appreciated. Also, the following libraries and their librarians, particularly rare book rooms and interlibrary loans, were invariably helpful treasure houses: Rider University Moore Library, Pennsylvania State University Pattee and Paterno libraries, University of Virginia's Alderman Library, Columbia University's Butler and Avery libraries, St. Mark's Library at the New York Theological Seminary, and the wonderful New York Public Library. Other professional and personal aid was always available from my colleagues at Rider, and Beverly Maximonis's secretarial support was as abundantly available as ever. Former and current students at Rider and elsewhere read many of the texts alongside the literature and raised questions in various thoughtful ways. Bob DeMaria first put me on to Blackwell, for which I am very grateful. Production staff and particularly the editor Andrew McNeillie at Blackwell Publishing were supportive and professional, making the process easy for all involved.

Finally, it is to PJ that I dedicate this book, whose confidence and patience and love saw me through the process.

The author and publishers gratefully acknowledge the following for permission to reproduce copyright material:

A/Y Memorandum Book. Records of Early English Drama: York. 2 vols., ed. and trans. Alexandra F. Johnston and Margaret Rogerson, Toronto: University of Toronto Press, 1979, reprinted by permission of Toronto University Press; Adam of Usk. *The Chronicle of Adam Usk, 1377–1421*, ed. and trans. C. Given-Wilson, Oxford: Clarendon Press, 1997, reprinted by permission of Oxford University Press; Bartholomeus Anglicus, *On the Properties of Things*, 3 vols., trans. John Trevisa, ed. M. C. Seymour, Oxford: Clarendon Press, 1975–88, reprinted by permission of Oxford University Press; *The Book of Vices and Virtues: A Fourteenth Century English Translation of the Somme le Roi of Lorens d'Orléans*, ed. W. Nelson Francis, Early English Text Society (EETS), o.s. 217, London: Oxford University Press, 1942, reprinted by permission of the Council of the Early English Text Society; *The Cloud of Unknowing and The Book of Privy Counselling*, ed. Phyllis Hodgson, EETS, o.s. 218, 1944, London: Oxford University Press, 1985, reprinted by permission of the Council of the Early English Text Society, *Dives and Pauper*, 2 parts, ed. Priscilla Heath Barnum, EETS, o.s. 275, 280, London: Oxford University Press, 1976, 1980, reprinted by permission of the Council of the Early English Text Society; Richard Fitzralph, "*Defensio curatorum.*" *Dialogus inter militem et clericum*, trans. John Trevisa, ed. Aaron Jenkins Perry, EETS, o.s. 167, London: Oxford University Press, 1925, reprinted by permission of the Council of the Early English Text Society; Geoffrey de la Tour Landry, *The Book of the Knight of the Tower*, trans. William Caxton, ed. M. Y. Offord, EETS, s.s. 2, London: Oxford University Press, 1971, reprinted by permission of the Council of the Early English Text Society; *Gesta Henrici Quinti (The Deeds of Henry the Fifth)*, ed. and trans. Frank Taylor and John S. Roskell, Oxford: Clarendon Press, 1975, reprinted by permission of Oxford University Press; *Heresy Trials in the Diocese of Norwich, 1428–31*, ed. Norman P. Tanner, Camden Society, 4th Series, 20, London: Royal Historical Society, 1977, reprinted by permission of the Royal Historical Society; Henry Knighton, *Knighton's Chronicle, 1337–1396*, ed. and trans. G. H. Martin, Oxford: Oxford University Press, 1995, reprinted by permission of Oxford University Press; *The Little Red Book of Bristol*, vol. 2, ed. Francis B. Bickley, Bristol: Council of the City and County of Bristol, 1900, reprinted by permission of the Bristol Record Office; "La Manere de la renonciacione del Roy Richard de sa corone et de la eleccione del Roy Henri le quatre puis le conqueste etc.," in

Chronicles of the Revolution, 1397–1400: The Reign of Richard II, ed. and trans. Chris Given-Wilson, Manchester: Manchester University Press, 1993, reprinted by permission of Chris Given-Wilson; Sir John Mandeville. *Mandeville's Travels*, ed. M. C. Seymour, Oxford: Clarendon Press, 1967, reprinted by permission of Oxford University Press; John Mirk, *Instructions for Parish Priests*, ed. Gillis Kristenson, Lund: Gleerup, 1974; *Paston Letters and Papers of the Fifteenth Century*, 2 vols., ed. Norman Davis, Oxford: Clarendon Press, 1971, reprinted by permission of Oxford University Press; *Rotuli Parliamentorum*, ed. J. Strachey et al., vol. 3, London, 1767, 415–53, in *Chronicles of the Revolution, 1397–1400: The Reign of Richard II*, ed. and trans. Chris Given-Wilson, Manchester: Manchester University Press, 1993, reprinted by permission of Chris Given-Wilson; William Thorpe, *Two Wycliffite Texts*, ed. Anne Hudson, EETS, o.s. 301, Oxford: Oxford University Press, 1993, reprinted by permission of the Council of the Early English Text Society; *A Tretise of Miraclis Pleyinge*, ed. Clifford Davidson, Kalamazoo, MI: Medieval Institute, 1993, reprinted by permission of the Board of the Medieval Institute; *Visitations of Religious Houses in the Diocese of Lincoln*, vol. 2: *Records of Visitations Held by William Alnwick, Bishop of Lincoln, 1436–1449*, Part 1, ed. A. Hamilton Thompson, London: Canterbury and York Society, 1919, reprinted by permission of the Lincoln Record Society and the Canterbury and York Society; Thomas Walsingham, *Annales Ricardi Secundi. Johannis de Trokelowe et Henrici de Blaneforde: Chronica et Annales*, ed. Henry Thomas Riley, London, 1866, 282, 286–7, in *Chronicles of the Revolution, 1397–1400: The Reign of Richard II*, ed. and trans. Chris Given-Wilson, Manchester: Manchester University Press, 1993, reprinted by permission of Chris Given-Wilson.

The publishers apologize for any errors or omissions in the above list and would be grateful to be notified of any corrections that should be incorporated in the next edition or reprint of this book.

N

Stirling
Dunfermline
Glasgow Edinburgh
Berwick-upon-Tweed
Holy Island
ARRAN
SCOTLAND
Bamborough
Otterburn Alnwick
CHEVIOT HILLS
NORTHUMBERLAND
HADRIAN'S WALL
Carlisle Durham
CUMBERLAND DURHAM
WESTMORLAND Mount
Grace Priory
Sheriff
ISLE OF MAN Boroughbridge Hutton Castle
York Bridlington
YORKSHIRE
Irish Sea Towton
Cawood Hull
LANCASHIRE
Sheffield
NOTTS LINCOLN
THE PEAK
CHESHIRE SHERWOOD Lincoln
Chester 'The FOREST
Gawain THE
Country' FENS
DERBY Nottingham
STAFFORD
Walsingham
SHROPSHIRE LEICESTER Bawdswell
King's Lynn
Shrewsbury Leicester RUTLAND Norwich
NORFOLK
WALES ENGLAND

CAMBRIDGE
Coventry Diss
WORCESTER Warwick HUNTS Bury St Edmunds
MALVERN HILLS WARWICK Cambridge SUFFOLK
HEREFORD NORTHAMPTON BEDFORD
HERTFORD ESSEX
GLOUCESTER OXFORD Harwich
BUCKINGHAM Ware
COTSWOLD Oxford CHILTERN HILLS Stratford-at-Bow
HILLS BERKS Windsor London
Bristol Greenwich
Bath WILTSHIRE Hampton Court Deptford Canterbury
SALISBURY SURREY NORTH DOWNS
PLAIN Amesbury KENT
Glastonbury Salisbury Stonehenge Winchester SUSSEX Dover
SOMERSET HAMPSHIRE SOUTH DOWNS
DEVON DORSET DOWNS NEW Southampton Hastings
Tintagel DORSET FOREST
DARTMOOR Exeter ISLE OF WIGHT
CORNWALL Plymouth
Dartmouth

0   50   100 miles
0   50   100 km

FRANCE

Introduction

This anthology makes available a selection of historical texts, cultural documents, and images in order to further readers' thinking about the works of Geoffrey Chaucer and other Middle English writers. Several of the historical writings have been regularly mentioned in literary and historical studies in the past, while some are less familiar – for instance, the *Anonimalle Chronicle*'s account of the 1381 revolt and Henry Knighton's description of the pestilence alongside Jean Froissart's description of a tournament Richard II held in 1390. The cultural documents are necessarily of many kinds, some again frequently noted in literary and historical criticism while others less so: parliamentary and local acts and trials, letters and testimonies, moral, homiletic, and educational tracts. The images are principally of manuscript pages and illuminations and, like the others, chosen for the student of Middle English literature.

These texts and images represent a cross-section of social, economic, political, ideational, and epistemological developments. The most important criterion for including a text or image is that it contain something, preferably several features, that shed light on the themes, ideas, and styles commonly found in Chaucer and other Middle English literature. This broad measure is nevertheless reasonably finite: rulers and their exploits, guilds, labor, sumptuary, censorship, marriage, gender, the fraternal orders – to name a few topics – are of particular interest to authors of this period. The second most important criterion is the sheer significance of a historical event or cultural factor. The usurpation of the throne in 1399 and the persecution of Lollards, for instance, are historically momentous and had noteworthy causes and lasting effects. Texts such as John Gower's *Confessio amantis* and William Langland's *Piers Plowman* acknowledge them explicitly, while they receive smaller or tangential references in others. The third measure for inclusion is the richness of the selection; that is, whether it is interesting in itself rather than merely in terms of some inert fact or idea that might simply be stated in summary form. The authors and artists who create these histories, cultural texts, and images appear actively engaged with the events and issues at hand, or are at least writing in a style or making an illumination that is complex enough to encourage comparison with more creative literature. In a few cases I have included more than one author's or artist's interpretations of a historical occurrence or cultural feature to allow readers to compare and contrast these interpretations themselves, as well as compare and contrast them with literary texts.

Even though today it seems we can only talk about more and less explicitly literary works rather than a clear distinction between literature and historical or other writing, I have pragmatically allowed current and hopefully up-coming literature textbooks – both anthologies and editions of individual authors – to shape my selection of documents to include here. That is, I rely on those publications to take care of literature, and I have tried to choose more explicitly historical and cultural texts. I have also been somewhat restrictive in my selections from among these usually less-consciously literary writings. Rather than simply aim to represent historical and cultural items from a primarily inert and generalized Middle Ages, this collection contains only fourteenth- and fifteenth-century texts and images that existed in England. The idea in limiting the selection to these two centuries and this country of origin or production is to introduce descriptions, arguments, narratives, and images that are often articulated in a temporally specific manner and in forms that correspond to or differ in interesting ways from contemporary poetry, prose, and drama. While the historical and cultural distinctions between England and the Continent were by no means clear, England of course claiming a good deal of France during the period, it was felt that sufficient translation, not only in the literal sense of "carrying across" but also of adaptation to the target audience – English readers and writers – made it possible to include only documents that existed in material form in England. My only regret is that because of the practical constraints of course offerings and literature textbooks produced, my selection is narrowly English and excludes substantial material on Ireland, Wales, and Scotland. Obviously, on a more practical level, the strictures of time period and country have also helped to limit the potential number of inclusions from approximately four hundred documents I considered.

The principal idea that informs the collection is that fourteenth- and fifteenth-century English literature may most fruitfully be read alongside less deliberately literary texts. The "textual environments," in Paul Strohm's useful phrase, of the poems, prose, and dramas are diverse but finite.[1] As even a cursory examination of the Chaucer or Middle English selections we most commonly read reveals, medieval literature demands that we look beyond the borders of its lyrics and narratives. It is messy, habitually pointing to forces and texts outside the enclosure of a whorling hypotactic opening "Whan . . ." and the declarative and conventionally terminating ". . . Amen." Readers of medieval literature may begin at the most material and seemingly concrete starting point, the physical page of a poem, prose work, or drama, but they quickly find that manuscript survival and versions, authorial anonymity and scribal preferences, intrusive glosses and expository illuminations, combine to multiply and connect such a beginning to a web of historical starting points beyond the single text. Moving off the vellum or paper, one is immediately struck by the openly allusive nature of Middle English literature. It may refer to itself, even to the act of authorial com-position, but it also loves to echo – often concurrently – a range of religious and secular, and Latin, French, and English discourses. In the process the works, passages, lines, even words, suggest historical and other events, both large scale and more mundane, forcing a binocular perspective on the historical level as much as on the practical, one eye on the line and another on the footnotes. A reader familiar with the literary work at hand and yet still wishing to avoid delving into historical and cultural contexts might resort to beginning his or her research from the other end, commencing with the most recent reception of a text. However, there again the critical responses thread together back into the past beyond medievalisms and John Dryden until one ends up examining fourteenth- and fifteenth-century responses; reception becomes an issue of near-contemporary influence, scribal recension, even authorially reworked texts and an author's anticipation of responses to his or her own works.

The student of Middle English literature has to love the mess yet try to find a way to enjoy such complexities while not losing focus, perhaps out of baffled exhaustion. Studying this conglomeration of materials is undoubtedly challenging and demands a range of skills that other periods do not always require. While the fundamental goal of this volume is utilitarian, it is hoped it will encourage more of an interdisciplinary approach, that is, thinking about how, on the one hand, historical and cultural items and, on the other, literary texts of various kinds register each other, correlate, and "quite." It is for the student of the literature who wants to rise to the challenge of considering him or herself a "literary historian," an appellation that compresses the potentially daunting idea that the specialities of literary and historical study are both possible nowadays despite the inadequate time institutions and society at large make available for such development. In fact, a trinity appears to characterize the goal of medieval studies today, of literary and historical abilities as well as theoretical sophistication. Literary theory offers not only the chance to reconsider one's assumptions but also expands the field of interpretation so that more and more thoughtful readings become possible. Indeed, theory has always been essential to medieval study, for instance leading to the inclusion of more texts in the medieval canon, not only texts by women but works of different genres such as nonfiction prose as well as writings that were formerly labeled as simply minor, derivative, or somehow not literary enough. Textual–literary study, historical examination, and theoretical abilities are three very powerful tools that one can see employed in ever more eloquent combinations in articles and books on medieval literature, making the Middle Ages an exciting period for those who like playing in a multiform and diachronic field that may be characterized by what the sciences currently call "complexity."

Students of medieval literature already have resources and training they can draw on to comprehend and think imaginatively about the materials in this volume, not the least of which is a tendency to read all phenomena, whether textual, cultural, or historical, with sensitivity. Cultural critic Stuart Hall is worth quoting at some length here because he suggests why we might already be at an advantage: "Meaning is a social production, a practice. The world has to be *made to mean*." A person looking at incidents in the past, for instance, consequently wants to ask

> which kinds of meaning get systematically and regularly constructed around particular events. Because meaning was not given but produced, it followed that different kinds of meaning could be ascribed to the same events. Thus, in order for one meaning to be regularly produced, it had to win a kind of credibility, legitimacy or taken-for-grantedness for itself. That involved marginalizing, down-grading or de-legitimating alternative constructions. Indeed, there were certain kinds of explanation which, given the power of and credibility required by the preferred range of meanings, were literally unthinkable and unsayable.

So questions might include:

> First, how did a dominant discourse warrant itself as *the* account, and sustain a limit, ban or proscription over alternative or competing definitions? Second, how did the institutions which were responsible for describing and explaining events of the world . . . succeed in maintaining a preferred or delimited range

of meanings in the dominant systems of communication? How was the active work of privileging or giving preference accomplished?[2]

Literary historians are well-suited to analyzing what might be characterized as the rhetorical aspects of historical writings and even images, the conventions, modes, and strategies writers and artists employ in representing events and why they might employ these devices. Such skills are also essential in examining what are essentially and invariably *interpretations* of historical events and cultural features in order to consider the diversity, "credibility," and "marginalizing" power of their representations.[3]

The final service the book is intended to provide is simply to make the documents, many of them key acts, laws, statements, and observations, available to readers. It is remarkable how difficult it remains for the student to put his or her hands on printed versions of texts such as the 1349 Ordinance of Laborers or Archbishop Arundel's anti-Wycliffite and anti-vernacular 1409 *Constitutions,* documents now frequently referred to even in the most condensed introduction to literary texts and historical periods. This situation continues to demand not only some fairly advanced research skills to track down and make sense of the documents, but also a comprehensive library collection with aggressive collecting begun at least in the nineteenth century. Readers will therefore perhaps find several of the documents familiar and now more readily available, while others will be new, but all will resonate with the literature in interesting and (hopefully) currently unimagined ways.

A very brief overview of fourteenth- and fifteenth-century historical writings, cultural texts, and art works should give some orientation to these materials. Historical writing during the period may be classified into two major types, the universal chronicle and the contemporary, local history.[4] The universal chronicle, more so than the other histories, expressly sought to encourage the reader to comprehend God's divine purpose and to learn, from examples from the past, how the virtuous are rewarded and the evil punished. More (what we might consider today) encyclopedic than historical in scope, universal chronicles usually begin with Creation and continue in linear chronological sequence up until the present, which points towards Judgment. They discuss many countries, rulers, and kinds of events, and the sources for these histories are usually documentary in form, frequently other earlier chroniclers. Developing alongside this more traditional type of universal history were records of contemporary and local events. These are new forms of historical writing in fourteenth- and fifteenth-century England. The intentions behind these focused histories tend to be more diverse:

almost in legal fashion to record events for future use, to provide news of current circumstances and incidents, and more explicitly to entertain. Rather than geographically and temporally large in scope, these histories treat only royal and other political happenings or provincially specific events the writer has observed or learned from during his lifetime (and from what we know, the writers were exclusively male). Sources are first-hand observation, local documents, and word-of-mouth. Although historical accuracy was not of principal concern to the universal or more localized chronicle writers, they both valued reliable and authoritative sources; they are willing to dispute claims, and overall they astutely judge sources that vary in their facts or interpretations of circumstances. An overarching change in the fourteenth and fifteenth centuries concerns the authors of both kinds of histories, who are overwhelmingly clerical at the start of the period but gradually change from religious clerics to secular clerics and finally to educated laymen as the decades progress. Correspondingly, chronicles come to be written not only in Latin and Anglo-Norman French, but also in English, along with increasing numbers of translations into the vernacular.

The diverse cultural documents of the period – the legal texts, religious discussions, and observations about the social and natural world – also seek to edify. They form a continuum from more explicitly purposeful and didactic texts at one end to descriptive and analytical reports at the other. The more purposeful documents may have the force of statutes, ordinances, or other laws, or are merely warnings or advice, but in this period a law could be more an expression of a wish that something be done rather than being enforced, while a less institutional articulation of a desire that people act in a certain manner may express already popular codes of thinking and behavior. The other cultural texts, which are more descriptive than overtly pedagogical, predominantly employ different rhetorical modes. They seek to engage their audiences with animated depictions of the contemporary world, making diverse phenomena immediate and relevant to their readers. Religious writers are responsible for the majority of both kinds of cultural text, but again throughout the centuries we increasingly hear the voices of the nobles or gentry and the new middle class, people such as the wealthy landowners the Pastons or William Caxton, whose first employment was apprenticing for the merchant guild in London.

The images may be classed under both kinds of documentary form, historical and cultural. Surviving art works from the fourteenth and fifteenth centuries include panel and wall paintings, stained glass, embroideries, and illuminations, as well as more everyday objects. While medieval art works are often described in the context of specifically art-historical developments, it is not so strange that all but one of the images included here is or was originally part of a book. Even the exception, the Wilton Diptych, is a hinged art work, made to be packed up and carried along with a royal household, which is more than can be said for the colossal Vernon manuscript. Medieval art of the fourteenth and fifteenth centuries, so often associated with books, offers a unique opportunity for another form of interdisciplinary work and with it, another set of issues. For instance, as Michael Camille has shown most forcefully, the literary historian needs to resist the tendency to see marginal borders and images as merely decorative or illustrative.[5] Art works can work alone or in combination with texts to, in Stuart Hall's words, "legitimate" the "social construction of meaning," certainly to develop it. What was Lord Lovell memorializing when he commissioned the particular image we see in the lectionary, an unusual donor image which accompanies a traditional collection of readings? What kinds of ideas is Richard II projecting in the Wilton Diptych? What impression of Chaucer's works do the various artists as well as scribes involved in producing his books have? How are these interpretations of Chaucer's works similar to and different from other contemporary responses such as Thomas Hoccleve's?

During this period, in areas and centers such as East Anglia, the Midlands, Essex, and London around St. Paul's Cathedral (which becomes dominant), as well as in households (administered by men and women), skilled lay workers made the majority of illuminated luxury books. At least two different craftspeople – writers and limners – worked in two distinct stages. A scribe might buy the parchment, rule the page layout, and copy the text. This "writer" or "stationer" might then pass the book on to the limner, who would then outline or sketch images in graphite, then gild, paint, and finally edge the figures and the jagged borders of gold leaf. In this illumination stage, this "lightening" of pages, the limner employed colored ink line drawing, painting with dark and bright colors, and the pressing on and burnishing of gold leaf. Unlike less lavish books, illuminated texts were luxury items and therefore, as with much poetry produced for England's courts and wealthy landowners, such cultural products need to be considered in light of their restricted audiences. Lay owners of illuminated manuscripts in the fourteenth and fifteenth centuries far outnumbered religious buyers. Such books were kept within the owner's manor, household, college, or chapel, to remain out in some suitable place for looking at and reading. In terms of changes throughout the period, Lucy Sandler notes that of the 158 surviving illuminated books she examined that were produced between 1285 and 1385, none was in English, whereas in Kathleen

Scott's very useful study of the following century, 1390–1490, these figures are very different. Of 140 surviving illuminated books from the later period, 11 are in French, 88 in Latin, and 54 in English.[6]

The documents in this collection are grouped together into six thematic chapters (seven including the images), as the table of contents makes clear. Although the chapters overlap in important ways, they represent perhaps a more preferable form of organizing the selections than "hap or fortune," or simple chronological order, especially because the texts are roughly contemporary with each other. I chose these six categories because they seem to correspond to six general current topics in literary criticism on Chaucer and Middle English literature. Where a selection seems to the reader to belong in another place, I simply beg for the understanding that I too considered where to put it. The one outstanding example is the literature of the revolt, which I choose to include in Labor and Capital rather than Force and Order because it corresponds more closely to other selections in that category than texts elsewhere, an indication of its principally economic causes. Each individual selection's descriptive title is designed to help direct readers to desired subject matter. Cross-references throughout the volume, plus the index, should also assist in finding requisite texts. On page viii and following I have provided a list that suggestively keys selected literary works to the documents contained within this anthology, based on critical discussions of the literary works and with the understanding that other possibilities for literary-historical analysis exist. On page xvi I have also included a chronology of historical and literary events side by side to encourage thinking about the moments texts were composed or circulated.

Within each chapter, concise introductions to the selections place them, where possible, in historical, authorial, and manuscript contexts. These introductions also provide brief select bibliographies of other related medieval works and the most helpful and important secondary studies, which are oriented more towards historical studies than literary ones, again to help the student of Middle English literature who might be less familiar with the historical material. Anyone wishing to pursue further study should keep in mind that the introductions and notes to the editions of the texts are often the best places to start. At the risk of redundancy, some bibliographical works are listed in more than one introduction because they contain material that seems especially valuable to more than one topic. I have included the manuscript or book date (where known) of each selection also to encourage the reader to consider the period of a text's circulation. English dialects are noted also in order to indicate each document's geographic area of origin. I have provided a glossary at the back of the book for commonly occurring words. Glossarial notes within the texts provide the meaning for the first occurrence of less common words. The select bibliography at the back of the book will also help direct the student of medieval English literature. The appendix of currency and measures explains the medieval systems and their terminologies, and provides metric conversions. It also includes (despite the care with which they must be treated) tables of sample incomes and prices from the period.

The idea for this collection has evolved out of my own and many others' experiences teaching Chaucer and late-medieval English literature, where instructors have wanted to couple each of the literary selections with one or more primary historical documents. While readers may immediately think of Robert Miller's *Chaucer: Sources and Backgrounds*, Miller's book, like the more comprehensive *Sources and Analogues of Chaucer's Canterbury Tales* and other collections of "sources," is almost entirely literary in focus, containing what medieval readers understood as fables and "worldy enditynges," stories and poems that Chaucer drew on directly for his writings. More strictly historical anthologies of primary documents that exist invariably cover a wide range of periods and primarily continental items, and they are designed as general introductions to medieval history. Still others are out of print or too unwieldy despite the extremely useful role they play in making frequently out-of-the-way selections available to a wider public, the *English Historical Documents* volumes in particular; these I have listed also in the bibliography at the back of the book. Edith Rickert's *Chaucer's World* is an early precedent to this volume, a remarkable work (in a career of remarkable achievements) that demonstrates great foresight in providing what Rickert's posthumous editors called "a mosaic of fourteenth-century life."[7] My focus has been perhaps to pick only certain colors in a mosaic that speak most directly to current critical interests, a perspective that has benefited from Rickert's and others' painstaking identification of prominent themes that are common to historical and literary texts.

Editorial Practice

The original documents exist in Latin, French, and a variety of Middle English dialects. Where a Middle English text or translation from the period exists, I have chosen it. Some of the remaining documents are newly translated, some are twentieth-century translations, and some older translations, depending on the quality of available texts. Manuscript variants are not noted. Previous editors' and my alterations to editions are indicated in

square brackets. Readers should refer to the original editions for variants
and other apparatus. Abbreviations and contractions are silently expanded.
The thorn character is transcribed as *th*, the yogh character as *g*, *gh*, *w*, *y*, or
z as appropriate. The consonantal *i* is transcribed as *j*, but the *i/y* variation
remains; *u/v* are normalized according to modern practices; initial *ff* appears
as *f* or *F*. Capitalization, word division, punctuation, paragraphing, numerals,
dates, and currencies are modernized as appropriate.

Notes

1 Paul Strohm, *Hochon's Arrow: The Social Imagination of Fourteenth-century Texts*
(Princeton, NJ: Princeton University Press, 1992), 3–9.
2 Stuart Hall, "The Rediscovery of 'Ideology': Return of the Repressed in Media
Studies," in *Culture, Society, and the Media*, ed. M. Gurevitch et al. (New York:
Routledge, 1982), 67–8.
3 Further discussion of what Early Modern scholar Louis Montrose calls "the
textuality of history" may be found in New Historicist writings such as those
contained in *The New Historicism*, ed. H. Aram Veeser (New York: Routledge,
1989).
4 This distinction and other ideas in this section are primarily based on observations
made in Antonia Gransden, *Historical Writing in England*, vol. 2: *c. 1307 to the
Early Sixteenth Century* (London: Routledge, 1982) and John Taylor, *English
Historical Literature in the Fourteenth Century* (Oxford: Clarendon Press, 1987).
5 Michael Camille, *Image on the Edge: The Margins of Medieval Art* (Cambridge,
MA: Harvard University Press, 1992).
6 Lucy Sandler, Introduction, *Gothic Manuscripts, 1285–1385*, A Survey of Manuscripts Illuminated in the British Isles 5 (London: Harvey Miller, 1986); Kathleen
Scott, Introduction, *Later Gothic Manuscripts, 1390–1490*, A Survey of Manuscripts
Illuminated in the British Isles 6 (London: Harvey Miller, 1996).
7 *Chaucer's World*, compiled by Edith Rickert, ed. C. C. Olson and M. M. Crow
(1948; New York: Columbia University Press, 1968), xi.

1
Conventions and Institutions

Benedictine Rule

Monastic orders existed in Ireland and Wales in the fifth century, first
arrived in England in the sixth and seventh centuries, and in the eighth
century the Rule of St. Benedict (480–ca. 550), Benedict's set of codes for
behavior, also came to be known in the British Isles. Receiving additional
impetus after 1066 and then again with the arrival of orders of canons and
friars in the twelfth and thirteenth centuries, the monastic orders had their
maximum numbers at the beginning of the fourteenth century, declined
with the pestilence later in the century, then recovered significantly. From
their inception many monastic houses received large endowments, were
powerful landholding institutions, and were deeply and directly involved in
the economic, legal, and social lives of all of society's strata in both immediate and extended geographical areas.

William Caxton (ca. 1422–92) began his career as a merchant. In the
1440s he went to Bruges, Cologne, and Ghent where he began his career as
a printer and translator. He returned to England in 1476 with movable type
and proceeded to publish over one hundred titles in the remaining sixteen
years of this life, including several of Chaucer's, Gower's, Lydgate's, and
Malory's works as well as his own translations.

Six English translations of the Benedictine rule survive from the eleventh
century to 1516. None of the translations is dependent on each other, nor
is any direct French or Latin source known. Caxton's edition from about
1490 also contains Heinrich Suso's *Horologium sapientiae* and other texts,
and it, like several manuscript versions, is addressed to both men and women.
Also like the other versions, Caxton's print lays out the qualifications and

duties of the abbot and abbess, the process of admission to the order, directions for divine service, cultivation of obedience and the twelve rungs of the ladder of humility, and the practical regulation of dress, food, and manual duties.

Primary documents and further reading

Blake, N. F. (1969) *Caxton and His World*. London: André Deutsch.
Knowles, D. (1948–59) *The Religious Orders in England*, 3 vols. Cambridge: Cambridge University Press.
Knowles, D. and R. N. Hadcock (1971) *Medieval Religious Houses: England and Wales*. New York: St. Martin's Press.
Pantin, W. A. (ed.) (1931, 1933) *Documents Illustrating the Activities of the General and Provincial Chapters of the English Black Monks, 1215–1540*. Camden Society, 3rd series, 45, 47. London: Royal Historical Society.

Caxton, W. (trans.) "The Caxton Abstract of the Rule of St. Benet." In E. A. Koch (ed.) (1902) *Three Middle English Versions of the Rule of St. Benet and Two Contemporary Rituals for the Ordination of Nuns*. EETS, o.s. 120. London: Kegan Paul, Trench, Trübner, 120–38 (selections).
Language: English (Southeast Midland)
Book date: ca. 1490

[B]ere in thy mynde this synguler note that the hede or the sovereyn wyth all the congregacion streytly be bounde to folowe the rule in every poynte and that none of theim be soo bolde to decly[n]e or departe therfro so that none folowe the wyll of theyr owne mynde oonly but ever be redy to be reformyd. The subgettes also owe to be ryght ware that they make no strife wythyn or wythout wyth theyr sovereyns; yf that they doo, anone lete hem have the streyt reguler punysshment wyth the fere of God and in kepynge the rule, remembrynge that the hede withoute ony dowte shall yeve a full streyte accompte oo day of all their jugementes and byhavour to God atte ferefull daye of rekenynge . . .

Also, the sovereyn and the subgettes owe ever to flee idylnesse, the norisshe[1] of al synnes, and to be ocupyed ever in vertu, lovyng God wyth all their herte, of all theyr soule, and of all their strength, and theyr neyghbour as theyr selfe, doyng ever unto theym as they wolde be done unto, dyspisyng theyrselfe, and folow Crist by the crosse of penaunce. Also, they must chastyse theyr body and flee the pleasur therof and to use fastynge, and

---

[1]   nourisher.

refresshe the poore peple wyth dedes of mercy, goostly and bodely, and medle lytyll wyth worldly actes, no thyng preferryng above the love of God, wrath or deceyte never to kepe in herte or to promyse ony false peas, kepynge ever charytee, and use never to swere, leeste that by custome ye fall in perjurie, and sey ever the trouth in herte and mouth, never yeldyng evyll for evyll but rather good for evyll, doyng no wronge to ony but for to suffre paciently whan it is done to you. Love your enmyes, and curse hem not, and be redy to take persecucion for a rightwys mater; never be prowde or dronklew nor moche etyng or slouthfull, not grutchynge or bakbytynge, ever puttynge your trust in our Lord God. Whan that ye see ony goodnes in your-selfe, anone put it to oure Lorde and not to your-selfe. All thinge that is evyll ascryve to your-selfe. Fere ever the daye of jugement and the dungeon of hell, desyrynge wyth all your mynde and herte the everlastyng lyfe, and have evere deth suspecte afore your eyen, and gyde ever your dedes wysely in every hour, and be certeyn that God beholdith theim in everi place, and every evyl thought that commyth to your mynde, anone put it awaye by thynkyng of Cristes passyon, and shewe theym by confessyon to your goostly fader, and kepe ever your tongue from evyll and schrewde langage, and speke lytyll and well, and ever avoyde vayn wordes and dissolute laughter and japes, and be glad to here gode lectures and lyves of sayntes with preyer, dayly waylyng your synnes and the synnes and ignoraunce of the peple wyth amendes makyng. The preceptes of your sovereyn in all thynges obey, lefull as to God, and fulfyll them. Love ever chastyte; and flee ever envy, hatrede, and stryff; and worship your elders; and favour the yong in all love and drede of God. Ever pray for your enmyes and, or the sone goo downe, be in perfyte peas wyth theym dayly to your power, and never dyspeyr of the grete mercy of God. Loo, thyes ben the instrumentes of the spirituell crafte and occupacion, the which exercisid and doon, oure Lorde hath promysed to you and us that eye never sawe, nor ere ever herde, nor cowde ever in-to mannys herte ascende, the whiche to al his lovyng servantes he hath ordened. Amen.

Obedyence is a grete vertu done without grutchyng or taryenge. It is the fyrst steppe unto mekenes, and it is right specyous and nedefull to be had for all peple and namely for relygyous persones. True obediencers, assone as thei be called or commaundid of theyr sovereyn, anone after the worde seyde, they be redy wyth all gladnesse to doo the dede so commaundid, settyng asyde all other thynges undone and their owne wyll in every poynt, and that wyth all quyknesse of herte and body for drede of our Lorde. Wherfore, he callyth suche a lyfe a streyt waye to heven and not a comyn waye where synners take her owne wyll, and be not undir the yocke of obedyence to an other. Wythouten doubte trew obedyencers folow surely oure Lorde and his wordes where he seyth, "I come not in-to thys world to doo myn owne wyll but the wyll of my fader the whiche sent me."[2] Thenne this obedience is gretly acceptable to God and swete to al Cristen peple whan it is done quikly and wythoute grutchynge or frowarde[3] countenaunce in worde or in herte. Our Lorde loveth a thyng done unto hym cherefully in soule, and such obedience done to the sovereyn is done to God and for God, as he seyth hymselfe. Yf one obey with grutchyng either in worde or in their herte, fulfyllyng the commaundement of theyr sovereyn, yet it is not acceptable to God, the whiche beholdyth the herte ever and the wyll of the doer therof, and he shal have noo grace but rather payne ordeined for grutchers, without he amende him.

As for silence, doo aftir the cheyf prophete of God, David, where he seyth in the sauter, "I have seyd that I shall not offende in my tongue. I have put a kepyng to my mowth and am dompe and therwith made meke and silent."[4] In moche speche, as it is writen, synne cann not be avoyded; also, in the power of the tongue is deth and lyfe. As it accordith to a mayster to speke and teche, so it behoveth the disciple to here and be silent; wordes of unclennes voyde or, mevynge to disolucyon or to laughter, ben dampned by the rule in ony place to be had, and it is commaundid streytly by the same, none to be so bolde to open their mowth in suche maner of talkyng. Also, silence is to be kept by the rule at all tymes and spyrituelly at nyght after complyn, and noo licence thenne is to be gyven to any for to speke but oonly to officers or to theim that grete nede causith to speke with sadnesse and honestee, and silence also is to be kept at all refeccions and meles and in other places, and at other tymes specyfyed by the rule. Yf theyr be founde ony gylty in theis premyses, thei ought to be punysshid streytly and grevously.

Holy scrypture cryeth and seyth, "He that wyll high hymselfe shal be made lowe, and he that mekyth hym selfe shall be made high."[5] In thys is shewid that exaltacyon is the doughter and nygh of kyne to pryde, whiche is mortall. Yf we wyll atteyne and come to the heyth of perfyte mekenes, the whiche wyll bringe us to the honour of heven in body and soule, lete us lyft up our herte and mynde unto heven by the skale and lader of Jacob, descendyng wyth the angels from ony exaltacyon, and clymme up to theym by mekenes and humyliacion . . .

[The twelve steps are then specified; the sixth and twelfth follow here.]

[2]   John 6.38.
[3]   ugly.
[4]   Psalms 38.2–3.
[5]   Luke 14.11, 18.14.

The sixth degre of mekenes is whan one is well content wyth symple araye or habite, and is glad to be set lytill by and to be take as a drudge or outcast of the religion, and to be ever redy to doo al thynges that is boden hym to doo, jugyng him an idyll servaunt and unworthy to God and man . . . The twelfth degree is whan one, not oonly in his mowthe but aswell in his body, shewyth meknesse to all that beholde hym as in al his dedes in chaptour, in chirche, in garden, in felde, sittynge, walkynge, or standynge, and his hede enclynynge and his sight to the grounde, shewynge hym selfe every houre gylty of hys synne, havynge ever suspect for to be brought to the ferefull jugement of God, seyeng thus wyth the publycan, "Good Lorde, I a synner am not worthy to lyfte up myn eyen to heven."[6] Who som ever hath ascendyd al thise degrees of mekenesse shall anone have the charyte of God perfitely, the whyche thenne puttyth awaye all drede in suche thynges, the whyche he dyde afore with drede, and also dooth thenne al his actes of accustome as it were naturalle to hym, cherefully and wythoute labour, and that not for the drede of hell he dooth it, but for fervent love that he hath to God by a custome and delyte of vertue, the whyche grace is yeven of the holy gooste . . .

The grete vice and syn of properte in relygyon is namely to be cutte awaye by the rote. Presume none in relygyon to yeve ony thyng or to take wythout the wyll and commaundement of the sovereyn, nor it is leefull ony to have a thyng to theyrself propre, not as moche as their owne body, or to have their own wyll in their power. All thynges to theim necessary is to be had of the sovereyn accordynge to theyr nede, not acceptynge ony persone more than an other but accordyng to nede and in-firmyte. And all thynges must be commyn emonge theym accordyng to the lyfe of the apostles. None presume to sey: "Suche a thynge is myne." Yf ony be founde gylty in this venemouse offence of properte, lete hem twyes or thries be correct; yf they doo not amende, see thenne to their cha[s]tysment. Yf at ony tyme one nede a lytyll thyng, thanke he our Lorde and say he ever "*Deo gracias*," not beyng sory that another that nede hath, that pite is shewid uppon hym. And he that hath suche pite shewyd upon hym shal not therof be proude by contenaunce or by worde, and thus shall all the congregacyon be in rest and charitee, and grutchynge layd a syde, the whiche is perilous to be had eyther by worde or sygne. Yf ony therin be founde culpable, anone put theim to streyt disciplyne.

Eche one be besy to serve other, and none is to be exscusid from the dressing bord of the kechyn wythout they be seke or other wyse occupyed for the commyn well. In suche meke and low service is goten grete mede,

---

[6]   Luke 18.13.

charite, and rewarde, and whan they shall departe wekely from the kechyn by cours, they owe to make al thynges clene at theyr departyng, and the clothes that the covent hath fyled with theyr handes or fete, they shall delyver clene also wyth all mekenes. And moreover theyr owne fete they shall make clene in theyr departyng, and delyver al the naprye[7] and clene clothes to the celerer. Suche servytoures by the rule may take a lytyll refresshing of mete and drynke afore high dyner for by-cause of their attendaunce and servyse at the same . . .

In the tyme of Lent echon by theyr-selfe have the Bible, the whiche they owe to rede complete and hole besyde theyr servyse, and the seyde Bible is to be delyverd unto theym atte begynnynge of Lent. And the serchers of the relygyon owe to see warely about that they be occupyed in lecture therof Sonday and other, and not aboute fables, japes, or sluggisshenes. Yf ony suche be founde, see that they be spoken unto sharply ones or twyes, and yf they amende not theyr-wyth, lete theym be correct soo that all other maye beware by theym. If theyr be ony so slouthfull or neclygent that they maye not or wyll not be occupied in redyng or holy medytacyon, thenne lete theym be assigned to other occupacyons to doo so that they be never unoccupied in vertu. If they be seke or feble for age, thenne such an occupacyon is to be put unto theym that they maye awaye wyth and not to be ydyll, by the discrecion of the sovereyn.

How be it that a relygious persone owe every tyme to kepe Lent, yet for by-cause that fewe have thys vertu, therfore we advise and counseyll, seyth Saynt Benet,[8] all of the relygyon spiritually theys forty dayes of Lent to kepe in all clennesse of lyfe, and to put utterly awaye all theyr neclygences and olde custome of synne, and thenne more spiritually to gyve theim to prayer, waylyng and wepinge, redinge, and abstinence in mete and drynke, wythdrawynge somwhat of theyr takynge in mete and drynke other wyse than they dide afore, and that wyth good wyll, offerynge it in his mynde to God and to the poore peple, and to wythdrawe some what of slepe and speche and wanton behavour. And as for abstynence of mete and drynke, it owe to be doon wyth the consente ever of the sovereyn and the helpe of prayer. For yf it be otherwyse doon, it is to be taken of presumpcyon and vayne glory, and thenne it hath noo mede . . .

Clothynge to the covent, and habyte, is to be yeven accordyng to the hete of the yere or to the coldenes of the countre that they dwell in, lasse or more as nede is. And the sovereyn must have consideracion therof and to

---

[7]   linen.
[8]   Rule 49.1–3.

bye suche cloth that is made in that countre or provynce of the vilest and lyghtest pryce. And as oft as they shal take new, thenne to rendre up the olde for the use of pore peple. Of other thynges necessary for theyr body daye and nyght in wynter and somer, and of theyr celles and lodgyng, and of their behavour in theim with other, the hole rule certifieth, and how the sovereyne shal dylygently serche that thei lacke no thyng to theym necessary soo that all occasion of grutchyng, or for ony thynge werkynge, or for ony thynge kepyng have no place in the relygyon, ever remembryng the wordes wrytyn in the Actes of the Apostles where it is seyde that it was distribute and delyverd to echone of theym as theyr nede required . . .[9]

[A] monestary is to be sette in suche a place where all thynges necessary soone maye be had so that the covent nede not to passe the boundes of the clausures therof, the whiche yf thei dide, shulde be perylle for theyr soules. Saynt Benet woll that the rule be red effectuelly oftymes in the yere afore the congregacion for by-cause none of hem shal pretende ignorance or ony exscuse.

Whan ony of the bredern must doo a journey without the clausure of the place, after licence had, he shall commende hym to the prayer of his sovereyn, and ever at last oryson in the servyse of God shal a prayer be sayd for him and all that is absent. And the daye that they come home ayen, they shal lye prostrate all the servyse tyme and desyre the covent to praye for theym for theyr excesses done in the journey, as in syght, heryng of ony vanytees or evyll thynges, or ony voyde wordes. And they shall not tell ony thyng that they sawe or herd in theyr journey, for it is a grete meane to the destruccion of suche a place of relygion. And he that presumyth to doo the contrary or to goo oute of the clausure of the monestary to ony place, thought it be never so lytil, wythout commandement or licence of the sovereyn, owe to be streytly punysshyd.

Friars

The mendicant orders first arrived in England in the thirteenth century and the number of adherents rapidly grew. Two of the four principal orders – the Friars Preachers (Dominicans or Black Friars) and the Friars Minor (Franciscans or Grey Friars) – quickly became integral in the life of universities and commercial centers in the country, the Franciscans producing the remarkable theologians Roger Bacon, John Duns Scotus, William of Ockham,

[9] Acts 4.35.

and John Pecham. Both orders also established houses for women, which flourished in the fourteenth century. Along with the remaining two orders – the Augustinians and the Carmelites (White Friars) – the four mendicant orders had their maximum number of followers (in approximately 190 houses) in the early fourteenth century before the pestilence. Friars ideally gave up permanent residence in one locality and material possessions; maintained contact with communities through preaching, confessions, and burial of the dead; and were obedient to provincial superiors and ultimately the pope.

Anti-fraternal criticism began almost with the inception of the mendicant orders because of their real or perceived competition with parish priests and other secular clergy over the offices of preaching, confession, and burial as well as the income derived from these sources. Reproof and satire gained additional impetus from William of St. Amour, a master at the University of Paris, who wrote *De periculis novissimorum temporum* (*On the Perils of the Last Times*) in 1256, a work that questioned the fraternal orders' very right to exist as true apostolic functionaries and that was sharply critical of fraternal hypocrisy, in particular the desire for material gain despite claims to poverty. Petrarch, Boccaccio, Jean de Meun, William Langland, Geoffrey Chaucer, and John Gower all satirize the friars, a practice which came to have additional significance in England because of Lollardy, new developments in the debates among clergy members, and Richard Fitzralph.

Richard FitzRalph (ca. 1300–60), archbishop of Armagh and primate of Ireland, was, until the 1350s and 1360s, best known in his role as a refuter of Armenian heresies for the pope in Avignon and as a preacher and theologian in England. Either coming upon or partially instigating an anti-mendicant controversy in London and elsewhere in 1356–7, FitzRalph proceeded to preach a number of anti-fraternal sermons in the vernacular, which led the four orders to respond, in turn requiring the archbishop to defend his position in front of the papal court. On November 8, 1357, he preached before Innocent VI what became known as *Defensio curatorum*, which outlined his objections to the friars, a text that survives in over seventy manuscripts.

John Trevisa (ca. 1342–1402), having attended Oxford, became a priest and vicar for Thomas, fourth Lord Berkeley, for whom he completed six translations of Latin texts, including Ranulf Higden's *Polychronicon* (see "The English and England," p. 50 and "The English Language," p. 259), Batholomeus Anglicus' *De proprietatibus rerum* (see "Humors," p. 13), and two original works in English on translation. The date of his translation of the *Defense of the Curates* is unknown. The translation survives in six manuscripts.

Primary documents and further reading

Erickson, C. (1975) "The Fourteenth-Century Franciscans and their Critics I." *Franciscan Studies* 35: 107–35.

—— (1976) "The Fourteenth-Century Franciscans and their Critics II." *Franciscan Studies* 36: 108–47.

FitzRalph, R. (1960) [1614] *Defensio curatorum. Monarchia s. romani imperii*, vol. 2, ed. M. Goldast. Graz: Akademische-Druck. U. Verlagsanstalt, 1391–1410.

Hagen, K. T. (1996) "A Frere Ther Was, A Wantowne and a Meryee." In L. C. Lambdin and R. T. Lambdin (eds.) *Chaucer's Pilgrims: An Historical Guide to the Pilgrims in The Canterbury Tales*. Westport, CT: Greenwood Press, 80–92.

Knowles, D. (1948–59) *The Religious Orders in England*, 3 vols. Cambridge: Cambridge University Press.

Mann, J. (1973) *Chaucer and Medieval Estates Satire*. Cambridge: Cambridge University Press.

Miller, R. P. (ed.) (1977) *Chaucer: Sources and Backgrounds*. New York: Oxford University Press.

Scase, W. (1989) *Piers Plowman and the New Anticlericalism*. Cambridge: Cambridge University Press.

Szittya, P. R. (1986) *The Antifraternal Tradition in Medieval Literature*. Princeton, NJ: Princeton University Press.

Walsh, K. (1981) *A Fourteenth-century Scholar and Primate: Richard FitzRalph in Oxford, Avignon, and Armagh*. Oxford: Clarendon Press.

Richard FitzRalph. British Library MS Harley 1900, fols. 7r–15v. "*Defensio curatorum.*" *Dialogus inter militem et clericum*, trans. John Trevisa, ed. A. J. Perry. EETS, o.s. 167. London: Oxford University Press, 1925, 43–73 (selections).
Language: English (Southwestern)
Manuscript date: ca. 1400

Y seide, and efte y seye, if me axeth what persoon is most worthi to be chose for singuler[1] of parischons,[2] a frere or the ordynarie, y say that the ordynarie is more worthi to be chose for schrifte than eny frere. For he is more profitable, and schrifte that is schewide singulerliche to hym voydeth mo desavauntes[3] and damages. First y saye that the ordinarie is the more siker[4] persone, for . . . he is y-fonge[5] a persoon of God and of holy chirche

[1]   personal well-being.
[2]   parishioners.
[3]   more disadvantages.
[4]   reliable.
[5]   accepted as.

and of the comyn lawe, and the frere is forbode by the lawe. Thanne the ordynarie is the more siker persone. Also, the ordinarie is more y-bounde to his parischons than is a frere. Thanne the parischon may verreilich and more sikerliche triste that the ordynarie wole more bisiliche ordeyne for his savacioun than wole eny frere that is a straunge persoone, as a bodiliche leche[6] that is prevy and y-knowe is more y-holde to the seke man than a straunge leche. Also, by the comyn cours, the parischon douteth nought nother schal doute of his ordinarie, wether his power to assoile his sugetis[7] be y-bounde other no, but of freres he may have verreiliche suspecioun and trowe that her power is y-bounde for diverse cursyngis, and with oute eny doute hit is more siker to be schryve to hym that hath fre power than to hym that his power is y-bounde. Thanne the ordinarie is the more siker persone and the more certeyn. And that me may trowe that freres beth acursed, hit is preved, first by the decretal in *Clementinis de decimis.* There it is seide that "Alle men of religioun that haveth no benefice beth a-cursed if thei withholdeth, other withdraweth, other fondeth to appropre to hem without a laweful cause, by any maner, colour, other sleighthe,[8] rightes other tethinges that beth dewe to holy chirche."[9] And it semeth no dowte, by Goddes owne lawe, that tethinges of byqueestes and of fre giftes is detty[10] and dewe to parische chirches and to curatours therof. And so seyn the doctors Innocencius and Hostiensis.[11] Thanne alle freres that bynymeth[12] parische chirches the tethinge of that is y-geve hem other biquethe, beth acursed. For thei payeth nevere tethinge of siche byquystes and giftes, as it is comynliche seide . . .

Also, that the ordynarie is more siker to the paryschon, hit is preved other wise in this maner: for the parischon may skilfulliche deme that his ordynarie is a juge lasse suspect and more skilful[13] for to enjoye[14] hym skilful penaunce and profitable for his synnes. For he schal nought suppose nother have suspecioun that his ordynarie hereth his schrifte for covetise of getyng and of wynnyng of bodilich help and socour, for the ordynaries liflode[15] longeth

[6]   doctor.
[7]   subjects.
[8]   sleight.
[9]   Clement V (d. 1314), *Clementines.*
[10]   owing.
[11]   Innocent IV (ca. 1190–1254), Henry of Suso (d. 1270).
[12]   deprive.
[13]   reasonable.
[14]   enjoin.
[15]   livelihood.

to his offys by lawe of God and of holy chirche. Of freres thei may suppose and wene that thei doth hit for to have socour and help of her liflode, for in here appele that thei made agenes me in Engelond hit is conteyned that by her fundacioun thei beth y-bounde to beggerie and to the heighest poverte, nought with-stondyng that thei tellith that thei haveth powere to here the schriftes of alle men that wole be schryve to hem. Therfore, the parischen may skilfulliche suppose and have suspicioun that, bycause of getyng somme releve of her beggerie, thei beth so busy to here schriftes. Thanne may the parischon skilfulliche argue in his herte why wolde this begger sitte and here my schrifte and leve his beggyng and getyng of his liflode but he hope to have of me siche maner help, and nede driveth to synne, by the which synne the nede myght be releved, as Proverbs 30,[16] Salomon, seith and prayeth: "Geve me nother beggerie nother riches, but geve me onliche what is nedeful to my liflode lest y be excited to denye and saye who is oure Lorde, and conpelled by nede for to stele and forswere the name of my God." Thanne hit folewith that for all maner synnes, he wole joyne me almes dede for to releve his owne beggerie, and so y schal nought be cleneliche by-quyt of my synnes. Therfore, whanne hise disciples axide of oure Lord, "Why myght we nought cast hym out?" and spake of a fende, oure Lord answerde and seide: "These manere fendes beth nought cast out but with bedes and fastyng," Matthew 16.[17] Of this worde hit is y-take that as for evereche diverse sekenesse of body diverse medicyns helpith, so for evereche gostlich seknese most be ordeyned his propre medicyn. And this begger that is bisy about his beggerye wole nought with-out suspecioun ordeyne me siche medicyns for my synnes . . .

Curatours haveth another grete damage by cause of mysuse of privy-leges: that freres haveth touchyng[18] the thre quarters of alle profites that fallith to hem, other wise of biquyst other of gifte, distinctliche other indistinctliche,[19] and al maner mysuse that thei useth of that is conteyned in the chapitre *dudum*,[20] and touchyng the ferthe part that is i-graunted to curatours and y-taxed there, the whiche ferthe part of many biquystes, offryngis, and giftes freres payeth nought to curatours, but freres appropreth hit to hem-silf with many cautels and wyles as curatours tellith so that bitwene hem and freres as it were in evereche place among Cristen men is

---

[16]   Proverbs 30.8–9.
[17]   Matthew 17.18–20.
[18]   handling of.
[19]   individually or indiscriminately.
[20]   before.

ple[21] and strif withoute ende. So that in many placis charite is fer, and after wordes cometh strokes . . .

Thanne hit folewith that these of the ordres of beggers multeplieth hem in this maner agenus the ordenaunce of God almyghtyes witt and his wisdom, and bynymeth therby the fleece of the peple and of the clergie, and chargith hem in everech place. For now unnethe may any grete men other smaal, lewed or lered, take a morsel of mete but siche beggers come unbede and begge nought as pore men schuld atte gate other atte dore, axing almes mekelich as Fraunces taught and hoteth[22] in his testament,[23] but thei cometh into houses and courtes, and beth y-harberwide,[24] and etith and drynketh what thei ther fyndeth unbede and unprayed. And notheles thei bereth with hem corn,[25] other mele, brede, flesche, other chese; though there be but tweyne in the hous, thei bereth with hem that oon. And no man may hem werne but thei put of[26] al kyndeliche schame. And it is wonder that thei dredith nought the sentence of Pope Gregorye that writeth in a comyn privelege to prelates of holy chirche in this maner: "For ofte vices of privy riches entreth, and Sathanas his angel degiseth[27] hym in the liknesse of an angel of light. By this present auctorite, we comaundeth and hoteth that if eny that tellith that thei beth of the ordre of frere prechours precheth in yowre contrayes and turneth hem to begging of money wharby the ordre of hem that haveth made professioun to povert myght be diffamed, take ye hem as fals faytours[28] and dampneth hem."[29] Thei beth now so sotyl in this crafte of beggerie that pore vikers and persons and al the peple pleyneth therof, neigh in everech place. This semeth a wonder maner lyvyng in hem that seyn, that thei mot holde the gospel by her professioun and doth agenus Cristes owne sentence that sente his disciples to prech the gospel and seide: "Passe ye nought from hous to hous," Luke 10.[30] Also thei doth agenus another scripture that seith: "Voide and war that thou be noght herberwed from hous to hous," Ecclesiasticus 29.[31] Bot thei goth so about

[21] contention.
[22] commands.
[23] Rule 1.9.
[24] lodged.
[25] grain.
[26] off.
[27] disguises.
[28] beggars.
[29] Gregory I the Great (ca. 540–604), *Liber regula pastoralis.*
[30] Luke 10.7.
[31] Ecclesiasticus 29.30.

from court to court and from hous to hous, for her cloystre schulde nought be her prison. Ys nought this grete damage to the clergie and to the peple also? Sothlich hit semeth so to many men, and al hit hath occasioun of the mysuse of pryvyleges, for thei tellith that thei useth so the privyleges of prechyng and of heryng of schriftes, neigh everech man schameth to werne hem other to put hem of.

And also these privyleges and other thingis that schal be touched withynne doth freres many damages. For hit semeth that these privyleges infecteth hem with many maner synnes: with the synne of injurie and of wrong, with the synne of unbuxomnesse,[32] with the synne of covetise, and with the synne of pride . . .

Also, Seynt Fraunceys in his rule hoteth in this maner: "Ich hote heighlich alle freres that thei have noon suspect company as counseil of wymmen; also, that thei come nought in abbayes of monchons[33] out-take[34] thilke freres that have special leve of the court of Rome; also, that thei be nought gossippes to men nother to wymmen leste sclaundre arise by occasioun therof among freres."[35] And freres procureth the contrarie for to here the privyeste counseile of wymmen, of queenes, and of alle othere, and leggeth[36] hed to hed. With grete obedience thei folewith Seynt Job that seide: "Ich have made covenaunt with myn eighen that y wolde thenke of a mayde."[37] And so now by sich company thei disputeth with ladyes in chambre; therfore, in al the worlde wide sclaunder springeth of freres, the wiche sclaundre y wolc nought reherse at this tyme. Of many hit semeth openlich that thei infecteth hem-silf with the synne of unobediens and unbuxumnesse by the mys-use of siche privyleges and of her owne reule by occasioun of siche privyleges.

Humors

Humoral theory in England in the fourteenth and fifteenth centuries belonged both to the world of the practitioner and the academic. It originated in Aristotle's idea of balance within the body and achieved its fullest articulation in the works of Galen (129–ca. 216), which became central

[32] disobedience.
[33] nuns.
[34] except.
[35] Rule 1.12.
[36] lie.
[37] Job 31.1.

to the curriculum of medical study in Europe. The enormous quantity of medical manuscripts in England (over 7,000 in English alone from the mid-fourteenth to fifteenth centuries) testifies to the thorough extent to which medical discourses permeated society.

Bartholomeus Anglicus wrote his *De proprietatibus rerum* in the mid-thirteenth century. Bartholomeus was probably born an Englishman, studied in Paris, became a Minorite in France, and went on to lecture on theology in Paris. His text is encyclopedic, not a strictly medical work, and contains information about spiritual and human matters, including all the branches of human knowledge. John Trevisa completed his translation of *De proprietatibus rerum* in 1398, a translation which survives in eight manuscripts alongside several Latin versions (see "Friars," p. 7, for a general introduction to Trevisa, as well as "The English and England," p. 50, and "The English Language," p. 258). These eight manuscripts are large and professionally produced. About 1495 Wynkyn de Worde published one of Trevisa's translations, possibly a later printing of one completed by Caxton in Cologne in 1471–4.

Primary documents and further reading

Gottfried, R. S. (1986) *Doctors and Medicine in Medieval England, 1340–1530*. Princeton, NJ: Princeton University Press.

Green, M. H. (ed. and trans.) (2001) *The Trotula: A Medieval Compendium of Women's Medicine*. Philadelphia: University of Pennsylvania Press.

Jones, I. B. (1937) "Popular Medical Knowledge in Fourteenth-century English Literature." *Bulletin of the Institute of the History of Medicine* 5, 2 parts: 405–51, 538–88.

Ogden, M. S. (ed.) (1971) Guy de Chauliac, *The Cyrurgie*. EETS, o.s. 265. Oxford: Oxford University Press.

Robbins, R. H. (1970) "Medical Manuscripts in Middle English." *Speculum* 45: 393–415.

Ussery, H. (1971) "Chaucer's Physician: Medicine and Literature in Fourteenth-century England." *Tulane Studies in English* 19: 1–158.

Voigts, L. E. (1984) "Medical Prose." In A. S. G. Edwards (ed.) *Middle English Prose: A Critical Guide to Major Authors and Genres*. New Brunswick, NJ: Rutgers University Press, 315–35.

—— (1995) "Multitudes of Middle English Medical Manuscripts, or the Englishing of Science and Medicine." In M. R. Schleissner (ed.) *Manuscript Sources of Medieval Medicine: A Book of Essays*. New York: Garland, 183–95.

von Fleishhacker, R. (ed.) (1894) *Lanfrank's "Science of Cirurgie,"* Part I. EETS, o.s. 102. Berlin: Asher.

Bartholomeus Anglicus. British Library MS Additional 27944, fols. 28v–36v. *On the Properties of Things*, trans. John Trevisa, 3 vols., ed. M. C. Seymour. Oxford: Clarendon Press, 1975–88. 1: 129–62 (selections).
Language: English (Southwestern)
Manuscript date: ca. 1410

To trete of the propretees of mannes body and of the parties therof, we schul first biginne to trete of the qualitees of the elementis and of the humoures of whiche the body is maad . . .

Elementis beth foure, and so beth foure qualitees of elementis of the whiche everiche body that hath a soule is componed[1] and imade as of matir, and nameliche mannes body that is nobilest among alle the elementis and most nobilliche is i-ordeined among alle thinges that beth componed and imade of divers thinges. Mannes body is i-ordeyned to be the propre instrument of the resonabil soule in his workes of kinde and of wille.

Mannes body is made of foure elementis — of erthe, watir, fire, and aier — and everiche therof hath propre qualitees. Foure ther beth iclepid the firste and principal qualites, that is to wite, hete, coold, drye, and wetenesse, and ben iclepid the firste qualites for they sliden first of the elementis into the thinges that ben imaade of elementis. They ben also iclepid the principal qualitees for of hem cometh al the secundarye effectis. Tweyne of these qualites ben iclepid *active* "able to worche," hete and cooldnes. The othir tweyne, drynesse and wetnesse, ben iclepid *passive* "able to soffre." And so as these qualites have maistrie, the elementis ben iclepid *active* othir *passive* "able to do or soffre." The firste tweyne ben principallich iclepid *active*, noght for they worchin alone, for the passive qualites worchith also, [for] non qualite is in the body an ydel; but therfore they beth iclepid *active* for, be the worchinge of hem, the othir beth ibrought inne and ikept and isaved . . .

For *libro 1 capitulo 16* Constantinus[2] seith if the body is hote, thanne is moche fleisch and litil fatnesse, rede colour, moche here (blak othir rede), hote touche and gropinge, good witt, a man of gret facounde[3] and of gret mevynge,[4] hardy and wratheful, lovy[5] and lecherous, and desiringe moche, and hastilich defienge[6] for good digestioun, of scharp voys, an schamefast, of strong and swift puls . . .

[1] mixed.
[2] Constantine the African (d. 1087), *Royal Book.*
[3] eloquence.
[4] moving.
[5] given to amorous activities.
[6] digesting.

Also, coolde is the modir of whightnesse and of palenes, as hete is the modir of blaknes and of rednes. And so in hote londes cometh forth blake men and browne, as among the Moores, in coolde lond white men, as amoung the Sclaves. So seith Aristoteles *in libro de celo et mundo*[7] and tellith the resoun why and seith that in coolde londes the modres of wommen ben disposid to conseive suche children. Therfore, they beren children with whyte skynnes that haveth longe, yelewy, neissche,[8] and streite here. The contrarie is in hote londes there wymmen bereth children that ben blake and hath litil here and crips,[9] as in blo men londe.[10] Thenne coolde schewith itself in the body what he is and hath the maistrie withinne, for in the body ther coolde hath the maistrie the colour is white, here is neissche and streight, hard wit[11] and forgeteful, litil appetite, miche slepe, hevy goinge and slowe. So seith Constantinus *libro primo capitulo 17.* This schal not alwey be undirstonde in everich colde nedeliche,[12] but in comparisoun to the complexioun of the heete that hath the maistrye and in proporcioun of the hote lond to the coolde lond, auctoures seith suche thingis and lefte hem iwrite in here bookes to hem that camen aftir hem . . .

An humour is a substaunce fletinge[13] in dede, and is ibred and cometh of gederinge of the element qualitees, and apt to norische and fede the membres and to counforte the worchingis therof kyndeliche, or hapliche[14] to lette the worchingis therof. For humour is the firste principal material of bodies that haveth felinge and chief help in here worchinge, and that bycause of norischinge and of fedinge. Constantinus seith that the humoures beth iclepid the children of the elementis, for everiche of the humours cometh of qualite of elementis. And there beth foure humours: blood, flewme, colera, and melencolia. And beth iclepid symple in comparisoun to the membres and lymes, thouh they be componed in comparisoun to the elementis whos children they beth.

Thise foure humours, if they beth in evene proporcioun in quantite and qualite, he fedith alle bodyes that hath blood and maketh hem parfite and kepith in [dewe] beinge and state of helthe; as agenward, if they beth

---

[7]   Aristotle (384–322 BCE), *De caelo et mundo.*
[8]   soft.
[9]   curly.
[10]   Ethiopia.
[11]   slow to understand.
[12]   necessarily.
[13]   flowing.
[14]   potentially.

uneven in proporcioun and infecte, thanne they bredith eveles. Thise humours beth nedeful to the makinge of the body and to the reuleynge and kepinge therof, and also to restore what is ilost in the body . . .

Thise foure humours beth ibred in this manere. Whan mete is ifonge[15] in the place of seethinge,[16] that is the stomak, first the more sotil partie and fletinge therof that phisicians clepith *pthisinaria* is idrawe be certeyn veynes to the lyvour and ther, by the worchinge of kinde hete, it is ichaungid into the foure humours. The bredinge of hem bigynneth in the lyver, but it endith there [not] atte fulle. First, by worchinge, hete turneth what is coolde and moist in[to] the kynde of flewme, and thanne what is hote and moist into the kynde of blood, and thanne what is hote and drye into the kynde of colera, and thanne what is coolde and drye into the kinde of malancolia. Thanne the proces is suche: first, fleume is bred as an humour half sode;[17] secounde, blood that is parfitliche isode; the thridde, colera that is oversode;[18] the laste is malencolia that is more erthi and the drestis[19] of the othir. And so suche is the ordre, as Avicenne seith: the bredinge of elementis is streite and agenward into the same, for aier is ibred of fire, and fire of aiere, and everiche element of othir . . .[20]

Thenne of the sentence of the forseid auctours[21] gedre thu schortliche that kinde blood is pure, hoot and moist, sotile[22] and swete, and also it kepith the kinde vertu of fedinge.[23] And blood is the sete of the soule and conteyneth hym, and maketh parfite [youthe], complexioun a chaungith, and kepith and saveth the herte and the spiritis, and maketh hem glad, and waketh love, schedith him in the uter partie of the body and maketh it of good colour and hiewe. And if blood is wel and temperat, he kepith hele and helthe. And if he is corrupt, it bredith corrupcion, as in *lepra*[24] that is corrupt blood in the wellis.[25] Medlid [with] othur humoures, it temprith the malice therof. And blood by his vertu swagith the smertinge of eighen . . .

---

[15]   received.
[16]   digesting.
[17]   cooked.
[18]   over-cooked.
[19]   dregs.
[20]   Avicenna (980–1037).
[21]   Isidore of Seville (570–636), Constantine the African, and Aristotle.
[22]   thin.
[23]   it retains the natural power of food.
[24]   leprosy.
[25]   source.

In wommen, for to grete moisture and defaute of hete, if it is iholde over dewe tymes, it is cause and occasioun of ful gret greves. For somtime it stuffith the spiritual membres, and somtyme frenesye[26] and othir eveles that beth opunliche iknow, as that corrupt blood to longe iholde is ise[n]t to divers place of the body, as it is more openlich conteined *in libro passionarum Galieni.*[27] Therfor, agens suche periles best remedye is to voyde suche corrupt blood that greveth so the body that he is inne, for also it chaungith wondirliche and infectith othir bodyes. For *libro 10 capitulo 2* Isidre seth by the touch of the blood *menstruales* fruyt growith noght but drieth and beth ibrent, and dyeth herbes, and treen leseth here fruyt, irne[28] is frete[29] with roust, bras and metal wexith blake. If hounde etith therof, he waxith wood.[30] Also a thing hatte[31] *glutinum aspalti* is so hard that it may nought be todeled[32] with watir nothir with irne, and if the blood *menstrualis* touchith, that *glutinum aspalti* al tofalleth anon, as Isidir seith. This blood is bred in wymmennes bodyes of superfluite of moisture and feblenes of hete. And for it schulde not greve kinde, it is igedred into the modir as filthe into a goter. If it is iput out therof in dwe maner, it clensith and releveth al the body, and clensith the modir also, and disposith and maketh able to conceyve . . .

The superfluyte of [flegm] is knowen, as Constantinus seith, be thise signes and tokens: for a verray fleumatik man is in the body lustles, hevy, and slowgh; dul of wit and of thought, forgeteful; neissche of fleissche and quavy,[33] bloo of colour, whitliche in face, ferdeful of herte; ful of spittinge, snyvel, and rokeinge;[34] ful of slouthe and of slepinge; of a litil appetite and of litil thurst but if the flewme be salt, for than for mellinge[35] of hote humour he filith salt savour in his mouthe; neische, yelowh, and streit of here; neische, grete, and slough of puls. His urine is white and thicke, rawe and evel icoloured. He is fat and greet and schort; and his skin is pleyn and smethe, [bare withouten eer].[36] He metith[37] and hath swevenes[38] of grete watris and

26   madness.
27   Pseudo-Hippocrates (Gariopontus, d. ca. 1050), *Passionarius,* here attributed to Galen.
28   iron.
29   corroded.
30   mad.
31   called.
32   mixed.
33   soft, flabby.
34   spitting, vomiting? (obscure).
35   mixing.
36   hair.
37   dreams.
38   dreams.

snowe and reyne and of seilynge on coolde watir and of swymmynge therinne. Men of that complexioun hath often coolde yveles and beith itravayled[39] therwith and nameliche in wintir, for thanne the qualitees of fleume, coolde and moist, beth istrengthid. So seith Constantin . . .

Thenne this kyndeliche colera, if it passe noght the boundis of kynde, it maketh othir humours sotile, and comfortith digestioun, and clensith drasten[40] and corrupcioun, and maketh the body to strecche in lengthe, brede, and thickenesse, and bredith boldenes and hardynes and mevynge and lightnes and wrethe[41] and appetite of wreche[42] and also of the werkes of Venus, and helpith the *vertu explusive*,[43] and clerith thicke matere and maketh it meve from the middel to the uttir parties, and chauingith the uttir parties in colour of citrine[44] and blak. And so colerik men beth generalliche wratheful, hardy, unmeke, light,[45] unstable, inpetuous; in body long, sklendre, and lene; in colour broun; in eer blak and crips, [hard] and stif; in touche hoot; in puls strong and swifte. The urine of hem is thinne in substaunce and subtile, in colour fury,[46] schinynge, and clere . . .

If this humour [melancholy] have maistrye in any body, thyse beth the signes and tokenes. First, the colour of the skyn chaungith into the blake or into bloo colour; sour savour and sharp and erthey is ifeled in the mouth by the qualite of the humour; the pacient is faynt and ferdful in herte withoute cause. Galien seith if the dredes of suche endureth withouten cause, his passioun is melencolia. And so al that hath this passioun withouten cause beth often dredeful and sory, and that for the melencolif humour constreyneth and closith the herte. And so if men asketh of suche what they drede and wherfore thei beth sory, they haveth none answere. Somme weneth that they schullen dye anon unresonabliche. Somme dredith enemyte of som oon. Som loveth and desireth deth. *In libro passionum* Galien seith no wondir though he that soffreth *coleram nigram* be sorry and have suspeccioun of deth, for no thing is more dredeful outward in the body than derknes. And so whanne any derk thinge heleth the brayn as malincolie flewme, it nedith that the pacyent drede, for he bereth with hym the cause why he

---

[39]   belabored.
[40]   dregs.
[41]   wrath.
[42]   vengeance.
[43]   "*vertu explusive*" is a Galenic faculty, dealing with elimination of wastes.
[44]   yellowish or yellow-red.
[45]   cheerful.
[46]   fiery.

schulde drede. And therfore he meteth dredeful swevenes and of derknes, griselych to se, and stinkinge of smelle, and soure in savour.

Of alle thise cometh *passio melancolya*. Also, it cometh of [*mania*,] "madnes," and of disposicioun of melancolie whanne suche hath likinge and laugheth of sorewful thinges and maketh sorowe and dool for joyeful thingis. Also, suche holdeth here pes whanne they schulde speke and speke to moche whanne they schulde be stille and holde here pees. Also somme trowith that they beth erthene vessellis and dredeth to be touchid lest they beth ibroke. And somme weneth that they closeth and conteyneth the world in here fist and alle thingis in here hondes, and therfore they putte noght here hond to take mete; they dredeth that the worlde schulde tofalle and be lost if they streight out here hondes. Also somme weneth that an aungel holdeth up the worlde and wolde forwery[47] late the worlde falle, and therfore they heveth up here hondes and schuldres to holde up the worlde that hem semeth is in point to falle and breideth[48] strongliche and streyneth if fisicians maketh hem holde doun here hondes. Also somme weneth that they have none heedes, and somme that they have leden hedes or asse hedis or som othir weyes evel ischape. Also somme, if they here the kockes crowe, they rereth up here armes and crowith, and trowith that hemsilf be kockes, and at the laste they ben hoos[49] for grete cryenge and doumbith. Also somme falleth into wel evel suspicions withouten recovere, and therfore they hatith and blameth and schendith hire frendes and somtyme smytith and sleeth hem.

Melencolik men fallith into thise and many othir wondirful passiouns, as Galien seith and Alisaundir[50] and many othir auctours, the which passiouns it were to longe to rekene al on rowe. And this we seeth alday with oure eighen, as it fel late of a nobleman that fel into suche a madnes of melancolye that he in alle wise trowed that he himself was a catte, and therfore he wolde nowher reste but undir beddes there cattis waitid aftir myse.[51] And in cas in wreche of his synnes Nabugodonosor was ipunyschid with suche a payne, for it is iwriten in stories that seven yere hym semed that he was a best thurough divers schappis: lyoun, egle, and ox.[52]

---

[47]   wearily.
[48]   start.
[49]   hoarse.
[50]   Alexander of Tralles (d. 605).
[51]   mice.
[52]   Daniel 4.25–34.

Marriage

Three principal bodies of texts discussed marriage in late medieval Europe: theology, law, and literature. Theologians focused on marriage not only as a socially sanctioned state of mutual love between a man and a woman, but also as many possible relationships among the individual, the Church, and Christ. Hence, earthly marriage, and particularly the wife, ranked lower on a scale below other possible marriages, the married woman less favored than a virgin bride of Christ. The Fourth Lateran Council of 1215 set the prohibition against marriage between first cousins, but this tells us little of the reality of people's abilities and desires to choose. The same council, however, accepted the idea that free consent was necessary, but in England in the later Middle Ages the king and lords frequently imposed a marriage tax on tenants who married people out of their feudal property or who simply wanted freely to choose their own partners. The legal implications of the marriage bond were different for men and women. In general marriage was a disadvantage for a woman, who became a *feme covert*; without special provisions, she was legally "covered" by her spouse, who gained control over land and goods.

Geoffrey de la Tour Landry, a knight from the province of Maine-et-Loire, composed his *Book* for his daughters in 1371–2. Geoffrey states in his prologue that, having composed a book of instruction (now lost) for his sons, he decided to make his book for his daughters because he still remembers his wife who died some twenty years before, he has seen his fellow courtiers deceiving women with their words and deeds, and he wishes his daughters to "turne to good and worshipe above all ertheli thinges." He states that he employed two of his priests and clerks to compile tales of good and evil women for his daughters" instruction from the Bible, histories of kings, and chronicles; he adds examples from his own life as well as commentary. Over twenty French manuscripts of the book survive. Two English translations remain: a mid-fifteenth century manuscript and Caxton's translation from 1483–4 (from which the following excerpt and that in "Sumptuary," p. 215, are taken). Geoffrey's *Book* is a frequently transfixing misogynist text of moral prescription and exempla.

Dives and Pauper consists of a fictionalized dialogue between the wealthy and learned Dives and the authorial poor wandering preacher Pauper. It is a long didactic treatise on the ten commandments written by an unknown friar in the first quarter of the fifteenth century and survives as a whole or in part in eleven manuscripts and three early printings. The majority of the text concerns the ways in which Christian doctrine intersects with human worldly practices (frequently legal practices). Parts of the text take up issues of interest to Wycliffite writers and their opponents. The following excerpt (and the other, in "Sumptuary," p. 215) is from chapter 4 on adultery, the subject of the seventh commandment.

Primary documents and further reading

Geoffrey de la Tour Landry (1973) *The Book of the Knight of La Tour-Landry, Compiled for the Instruction of His Daughters*, ed. T. Wright. EETS, o.s. 33 (1868). Oxford: Oxford University Press.

Helmholz, R. H. (1974) *Marriage Litigation in Medieval England.* Cambridge: Cambridge University Press.

Ho, C. (1994) "As Good as Her Word: Women's Language in *The Knight of the Tour d'Landry.*" In L. O. Purdon and C. L. Vitto (eds.) *The Rusted Hauberk: Feudal Ideals of Order and Their Decline.* Gainseville: University of Florida Press, 99–120.

Krueger, R. L. (1993) "Intergeneric Combination and the Anxiety of Gender in *Le Livre du Chevalier de la Tour Landry pour l'Enseignement de Ses Filles.*" *L'Esprit Créateur* 33: 61–72.

Loengard, J. S. (1990) " 'Legal History and the Medieval Englishwoman' Revisited: Some New Directions." In J. T. Rosenthal (ed.) *Medieval Women and the Sources of Medieval History.* Athens, GA: University of Georgia Press, 210–36.

Montaiglon, A. de (1854) *Le Livre du Chevalier de La Tour Landry pour l'enseignement de ses filles.* Paris.

Noonan, J. T. (1973) "Marriage in the Middle Ages: Power to Choose." *Viator* 4: 419–34.

Power, E. (ed. and trans.) (1928) *The Goodman of Paris.* London: Routledge.

Sheehan, M. M. (1996) *Marriage, Family, and Law in Medieval Europe: Collected Studies*, ed. J. K. Farge. Toronto: University of Toronto Press.

Geoffrey de la Tour Landry (1971) *The Book of the Knight of the Tower*, trans. W. Caxton, ed. M. Y. Offord. EETS, s.s. 2. London: Oxford University Press, 168–70.
Language: English (Southeast Midland)
Book date: 1484

How men ought to love after his estate and degree.

"What saye yow, lady,[1] wold ye have kept them so straitly that they shold not take somme plesaunce more to somme than to the other?"

"Syre, I wylle not that they have or take ony plesaunce of them that ben of lower estate or degree than they be of, that is to wete, that no woman

---

[1] the lady of the tower.

unwedded shalle not sette her love upon no man of lower or lasse degree than she is of. For yf she tooke hym, her parentes and frendes shold hold her lassed and hyndered.[2] These, whiche loven suche folke, done ageynste theyre worship and honoure. For men ought to desyre ne coveyte nothynge so moche in this world as worship and the frendship of the world and of hir frendes, the whiche is lost as soone as she draweth oute her self oute of the governement and fro the counceyll of them, as I myght telle, yf I wold, an ensample of many whiche therfore ben dyffamed and hated of theyr parents and frendes.

"And therfore, syre, as I theyr moder charge and deffende them: that they take no playsaunce,[3] ne that in no wyse sette theyr love to none of lower degree than they be come of, ne also to none of hyhe estate, whiche they may not have to their lord. For the grete lordes shalle not take them to theyr wyves, but alle theyr lovynge loke and semblaunt, they do it for to deceyve them and for to have the delytes and playsaunce of theyr bodyes, and for to brynge them in to the folye of the world."

How wedded wymmen, whiche have sette theyr love to some of lower degree than they be of, are not worthy to be callyd wymmen.
"Also, they whiche putte and sette theyr love on thre maner of folke – that is to wete, wedded men, prestes, and monkes, and as to servauntes and folke of noughte – these maner of wymmen, whiche take to theyr peramours and love suche folke, I hold them of none extyme ne valewe but that they be more gretter harlottes than they that ben dayly at the bordell. For many wymmen of the world done that synne of lechery but only for nede and poverte, or els by cause they have ben deceyved of hit by false counceylle of bawdes. But alle gentylle women whiche have ynough to lyve on, the whiche make theyre peramours or lovers suche maner of folke as before is sayd, it is by the grete ease wherin they be and by the brennynge lecherye of theyr bodyes. For they knowe wel that, after the lawe of theyr maryage, they may not have for theyr lordes ne to be theyr husbondes men of the chirche ne other of no valewe. This love is not for to recovere ony worship but alle dishonour and shame."

How hit is almesse[4] to enhaunce a man in to grete valour.
"At the leste, syth ye wylle not graunte ne accorde that youre doughters love no man peramours as longe as they shalle be unwedded, please it yow

---

[2] lowered and belittled.
[3] pleasure.
[4] alms, good deeds.

to suffre that whanne they shall be wedded, they may take somme plesaunce of love for to hold and behave them self the more gaye and joyefull, and for the better knowe theyr behavynge and maner emonge folke of worship. And as before this tyme I have sayd to yow, it were to them grete welthe and worship to make a man of none extyme ne of valewe to become of grete valour."

The answere of the lady of the towre.
"Sire, to thys I ansuere yow: I wylle well and am content that they make good chere to all worshipfulle men, and more to somme than to the other, that is to wete, to them of gretter name and more gentyl, or els better men of theyr persones, and after that they bere to them worship and honour, and that they synge and daunce before them honourably. But as for to love peramours sythe they shall be wedded – withoute it be of suche love as men ought to bere unto folke of worshippe – for to love and worshippe them after that they be worthy and of valour, and whiche have had grete payne and travaylle to gete and acquere glorye and worshyp by theyr valyaunce in armes, these must be loved, doubted,[5] served, and honoured withoute havynge in them ony plesaunce, sauf only for the bounte of them. But to saye and hold hit good that a wedded woman shold love and have a peramour, ne take the othe and feythe of none, to thende that they be theyr lovers and peramours, ne also to gyve also to gyve their feith and othe to none, I trowe and wene certaynly that no lady ne damoysell, wedded ne woman of other estate, shall not put her estate and worship in this balaunce . . ."

Glasgow University Library MS Hunterian 270, fols. 161v–172r. In P. H. Barnum (ed.) (1980) *Dives and Pauper*, 2 parts. EETS, o.s. 275, 280. London: Oxford University Press, II: 65–89 (selections).
Language: English (Southwestern)
Manuscript date: ca. 1450

DIVES: Whan gaf God lawys of matrimonye, and what lawys gaf he?
PAUPER: Whan God hadde mad Adam, he put a gret slep in hym and in his slep he took out on of his rybbys and fylde up the place with flesch, and of that rybbe he made Eve and broughte hir to Adam. Than Adam awooc and, as God inspyred hym, he tolde the lawys of wedlac and seyde thus: "This bon is now of myn bonys and this flesch of myn flesch, for this thing man

---

[5]   feared.

shal forsakyn fadyr and modyr, and clevyn to his wyf, and ther schul ben two in on flesch," Genesis 2[6]. In whiche wordys, whan he seide that man for his wyf schulde forsakyn fadyr and moodir, and clevyn to his wif, he schewyd the sacrament of trewe love and unyte that owith to ben atwoxsyn[7] housebonde and wyf, and be the same wordis he schewyd what feith owith to ben atwoxsyn hem, for he shal clevyn to hys wyf and medlyn with hyr and with non othir, and she with hym and with non othir. And in that he seyde that ther shuldyn ben two in on flesch he schewyd that thei shuldyn medlyn togedere principaly to bryngyn forth childryn to Godys worchepe, for in her child, housebond and wyf ben on flesch and on blood. Also, in that he seyde that the housebonde schulde clevyn to his wyf, he defendyth[8] fornicacion and avouterie. And in that he seyde in the singuler numbre – "to hys wyf" and nout "to his wyfys" – he defendyd bygamye, that a man schulde nout han to wyfys togedere ne on woman to house-boundys togedere. And in that he seyde that thei two schuldyn ben in on flesch he defendyd sodomye. And also be the same wordis he schewith that iche of hem hat power ovyr otheris body and non of hem may conteynyn but thei ben bothin therto of on assent. DIVES: Why made God woman mor of the rybbe of Adam than of anothir bon? PAUPER: For the rybbe is nexst the herte, in tokene that God made hyr to ben mannys felawe in love and his helpere. And as the rybbe is nexst the herte of alle bonys, so schulde the wyf ben nexst in love of all women and of alle men. God made nout woman of the foot to ben mannys thral ne he made hyr nout of the hefd to ben hys maystir but of his syde and of his rybbe to ben his felawe in love and helper at nede. But whan Eve synnyd, than was woman maad soget to man, that the wyf schulde ben rewlyd be hyr housebonde and dredyn hym and servyn hym as felaw in love and helper at nede and as nest solas[9] in sorwe, nout as thral and bonde in vyleyn servage, for the housebonde owyth to han his wyf in reverence and worchepe in that they ben bothin on flesch and on blood. DIVES: Why made nout God woman be hyrself of the erde as he dede Adam? PAUPER: For to moryn[10] her love togedere and also to gevyn woman materie of[11] lownesse. First, for moryng of love, for in that woman is part of mannys body man must lovyn hyr as hys owyn flesch and blood,

---

[6] Genesis 2.23–4.
[7] between.
[8] forbids.
[9] nest of consolation.
[10] increase.
[11] reason for.

and she must also lovyn man as hyr begynnyng and as hyr flesch and hyr blood. Also, she owyth takyn gret materie of lownesse and thynkyn that man is hir perfeccioun and hyr begynnynge, and han man in reverence as hyr perfeccioun, as hyr principal, as hyr begynnyng, and hyr firste in ordre of kende. God made al mankende of on, for he wolde that al mankende schulde ben on in charite as they comyn al of on.

DIVES: Wether is avouterie gretere synne in the man than in the woman?
PAUPER: Comounly it is mor synne in the man than in the woman, for the heyere degre, the harder is the fal and the synne mor grevous. Also, man is mor myghty be weye of kende to with-stondyn and hat mor skyl and resoun wherby he may withstondyn and bewar of the fendis gyle. And in that he is mad maystir and governour of woman to governyn hyr in vertue and kepyn hyr from vycis, if he falle in vycis and in avouterie mor than woman, he is mychil to blame and worthi to ben reprovyd schamfully. Therfor, Sent Austyn, *libro De decem cordis*, undirnemyth[12] housebondys that fallyn in avouterie and seith to iche of hem in this maner: "God seith to the that thu schal don non lecherie, that is to seye, thu schalt medelyn with no woman but with thin wyf. Thu askyst this of thin wyf, that she medele with non but with the, and thu wilt nout yeldyn this ne kepyn this to thin wyf. And ther thu aughtyst ben aforn thin wyf in vertu thu fallys[t] doun undir the byr of lecherie. Thu wilt that thin wyf be ovyrcomere of lecherye and han the maystry of the fend, and thu wilt ben ovyrcomyn as a coward and lyn don in lecherye. And noutwithstondyng that thu art hefd of thin wyf, yet thin wyf goth aforn the to God, and thu that art hefd of thin wif gost bakward to helle. Man," seith he, "is hefd of woman,[13] and therfor in what houshold the woman lyvyth betere than the man, in that houshold hongyth the hefd donward for, sith man is hefd of woman, he owith to lyvyn betere than woman and gon aforn his wif in alle goode dedys that she mon suhyn[14] here housebounde and folwyn hyr hefd. The hefd of iche houshold is the housebonde, and the wyf is the body. Be cours of kende, thedir that the hefd ledyth, thedir schulde the body folwyn. Whi wil than the hefd that is the housebounde gon to lecherie and he wil nout that his body, his wyf, folwe? Why wil the man gon thedyr whydir he wil nout that his wif folwe?"[15] And a lytyl aftir in the same booc Sent Austyn seith thus: "Day be day pleyntis ben maad of mannys lecherie although her wyfys dur nout plenyyn

---

[12] reproves.
[13] 1 Corinthians 11.3; Ephesians 5.23.
[14] follow.
[15] Augustine (354–430), *Sermons*.

hem on her housebondys. Lecherie of men is so bold and so custumable[16] that it is now takyn for a lawe insomychil that men tellyn her wyfys that lecherie and avouterie is leful to men but nout to women," thus seith Sent Austyn. DIVES: And sumtyme it is herd and wust that wyfys ben takyn lychynge with her servans and brout to court afor the juge with mychyl schame. But that ony housebounde is so brout to court aforn the juge for he lay with ony of his women, it is seldam seyn. PAUPER: "And though," as seith Sent Austyn in the same booc, "it is as gret a synne in the housebonde as in the wif and somdel mor, but forsothe," seith he, "it is nout the trewthe of God but the schrewidnesse of man that makyth man lesse gylty than woman in the same synne." Men ben nout so oftyn takyn in avouterie ne punchyd for avouterie as women ben, nout for thei ben lesse gylty but for that thei ben mor gylty, and mor myghty, and mor sley to meyntethin her synne, and nyh iche of hem confortith othir in his synne. Men ben witnessis, jugis, and doerys to punchyn avouterie in woman. And for thei ben ovyrdon[17] gylty in avouterye, therfor thei travaylyn nyh alle with on assent to meyntethin her lecherie. In woman is seldam seyn avouterie, and therfor it is wol slaundrous whan it fallyt and hard punchyd. But in men it is so comoun that ther is unethis ony slaundre therof. Women dur nout spekyn agenys the lecherye of men, and men wyl nout spekyn to reprovyn lecherye of man for thei ben so mychil gylty . . .

DIVES: Women mon betere ben chast than men for thei han mychil kepyng[18] upon hem. The lawe byndith hem to chaste. Her housebondis ben besy to kepyn hem, and harde lawys ben ordeynyd to punchyn hem if they don omys. PAUPER: To this answerith Sent Austyn in the same booc and seith thus: "Mychil kepynge makith woman chast, and manhod schulde makyn man chast. To woman is ordeynyd mychil kepynge, for she is mor frele. Woman is aschamyd for hyr housebound to don omys, but thu art nout aschamyd for Crist to don omys. Thu art mor fre than the woman for thu art strangere and lythlyere,[19] thu myght ovyr-comyn the flesch and the fend if thu wilt, and therfor God hat betakyn the to the. But on woman is mychil kepyng of hir housebonde, dredful lawys, good norture, gret schamfastnesse, and god principal; and thu, man, hast only God abovyn the. Thin wif fleth lecherie for dred and schame of the, for dred of the lawe, for good norture, and pryncipaly for God. But for alle these thu kepist the nout

---

[16]   customary.
[17]   excessively.
[18]   attention.
[19]   stronger and more lithe.

chast ne thu levyst nout thin lecherie neyther for dred of God, ne for Godis lawe, ne for schame of the world, ne for schame of thin wyf to whom thu art boundyn to ben trewe, ne thu wilt levyn it for no good norture but lyvyn as an harlot and usyn harlotis manerys; thu art nout aschamyd of thin synne," seith Sent Austyn, "for so many men fallyn therynne. The schrewidnesse of man is now so gret that men ben mor aschamyd of chaste than of lecherie. Manquellerys,[20] thevys, perjurerys, fals witnessis, raveynouris,[21] and false men ben abhominable and hatyd amongis the peple, but hoso wil lyn be his woman and ben a bold lechour, he that is lovyd, he that is preysyd, and alle the woundis of his soule turnyn into gamyn. And if ony man be so hardy to seyn that he is chast and trewe to his wif, and it be knowyn that he be swiche, he is aschamyd to comyn amongis men that ben nout lyk hym in manerys, for thei schul japyn hym, and scornyn hym, and seyn that he is no man, for manys schrewydnesse is now so gret that ther is no man holdyn a man but he be ovyrcomyn with lecherie, and he that ovyrcomyth lecherie and kepit hym chast, he is letyn[22] no man." These ben the wordis of Sent Austyn in the same booc . . .[23]

[T]he lawe put many cas in whyche the housebounde may nout accusyn his wyf of lecherie; first, if he be gylty in the same . . . Also, if he geve hyr occasion to don fornicacioun be withheldynge of dette of his body . . . Also, if she be defylyd be strencthe and gret violence agenys hyr wil . . . Also, if she wene that her housebond be ded . . . And if she be weddyd to anothir wenyng that hyr housebound be ded, whan he comyth hom, she must forsakyn the secunde housebonde and wendyn agen to the firste; and but she forsake the secunde onon as she knowith that hyr firste housebounde is on lyve ellys she fallith in avouterye and hir firste housebonde may accusyn hyr and forsakyn hyr. Also, if she be deceyvyd and medelyth with anothir wenynge that it wer hyr housebonde . . . Also, if he knewe hyr lecherie and suffryth hyr in hyr synne and medelyth with hyr aftir that he knowyth hyr synne or forgevy[th] it hyr and reconcylith hyr to hym, than may he nout accusyn hyr . . . Also, if hyr housebonde put hyr to don omys . . . Also, if an hethene man forsake his hethene wif and she be weddyt to anothir hethene man and aftir thei ben bothin turnyd to Cristene feith, than is he bondyn to takyn hyr agen but she felle in ony othir fornicacioun, nout-wythstondynge that she be knowyn flechly of the secunde house-bonde . . .

[20]   man-killers.
[21]   thieves, rapists.
[22]   considered.
[23]   *Sermons.*

DIVES: Reson and holy writ cachyn me to grantyn that bothin avouterie and symple fornicacion ben wol grevous synnys, but mor grevous is avouterie, and fayn Y wolde kepyn me from bothin synnys. But women ben the fendis snaris and so temptyn men to lecherie that it is wol hard to me for the kepyn me. *"Adam, Sampsonem, Petrum, David, and Salomonem femina decepit; quis modo tutus erit?"* "Woman deceyvyd Adam and Sampson, Petir, Davyd, and Salomon; ho may than ben sykyr from womanys gyle?"[24] PAUPER: Many man hat ben deceyvyd be wyckyd women mor be his owyn folye than be deceyt of woman, but many mo women han ben deceyvyd be the malyce of men than evere wer men deceyvyd be malyce of woman. Therfor, the woman lechour is clepyd the snare of the fendis that huntyn aftir mannys soule, for Salomon seith: *"Inveni amario-rem morte mulierem, etc.,"* "Y have foundyn woman mor byttyr than deth. She is the snare of the hunterys, hyr herte is a net and hyr hondis ben harde bondys. He that plesith God schal ascapyn hyr, but the synful man schal be takyn of hyr," Ecclesiastes 7[25] But men ben clepyd nout only the snare of the fend but also thei ben clepyd his net sprad abrod on the hyl of Thabor for to takyn many at onys, Hosea 5[26]. Mannys malyce is clepyd a net sprad abrod on an heye hil for it is opyn and boldeliche don, nout in a fewe but in manye, and therfor whan holy wryt reprovyt the malyce of men, he spekith in the plurer numbre as to manye, but whan he reprovyth the malyce of woman he spekyt in the singuler numbre as to fewe in tokene that ther ben mor schrewis of men than of women and comounly mor malyce in men than in women, althou sum woman be wol malicious. Fyghtynge, roberye, manslaute, opyn lecherie, glotonye, gyle, falsnesse, perjurie, tretourie, fals contr[y]vynge, and swyche othir horrible synnys regnyn mor in man than in woman.

This fals excusacioun that men so excusyn her synne be the malyce of woman began in Adam and les[27] Adam and al mankende, for synfullyche he excusyd hys synne be woman whan God undirnam[28] hym of hys synne and putte woman in defaute; and also he put God in defaute that made woman and answeryd wol proudlyche, as men don these dayys, and seide to God: "Woman that thu geve to me to ben myn felawe gaf me of the tre, and Y

---

[24] Salimbene de Adam (1221–ca. 1287).
[25] Ecclesiastes 7.27.
[26] Osee 5.1.
[27] lies with.
[28] reproved.

eet therof,"[29] as ho[30] seye: "Haddist thu nout govyn hyr to me to ben myn felawe, Y schulde nout a synnyd." And so noutwithstondynge that he was mor in defaute than woman, yet he wolde nout knowlechyn ony defaute but he putte woman and God principaly that made woman in defaute. DIVES: Hou was Adam mor in defaute than woman? PAUPER: For to hym pryncipaly God gaf the precept that he schulde nout etyn of that tre, and Eve knew it nout but be Adam. Woman was temptyd be the fend wondirfolyche in the neddere, whyche wente that tyme righth up and hadde a face lyk a woman, as seith Bede and the Maystyr of Storiis,[31] and she was deceyvyd with his fayre behestis and his false slye speche, for he hyghte[32] hyr that thei schuldyn nout deyyn but ben as Goddis, connyng good and wyckyd. Adam hadde non temptacioun fro outward but a symple word of his wyf that profryd hym the appyl, for we fyndyn nout that she seyde to hym ony deceyvable word. And therfor sith man was forbodyn of Godys mouth, and she nout but be man, and man hadde lesse temptacioun than woman and therto in nothing wolde accusyn hymself ne yeldyn hym gylty but putte defaute al in woman and in God, therfor he synnyd mor than woman, for woman yald hyr gylty,[33] but she askyd no merci. She made non swyche excusacion but in gret party yald hyr gylty in that she seyde, "The neddere hat deceyvyd me."[34] For in that she knowlechyd that she was deceyvyd, she knowlechid that she hadde don omys, and unwiselyche, and othirwyse than sche aughte a don. And for that woman lowyd hyr and knowlechyd hyr unwisdam and hyr folye, therfor God putte in woman that tyme onon hope of our savacioun whan he seyde to the neddere: "Y schal puttyn enmyte atwoxsyn the and woman, and atwoxsyn thi seed and hyr seed, and she schal brekyn thin hefd."[35] That was the fend, whyche was hefd and ledere of the neddere that tyme. The seed of the fend ben wyckyd warkys and wyckyd folc, to whyche God seyde in the gospel: "*Vos ex patre diabolo estis*," John 8, "Ye ben of the fadir the fend."[36] The seed of woman gostlyche ben hyr goode dedys, with whyche the fend and the fendis lymys han gret envye, and comounly women wlatyn[37] mor horriblete of synne than don men. And

---

[29]   Genesis 3.12.
[30]   though he.
[31]   The Venerable Bede (672–735); Peter Comestor (d. 1178).
[32]   promised.
[33]   yielded herself as guilty.
[34]   Genesis 3.13.
[35]   Genesis 3.15.
[36]   John 8.44.
[37]   abandon.

be our lady, blyssyd mote she ben, the fendys power is dystryyd. Also, the seed of woman was Crist, born of the maydyn Marie withoutyn part of man, and so ther was nevere man propyrly seed of woman but Crist alone, and alwey is enmyte betwoxsyn Crist and the fend and his seed . . .

And so ben men yit these days ovyrcomyn with lecherye withoutyn womanys companye and withoutyn doyng of women for, as Crist seyth in the gospel, "Hoso loke on a woman in wil to don omys with hyr, though she thinke nout on hym, he that doth lecherye";[38] and if he handele hyr, or smelle hyr, or speke to hyr, or go to hyr, or seke be whilys and sleyghthis to han his lust of hyr, thou the woman consente nout to hym and though he be lettyd of his wyckyd wil, yit is he gylty in lecherye and doth agenys this comandement of God: "Non mechaberys."[39] Men lechourys gon and rydyn fro town to town to getyn women at her lust. Thei sekyn the women and nout the women hem. They castyn many wylys to getyn womanys assent in synne. Men comounly ben warkeris and begynnerys of lecherie, and than wether the woman assente or nout assente, yit the man is gylty. And for oftyntyme it fallit that whan men wendyn ben sekyr of the womanys assent, than the woman wil nout assentyn for dred of God; and if she assentyd aforn and hyghte the man to folwyn his lust and aftir repentyth hyr and withdrawith hyr from hys wyckyd companye, than schal that lechourys man diffamyn al women and scyn that thei ben false and deceyvable, for swyche lechouris spekyn mest vylenye of women for they mon nout han her foul lust of hem at wille. And for thei mon nout defylyn hem with her body, they defylyn hem with her tunge and spekyn of hem wol evele and diffamyn hem falslyche and procuryn to hem the harm that they mon . . .

DIVES: And, though, many woman wil assentyn to lust of the flesch wol lyghthlych if it be profryd. PAUPER: That is soth, but women be nout so redy to assentyn as men ben to profryn it, and he that profryth it and begynnyth, he assentyth first and is mor in defaute. DIVES: Thu excusist mychil women and accusist men. PAUPER: Y accuse non good man but wyckyd men, lechouris, ne Y excuse no wyckyd woman but goode women that ben falslyche defamyd of lecherie, nout only in here personys but in her kende generaly, for the proude malyce of man diffamyth unskylfolyche[40] the kende of woman and, as Adam dede, put his synne on woman and nout wil accusyn hys owyn malyce to getyn mercy.

---

[38]   Matthew 5.28.
[39]   "Thou shalt not commit adultery," Exodus 20.14.
[40]   unjustly.

Pilgrimage

The spiritual, moral, physical, and pecuniary aspects of pilgrimages were the subject of debate throughout the Middle Ages, but contention intensified in the fourteenth and fifteenth centuries in England as it did on the Continent. Archbishops, bishops, and others encouraged the view that pilgrimages were effective in remitting sins, while popular belief in the efficacy of visiting shrines of saints for curative reasons remained strong. On the other hand, arguments arose against physical pilgrimages and for the superiority of an exclusively spiritual journey, which may include enclosed or private forms of asceticism and hardship as well as penance that did not involve travel. Also, geographic pilgrimages as penance were not always voluntary during this period, and it became increasingly common for people to be sentenced to perform pilgrimages for violations such as adultery, disturbing the peace, theft, assault, poaching, and even more serious crimes. These actions fed tensions about class inequities as well as led to concern about the danger caused by involuntary pilgrims. Corruption and excesses associated with pilgrimages also received criticism; how important for contrition was the buying of badges, likenesses of saints, relics, wax talismans, candles, and other paraphernalia? That both willing and sentenced pilgrims could pay off their pilgrimage through various forms of donation or by having a proxy perform the pilgrimage also raised questions about penance as well as social justice. Uneasiness about the veneration of saints and physical representations of spiritual figures logically became associated with discussions about pilgrimages, especially from Lollards. Their criticism of the many aspects of pilgrimages is one of their most distinctive and common objections (see "Lollard Trials," p. 59, and "Plays and Representations," p. 262).

William Thorpe was educated (possibly at Oxford) and took orders as a priest. Some time between 1382 and 1386 Robert Braybrooke, bishop of London (1382–1404), tried Thorpe for heresy and imprisoned him there. In 1397 he was released from that imprisonment (or possibly a second term in prison). Ten years later on August 7, 1407, Thorpe was examined before Thomas Arundel (archbishop of York 1388–97, archbishop of Canterbury 1396–7, 1399–1414) and three clerks in Saltwood Castle in Kent. According to a "litil rolle" in the archbishop's hands, a bailiff from Shrewsbury claimed that Thorpe had preached that the sacrament remained material bread after consecration, that images should not be worshipped, that people should not go on pilgrimages, that priests have no right to receive tithes, and that it is not lawful to swear in any manner. Thorpe denies the specific charges in his *Testimony* and submits himself to God and the Church as long as they accord with his ideas; his account ends with him being sent to prison. Thorpe's *Testimony* survives in four versions; Rawlinson C.208 is the earliest.

Whether the events recounted in Thorpe's text are truthful or not is open to debate, and the issue becomes even more interesting because of his realist style: dramatic arguments, detailed depictions of the actions of those present, descriptions of Thorpe's own thoughts and feelings. The reasons why a person would openly proclaim in writing his continuing adherence to Lollard beliefs are difficult to understand, especially if he recanted. If Thorpe wrote his account in prison, it is puzzling how such a manuscript would have circulated.

Primary documents and further reading

Copeland, R. (1996) "William Thorpe and His Lollard Community: Intellectual Labor and the Representation of Dissent." In B. A. Hanawalt and D. Wallace (eds.) *Bodies and Disciplines: Intersections of Literature and History in Fifteenth-century England*. Minneapolis: University of Minnesota Press, 199–221.

Finucane, R. C. (1995) *Miracles and Pilgrims: Popular Beliefs in Medieval England*. New York: St. Martin's Press.

Jurkowski, M. (2002) "The Arrest of William Thorpe in Shrewsbury and the Anti-Lollard Statute of 1406." *Historical Research* 75: 273–95.

Loxton, H. (1978) *Pilgrimage to Canterbury*. Newton Abbot, Devon: David and Charles.

Somerset, F. (1998) *Clerical Discourse and Lay Audience in Late Medieval England*. Cambridge: Cambridge University Press.

Sumption, J. (1975) *Pilgrimage: An Image of Mediaeval Religion*. Totowa, NJ: Rowman and Littlefield.

Webb, D. (2000) *Pilgrimage in Medieval England*. London: Hambledon Press.

William Thorpe. Bodleian Library MS Rawlinson C.208, fols. 51v–57r. In A. Hudson (ed.) (1993) *Two Wycliffite Texts*. EETS, o.s. 301. Oxford: Oxford University Press, 61–5.
Language: English (Southeast Midland)
Manuscript date: ca. 1410

And thanne the archebischop seide to me, "What seist thou now to the thridde poynt that is certefied agens thee, preching at Schrovesbirie opinli that pilgrimage is unleeful? And over this thou seidist there that tho men and wymmen that goen on pilgrimage to Cantirbirie, to Beverleye, to

Bridlyntoun, to Walsyngam, or to ony suche pilgrymage ben acursid and madd foolis spendi[n]ge her goodis in wast."[1]

And I seide, "Sere, bi this certificacioun I am acusid to you that I schulde teche that no pilgrimage is leeful. But, ser, I seide nevere thus, for I knowe that there is trewe pilgrimage and leeful and ful plesynge to God. And therfore, ser, howevere myn enemyes have certified to you of me, I toolde at Schrovesbirie of two manere of pilgrimagis, seiinge that ther ben trewe pilgrimes and fals pilgrimes."

And the archebischop seide to me, "Whom clepist thou trewe pilgrimes?"

And I seide, "Sere, with my forseid protestacioun, I clepe hem trewe pilgrymes travelynge toward the blis of hevene, whiche in the staat, degree, or ordre that God clepith hem to, bisien hem feithfulli for to occupie alle her wittis, bodili and goostli, to know treweli and to kepe feithfulli the heestis of God, hatynge evere and fleynge alle the sevene dedli synnes and every braunche of hem; reulynge vertuousli, as it is seide bifore, alle her wittis; doynge discretli, wilfully, and gladli alle the workis of mercy, bodili and goostli, aftir her kunnynge and her power; ablynge[2] hem to the giftis of the Holi Goost; disposynge hem to resceyve into her soule and to holde therinne the eighte blessingis of Crist,[3] bisiynge hem to knowe and to kepe the sevene principal vertues. And so thanne thei schulen deserve herthorugh grace for to usen thankfulli to God alle the condiciouns of charite, and thanne thei schulen be movyd with the good spirit of God for to examyne ofte and bisili her conscience, with that neither wilfulli ne witingli thei erren in ony article of bileve, havynge contynuely, as freel kynde wole suffre, al her bisinesse to dreede and fle the offence of God, and to love over al thing and seche to done ever his plesynge will. Of these pilgrymes I seide whatever good thought that thei ony tyme thenken, what vertues worde that thei speken, and what fructuouse werk that thei worchen, every such thought, word, and werk is a stap noumbrid of God toward him into hevene. These blessid pilgrymes of God, whan thei heeren of seyntis or of vertuouse men or wymmen, thei bisien hem to knowe the lyvynge of seyntis and of vertues men and wymmen, how thei forsoken wilfulli the prosperite of this lyf, how thei withstoden the sugestiouns of the fend, and how thei ref[r]eyneden her fleischli lustis, how discreet thei weren in [penaunce doynge, how pacient thei weren in] alle her adversitees, how prudent thei weren in conselynge of

---

[1]   Canterbury had the shrine of Thomas à Becket (archbishop of Canterbury 1162–70), Beverley a shrine to St. John, Bridlington a shrine to St. John of Bridlington (prior 1362–ca. 1375), and Walsingham a shrine to the Virgin.
[2]   preparing.
[3]   Matthew 5.3–11.

men and of wymmen, movynge hem to haten evere al synne and to fle it, and to schame evere greetli therof, and to love alle vertues and to drawe to hem, ymagynynge how mekeli Crist and his sueris[4] bi ensaumple suffry[d]e[n] scornes and sclaundris, and how pacientli thei aboden and token the wrath ful manassynges of tirauntis, how homely[5] thei weren and servysable to pore men for to releve hem and conforte hem bodili [and gostli] aftir her kunnynge and her power, and how devoute thei were in preieris, how fervent in hevenli desiris, and how thei absentid hem fro spectaclis and fro veyn sightis and heeringe, and how stable of contenaunce thei weren, how herteli thei weileden and sorewiden for synne, how bisi thei weren to lette and to distroie alle vicis, and how laborouse and joieful thei weren to sowe and to plante vertues. These hevenli condiciouns and suche other have tho pilgrimes either thei bisien hem to have, whos pilgrimage God accepith.

"And agenward," I seide, "as her werkis schewen, the moost part of hem, bothe men and wymmen, that gon now on pilgrimage, have not these forseide condiciouns neither loven to bisien hem feithfulli to have hem. For, as I wel knowe, sith I have ful ofte assaied, examyne (whoevere wole and can) twenti of these pilgrimes, and there schulen not be founden ofte three men or wymmen among these twenti that knowen thriftili oon heest of God, neither thei cunnen seien the Pater Noster, neither the Ave, neither the Crede in ony manere langage. And, as I have lerned and also I knowe sumdel bi experience of these same pilgrimes, tellinge the cause whi that manye men and wymmen now gon hidir and thidir on pilgrymage, it is more for the helthe of her bodies than for the helthe of her soulis, more for to have richessis and prosperite of this world than for to be enrichid with vertues in her soulis, more for to have here worldli or fleischli frendschip than for to have frendschip of God or of hise scintis in hevene; for whatevere thing man or womman doith, neither the frendschip of God ne of ony seint mai be hadde withouten kepynge of Goddis heestis.

"Forthi with my protestacioun, I seie now as I seide in Schrovesbirie, though thei that have siche fleischli willis traveilen soore her bodies and spenden myche moneye to sechen and visiten the bones either ymagis, as thei seien thei don, of that seint or of that, siche pilgrymage is neithir preisable ne thankful to God neither to ony seint of God sith in effecte alle siche pilgrymes dispisen God and alle hise seyntis. For the heestis of God thei wolen neither knowen ne kepe, neither thei wolen conforme hem to lyve vertuesly bi ensaumple of Crist and of hise seyntis. Wherfor, ser, I have prechid and taughte opinli and privyli, and so I purpose al my lyf time to do

---

[4]   disciples, followers.
[5]   plain, unpretentious.

with Goddis helpe, seiinge that siche madde peple wasten blamfulli Goddis goodis in her veyne pilgrymageyng, spendynge these goodis upon vicious[6] hosteleris and upon tapsters, whiche ben ofte unclene wymmen of her bodies, and at the laste tho goodis, of the whiche thei schulden do werkis of mercy aftir Goddis heeste to pore nedi men and wymmen, these pore men goodis and her lyflode these renners aboute offren to riche preestis, whiche have moche moore lyfelode than thei neden. And thus tho goodis thei wasten wilfulli and spenden hem unjustli agens Goddis heeste upon strangeris, with the whiche thei schulden helpe and releeven aftir Goddis wille her pore and nedi neighebores at home. Yhe, and over this foli, ofte tymes dyverse men and wymmen of these that rennen thus madly hidir and thidir on pilgrimagynge, borow[e]n herto mennys goodis, yhe, and sumtyme thei stelen mennes goodis herto, and thei yelden hem nevere agen.

"Also, sire, I knowe wel that whanne dyverse men and wymmen wolen goen thus aftir her owne willis and fyndingis out on pilgrimageyngis, thei wolen ordeyne biforehonde to have with hem bothe men and wymmen that kunnen wel synge rowtinge[7] songis, and also summe of these pilgrimes wolen have with hem baggepipis so that in eche toun that thei comen thorugh, what with noyse of her syngynge, and with the soun of her pipinge, and with the gingelynge of her Cantirbirie bellis,[8] and with the berkynge out of dogges aftir hem, these maken more noyse than if the king came there awey with his clarioneris and manye other mynystrals. And if these men and wymmen ben a monethe oute in her pilgrymage, manye of hem an half yeere aftir schulen be greete jangelers, tale tellers, and lyeris."

And the archebischop seide to me, "Lewid losel,[9] thou seest not fer inowgh in this mateer, for thou considrist not the grete traveile of pilgrymes, and therfore thou blamest that thing that is preisable. I seie to thee that is right wel don that pilgrimes have with hem bothe syngeris and also baggepipes that, whanne oon of hem that gon barefot smytith his too agens a stoon and hurtith him soore and makith him blede, it is wel done that he or his felowe take thanne up a songe either ellis take out of her bosum a baggepipe for to dryve awei with siche myrthe the hurt of his sore, for with siche solace the traveile and werinesse of pilgrymes is lightli and myrili brought forth."

And I seide, "Sere, Seint Poul techith men to wepe with men wepinge."[10]

[6] corrupting.
[7] bellowing.
[8] Pilgrims frequently attached small bells to their horses' bridles.
[9] wretch.
[10] Romans 12.15.

And the archebischop scornede me and seide, "What janglist thou agens mennys devocioun? Whatevere thou and siche other seyen, I seie that the pilgrimage that is now usid is to hem that done it a preparacioun and a good m[e]ene to come the rather[11] to grace. But I holde thee unable to knowe this grace, for thou enforsist thee to lette the devocioun of the peple sith, bi autorite of holi writt, men mowen lefulli have and use siche solace as thou reprevest. For Davith in his laste psalme techith men to usen dyverse intrumentis of musik for to preise with God."[12]

Prioresses

In the year 1000 only six or seven religious houses for women existed in England. When religious houses were dissolved in the sixteenth century, approximately seventy-five Benedictine nunneries were active. Nuns' primary duties were prayer, contemplation of religious texts, and duties that sustained their house. Nunneries' wealth varied widely, from those that received royal patronage or that benefited from the bequests of affluent families, to houses that were in constant peril of economic failure.

Prioresses and abbesses often were women of some social standing. They were in charge of not only the spiritual but also the physical well-being of usually about twelve sisters; they had to be adept at managing property, assigning work, buying and selling goods, finances, overseeing support staff, novices' education, and discipline. The Ankerwyke priory of Benedictine nuns in Buckinghamshire west of London was founded about 1160 and contained eight nuns in 1441. The properties mentioned in the bishop's record that were administered by the prioress, Dame Clemence Medforde, were all within a 20-mile radius of the abbey.

The following excerpt is fairly typical of bishops' visitation accounts, revealing situations in which rules are frequently broken while accusations and revenge are common among the inhabitants of houses. It follows the usual form of such documents: introduction, *detecta* (the house members' depositions) and *comperta* (the bishop's findings) here combined, publication of the findings before the convent, and injunctions. Of bishop William Alnwick's forty-two surviving accounts from 1438–45, nine contain injunctions in English, all of which are addressed to women's houses. (Alnwick also presided over Lollard cases, for which see "Lollardy Trials," p. 59).

---

[11]   sooner.
[12]   Psalms 150.3–5.

Primary documents and further reading

Caxton, W. (trans.) (1902) *Three Middle English Versions of the Rule of St. Benet and Two Contemporary Rituals for the Ordination of Nuns*, ed. E. A. Koch. EETS, o.s. 120. London: Kegan Paul, Trench, Trübner.

Clark, A. (ed.) (1905–11) *The English Register of Godstow Nunnery, Near Oxford*, 3 parts. EETS, o.s. 129–30, 142. London: Kegan Paul, Trench, Trübner.

Hogg, J. (ed.) (1978–80) *The Rewyll of Seynt Sauioure*, 4 vols. Salzburg: Institut für Englische Sprache und Literatur.

Hourigan, M. (1996) "Ther Was Also A Nonne, A Prioresse." In L. C. Lambdin and R. T. Lambdin (eds.) *Chaucer's Pilgrims: An Historical Guide to the Pilgrims in The Canterbury Tales*. Westport, CT: Greenwood Press, 38–46.

Oliva, M. (1998) *The Convent and the Community in Late Medieval England: Female Monasteries in the Diocese of Norwich, 1350–1540*. Woodbridge, Suffolk: Boydell.

Power, E. (1964) [1922] *Medieval English Nunneries, c. 1275 to 1535*. New York: Biblo and Tannen.

Tolkien, J. R. R. (ed.) (1962) *Ancrene Wisse: The English Text of the Ancrene Riwle*. EETS, o.s. 249. London: Oxford University Press.

Thompson, A. H. (ed.) (1919) *Visitations of Religious Houses in the Diocese of Lincoln*, Vol. 2: *Records of Visitations Held by William Alnwick, Bishop of Lincoln, 1436–1449*. Part 1. London: Canterbury and York Society, 1–9 (selections).
Language: Latin and English (Northeast Midland)
Manuscript date: 1441

The visitation of the priory of Ankerwyke of the order of St. Benet, the diocese of Lincoln, begun and performed in its chapterhouse, on the tenth day of the month of October in the year of our Lord, 1441, by the reverend father in Christ and lord, William, by the grace of God bishop of Lincoln, in the sixteenth year of his consecration and sixth of his translation . . .[1]

[1.] Dame Margery Kyrkeby says that all the houses and buildings within the priory are going to ruin, and three useful and necessary houses have fallen down, thrown to the ground because of the carelessness and negligence of the prioress, namely the sheepfold (which was worn out by the fault of the prioress, who was then at a wedding at Bromhall),[2] another house in which dairy products are made, also a barn of which the timber, because it was not gathered together, is now burned. She[3] confesses being

---

[1]   William Alnwick, bishop of Norwich 1426–36, and Lincoln, 1436–49.
[2]   About 6 miles from Ankerwyke.
[3]   I.e., Clemence Medforde, the prioress.

at the wedding; she confesses the burning and also the remainder of the article.

[2.] Also, that the prioress alone keeps and all her time has kept the common seal of the house so that she can do with it whatever she wishes without the knowledge and consultation of the nuns. She confesses that she alone has kept the seal in her turn for the time, years and days, and sometimes with other fellow nuns, provided there have been any who are discrete there.

[3.] Also, there used to be customarily many notable vestments; where they have gone or whether they be there is not known; it is believed, however, that they have been removed from the house. She says that all the things that she received from the last prioress remain there in the house, about which she shows a schedule concerning the donation of the vestments and jewels.

[4.] Also, they had four chalices, and now they do not even have one. She confesses that there were four, of which two were in the house; the third is in pawn to Thomas Stanes [with the consent of the convent]; the fourth has been taken apart, also with the convent's consent.

[5.] Also, the prioress caused a silver thurible and a silver chalice, the heaviest which they had, to be broken up to make a cup for use at table, and she gave the chalice and censer as broken silver to one brother William Tudyngtone, a monk of Chertsey,[4] so that he might take an order to make the aforesaid cup from it and because the prioress had been given to understand that he had paid for the making of the chalice . . .[5] and she did not have enough to pay him. The cup remains in the hands of the said monk. She confesses the article, but she first had communication, as she asserts, with the convent, who all say that concerning this a discussion was not held in the chapter nor was the consent of all had, but only that the majority had no knowledge of the deed before it was done.

[6.] Also, she says that there used to be ten beautiful psalters kept in the house, some of which the prioress has given away and alienated. She confesses that she lent three, one to the prioress of Bromhall; she denies she did it without the consent of the convent.

[7.] Also, that in the past year in a place called "ly parkis," two miles distant from the priory, she sold a hundred oaks without asking any counsel or consent of the convent and under no compulsion of necessity. She denies the article.

---

[4] A Benedictine abbey of St. Peter in Surrey, about 20 miles southwest of Westminster.

[5] A sum is illegible here.

[8.] Also, at Alderbourne[6] she caused beeches to be felled at an unseasonable time so that they will never grow again, and therefore they are destroyed forever. She denies the article.

[9.] Also, the prioress has never rendered an account of her receipts and expenses, and yet all alone she receives, pays, and administers everything without any communication with the convent, even taking care of weighty business and leases and, even though she says that at the time of her installation the house had three hundred marks debt, this deponent says distinctly that then it was only thirty pounds in debt, and this amount was paid from other sources and in no way from the goods of the prioress or priory. She confesses that she never has rendered an account; she confesses also that she alone has received and administers everything without the knowledge of the convent. She denies that she has made leases unless it be with the knowledge of the convent.

10. Also, she caused a wood called Rowel, situated at Parnysshe,[7] to be felled unseasonably, leaving the boughs to lie after felling so that it is not likely that the wood will grow again for the profit of those now living. She denies the article.

11. (See 1.) Also, she says that the prioress has destroyed an entry, namely "a gatehouse," through which necessary items were brought in and chaff and other refuse were removed, and now that this entry has been blocked up they are carried out through the church to the great disgrace of the house. She confesses the whole article but says that she did it for greater seemliness in order to shut the pigs and other beast out of the cloister, which formerly, coming in through that entry, befouled it.

12. Also, to the fault of the prioress, six nuns have now left the house in apostasy. She confesses that so many nuns have left but without her knowledge.

13. Also, she has appropriated to herself in the dormitory four nuns' places and has blocked up the view of the Thames, which was a great comfort to the nuns. She confesses blocking up the view because she saw that men stood in the narrow space close to the window and talked with the nuns; she confesses the appropriation of the places.

14. Also, the prioress wears very expensive gold rings with diverse precious stones and also girdles silvered and gilded over, and silken veils, and her veil is too high on her forehead so that her forehead, being entirely uncovered, can be seen by all, and she wears furs of vair. She confesses the

6   In Buckinghamshire, west of Uxbridge.
7   Probably in Egham, Surrey.

use of several rings and girdles, and silken veils and the high carriage of her veils; she confesses also the use of vair furs. She has sworn that she will reform these things, having pledged to do so.

15. Also, she wears shifts of cloth of Rennes, which costs sixteen pence an ell. She denies the article.

16. Also, she wears kirtles laced with silk, and silver and silver gilt pins, and she has made all the nuns wear the same. She confesses the article with regards to herself; she has sworn that she will reform these things and has sworn to perform her penance, etc.

[17.] Also, she wears above her veil a cap of estate furred with budge. She confesses; however, it is because of various infirmities in her head. She has sworn as above that she will reform these things.

[18.] Also, she does not supply, nor for three years has supplied, fitting habits for the nuns to such an extent that the nuns go about in patched clothes. The threadbareness of the nuns was apparent to the lord.

[19.] Also, the prioress invited several outside people from the neighborhood to this visitation at great cost to the house, saying to them, "Stand on my side in this time of visitation, for I do not want to resign." She confesses the entertainment of her friends, but it was not to this end . . .

And on this Monday, namely the twenty-ninth of the said month of October, in this year and the aforesaid chapterhouse, the said reverend father sat in his capacity of judge in the business of his visitation and then ordered that the prioress and convent of the said place be called before him, who all appeared before him in person. And when they thus appeared, the same reverend father, the process of such business previously had and done, and also the adjournment of the same visitation having been first recited by him and acknowledged by the same nuns, put forth in detail and rehearsed to the same prioress article by article all that had been made known to him concerning the prioress. These things having been put to her, some the same prioress confessed and some she denied, just as it is written down at the end of every article; and concerning her denials, so far as they concern dilapidation and so involve deprivation, the lord decreed that an inquiry should be made after the summons of the same prioress and the others who ought to be summoned for this purpose, reserving to himself the power of proceeding against her as regards the rest according to her responses and the process held concerning them. And because the same prioress complained of sister Margery Kyrkeby in that she had called the same prioress a thief, the same Margery, being judicially impeached touching this, expressly denied the charge and cleared herself of it based alone on her own testimony. Afterwards, because the prioress confessed that for a long time past, even for very many days and years, she had had in her own keeping the common seal and very many, even all, of the archives of the house, the lord ordained that all these should be kept in one chest under two locks, the keys of which the prioress should wear one and sister Margery Kyrkeby, chosen for this by the convent, the other; and that nothing should be sealed with the said seal unless with the common counsel and consensus of the more reasonable part and majority of the convent and in the chapterhouse; and until provision of such locks should be made, the lord had the common seal shut up in a little box under his own seal. And then the same reverend father warned the said prioress, in virtue of the obedience proffered by her, to admonish and correct her sisters who are at fault in any way in the chapter, not in the hearing of any secular people, in a motherly and sisterly and temperate manner, and in no way severely, as has been her way, and in all other respects to treat them gently and supply and cause to be supplied to them sufficient raiment, habits, bed clothes, and nourishment. He also enjoined the individual members of the convent, under pain of imprisonment, that they should humbly obey the prioress in all lawful things and pay her reverence and show her honor, not any disobedience or disgrace. And because the young nuns asked that a governess in reading, song, and the regular observances should be appointed them, the lord, with the consent of all, appointed sister Juliane Messangere, enjoining her to perform the charge laid upon her and to instruct them in good manners and in no way so that they go contrary to the prioress in anything . . .

[T]he same deputy, wishing first and before all to obtain the clearest and fullest information and assurance concerning the observance or want of observance of such injunctions, as he affirmed, caused all the nuns except the prioress to go out of the chapterhouse and, proceeding in such business of the inquiry and having required the same prioress to tell the truth in virtue of obedience, diligently examined her concerning all and each individual injunction, and whether she, her fellow nuns, and the sisters have observed or not observed the same injunctions or any of them. And she, answering, said that these injunctions were and are in effect and according to her power well observed as regards both her and her sisters except the injunction whereby she is bound to supply to her sisters sufficient raiment for their habits and, concerning the non-observance of that injunction, she responds that she cannot observe it because of the poverty and insufficiency of the resources of the house, which have been much lessened because of the lack of a surveyor or steward. For which reason she besought the lord's goodwill and assistance that he would deign with charitable consideration to make provision for such a steward or director.

[Injunctions:] Wyllyam, by the grace of God, bysshope of Lincoln, to our wele belufed doghters in Cryste, the prioresse, and the covent of the priorye of Ankerwyke, of the ordere of Seynt Benette, of our diocyse, helthe, grace, and our blessyng. Now late we visytyng yow and your saide pryorye, by our inquisicyon then made fonde certeyn grete and notable defautes, grete and dewe [refor]macyone requiryng, for the reformacyone whereof we sende yowe here theise our injunccyons, comaundementes, and ordynaunces by yow to be keppede undere the peynes here by nethe writen.

1 . . . In the fyrste we commaunde, charge, and enjoyne yowe, prioresse, undere payne of grete contempte, that nyghtly ye lygge in the dormytorye to oversee your susters how thai are there governede after your rewle, and that often tyme ye come to matynes, messe, and other houres, ther to be present in the qwere but if grete sekenesse or unevytable occupacyons lette yowe. And also if hit happe yow to come late to the qwere at any houre, that ye make not the qwere to begynne agayne any houre than begunne, ne that ye putte the qwere to any other observaunce in saying of devyne servyce other wyse than the laudable custome of the place has been here afore.

2 . . . Also, we enjoyne yow, pryoresse, undere the same peyne, that oftentymes ye come to the chapitere for to correcte the defautes of your susters, and that as wele then as att other tymes and places ye treyte your saide su[sters] moderlie wyth all resonable favour, and that ye rebuke ne repreve thaym cruelly ne fervently at no tyme, specyally in audience of seculeres, and that ye kepe pryvye fro seculeres your correccyons and actes of your chapitere.

3. Also, undere the same peyne we enjoyne yow, prioresse, that aftere your rewle ye kepe the fraytour[8] but if resonable cause excuse yowe ther fro.

Also, we enjoyne yowe of the covent and everyche oon of yowe undere peyn of imprisonyng, that mekely and buxumly ye obeye the prioresse, procedyng discretely in hire correccyone, and also that in every place ye do hire dewe reverence, absteynyng yowe fro alle elacyone of pryde and wordes of disobeysaunce or debate.

4. Also, we enjoyne yowe, prioresse and covente and everyche one of yowe undere peynes here above and bynethe wryten, that ye absteyne yow fro all drynkenges after complyne but if sekenesse cawse the contrary and that every day and on one as complyne is sayde, ye alle go to the dormytorye, not to come owte save to matynes un to pryme be runge on the morwe next aftere.

---

[8]   refectory.

5. And also that none of yow, the prioresse ne none of the covente, were no vayles of sylke, ne no sylvere pynnes, ne no gyrdles herneysed wyth sylvere or golde, ne no mo rynges on your fyngres then oon, ye that be professed by a bysshope, ne that none of yow use no lased kyrtels, but butonede or hole be fore, ne that ye use no lases a bowte your nekkes wythe crucyfixes or rynges hangyng by thayme, ne cappes of astate obove your vayles . . . othere then [your r]ule askes, and that ye so atyre your hedes that your vayles come downe nyghe to your yene.

6. Also, we enjoyne yow, prioresse, undere paynes of contempte and grete cursyng that ye ministre to your susters of the covent sufficyently in mete and drynke, and also in clothes to thair habite and beddes, as your religyone wylle demaunde; and also that when frendes of your sustres come to visite thaym honestly, ye receyve hem and suffre thaym to speke wyth hem so that no sclaundere ne token of evelle falle ther bye to your saide susters ne to your place. And what ever thise saide frendes wyll gyfe your sustres in relefe of thaym, as in hire habyte and sustenaunce, ye suffre your sustres to take hit so that no abuse of evel come therbye noyther to the place ne to the persones therof.

7. Also, we enjoyne yowe, prioresse, undere peyne of cursyng, that fro hense forthe ye susteyne ne seculere persones wythe the commune godes of the place neyther wyth ynne ne wythe owte; and that fro hens forthe ye receyve no mo in to nunnes then may competently be susteyned of the commune godes of the place, ne that for receyvyng of any in to nunnes, ye exacte, ne receyve by paccyon, ne covenaunt, or promysse none wardly gode otherwyse then thai or thaire frendes of thair charitee wylle gyfe yowe.

8. Also, we charge yow, prioresse, undere the same payne of cursyng, that ye hafe an honeste woman servaund in your kychyne, brewhowse and bakehowse, deyhowse,[9] and selere wythe an honeste damyselle wythe hire to saruf[10] yowe and your sustres in thise saide offices so that your saide sustres for occupacyone in ony of the saide offices be ne letted fro divine seruice ne fro lernyng of thaire servyce and observaunces of religyone, lyke as we assygnede thaym a nunne to informe thaym ther yn.

9. Also, we enjoyne yowe, prioresse, undere payne of deposicyone, that fro hense forthe the commune seale and all the munymentes of your place be surely keppede in a chyste undere two lokkes of diverse forme and makyng, the keyes where of oon shalle remeyne in your kepyng and an other in the kepyng of dame Margery Kyrkeby, chosen ther to by the

---

[9] dairy.
[10] serve.

covent, and that nothyng be sealed wythe the saide seale but in the chapitere and by the fulle assent of the more parte of the covent.

10. Also, we charge yow, prioresse, undere the payne of perpetuelle privacyone fro your state and dignytee of prioressye, that fro hense forthe ye graunte, gyfe, ne selle to any manere persone fee, rente, annuytee, corrodye, ne lyverye to terme of lyve, certeyn tyme ne perpetuelly, ne that ye gyfe ne selle no wodes ne tynbere wythe owtene specyalle leve of us or our successours, bysshops of Lincolne, asked and had, and wythe the assent of the more partye of the covent . . .

11. Also, we charge yow, prioresse, unde[r] peyne of cursyng, that ye do take downe that perclose[11] that ye dyde make in the dormytorye and that ye oversee that every nunnes celle be open in toward the dormytory, as your rewle demaundes.

12. Also, we enjoyne yow, pryoresse, undere peyne of suspensyone fro alle administracyone in spirituele and temporele, that as ye may resonabylly come to aftere the suffycyence of your commune godes, ye do repare the howses and beeldynges wythe yn your place, specyally thoe that are falle to ruyne in your tyme and defawte, and also your tenementes owtward, the whiche are ryght ruynouse, as we are informede; and also that wyth yn this and the fest of Paske next folowyng,[12] ye do bryng in to the place alle the jewels of the place, as chalices, censures, psawters, and other what ever thai be the whiche ye hafe oythere lente owte or laide to wedde.[13]

13. And also that every yere be twyx the festes of Seynt Mighelle in Septembre and Seynt Martyne in Novembre ye shew to your susters in playn chapytere or to whome you wylle assigne a fulle and playn accompte of your mynystracyone in all the commune goodes of your place what is dewe and receyved and how th[ai a]re dispendede.

[11]   screen.
[12]   Easter.
[13]   I.e., in pawn.

2

Force and Order

Battle of Agincourt

The Hundred Years' War is a misnomer not only because the hostilities between England and France lasted from 1337 to 1453, but also because, as with much medieval warfare, engaged fighting was comparatively infrequent during this period. Major battles usually lasted less than two weeks, commonly with less than 3,000 people on each side, siege being a far more common form of achieving victory. Cause for war began mounting when the French king Charles IV died in 1328 with no heir. Edward III, his nephew, had a good claim to the throne, but the French peers chose Charles's cousin, Philip VI of Valois. In May 1337 Philip VI confiscated Edward's duchy of Gascony in southwestern France, and in October Edward laid claim to the French throne. The war would not close until England's alliance with Burgundy ended in 1435 and the English lost their last foothold in France, Castillon, in 1453.

Henry V's expedition through northwestern France began in August 1415 with a protracted siege on the town of Harfleur at the mouth of the Seine. In October Henry decided to lead the remains of his army to Calais instead of immediately departing by sea for England. The French, sensing an easy victory, finally encountered the English at Agincourt in the afternoon of October 24. English and French chronicles state different numbers of forces on the two sides that prepared for battle that evening, but the ratio seems to have been eight French to one Englishman. The *Gesta Henrici Quinti* estimates a slightly greater disparity, with 60,000 French to 6,000 English. After a night in the open air and rain, the English amassed in three groups of men-at-arms, each group flanked by archers. When the two forces finally encountered each other, the archers created havoc on the thick of the French horses and armed men, who were already weighed down by armor in the mud of a freshly ploughed field. The English forces were then able to move in and counter-attack on horseback and foot.

The anonymous royal chaplain and writer of the *Gesta* claims – and is generally agreed – to have been an eyewitness to several events he relates in the prose chronicle: the king's suppression of the 1414 Lollard uprising, the English army's expedition in France, Henry's triumphant return to London in November of the same year (see "Processions," p. 209), and the 1416 meeting between the king and Emperor Sigismund. The writer's descriptions of Henry V, of the intervention of divine grace, and of Emperor Sigismund signal that the *Gesta* is not only a reliable and important account, but that it was also intended to be politically persuasive. Henry is characterized as a devout king, who succeeds in the face of immediate adversity and who desires peace but has been forced into war by the intransigent French. God intercedes at crucial points in the king's attempts to reclaim his rights to France, and all successes are due to God's perception of the just nature of Henry's cause. While the audience is not definitively known, the *Gesta* circulated quickly after its composition. Its most important effect may have been on parliament and religious leaders, garnering financial and spiritual support for the king's next expedition to France, for which Henry was preparing during the time of the chronicle's writing. It was also probably intended for Sigismund in order to combat French hostility at the Council of Constance (see "The English and England," p. 50).

Primary documents and further reading

Allmand, C. (2002) *The Hundred Years War: England and France at War, c. 1300– c. 1450*, Revd. edn. Cambridge: Cambridge University Press.

Curry, A. (ed.) (2000) *The Battle of Agincourt: Sources and Interpretations*. Woodbridge, Suffolk: Boydell.

Jacob, E. F. (1961) *The Fifteenth Century, 1399–1485*. Oxford: Clarendon Press.

Sumption, J. (1990–9) *The Hundred Years War*, 2 vols. Philadelphia: University of Pennsylvania Press.

British Library MS Cotton Julius E.iv, fols. 119v–120r. In F. Taylor and J. S. Roskell (ed. and trans.) (1975) *Gesta Henrici Quinti (The Deeds of Henry the Fifth)*. Oxford: Clarendon Press, 86–93.

Language: Latin

Manuscript date: 1416–17

And then, when the enemy were nearly ready to attack, the French cavalry posted on the flanks made charges against those of our archers who were on both sides of our army. But soon, by God's will, they were forced to fall back under showers of arrows and to flee to their rearguard, save for a very few who, although not without losses in dead and wounded, rode through between the archers and the woodlands, and save, too, of course, for the many who were stopped by the stakes driven into the ground and prevented from fleeing very far by the stinging hail of missiles shot at both horses and riders in their flight.

And the enemy catapults, which were at the back of the men-at-arms and on the flanks, after a first but over-hasty volley by which they did injury to very few, withdrew for fear of our bows.

And when the men-at-arms had from each side advanced towards one another over roughly the same distance, the flanks of both battle-lines, ours, that is, and the enemy's, extended into the woodlands, which were on both sides of the armies. But the French nobility, who had previously advanced in line abreast and had all but come to grips with us, either from fear of the missiles, which by their very force pierced the sides and visors of their helmets, or in order the sooner to break through our strongest points and reach the standards, divided into three columns, attacking our line of battle at the three places where the standards were. And in the mêlée of spears which then followed, they hurled themselves against our men in such a fierce charge as to force them to fall back almost a spear's length.

And then we who have been assigned to the clerical militia and were watching, fell upon our faces in prayer before the great mercy-seat of God, crying out aloud in bitterness of spirit that God might even yet remember us and the crown of England and, by the grace of his supreme bounty, deliver us from this iron furnace and the terrible death which menaced us. Nor was God unmindful of the multitude of prayers and supplications being made in England, by which, as it is devoutly believed, our men soon regained their strength and, valiantly resisting, pushed back the enemy until they had recovered the ground that had been lost.

And then the battle raged at its fiercest, and our archers notched their sharp-pointed arrows and loosed them into the enemy's flanks, keeping up the fight without pause. And when their arrows were all used up, seizing axes, stakes and swords, and spear-heads that were lying about, they struck down, hacked, and stabbed the enemy. For the Almighty and Merciful God, who is ever marvellous in his works and whose will it was to deal mercifully with us, and whom also it pleased that, under our gracious king, his own soldier, and with that little band, the crown of England should remain invincible as of old, did, as soon as the lines of battle had so come to grips and the fighting had begun, increase the strength of our men, which dire want of food had previously weakened and wasted, took away from them their fear, and gave them dauntless hearts. Nor, it seemed to our older men, had Englishmen ever fallen upon their enemies more boldly and fearlessly or with a better will.

And the same just judge, whose intention it was to strike with the thunderbolt of his vengeance the proud host of the enemy, turned his face away from them and broke their strength – the bow, the shield, the sword, and the battle.[1] Nor, in any former times, which chronicle or history records, does it ever appear that so many of the very pick and most sturdy of warriors had offered opposition so lacking in vigour, and so confused and faint-hearted, or so unmanly. Indeed, fear and trembling seized them, for, so it was said among the army, there were some of them, even of their more nobly born, who that day surrendered themselves more than ten times. No one, however, had time to take them prisoner, but almost all, without distinction of person, were, as soon as they were struck down, put to death without respite, either by those who had laid them low or by others following after, by what secret judgement of God is not known.

God, indeed, had also smitten them with another great blow from which there could be no recovery. For when some of them, killed when battle was first joined, fell at the front, so great was the undisciplined violence and pressure of the mass of men behind that the living fell on top of the dead, and others falling on top of the living were killed as well, with the result that, in each of the three places where the strong contingents guarding our standards were, such a great heap grew of the slain and of those lying crushed in between that our men climbed up those heaps, which had risen above a man's height, and butchered their enemies down below with swords, axes, and other weapons.

And when at long last, after two or three hours, their vanguard had been riddled through and through, and broken up, and the rest were being put to flight, our men began to pull those heaps apart and to separate the living from the dead, intending to hold them as prisoners for ransom.

But then, all at once, because of what wrathfulness on God's part no one knows, a shout went up that the enemy's mounted rearguard (in incomparable number and still fresh) were re-establishing their position and line of battle in order to launch an attack on us, few and weary as we were. And immediately, regardless of distinction of person, the prisoners, save for the

---

[1]   Psalms 75.4.

dukes of Orleans and Bourbon, certain other illustrious men who were in the king's "battle," and a very few others, were killed by the swords either of their captors or of others following after, lest they should involve us in utter disaster in the fighting that would ensue.

After but a short time, however, the enemy ranks, having experienced the bitter taste of our missiles and with our king advancing towards them, by God's will abandoned to us that field of blood together with their wagons and other baggage-carts, many of these loaded with provisions and missiles, spears, and bows.

And when, at God's behest, the strength of that people had been thus utterly wasted and the rigours of battled had ended, we, who had gained the victory, came back through the masses, the mounds, and the heaps of the slain and, seeing them, reflected (though not without grief and tears on the part of many) upon the fact that so great a number of warriors, famous and most valiant had only God been with them, should have sought their own deaths in such a manner at our hands, quite contrary to any wish of ours, and should thus have effaced and destroyed, all to no avail, the glory and honour of their own country. And if that sight gave rise to compunction and pity in us, strangers passing by, how much more was it a cause of grief and mourning to their own people, awaiting expectantly the warriors of their country and then seeing them so crushed and made defenseless. And, as I truly believe, there is not a man with heart of flesh or even of stone who, had he seen and pondered on the horrible deaths and bitter wounds of so many Christian men, would not have dissolved into tears, time and again, for grief. Indeed, having previously been despoiled by English pillagers, none of them, however illustrious or distinguished, possessed at our departure any more covering, save only to conceal his nature, than that with which nature had endowed him when first he saw the light.

The English and England

Medieval writers from Bede, Geoffrey of Monmouth, and Layamon to the authors of fourteenth- and fifteenth-century romances, historical writings, and religious works described England in sociological terms. This kingdom, country, or nation, as Benedict Anderson observes of a later age, is here already imagined as a community of humans that is "limited" and "sovereign" even if its inhabitants are imprecise in answering where and when the entity sometimes called *England* begins and ends, and even if they continually speculate about its popular, regal, and heavenly sovereignty.

Ranulf Higden's *Polychronicon* is one of several chronicles written during Edward III's reign that contributed to a new consciousness about England as a nation. Higden (ca. 1275–ca. 1360), a Benedictine at the abbey of St. Werburgh's in Chester, began his universal and encyclopedic history about 1327, revising and adding to it until his death. Famous during his lifetime, his work survives in over 125 fourteenth- and fifteenth-century manuscripts, and its popularity is also confirmed by John Trevisa's English translation as well as an anonymous fifteenth-century translation (both printed alongside the Latin text in the Rolls Series). Trevisa finished translating the *Polychronicon* in 1387, adding his own materials (see also "Friars," p. 7, "Humors," p. 14, and "The English Language," p. 259). Trevisa's vernacular translation survives in 14 manuscripts, whereas some 118 complete or substantial manuscripts in Latin exist. Caxton and Wynkyn de Worde both printed redactions of his text with further alterations.

The Great Papal Schism, which began in 1378 when Clement VII was set up as antipope in Avignon against Urban VI in Rome, had disastrous consequences not only for the Church, but also for hopes of peace between England and France (see "Battle of Agincourt," p. 46). The Council of Constance, which met at the request of Emperor Sigismund in 1414–18, began with relative agreement, in particular that four "nations" would be able to vote: Italy, France, Germany, and England. However, in October 1416 the distinguished French cardinal, Pierre d'Ailly (1351–1420), called into question the national divisions, arguing that the Roman Church was comprised of four different divisions: French, German (which would include the English), Spanish, and Italian. He also cited another papal bull of Benedict XII that Western Christendom was divided into 36 Benedictine provinces of which only four encompassed Britain and one the sees of Canterbury and York. Despite objections from the emperor, the French kept the issue alive until March 1417, when Sigismund finally put a stop to their attempt to reduce England's representation. At the end of the month Thomas Polton, an English notary, delivered the English response for the record even though it was never publicly read at the Council.

Primary documents and further reading

Foedera: Conventiones, literae et cuiuscunque generis acta publica (1728) Vol. 9, ed. T. Rymer. London: J. Tonson.
Fowler, D. C. (1994) "John Trevisa." In M. C. Seymour (ed.) *Authors of the Middle Ages: English Writers in the Late Middle Ages*, vol. 1, no. 2. Aldershot: Variorum.

Gransden, A. (1982) *Historical Writing in England II: c. 1307 to the Early Sixteenth Century.* Ithaca, NY: Cornell University Press.

Loomis, L. R. (1939) "Nationality at the Council of Constance: An Anglo-French Dispute." *The American Historical Review* 44: 508–27.

Taylor, J. (1966) *The Universal Chronicle of Ranulf Higden.* Oxford: Clarendon Press.

Waldron, R. (1988) "John Trevisa and the Use of English." *Proceedings of the British Academy* 74: 171–202.

Ranulf Higden. St. John's College, Cambridge, MS 204. In C. Babington and J. R. Lumby (eds.) (1869) *Polychronicon*, vol. 2, trans. J. Trevisa. London: Longman, 165–75.
Language: English (Southwestern)
Manuscript date: ca. 1400

De gentibus huius moribus. Capitulum sexagesimum.[1]

Giraldus in Itinerario.[2] For the maneres and the doynge of Walsche men and of Scottes beeth to fore honde somdel declared, now of the maneres and of the doynges of the medled[3] peple of Engelond nedeth forto telle. But the Flemynges that beeth in the westside of Wales beeth now by torned[4] as though they were Englische by cause of companye with Englische men, and they beeth stalworthe and stronge to fighte, and beeth the moste enemyes that Walsche men hath, and useth marchaundyse and clothynge, and beeth ful redy to putte hem self to aventures and to peril in the see and in the lond, by cause of greet wynnynge, and beeth redy for to goo somtyme to the plowgh and somtyme to dedes of armes whan tyme and place axeth. Hit semeth of this men a grete wonder that in a boon[5] of a wethres right schuldre, whan the flesche is aweye i-sode[6] and nought i-rosted, they knoweth what hath be do, is i-doo, and schal be doo, and as hit were by a spirit of prophecie and a wonderful craft, they telleth what me doth in fer contrayes, tokens of pees and of werre, the staat of the reeme, sleynge of men, and spouse-breche; soche they declareth certeynliche by schewynge of tokenes and of synnes[7] that beeth in suche a schulder boon.

---

[1] Concerning the character of the people. Chapter Sixty.
[2] Higden here notes his source, Gerald of Wales (ca. 1146–1222), *Itinerarium Cambriae* (*Journey through Wales*).
[3] mixed.
[4] become.
[5] bone.
[6] boiled.
[7] signs.

Ranulf says: But the Englische men that woneth in Engelond, that beeth i-medled in the ilond, that [beth] fer i-spronge from the welles that they sprong of first, wel lightliche with oute entisynge of eny other men, by here owne assent tornen to contrary dedes. And also unesy, also ful unpacient of pees (enemy of besynesse) and wlatful[8] of sleuthe (*Willelmus de Pontificibus, libro tertio*),[9] that whan they haveth destroyed here enemyes al to the grounde, thanne they fighteth with hem self and sleeth everiche other as a voyde stomak and a clene worcheth in hit self.

[Ranulf says:] Notheles, men of the South beeth esier and more mylde; and men of the North be more unstable, more cruel, and more unesy; the myddel men beeth somdele partyners with bothe; also, they woneth hem to glotonye more than other men, and beeth more costlewe[10] in mete and in drynke and in clothynge. Me troweth that they took that [vyce] of Kyng Hardeknute that was a Dane,[11] for he sette twyes double messe and also at soper. These men been speedful bothe on hors and on foote, able and redy to alle manere dedes of armes, and beeth i-woned to have the victorie and the maistrie in everich fight wher no treson is walkynge; and [beth] curious, and kunneth wel i-now telle dedes and wondres that thei haveth i-seie. Also they gooth in dyvers londes; unnethe beeth eny men richere in her owne londe othere more gracious in fer and in straunge londe. They konneth betre wynne and gete newe than kepe her owne heritage; therfore, it is that they beeth i-spred so wyde and weneth that everich other londe is hir owne heritage. The men beeth able to al manere sleithe[12] and witte, but to fore the dede blondrynge and hasty, and more wys after the dede, and leveth ofte lightliche what they haveth bygonne. *Polycraticon, libro sexto.*[13] Therfore, Eugenious the pope[14] seide that Englisshe men were able to do what evere they wolde, and to be sette and putte to fore alle othere, nere that light with letteth.[15] And as Han[nibal] saide that the Romayns myghte nought be overcome but in hir owne cuntray, so Englische men mowe not be overcome in straunge londes, but in hir own cuntray they beeth lightliche overcome.

---

[8] full of loathing.
[9] William of Malmesbury (ca. 1090–1143), *Gesta pontificum Anglorum* (*History of the Bishops of England*).
[10] extravagant.
[11] Harthacnut (r. 1040–2).
[12] wisdom.
[13] John of Salisbury (ca. 1115–80), *Polycraticus.*
[14] Eugenius III (1145–53).
[15] except for where that light wit ("with") impedes them.

Ranulf says: These men despiseth hir owne and preiseth other menis, and unnethe beeth apaide with hir owne estate; what byfalleth and semeth other men, they wolleth gladlyche take to hem self; therfore, hit is that a yeman arraieth hym as a squyer, a squyer as a knyght, a knight as a duke, [and] a duke as a kyng. Yit som gooth a boute to alle manere staate and beeth in noon astaat, for they that wole take everiche degree beeth of non degree, for in berynge they beeth menstralles and heraudes, in talkynge grete spekeres, in etynge and in drynkynge glotouns, in gaderynge of catel hoksters and taverners, in aray[16] tormentoures, in wynnynges Argi, in travaile Tantaly, in takynge hede Dedaly, and in beddes Sardanapally, in chirches mamettes,[17] in courtes thonder, onliche in privelege of clergie and in provendres they knowlecheth hem silf clerkes.

Trevisa: "In wynnynge they beeth Argy, in travaile Tantaly, in takynge hede Dedaly, and in beddes Sardanapally." For to understonde this reson aright, foure wordes [therof] moste be declared, that beeth these foure: *Argi, Tantaly, Dedaly*, and *Sardanapally*; therfore, take hede that Argus in an herde, Argus a schippe, a schipman, and a chapman.[18] But here it is more to purpos that poetes feyneth oon that was somtyme al ful of eyghen in everiche side, and heet *Argus*, so that this Argus myghte see to fore and byhynde, upwarde and dounward, and al aboute in everiche a side, and by a manere likenesse of this Argus, he that is war and wys, and kan see and be war in everiche side is i-cleped Argus, and ful of yghen as Argus was. Than forto speke to meny such he moste be i-cleped Argi in the plural nombre. Than in that cronyke he seith[19] that they beeth Argy in wynnynge, hit is to mene that they beeth ware and seeth aboute in every side where wynnynge may arise. That other word is *Tantaly*; therfore, take hede that the poete[20] feyneth that Tantalus was a man and slowh his owne sonne; therfore, he was i-dampned to perpetual penaunce, as the poete feyneth that Tantalus stondeth alway in a water up anon to the over brerde[21] of the nether lippe and hath all way evene at his mouth ripe apples and noble fruyt, ne water cometh with ynne his mouth, he is so i-holde up; and so he stondeth in that array bytwene mete and drynke, and may nother ete ne drynke, and is an hongred and athirst that woo is hym on lyve. By a manere likeness of this Tantalus, they that dooth right nought, there moche thing is to doo in every side,

[16]   conduct.
[17]   idolaters.
[18]   merchant.
[19]   I.e., Higden.
[20]   Ovid.
[21]   outer edge.

beeth i cleped *Tantaly*. Hit semeth that this sawe[22] is to mene, in travaille they beeth Tantaly, for they dooth right nought therto. The thridde word is *Dedaly*, take hede that Dedalus was a wel sligh man, and by likness of hym men that beeth slighe beeth i-cleped *Dedaly* in the plurel noumbre, so it is to mene as hit semeth in this sawe, in takyge hede and in cry they beeth Dedaly, that is fel[23] and sly. The ferthe word is [*Sardanapalli*; therfore, take hede that] Sardanapallus was a kyng, *rex Assyriorum*, and was ful unchast, and by a manere liknesse of hym they that beeth swithe[24] unchast beeth i-cleped *Sardanapally*.

Ranulf says: But among alle Englische i-medled to giders is so grete chaungynge and diversite [of clothinge and] of array [and so many manere and dyverse shappes, that wel nyghe is there ony man knowen by his clothynge and his arraye] of what degree he is. Therof prophecied an holy anker to Kyng Egilred his tyme in this manere. *Henricus, libro sexto*.[25] Englisshe men for they woneth hem to dronkelewnesse, to tresoun, and to rechelesnesse of Goddes hous first by Danes and thanne by Normans and at the thridde tyme by Scottes, that they holdeth most wrecches and leste worth of alle, they schulleth be overcome; than the worlde schal be so unstable and so dyvers and variable that the unstabilnesse of thoughtes schal [be] bytokened by many manere dyversite of clothinge.

Magnum occumenicum Constantiente Concilium, vol. 5, ed. H. von der Hardt. Rerum universalis concilii Constantiensis. Frankfurt: Christiani Genschii, 1699, 85–93.
Language: Latin

[B]esides dukedoms, lands and islands, and dominions in great number, there are eight kingdoms, namely England, Scotland, and Wales (these three make up Great Britain), also a kingdom of the sea,[26] and in Ireland, which adjoins England, four great and notable kingdoms, namely Connaught, Galway, Munster, and Meath, just as the registrars of the Roman curia, clearly and with a seal, mention them together in the catalogue of Christian kings. There is also the notable principality of John,[27] prince of

---

[22]   report.
[23]   shrewd.
[24]   very.
[25]   Aethelred II, the Unready (r. 978–1016) in Henry of Huntingdon, *Historia Anglorum*.
[26]   Louise Loomis conjectures this is the Isle of Man, "*regnum . . . de Man*," rather than "*regnum . . . de mari*" as in the text.
[27]   John of Lancaster (1389–1435), Duke of Bedford.

the Orkney and other islands, which number around sixty. These islands are equal to or larger than the previously mentioned kingdom of France. But that supplementary decree,[28] we declare, limits the eight provinces for the assemblies of synods of the chapters of black monks (which, as is well known, are in, of, and under the power of the English or British nation) to four provinces, namely to the Irish for one, to Canterbury and York for the second, to the kingdom of Scotland for a third, and to Burgundy for a fourth. Out of this supplementary decree and because they base the premise of their writing upon that decree, it is clearly proved that they are wrong to write – or rather (always saving their graces) they write less well – that the English nation has one province, in accordance with the limitation of the aforementioned supplementary decree that it is only one thirty-sixth part of obedience to the pope. Indeed, there are ten provinces in it, of which eight (as defined above) are subject to the English nation, and the king of England now peacefully possesses seven of them under temporal rule and will soon, with the grace of God, possess the rest. The aforementioned English nation also has one hundred and ten dioceses, as is discussed below.

Insofar as they also write that Wales is not subject to the king of England and neither are the prelates and clergy of those parts, and they do not want to be part of the English nation, as is evident in this council: after making our protestation in advance, it is answered that they should blush to write something so contrary to the well-known truth because all Wales obeys the archbishop of Canterbury in his office of primate in spiritual matters and the most serene king of England in temporal ones, and does so peacefully and quietly, inasmuch as is evident in part even to this council since a number of venerable doctors and other graduates and clerics from Wales are here among the glorious English nation. In accordance with this also it is evident that they speak less accurately of Ireland, which contains four provinces and sixty spacious and ample dioceses, which are recognized indubitably and by common knowledge to belong to the glorious English nation.

Insofar as they also suppose that suffragans of the kingdom of Scotland are not and do not want to be of the English nation: having made our protestation in advance, it is answered that the suffragans are (by common knowledge) and ought to be of the English, or British, nation, since they cannot make any denial that Scotland is part of Britain, though not so great a part as England (which is known to the entire world), and they even have the same language as the English.

---

[28]   Benedict XII's division of Britain into four provinces.

It is also strange that such authors want to write that Wales, Ireland, and even Scotland are not of the English nation because they are not subject to the king of England. This is a given and not a concession, which has no use with regards to the proposition because it is well known that it makes no difference whether a nation is subject only to a single ruler or to several. Are there not many kingdoms in the Spanish nation, which are not subject to the king of Castille, the ruler of the Spanish? And even so it does not follow that they are not of the Spanish nation. Are there not Provence, Dauphiny, Savoy, Burgundy, Lorraine, and several other lands that have nothing to do with our adversary France and nevertheless are contained in the nation of France, or the Gallic nation? And thus likewise among other nations?

Third, as well, having made in advance as always our protestation here repeated, it is answered: It is the truth that to make any comparison among kingdoms accords with neither law nor reason since such comparisons are odious and first devised by the prince of darkness. But inasmuch as those who write from the opposite position perceive the superiority and nobility of the kingdom of France to the kingdom of England yet speak without prejudice or making any comparison, and in order to satisfy those who write from the opposite position, we state that the renowned kingdom of England is recognized to be of no less antiquity or prestige than the aforementioned kingdom of France but rather is more truly of more ancient and greater faith, dignity, and honour, or at least equal in all things, even in royal power, and in the divine favours of the great number of its clerics and peoples, and in the richness of its possessions.

From the time of the second age of the world, the preeminent royal house of England has flourished and thus far has existed continuously and in fact. Moreover, the royal house of England has been found to bring forth, among the several holy branches it produced, which could not easily be counted, St. Helen, with her son Constantine the Great, Emperor, born in the royal city of York.[29] They returned several lands of the infidels and the cross of the Lord from the peoples of the infidels to the hands of Christians and into their trust. Furthermore, that most religious man first gave permission throughout the whole world to those who lived under his rule not only to become Christians but also to build churches; he also established rewards to be given to them, bestowed enormous donations, and initiated the construction of the temple of the first seat of St. Peter so as to relinquish the imperial residence and yield it to St. Peter and his

---

[29]   Medieval legend states that St. Helen, mother of Constantine the Great, the first Christian emperor (306–37), found the true cross.

successors in the future. He also first granted permission for Christians freely to convene general councils for the destruction of heresies and schisms. In addition, he honoured the church so much that he called the clerics themselves gods. Indeed, the most powerful royal house of England never departed from obedience to the Roman church but under it has fought thus far in a most Christian manner . . . [The English writers continue by disputing France's claim to contain more provinces, diocese, counties, and churches, as well as a greater area than England. They also claim an older Christian origin than France, citing the story that Joseph of Arimathea and twelve others made their way to England after the crucifixion and converted the English.]

It is also generally agreed, according to Albertus Magnus and Bartholomeus' *On the Properties of Things*,[30] that the whole world is divided into three parts, namely Asia, Africa, and Europe, and that Europe is divided into four kingdoms. These are: first that of Rome, next that of Constantinople, third that of Hibernia, which has now been transferred to the English, and the fourth kingdom is Spain. From which it is clear that the king of England and his kingdom come from those more eminent and ancient kings and kingdoms of all Europe. This prerogative is not said to obtain for the kingdom of France.

Therefore, from what quarter has this unfair comparison of the kingdom of France to the kingdom of England arisen? From what quarter do those lords who write thus find the boldness to write that the kingdom of France is comprised of six or more divisions than the kingdom of England? For it is reckoned that, just as some who favour France for the sake of their individual glory depict, in the *mappamundi*, the city of Paris as occupying more space than the entire kingdom of England, so too, it seems, those who write about the aforementioned inequality between kingdoms in terms of the extent of their land and other qualities would like to presume. But the opposite is true, as was said earlier.

In addition to this, with regard to the point they do not hesitate to write, it accords with neither law nor reason to consider the Gallic nation, as it is generally understood, as equal to the English nation, keeping in mind several points taken above on their own: we say, having made our protestation in advance, that one must wonder in no small way at the hatred of these men for the glorious English nation, who do not want it to be compared to the Gallic. Surely, are not the two nations equal in their laws,

---

[30]   Albert the Great (ca. 1200–80) and Bartholomeus Anglicus (ca. 1240).

claims, and many writings? For present are all the necessary elements of an autonomous nation with respect to the fourth or fifth part of obedience to the pope,[31] just as with the Gallic nation, whether a nation be understood as a people distinguished from another by its blood relationships and habit of unity or according to the diversity of its languages, which are the strongest and truest proofs of nationhood and its essential nature according to both divine and human law (as will be said later) or whether a nation should be understood as it ought to be as a territory equal even to the French nation in that it is one of four or five nations in obedience to the pope. The glorious English or British nation is of as great vigour and authority, if we may speak all the same without making comparison or prejudice against anyone, as the glorious Gallic nation . . .

Also, whereas the Gallic nation has for the most part a single language intelligible among the people on the whole at any rate or in part through the whole extent of the nation, the glorious English or British nation has in, of, and under its power five languages, nations which cannot understand one another, namely English (which the English and Scots share), Welsh, Irish, Gascon, and Cornish. And so with every right it should be able to represent as many nations as it has distinct languages.

Also, by the most powerful right it ought to represent as a single principal nation the fourth or fifth part in obedience to the pope in the general council and in other places, especially since in itself the English or British nation has equality in size and nature but also in extent of lands, kingdoms, dukedoms, counties, baronies, and other temporal dominions, and also in the excellence and size of its cathedrals, monasteries, colleges, and parochial churches, and other respects, and speaking without prejudice, just as the Gallic nation has in and of itself.

Lollardy Trials

Religious and secular authorities applied the name "Lollard" to people from a cross-section of medieval society who believed in one or more heretical ideas, many of them deriving from the writings of John Wyclif (ca. 1330–84), the Oxford theologian. His writings, beginning in the 1370s, articulated a set of ideas that questioned traditional discourse about Church authority, state prerogatives, the nature of the sacraments, and authority to translate, interpret,

[31]   The four divisions at the Council of Constance were Italy, France, Germany, and Britain. Spain also claimed representative status.

and preach scripture (see "Censorship," p. 242). Intersecting with a number of widely held discourses (such as anti-fraternalism; see "Friars," p. 7), Wyclif's ideas were condemned at the Blackfriars' Council in London in 1382, but the persecution of followers, many of them women, didn't begin in earnest until 1400.

From 1428 to 1431 William Alnwick, bishop of Norwich 1426–36 (then translated to the bishopric of Lincoln), continued proceedings against Lollards begun earlier in 1428 in Canterbury and in his own diocese (also see "Prioresses," p. 37). The two trials excerpted here are from what at one time were approximately 120 court records of heresy investigations between 1428 and 1431 kept by officials under Alnwick. They are of two kinds in the Westminster manuscript: examinations of suspects and (comprising the majority of the manuscript) abjurations, which were to be read out by the accused or court officers before sentencing. Margery Baxter's is of the former type and Hawise Moon's the latter. Baxter's reference to Moon is not unusual. As the notes to the other names in the selections indicate, Lollards tended to coalesce around a central figure or in a particular district.

Primary documents and further reading

Aston, M. (1980) "Lollard Women Priests?" *Journal of Ecclesiastical History* 31: 441–61.

—— (1984) *Lollards and Reformers: Images and Literacy in Late Medieval Religion.* London: Hambledon Press.

Cross, C. (1978) "'Great Reasoners in Scripture': The Activities of Women Lollards, 1380–1530." In D. Baker and R. M. T. Hill (ed.) *Medieval Women.* Oxford: Blackwell.

Dahmus, J. H. (1952) *The Prosecution of John Wyclif.* New Haven, CT: Yale University Press.

Hudson, A. (1988) *The Premature Reformation: Wycliffite Texts and Lollard History.* Oxford: Clarendon Press.

—— (ed.) (1997) *Selections from English Wycliffite Writings.* Toronto: University of Toronto Press.

McFarlane, K. B. (1972) [1952] *John Wycliffe and the Beginnings of English Noncon-formity.* London: English Universities Press.

McSheffrey, S. (1995) *Gender and Heresy: Women and Men in Lollard Communities, 1420–1530.* Philadelphia: University of Pennsylvania Press.

Marx, C. W. (trans.) (1992) "The Trial of Walter Brut (1391)." In A. Blamires (ed.) *Woman Defamed and Woman Defended: An Anthology of Medieval Texts.* Oxford: Clarendon Press, 250–60.

Westminster Diocesan Archives MS B.2, fols. 60r–61v, 102r–103v. In N. P. Tanner (ed.) (1977) *Heresy Trials in the Diocese of Norwich, 1428–31.* Camden Society, 4th series, 20. London: Royal Historical Society, 43–9, 140–3 (selections).
Language: Latin and English (Southeast Midland)
Manuscript date: ca. 1430

Depositions against Margery, wife of William Baxter, wright.

On the first day of the month of April in the year of the Lord 1429, Joanna Clifland, wife of William Clifland, residing in the parish of St. Mary the Less in Norwich, was summoned to appear in person before the reverend father in Christ and lord, William, bishop of Norwich by the grace of God, presiding in judgement in the chapel of his palace. On the said lord's order, she swore herself, while physically touching God's holy gospels, that she would speak according to the truth about each and every individual thing that she was asked concerning the matter of the faith.

When the oath had thus been made, Joanna Clifland said that on the Friday before the last feast of the Purification of the Blessed Mary,[1] Margery Baxter, wife of William Baxter, wright, lately living in Martham in the diocese of Norwich, while sitting and sewing with this witness in her room next to the fire place in the presence of this witness and Joanne Grimell and Agnes Bethom, servants to this witness, said and instructed this witness and her afore-mentioned servants that they should in no way swear, saying in the mother tongue, "Dame, bewar of the bee, for every bee wil styngge, and therefor loke that ye swer nother be Godd, ne be our Ladi, ne be non other seynt and, if ye do the contrarie, the be will styngge your tunge and veneme your sowle."

Then this witness says that the said Margery asked her what she did every day in church. And she replied to her saying that first after her entrance in the church, kneeling before the cross, she usually said five Paternosters in honour of the cross and a whole Ave Maria in honour of the blessed Mary, mother of Christ. And then the said Margery remarked reproachfully to this witness, "You do ill by kneeling and praying in this way before images in such churches because God never was in such a church, nor has ever departed, nor will depart from heaven, nor will he offer or grant you more favour for such genuflections, adorations, or prayers performed in such churches than a lighted candle concealed beneath the wooden lath cover of the baptismal font can provide light to those in church at night time because there is no greater honour to be shown to images in churches or images of the crucifix than is to be shown to the gallows from which your

---

[1]   February 2.

brother was hung," saying in the mother tongue,[2] "Lewed wrightes of stokkes hewe and fourme suche crosses and ymages, and after that lewed peyntours glorye thaym with colours, and if you strive to see the true cross of Christ, I will show you it here in your own home." And this witness said she would willingly see the true cross of Christ. And the aforesaid Margery said, "Look," and then stretched her arms out wide, saying to this witness, "this is the true cross of Christ, and this cross you can and should see and worship every day here in your own home, and so you labour in vain when you go to church to worship or pray to any dead images or crosses."

And then this witness said that the aforementioned Margery asked her what she believed concerning the sacrament of the altar. And this witness, so she asserts, replied to her, saying that she believed that the sacrament of the altar after consecration is the true body of Christ in the form of bread. And then the said Margery said to this witness, "You believe ill because, if every such sacrament is God and the true body of Christ, there are countless gods because a thousand and more priests every day make a thousand such gods and afterwards eat these gods and, having eaten them, discharge them through their posteriors into repulsively smelling toilets, where you can find plenty of such gods if you want to look. Therefore, know for certain that that which you call the sacrament of the altar will never by the grace of God be my God, for such a sacrament was falsely made and deceitfully ordained by priests in the church to induce idolatry in simple people because this sacrament is only material bread."

Then the said Margery, asked by this witness, said to her, as she says, that the Thomas of Canterbury that people call Saint Thomas of Canterbury was a false traitor and is damned there in hell because he wrongfully endowed churches with possessions, and he encouraged and started many heresies in the church, which deceive the simple people. Therefore, if God was blessed, Thomas was and is cursed, and if Thomas was blessed, God was and is cursed; and those false priests are lying who say that Thomas patiently endured his death before the altar because, as a false, senseless traitor, he was slain while he fled through the doorway of the church.

And then this witness said that the aforementioned Margery, asked by this witness, replied to her that the cursed pope, cardinals, archbishops, bishops, and in particular the bishop of Norwich and others who start and support heresies and idolatries, ruling in general over the people, shall have within a short time the same or worse punishment than had "that cursed Thomma of Canterbury, for thay falsly and cursedly desseyve the puple with

---

[2]   But changing to Latin half way through.

thair false mawmentryes and lawes" to extort money from simple people in order to sustain their pride, extravagance, and idleness; and know without doubt that God's vengeance will shortly come upon those who most cruelly killed God's most holy sons and teachers, that is holy father Abraham, William White (the most holy and learned teacher of divine law), and John Waddon, and others who followed Christ's law . . .[3]

Also, this witness said that the aforementioned Margery said to her that no child or infant born, having Christian parents, should be baptized in water following common use because such an infant is adequately baptized in the mother's womb, and thus that superstition and idolatry that those false and accursed priests do when they dip infants in fonts in churches, they do only to extort money from the people to support those priests and their concubines.

Also, that the same Margery said to this witness then present that the consent of mutual love alone between a man and a woman suffices for the sacrament of marriage without any expression of words and without solemnization in churches.

Also, that the same Margery said to this witness that no faithful man or woman is bound to keep fast in Lent, on the Ember days, Fridays, saints' days, and other days proclaimed by the church, and that anyone was lawfully able on those said days and times to eat meat and all other kinds of food, and that it was better to eat the meat remaining from Thursday's leftovers on fast days than to go to market and to incur debt buying fish . . .

Also, that the same Margery said to this witness that William White, who was condemned as a false heretic, is a great saint in heaven and a most holy teacher ordained and sent from God, and that every day she prayed to that holy man William White, and every day of her life she will pray to him because he is worthy to intercede for her before God of heaven, and that the said William White said to the same Margery, as this witness reports, that the said Margery should follow him to his place of supplication because she then would see that he had made many miracles because he wanted to convert the people through his preaching and make the people rise up and slay all the traitors who stood against it and his doctrine . . .

Also, that the same Margery taught and instructed this witness that she should never go on a pilgrimage to Mary of Falsingham nor any other saint or place.[4]

---

[3]   William White, the well-known priest and a preacher of heretical ideas in Kent and Norwich, was burned for heresy in 1428. John Waddon was also burned in Norwich in the same year.
[4]   Margery employs a pun on Walsingham, an important site of pilgrimage for the Virgin.

The same Margery also said that Thomas Mone's wife is the most learned and most wise woman about the doctrine of William White, and that the son of Richard Belward's brother was a good teacher and first instructed her in the doctrine and his beliefs.[5]

This witness also said that the said Margery asked this witness that she and the aforementioned Joanna, her servant, should come secretly to the said Margery's room at night, and there she would hear her husband read the law of Christ to them, which law was written in one book which the said husband usually read to Margery at night, and she said that her husband is the best teacher of Christianity . . .

In addition, the said Margery spoke to this witness in this way: "Joanna, it seems from your face that you intend and threaten to reveal the advice I have told you to the bishop." And this witness swore that she never wished to reveal her counsel in this matter unless Margery herself gave her occasion to do so. And then the said Margery said to this witness, "And if you were to accuse me to the said bishop, I will do to you as I did to a Carmelite friar of Yarmouth who was the most learned brother in the whole country." This witness replied to her, asking what she did to the said brother. And this Margery responded that she spoke with the said brother, reproaching him because he begged and because alms would not do or give him good unless he was willing to give up his habit and go to the plough, and in that way he would please the lord God more than by following the life of any other friars. And then the friar asked Margery if there was anything else she wished to say to or teach him. And Margery, so this witness says, expounded the gospels in English to the said brother. And then this friar withdrew from Margery, as this witness says, and afterwards the same friar accused Margery of heresy. And Margery, hearing that the friar thus accused her, herself accused the friar that he wanted to have known her carnally and, because she was unwilling to consent, the friar accused her of heresy. And therefore Margery said that her husband wanted to kill the friar for that reason and so, for fear, the friar kept quiet and retreated in shame from the region.

The said Margery also said to this witness that she often made an insincere confession to the dean of St. Mary of the Fields[6] to the effect that the dean thought her to be of good life, and for that reason he often gave Margery money. And then this witness asked her if she had not confessed all her sins to a priest. And Margery said that she never brought evil to any priest, and, therefore, she never wished to confess to a priest nor to obey any priest because no priest has the power to absolve anyone of his or her

[5]   See the following excerpt for Hawise Moon's confession.
[6]   The college of St. Mary of the Fields, Norwich.

sins, and priests sin grievously every day more than other men. And the same Margery further said that all men and women who are of the same opinion as Margery are good priests, and that holy church exists only in the places of those who are in her sect, and therefore Margery said that one should confess to God alone and no other priest.

Then the said Margery also said to this witness that the people honor the devils who fell from heaven with Lucifer, which devils, after they had fallen to earth, entered into images standing in churches, and they continued to live and still live latent in them in order that people worshipping them in this way commit idolatry.

Then she said that the said Margery told this witness that blessed water and blessed bread are nothing but trifles and of no value, and that all bells are to be pulled down from churches and destroyed, and that all those who oversee bells in churches are excommunicate.

The same Margery also said to this witness that Margery should not be burnt even if she were convicted of Lollardy because, so she told this witness, she had and has a charter of protection in her womb.[7]

Also, the same Margery said that she prevailed in judgement over the lord bishop of Norwich, Henry Inglese,[8] and the lords abbots who were with them . . .

Hawise Moone, wife of Thomas Moone of Lodne[9]
. . . In the name of God, tofore you, the worshipful fadir in Crist, William, be the grace of God bisshop of Norwich, Y, Hawise Moone, the wyfe to Thomas Moone of Lodne of your diocese, your subject, knowyng, felyng, and undirstandyng that before this tyme Y have be right hoomly and prive with many heretikes, knowyng [thaym] for heretikes, and thaym Y have receyved and herberwed in our hous, and thaym Y have conceled, conforted, sup-ported, maytened, and favored with al my poar[10] – whiche heretikes names be these, Sir William Whyte, Sir William Caleys, Sir Huwe Pye, Sir Thomas Pert, prestes, John Waddon, John Fowlyn, John Gray, William Everden, William Bate of Sethyng, Bartholomeu Cornmonger, Thomas Borell and Baty, hys wyf, William Wardon, John Pert, Edmond Archer of Lodne, Richard Belward, Nicholas Belward, Bertholomeu Monk, William Wright, and many others[11]

---

[7] If Margery was pregnant, she could not be executed until after delivery.
[8] I.e., Henry IV (r. 1422–61, 1470–1).
[9] Southeast Norfolk.
[10] power.
[11] See note 3 for White and Waddon. William Caleys, Hugh Pye, William Bate, and Edmund Archer were also burned as heretics. The others are relatives or members of a coherent group in Coddon, Norfolk, and Tenterdon, Kent.

– whiche have ofte tymes kept, holde, and continued scoles of heresie yn prive chambres and prive places of oures, yn the whyche scoles Y have herd, conceyved, lerned, and reported the errours and heresies which be writen and contened in these indentures, that is to say:

Fyrst, that the sacrament of baptem doon in watir in forme customed in the churche is but a trufle and not to be pondred, for alle Cristis puple is sufficiently baptized in the blood of Crist, and so Cristis puple nedeth noon other baptem.

Also, that the sacrament of confirmacion doon be a bisshop is of noon availe ne necessarie to be had for as muche as whan a child hath discrecion and can and wile undirstande the word of God, it is sufficiently confermed be the Holy Gost and nedeth noon other confirmacion.

Also, that confession shuld be maad oonly to God and to noon other prest, for no prest hath poar to remitte synne ne to assoile a man of ony synne.

Also, that no man is bounde to do no penance whiche ony prest enjoyneth [hym] to do for here synnes whyche thei have confessed unto the pr[est], for sufficient penance for all maner of synne is every persone to abstyne hym fro lyyng, bakbytyng, and yvel doyng, and no man is bounde to do noon other penance.

Also, that no prest hath poar to make Cristis veri body at messe in forme of bred, but that aftir the sacramental wordis said at messe of the prest, ther remayneth oonly material bred.

Also, that the pope of Roome is fadir Antecrist and fals in all hys werkyng, and hath no poar of God more than ony other lewed man but if he be more holy in lyvyng, ne the pope hath no poar to make bisshops, prestes, ne non other ordres, and he that the puple callen the pope of Roome is no pope but a fals extersioner and a deseyver of the puple.

Also, that he oonly that is moost holy and moost perfit in lyvyng in erthe is verry pope, and these singemesses that be cleped prestes ben no prestes, but thay be lecherous and covetouse men and fals deceyvours of the puple, and with thar sotel techyng and prechyng, syngyng and redyng piteously thay pile[12] the puple of thar good, and tharwith thay susteyne here pride, here lechery, here slowthe, and alle other vices, and always thay makyn newe lawes and newe ordinances to curse and kille cruelly all other persones that holden ageyn thar vicious levyng.

Also, that oonly consent of love betuxe man and woman, withoute con-tract of wordis and withoute solennizacion in churche and withoute symbred askyng,[13] is sufficient for the sacrament of matrymoyn.

---

[12] rob.
[13] consanguineous asking, i.e., reading of the marriage banns.

Also, it is but a trufle to enoynt a seke man with material oyle consecrat be a bisshop, for it sufficeth every man at hys last ende oonly to have mende of God.

Also, that every man may lefully withdrawe and withholde tythes and offringes from prestes and curates and yeve hem to the pore puple, and that is moore plesyng to God.

Also, that the temporal lordis and temporel men may lefully take alle possessions and temporel godys from alle men of holy churche, and from alle bysshops and prelates bothe hors and harneys, and gyve thar good to pore puple, and therto the temporel men be bounde in payne of dedly synne.

[Als]o, that it is no synne ony persone to do the contrarie of the preceptes [of] holy churche.

Also that every man and every woman beyng in good lyf oute of synne is as good prest and hath [as] muche poar of God in al thynges as ony prest ordred, be he pope or bisshop.

Also, that censures of holy churche, sentences and cursynges, ne of suspendyng yeven be prelates or ordinaries, be not to be dred ne to be fered, for God blesseth the cursynges [of] the bisshops and ordinaries.

Also, that it is not leful to swere in ony caas, ne it is not leful to pletyn[14] for onythyng.

Also, that is in not leful to slee a man for ony cause, ne be processe of lawe to dampne ony traytour or ony man for ony treson or felonie to deth, ne to putte ony man to deth for ony cause, but every man shuld remitte all vengeance oonly to the sentence of God.

Also, that no man is bounde to faste in Lenton, Ymbren Days,[15] Fridays, ne vigiles of seyntes, but all suche days and tymes it is leful to alle Cristis puple to ete flessh and [all] maner metis indifferently at here owne lust as ofte as thay have appetite as wel as ony other days whiche be not commanded to be fasted.

Also, that no pilgrimage oweth to be do ne be made, for all pilgrimage goyng servyth of nothyng but oonly to yeve prestes good that be to riche and to make gay tap[s]ters and proude ostelers.

Also, that no worship ne reverence oweth be do to ony ymages of the crucifix, of Our Lady, ne of noon other seyntes, for all suche ymages be but ydols and maade be werkyng of mannys hand, but worship and reverence shuld be do to the ymage of God, whiche oonly is man.

---

[14] take legal action.
[15] Ember days, i.e., any of four groups of three prayer and fasting days (Wednesday, Friday, and Saturday) after Pentecost, the first Sunday in Lent, the feast of St. Lucy, and the feast of the Holy Cross.

Also, that al prayer oweth be maad oonly to God and to noon other seyntes, for it is doute if thar be ony suche seyntes in hevene as these singemesse aproven and commaunden to be worsheped and prayed to here in erthe.

Because of whiche and many other errours and heresies, Y am called tofore you, worshipful fadir, whiche have cure of my soule. And be you fully informed that the said myn affermyng, belevyng, and holdyng be opin errours and heresies, and contrarious to the determinacion of the churche of Roome, wherefor Y willyng folwe and sue the doctrine of holy churche and departe from al maner of errour and heresie, and turne with good will and herte to the oonhed[16] of the churche. Considerand that holy churche spereth not hyr bosom to hym that wil turne agayn, ne God wil not the deth of a synner but rather that he be turned and lyve, with a pure herte Y confesse, deteste, and despise my sayd errours and heresies, and these said opinions Y confesse hereticous and erroneous and to the feith of the churche of Rome and all universall holy churche repugnant. And for as muche as be the said thinges that Y so held, beleved, and affermed, Y shewed meself corrupt and unfaithful, that from hensforth Y shewe me uncorrupt and faithful, the feith and doctrine of holy churche truly to kepe Y promitte. And all maner of errour and heresie, doctrine and opinion ageyn the feith of holy churche and determinacion of the churche of Roome – and namely the opinions before rehersed – Y abjure and forswere, and swere be these holy gospels be me bodely touched that from hensforth Y shal never holde errour ne heresie ne fals doctrine ageyn the feith of holy churche and determinacion of the churche of Roome. Ne no suche thinges Y shal obstinatly defende, ne ony persone holdyng or techyng suche maner of thynges Y shal obstinatly defende be me or ony other persone opinly or prively. Y shal never aftir this time be no recettour, fautour,[17] consellour, or defensour of heretikes or of ony persone suspect of heresie. Ne Y shal never trowe to thaym. Ner wittyngly Y shal felaship with thaym, ne be hoomly with tham, ne gyve thaym consell, sokour, favour, ne confort. Yf Y knowe ony heretikes or of heresie ony per-sones suspect or of thaym fautours, confortours, consellours, or defensours, or of ony persone makyng prive conventicules or assembles, or holdyng ony divers or singuler opinions from the commune doctrine of the churche, Y shal late you, worshipful fadir, or your vicar general in your absence or the diocesans of suche persones, have sone and redy knowyng. So help me God atte holy doom and these holy gospels.

[16]   unity.
[17]   supporter.

In wittenesse of which thinges Y subscribe here with myn owen hand a cross +. And to this partie indented to remayne in your registre Y sette my signet. And that other partie indented Y receyve undir your seel to abide with me unto my lyves ende. Yoven at Norwich in the chapell of your palays the fourth day of the moneth of August the yer of our Lord a thousand four hundred and thretty.

Usurpation

For a year, beginning in November 1386, twelve lords of a "great and continual council" ruled England instead of King Richard II. Appointed by parliament and replacing the ineffectual chancellor Michael de la Pole, earl of Suffolk, the council's principal task was to reform the expenses and revenues of the king's household. The king attempted a recovery of his power in August 1387, which culminated in a ruling by King's Bench that the council members had been "derogatory to the regality and prerogative of the lord king" and that those who had limited his ability to appoint the ministers and to summon and dismiss parliament as he wished were traitors (see the image "Court of King's Bench," p. 145). However, Richard's friends and supporters subsequently failed in their attempt fully to regain control by force. In the Merciless Parliament of February to June, 1388, five Lords Appellant presented charges of treason against these members of the king's court, who were then exiled, hanged, or beheaded.

Richard was unable fully to revenge these humiliations until 1397, when he had regained sufficient power to recall the King's Bench's ruling. Of the five appellants, Thomas of Woodstock, duke of Gloucester, was murdered; Richard Fitzalan, earl of Arundel and Surrey, was tried and executed; and Thomas Beauchamp, earl of Warwick, was banished. A little later, in September 1398, Thomas Mowbray, earl of Nottingham and duke of Norfolk, and Henry Bolingbroke, earl of Derby, were also exiled.

With the death of John of Gaunt in February 1399, Richard moved to deny Henry his inheritance. Henry responded in July by returning from France while Richard was in Ireland, and Henry quickly gained control of central and eastern England. After some delay, the king landed in south Wales and eventually met with Henry's representatives at Conway around August 15 after the royal forces had all but dispersed. After agreeing to surrender his person and to summon a parliament to settle matters, Richard met with Henry at Flint and was taken into custody in the city of Chester before being transferred to the Tower of London at the beginning of

September. Henry either had been planning all along to claim the throne or at some moment in the August–September period he decided on the more ambitious goal, and he appointed a commission to marshal arguments and evidence as to how this could be done, setting September 30 as the date for parliament's session. Several meetings between Richard and Henry's delegates, and then Henry himself, on September 28 and 29 secured Richard's agreement to a list of articles against him. These charges were read out in parliament on September 30 to cries of approval, Henry securing at the same time confirmation that the lords assented to his new kingship. The king was crowned two weeks later, and in mid-February the 33-year-old former king, now Richard of Bordeaux, died in captivity in the Lancastrian stronghold of Pontrefact.

The records of the negotiations between Richard and Henry, from the conferences at Conway to the meetings in the Tower, disagree on several points, depending on the authors' allegiances and the reasons why the documents were written. The version of the "Record and Process" in the parliamentary rolls is the official Lancastrian account and a deft piece of propaganda written some time after September 30. The Lancastrians were eager to promulgate the "Record and Process," not only by having a redaction entered in the rolls, but also by circulating it among select abbeys so that the narrative and charges would be entered in chronicles.

"La Manere de la Renonciacione" differs from the "Record and Process" in that it includes descriptions of what happened on September 28, whereas the "Record and Process" begins its narrative on the 29th. Several points in "La Manere" suggest a less clearly propagandist intent, and it may have been written by someone who was merely a witness to the events of the 28–30 September. It survives in one manuscript, possibly written at an East Kentish religious house, perhaps Canterbury, but quickly came into the hands of at least one other chronicler.

Adam of Usk (ca. 1352–1430) studied and taught law at Oxford before entering into service for Thomas Arundel, archbishop of Canterbury (1396–7, 1399–1414). He accompanied Arundel and Bolingbroke to Chester in 1399 and, upon returning to London with them and Richard, became part of the committee concerned with finding the evidence and arguments to provide a rationale for deposing and replacing the king. Nevertheless, his eyewitness account of the days leading up to the usurpation are written in a characteristically personal style with a relatively ambiguous tone. Usk's account is contained in his continuation of Ranulf Higden's *Polychronicon* (see "The English and England," p. 50), which he began to write in 1401 and which chronicles the years 1377–1421.

Thomas Walsingham (d. ca. 1422), monk of St. Albans abbey in Hertfordshire, was most likely also responsible for a continuation of Higden's
diverse history, and he chronicled the intervening years from Higden's
endpoint in 1340 to 1377. However, his most important work was his continuation of Matthew Paris's *Chronica Majora*, which he began about 1380.
Walsingham compiled his own *Chronica Majora* from a number of different authors to cover the years 1308–92, then continued his theocentric
history to 1420 while cloistered from 1396 until his death by using official
documents, letters, and oral accounts (see also the image "Royal Benefactors,"
p. 154). Often critical of Richard II and John of Gaunt, his account of the
usurpation relies on the "Record and Process" but provides slightly different information.

Primary documents and further reading

Creton, J. (1824) *Histoire du Roy d'Angleterre Richard,* ed. and trans. J. Webb.
    Archaeologia 20: 1–423.
Bennett, M. (1999) *Richard II and the Revolution of 1399.* Stroud, Gloucestershire:
    Sutton.
Ferster, J. (1996) *Fictions of Advice: The Literature and Politics of Counsel in Late
    Medieval England.* Philadelphia: University of Pennsylvania Press.
Giancarlo, M. (2002) "Murder, Lies, and Storytelling: The Manipulation of Justice(s)
    in the Parliaments of 1397 and 1399." *Speculum* 77: 76–112.
Given-Wilson, C. (1993) "The Manner of the King's Renunciation: A 'Lancastrian
    Narrative'?" *English Historical Review* 108: 365–70.
Gransden, A. (1982) *Historical Writing in England II: c. 1307 to the Early Sixteenth
    Century.* Ithaca, NY: Cornell University Press.
Patterson, L. (1993) "Making Identities in Fifteenth-century England: Henry V and
    John Lydgate." In J. N. Cox and L. J. Reynolds (eds.) *New Historical Literary
    Study: Essays on Reproducing Texts, Representing History.* Princeton, NJ: Princeton
    University Press, 69–107.
Saul, N. (1997) *Richard II.* New Haven, CT: Yale University Press.
Scanlon, L. (1990) "The King's Two Voices: Narrative and Power in Hoccleve's
    Regement of Princes." In L. Patterson (ed.) *Literary Practice and Social Change in
    Britain, 1380–1530.* Berkeley: University of California Press, 216–47.
Stow, G. B. (1984) "Richard II in Thomas Walsingham's Chronicles." *Speculum* 59:
    68–102.
Strohm, P. (1998) *England's Empty Throne: Usurpation and the Language of Legiti-
    mation, 1399–1422.* New Haven: Yale University Press.
Taylor, J. (1987) *English Historical Literature in the Fourteenth Century.* Oxford:
    Clarendon Press.
Thomas, A. H. and I. D. Thornley (eds.) (1938) *The Great Chronicle of London.*
    London: George W. Jones.

Walsingham, T. (1864) *Historia Anglicana*, vol. 2, ed. H. T. Riley. Rolls Series. London.

Rotuli Parliamentorum (1767) Vol. 3, ed. J. Strachey et al. London, 415–53. In C. Given-Wilson (ed. and trans.) (1993) *Chronicles of the Revolution, 1397–1400: The Reign of Richard II*. Manchester: Manchester University Press, 169–86 (selections).
Language: Latin and English (Southwestern)
Date: ca. 1400

The Record and Process of the renunciation of King Richard the Second since the Conquest and of the acceptance of the same renunciation, together with the deposition of the same King Richard, here follow:

Be it remembered that at about nine o'clock on Monday the feast of St. Michael the Archangel, in the twenty-third year of the reign of King Richard II,[1] the lords spiritual and temporal and other great persons – namely Richard le Scrope, archbishop of York; John, bishop of Hereford; Henry, earl of Northumberland; Ralph, earl of Westmorland; Hugh, Lord Burnell; Thomas, Lord Berkeley;[2] the prior of Canterbury; the abbot of Westminster; Sir William Thirning and John Markham, justices; Thomas Stowe and John Burbach, doctors of law; Thomas Erpingham and Thomas Gray, knights; and William Ferriby and Denis Lopham, notaries public, who had initially been deputed, with the consent and counsel of the lords spiritual and temporal – the justices, and others learned in civil and canon law and in the laws of the kingdom, [who were] gathered together in the usual meeting-place of the council at Westminster to undertake the following act, came into the presence of the said King Richard in the Tower of London. And there, in the same king's presence, it was recited by the earl of Northumberland, acting on behalf of and with the permission of all the aforesaid, how the same king at an earlier time, at Conway in North Wales, being then at liberty, had promised lord Thomas,[3] archbishop of Canterbury, and the aforesaid earl of Northumberland that he was willing to yield up and renounce his crowns of England and France and his royal majesty on account of his own inability and insufficiency which he himself admitted there,

---

[1]   September 29, 1399.
[2]   Richard le Scrope, archbishop of York 1398–1405; John Trefnant, bishop of Hereford 1389–1404; Henry de Percy, earl of Northumberland 1377–1405; Ralph de Neville, earl of Westmorland 1397–1425; Hugh, Lord Burnell (ca. 1347–1417); Thomas de Berkeley (ca. 1352–1417).
[3]   Thomas Arundel, archbishop of Canterbury 1396–7, 1399–1414.

which was to be done in the best manner and form that could be devised according to the counsel of learned men. In reply to this, and in the presence of the aforesaid lords and others, the king replied easily that he was willing to carry out what he had formerly promised in this regard; he wished, however, to speak with his kinsmen Henry, duke of Lancaster, and the aforesaid archbishop before thus fulfilling his promise. He also asked to be given a copy of the Cession made by him, that he might study it for a while; a copy was therefore given to him, and the said lords and others returned to their lodgings.

Later on that same day, after dinner, after the king had grown impatient for the arrival of the duke of Lancaster, who delayed a long time, at length the duke of Lancaster, the lords and other persons named above, and the archbishop of Canterbury came into the king's presence in the Tower, where Lords Roos, Willoughby, and Bergavenny were also present.[4] And after the king had spoken apart for a while with the said duke and archbishop of Canterbury, with whom, it seemed to those present, he conversed with a cheerful expression, he at length called forward all who were there and announced to them that he was ready to perform the Cession and Renunciation which he had promised. And although he was informed that, in order to save him the trouble of reading such a lengthy document, he could allow his Cession and Renunciation, which was written down on a parchment schedule to be read out for him by others, nevertheless he himself, willingly and, so it seemed, with a cheerful expression, took the schedule in his hands and announced that he wished to read it himself, and, quite distinctly, he read it out. Thus did he absolve his liegemen, and renounce, and yield up, and this he swore, and indeed he added further remarks and enlargements during the reading, and he signed it at the foot with his own hand as can be clearly seen on the aforesaid schedule, the tenor of which follows in these words:

"In the name of God, amen. I, Richard, by the grace of God king of England and France and lord of Ireland, absolve all my archbishops, bishops, and other prelates of the church in the said kingdoms and dominions whatsoever, both secular and regular, of whatever dignity, degree, estate, or condition they be, and all my dukes, marquises, earls, barons, knights, vassals, vavasours, and all my other liegemen whatsoever, whether ecclesiastical or secular, by whatever name they might be described, from their Oath of Fealty and Homage and any other oaths to me which they have taken,

---

[4] William de Ros (d. 1414), William de Willoughby (ca. 1370–1409), Beauchamp, Lord Abergavenny (d. 1411).

together with all bonds of allegiance, regality, and lordship, or of any other kind, by which they are or have been bound to me . . . And by these words I fully, willingly, directly, and totally renounce my right to the rule, governance, and administration of these kingdoms and dominions, and all and every type of power and jurisdiction in them, together with the name, honour, regality, and majesty of kingship . . . Saving the rights of my successors as kings of England in these kingdoms and dominions in all the foregoing for all time . . . I confess, acknowledge, recognize, and from my own certain knowledge truly admit that I have been and am entirely inadequate and unequal to the task of ruling and governing the aforesaid kingdoms and dominions and all that pertains to them, and that, on account of my notorious insufficiencies, I deserve to be deposed from them. And I swear upon these Holy Gospels, physically held here by me in person, that I shall never contravene the aforesaid Renunciation, Resignation, Demission, and Cession, nor in any way, by word or deed, on my own behalf or, so far as I am able, through any other person, either openly or secretly challenge them, or allow them to be challenged, but I shall regard the same Renunciation, Resignation, Demission, and Cession as established and accepted by me in perpetuity and shall firmly hold and observe them in each and every part, as God and these Holy Gospels shall judge me. Written by me, the aforesaid King Richard, with my own hand."

And immediately the same king added to this Renunciation and Cession in his own words that, were it in his power, he should like the duke of Lancaster to succeed him to the throne. Yet, since his power to decide such things, as he himself said, was now minimal, he asked the aforesaid archbishop of York and bishop of Hereford, whom he also appointed as his spokesmen to convey and announce his Cession and Renunciation to the estates of the realm, that they should declare his will and intention in this matter too to the people. And, as a sign of his will and intention, he publicly removed from his finger his golden signet ring and placed it on the aforesaid duke's finger, declaring that he wished this deed of his to be made known to all the estates of the realm. When this had been done, all who were there bade him farewell and left the Tower to return to their lodgings.

On the following day, Tuesday, the feast of St. Jerome, in the great hall at Westminster, which had been suitably prepared for the holding of a parliament, in the presence of the aforesaid archbishops of Canterbury and York, the duke of Lancaster, and the other dukes and lords both spiritual and temporal whose names are written above, as well as a great assembly of the people of the realm gathered there for the holding of parliament, with the duke of Lancaster occupying his proper and accustomed place, and the royal throne solemnly bedecked with cloth of gold standing vacant and without any president, the aforesaid archbishop of York and bishop of Hereford, in accordance with the king's injunction, publicly announced that the Cession and Renunciation had indeed been made by the king and that he had signed it with his own hand and had handed over his own signet, and they caused the Cession and Renunciation to be read out there, first in Latin and then in English. Whereupon the estates and people there present were immediately asked by the archbishop of Canterbury who, on account of the dignity and prerogative of his metropolitan church of Canterbury, has the privilege of speaking before all the other prelates and magnates of the realm in such matters, if they wished, for their own welfare and for the good of the realm, to accept that same Renunciation and Cession. To which the same estates and people replied that, considering the reasons given by the king himself in that Renunciation and Cession, it seemed most expedient to them, and unanimously and without dissent they accepted the Renunciation and Cession, each one singly and then jointly together with the people. Following this acceptance, it was publicly declared there that, as well as accepting this Cession and Renunciation, it would be of great benefit and advantage to the realm if, in order to remove any scruple or malevolent suspicion, the many wrongs and shortcomings so frequently committed by the said king in his government of the kingdom, which, as he himself confessed in his Cession, had rendered him worthy of deposition, were to be set down in writing in the form of articles publicly read out and announced to the people. The greater part of these articles was thus publicly read out, of which the full tenor is as follows . . . [There follows a copy of Richard's coronation oath.]

Here follow the charges against the king, for which he was deposed:

1. Firstly, the king is charged for his evil government, namely, that he gave the goods and possessions of the crown to unworthy persons and otherwise indiscreetly dissipated them, as a result of which he had to impose needlessly grievous and intolerable burdens upon the people, and committed innumerable other crimes. By his assent and command, certain prelates and other temporal lords were chosen and assigned by the whole parliament to labour faithfully at their own costs for the just government of the kingdom;[5] the king, however, made an agreement with his supporters, proposing to impeach of high treason the said lords spiritual and temporal thus employed about the government of the kingdom and coerced the justices of the realm

---

[5]   I.e., the so-named Wonderful Parliament or Great and Continual Council of 1386–7.

with threats of life and limb to confirm his wicked plans, intending to destroy the said lords.

2. Item: the king, when he was formerly at Shrewsbury, caused to come before him and others that supported him, in a chamber, various persons, including the majority of the justices, where, through fear and threats, he induced, compelled, and forced them each to answer certain questions on his behalf concerning the laws of the kingdom against their will and otherwise than they would have answered had they not been under compulsion but at liberty;[6] by authority of which questions the king planned to proceed to the destruction of the duke of Gloucester and the earls of Arundel and Warwick and other lords against whom he had conceived a great hatred because they wished him to be under good rule.[7] By divine providence and through the resistance and power of the said lords, the king was prevented from carrying out his plans.

3. Item: when the lords temporal, in order to defend themselves, resisted the king's evil designs, the king set a day for parliament to see justice done to them, whereupon they, putting their hope and faith in the meeting of parliament, retired peaceably to their houses, but the king then secretly sent the duke of Ireland[8] with his letters and his standard into Cheshire in order to raise to arms there a great number of men, and he incited them to rise up against the said lords and the magnates of the kingdom and the servants of the republic,[9] thus challenging the peace which he had publicly sworn to keep, as a result of which deaths, imprisonments, quarrels, and numerous other evils occurred throughout the kingdom, by which acts he committed perjury.

4. Item: although the king pardoned the duke of Gloucester and the earls of Arundel and Warwick and all their supporters in full parliament and with its assent, and for many years behaved towards them in peaceful and benevolent fashion, yet he continued to bear hatred in his heart towards them so that when an opportunity came, he ordered the seizure of the duke of Gloucester – his own uncle, the son of the celebrated Edward, former king of England, and constable of England – who had come humbly forward to

---

[6] The Questions to the Judges in August, 1387.

[7] I.e., three out of the five lords appellant, who called for the Merciless Parliament of February 1388: Thomas of Woodstock, duke of Gloucester 1385–97; Richard Fitzalan, earl of Arundel 1346–97; and Thomas Beauchamp, earl of Warwick 1370–97, 1399–1401. The other two were Henry Bolingbroke and Thomas Mowbray, earl of Nottingham 1383–99.

[8] Robert de Vere, earl of Oxford 1381–88, created duke of Ireland in 1386, which he forfeited in 1388.

[9] At Radcot Bridge in December 1387, where the three lords appellant swiftly defeated de Vere's forces.

meet his lord king in solemn procession, and the said earls of Arundel and Warwick;[10] the said duke he sent abroad to the town of Calais to be imprisoned by the earl of Nottingham, one of those who had appealed him, and there he caused him, without response or any legal process, to be secretly suffocated, strangled, and barbarously and cruelly murdered.[11] The earl of Arundel, although he pleaded both a charter of general pardon and a charter of pardon which had been granted to him, and requested that justice be done to him, he wickedly ordered to be decapitated, having surrounded the parliament with a great number of armed men and archers whom he had gathered there for the purpose of overawing the people;[12] the earl of Warwick and Lord Cobham he committed to perpetual imprisonment and confiscated, from them and their heirs, their lands and tenements, both those held in fee simple and those held in tail, expressly contrary to justice and to the laws of his realm, and to his oath, granting them to their appellants.[13]

5. Item: at the time when the king in his parliament caused the duke of Gloucester and the earls of Arundel and Warwick to be adjudged, in order that he would be free to pursue his cruel designs and wicked will against them and others, he gathered together a great number of malefactors from the county of Chester, some of whom travelled through the realm with him, both within the royal household and separately from it, cruelly killing some of the king's subjects, beating and wounding others, plundering the goods of the people, refusing to pay for their provisions, and raping and ravishing both married and unmarried women. And although serious complaints were made to the king about the excesses committed by them, yet he made no attempt to stop them but rather supported these men in their crimes, trusting in them and their protection against all others of his kingdom so that his faithful subjects had great reason to grieve and to be indignant.

6. Item: although the king caused a proclamation to be made throughout the kingdom that he had had his uncle the duke of Gloucester and the earls of Arundel and Warwick seized and arrested not for any conspiracies or insurrections committed by them within the kingdom of England but for numerous extortions, oppressions, and other deeds done by them at a later time contrary to his regality and to his royal majesty – for, as he said, it was not his intention that any member of the duke's or the earls' following, or any person that had ridden with them at the time of those

---

[10]   On July 10, 1397.
[11]   Early September, 1397.
[12]   On September 21.
[13]   The earl of Warwick was imprisoned on September 28 and John, Lord Cobham, also a member of the council of 1386–7, was banished in January 1398.

conspiracies and insurrections should be harassed or molested on account of that – nevertheless, he later impeached the said lords in parliament not for any such extortions or oppressions but for the aforesaid conspiracies and insurrections, for which they were adjudged to death, and he compelled with threats of death many of their followers and many of those who had ridden with them at that time to make fine and redemption as if they were traitors, which was to the great destruction of many of his people. Thus did he craftily, maliciously, and fraudulently deceive the said lords, their followers, and the people of the realm.

7. Item: although many of these people, while making fine and redemption in this manner, had obtained from the king letters patent pardoning them fully, yet they received no benefit from these letters of pardon until they paid new fines and redemptions in order to save their lives, by which they were gravely impoverished, which derogated greatly from the name and honour of kingship.

8. Item: in the last parliament held at Shrewsbury,[14] the king, desiring to oppress his people, subtly procured and caused to be granted that the power of parliament should, with the assent of all the estates of the realm, be delegated to certain persons who, once the parliament had been dissolved, were to terminate certain petitions which were pending but had not been decided in parliament; by authority of this concession, however, they proceeded by the king's will to deal with other general business relating to that parliament, which was derogatory to the state of parliament, to the prejudice of the whole realm, and a pernicious example. And in order that these actions might seem to have proper authority, the king of his own volition ordered the Rolls of Parliament to be erased and altered, contrary to the intention of the aforesaid grant.

9. [The king decreed that no one was to intercede or plead for a pardon for the exiled Henry, thus violating his oath.]

10. [The king sought papal confirmation of parliamentary statutes, which would therefore include threats against those who would contravene them, which was contrary to the crown and the good of the realm.]

11. [Despite the king's approval of a duel between Henry and Thomas Mowbray, earl of Nottingham, Richard instead banished Henry (on 16 September, 1398).]

12. [The king reneged on allowing Henry income while in exile.]

13. [The king selected sheriffs instead of officers, justices, and others appointing them.]

---

[14]   January 28–31, 1398.

14. [The king borrowed money from lords and others, and failed to pay it back by the agreed time.]

15. Item: whereas the king of England used to live honestly upon the revenues of the kingdom and the patrimony belonging to the crown without oppressing his people except at times when the realm was burdened with the expense of war, this king, despite the fact that throughout almost the whole of his time there were truces in operation between the kingdom of England and its enemies, not only gave away the greater part of his said patrimony to unworthy persons but, because of this, was obliged to impose grants upon his realm almost every year, which greatly oppressed his people and impoverished his nation, nor did he use these grants for the benefit or welfare of the English kingdom, but he dissipated it prodigiously upon the ostentation, pomp, and vainglory of his own person. He also owed great sums of money in the realm for victuals for his household and for other purchases despite the fact that his wealth and riches were greater than can be remembered for any of his progenitors.

16. Item: the king, not wishing to uphold or dispense the rightful laws and customs of the realm but preferring to act according to his own arbitrary will and to do whatever he wished, at times when his justices or others of his council expounded to him upon the laws of the realm and asked him to do justice according to those laws, frequently replied and declared expressly, with an austere and determined expression, that his laws were in his mouth, or, at other times, that they were in his breast, and that he alone could change or make the laws of his kingdom. And thus, led astray by his own opinions, he frequently failed to do justice to his liegemen but forced many, through fear and threats, to desist from the pursuit of common justice.

17. [The king arranged for a petition to grant him liberty to go against parliamentary statutes while they were still in effect, thus going against his coronation oath.]

18. [The king interceded to allow sheriffs to remain in office longer than the legal term of one year.]

19. [The king interfered in the appointment of knights of the shires and then used bribes and threats to get them to agree to items such as granting him the duties from will (at the parliament in Shrewsbury, 1398).]

20. [The king commanded sheriffs to obey all his mandates and to arrest anyone who said anything against the king.]

21. [The king forced people in seventeen counties to submit to him as traitors in order to extort their goods.]

22. [The king illegally ordered certain churchmen to provide him with supplies and money to fund his expedition to Ireland (in 1399).]

23. Item: in many great councils of the kingdom, when the lords of the realm, justices, and others were charged faithfully to counsel the king on matters concerning his welfare and that of his kingdom, the aforesaid lords, justices, and others, when offering their advice according to their discretion, were often so sharply and violently rebuked and reproved by the king that they dared not speak the truth in giving their advice on such matters.

24. [Richard took royal treasure with him when he went to Ireland, risking the impoverishment of the realm, and he ordered that "records of his estate and government of the kingdom" be erased.]

25. Item: the king was so variable and dissimulating in both word and letter, and so inconstant in his behaviour, especially in his dealings with the pope, and with kings, and with lords and others both within and beyond his own kingdom, that virtually no living person who came to know him could or wished to trust him. Indeed, so faithless and deceitful was he reputed to be, that he was a scandal not just to his own person and to the whole realm, but above all to foreigners throughout the world who heard about him.

26. Item: although the lands, tenements, goods, and chattels of each free man should not, according to the laws in force since ancient times, be seized except as a consequence of forfeiture, nevertheless the king, seeking to undermine those laws, frequently declared in the presence of many lords and others of the community of the realm that the lives of each of his subjects, together with their lands, tenements, goods, and chattels, were his and subject to his will, regardless of any forfeiture, which is entirely contrary to the laws and customs of the kingdom.

27. Item: although a statute was ordained, which has hitherto been maintained, "that no free man should be arrested, etc., or in any way destroyed, nor should the king proceed or order any process against him unless it be by lawful judgement of his peers or by the law of the land,"[15] yet by the will, command, and ordinance of the king, many of his liegemen, being maliciously accused of having allegedly said things either openly or privately to the disgrace, scandal, or dishonour of the king's person, were seized, imprisoned, and brought before the constable and marshal of England in the Court of Chivalry, in which court the said liegemen were not permitted to enter any response except that they were not guilty, nor to defend themselves otherwise than by their bodies, despite the fact that those who accused and appealed them were young, strong, and healthy, whereas the accused were aged, impotent, lame or infirm. From this the destruction not only of various lords and magnates of the realm but of each and every

---

[15]   Clause 39 of Magna Carta.

person belonging to the community of the realm could have resulted. Thus, when the king willfully contravened this statute of the realm, he undoubtedly thereby committed perjury.

28. [The king forced his subjects to swear oaths of allegiance to him.]

29. [The king impeded ecclesiastical cases against individuals, thereby infringing on the liberties of the church.]

30. Item: the king in parliament, with armed men standing around in a threatening manner, adjudged Thomas Arundel, archbishop of Canterbury, primate of all England and his spiritual father, who was through the king's cunning absent at the time, to perpetual exile[16] without any reasonable or legitimate cause, without lawful process, and contrary to the laws of the kingdom which he himself had sworn to uphold.

31. Item: perusal of the king's testament, written under his great and privy seals as well as his signet, revealed among other things the following clause: "Item, we wish that once the debts of our household, chamber, and wardrobe have been paid, for which we leave twenty thousand pounds, and when fuller provision has been made by our executors for the lepers and chaplains whom we appointed to be maintained at Westminster and Bermondsey, for which purpose we leave five or six thousand marks to be spent by the said executors, the remainder of our gold should pass to our successor on condition that he approves, ratifies, confirms, upholds, and strictly observes each and every one of the statutes, ordinances, establishments, and judgements made and given in our parliament held on the seventeenth day of September in the twenty-first year of our reign at Westminster[17] or in the same parliament when it was continued at Shrewsbury, and all the ordinances, judgements, and establishments made or given on the sixteenth of September in our twenty-second year at Coventry or afterwards on the eighteenth day of March at Westminster by authority of the same parliament, together with any ordinances or judgements which might in future be promulgated under the authority of the same parliament. If, on the other hand, our successor will not perform the above or refuses to do so, which we cannot believe will happen, then we wish that Thomas, duke of Surrey; Edward, duke of Aumale; John, duke of Exeter; and William le Scrope, earl of Wiltshire,[18] once they have paid the debts of our household, chamber,

[16]   September 25, 1397.
[17]   1397.
[18]   Thomas de Holand, duke of Surrey ca. 1371–1400; Edward "of York," duke of Aumale ca. 1373–1415; John de Holand, duke of Exeter ca. 1350–1400; William le Scrope, earl of Wiltshire ca. 1350–99.

and wardrobe, and set aside five or six thousand marks, as mentioned above, should have and keep the remainder for the defence and maintenance of the aforesaid statutes, ordinances, establishments, and judgements to the utmost of their ability, even unto death if need be, for each and every one of which injunctions we burden their consciences as they would wish to answer at the day of judgement." Which article clearly demonstrates that the king tried unswervingly to uphold and maintain those wrongful and iniquitous statutes and ordinances, which are repugnant to all law and reason, not only in his life but even in death, regardless of the danger to his soul and to his kingdom, and to the ultimate destruction of his liegemen.

32. [Even though the king had earlier forgiven Gloucester for his role in the Great and Continual Council, he later had him murdered.]

33. [Richard dissuaded archbishop Arundel from answering in parliament in 1397 charges brought against him and then banished him, falsely promising to end his exile soon.]

Following this all the estates assembled there were asked both individually and jointly to give their opinion on the aforesaid, and it seemed to them, bearing in mind also the king's own confession of inadequacy and the other things mentioned in his Renunciation and Cession, that the wrongs and defects specified were fully sufficient and notorious to justify the king's deposition; all the aforesaid estates unanimously agreed, therefore, that there was abundant cause, for the security and peace of the people, and the welfare of the realm, to depose the king . . . [The estates then appointed proctors to carry out the "sentence of deposition," which they wrote, read out, and took to the king.]

Immediately after this, since it was clear from the foregoing and what followed from them that the realm of England with its appurtenances was vacant, the said Henry, duke of Lancaster, rose from his place and, standing erect so that he could be seen by the people, humbly made the sign of the cross on his forehead and on his breast and, after first invoking the name of Christ, claimed this realm of England, now vacant as aforesaid, together with the crown and all its members and appurtenances, in his mother tongue, in the following words:

"In the name of Fadir, Son, and Holy Gost, I, Henry of Lancaster, chalenge this rewme of Yngland and the corone with all the membres and the appurtenances als I that am disendit be right lyne of the blode comyng fro the gude lorde Kyng Henry therde and thorghe that ryght that God of his grace hath sent me, with helpe of my kyn and of my frendes to recover it, the whiche rewme was in poynt to be undone for defaut of governance and undoyng of the gode lawes."

Following this challenge and claim, the lords spiritual and temporal and all the estates there present were individually and jointly asked what they thought of this challenge and claim, to which the same estates, together with all the people, unanimously and without any difficulty or delay agreed that the aforesaid duke should reign over them. Whereupon the king promptly showed to the estates of the realm the signet of King Richard which, as mentioned earlier, had been willingly handed over to him as a token, and the archbishop, taking the aforesaid King Henry by the right hand, led him to the royal throne. After the king had knelt for a short while to pray before the throne, the aforesaid archbishop of Canterbury, assisted by the archbishop of York, seated the king upon the throne to tremendous and joyful applause from the people. Presently, the said archbishop of Canterbury, having with difficulty on account of the joy of all present, imposed silence upon them, preached a short sermon . . . [The theme of Arundel's sermon was "A man shall reign over the people."[19] The archbishop preached on the instability and danger caused by an immature ruler, contrasting that former peril with the present, wherein a mature and wise man will reign.]

When this sermon was over, the lord King Henry, in order to set at peace the minds of his subjects, then and there publicly spoke these words:

"Sires, I thank God and yowe, spirituel and temporel, and all the astates of the lond, and do yowe to wyte it es noght my will that no man thynk yt be waye of conquest I wold disherit any man of his heritage, franches, or other ryghtes that hym aght to have, no put hym out of that that he has and has had by the gude lawes and custumes of the rewme except thos persons that has ben agan the gude purpose and the commune profyt of the rewme."

[Henry set dates for the next parliament, Monday, 6 October, and his coronation, Monday, 13 October, before all present retired to celebrate. On the following Wednesday, Lord William Thirning and his fellow proctors visited Richard in the Tower, read out the sentence of deposition, and confirmed that the people's homage to him had ended and would exist no more. The record states simply that Richard:] answerd and seyd that he loked not ther after, but he said that after all this he hoped that is cosyn wolde be goode lord to hym.

Corpus Christi College, Cambridge, MS 59, fols. 230v–231r. "La Manere de la renonciacione del Roy Richard de sa corone et de la eleccione del Roy Henri le quatre puis le conqueste etc." In C. Given-Wilson (ed. and trans.) (1993) *Chronicles of the Revolution, 1397–1400: The Reign of Richard II.* Manchester: Manchester University Press, 162–4.

[19]   1 Samuel 9.17.

Language: French
Manuscript date: ca. 1400

Firstly, on Sunday the eve of Michaelmas, after dinner,[20] the following people were, with the assent of all the great council of England, sent to King Richard, who was then in the Tower of London: the archbishop of York and the bishop of Hereford for bishops; the earls of Northumberland and Westmorland for earls; Lord Despenser, the former earl of Gloucester,[21] and Lord Bergavenny for barons; Sir Thomas Gray and Sir Thomas Erpingham for knights; Master Thomas Stow and Master John Burbach, doctors; and Master Denis Lopham and Master John Ferriby, notaries. This was in order to ascertain from the king on behalf of the aforesaid council whether he was willing to resign all the right that he had to the crown of England with its appurtenances, as he had previously promised to them that he would. The king said in reply that he would prefer first of all to see in writing the form of the resignation by which he was supposed to resign. Whereupon they handed him a bill in which it was explained how he had to resign all the right that he had to the crown of England and its appurtenances, that is to say, in the kingdoms of England, France, Ireland, and Scotland; the duchies of Guyenne and Normandy; the county of Ponthieu and the town of Calais; and in all the other castles, fortresses, and towns which he either held at present or claimed by right, both on this side of the sea and beyond it, and in every part of them, for himself and his heirs in perpetuity. To which he replied by saying that he wished to consider this until the following morning.

On the feast of Michaelmas, therefore, at nine o'clock in the morning, the same lords came to the Tower and with them the prior of Christchurch Canterbury, and they asked him if he had considered sufficiently what his reply to the aforesaid bill would be. He replied shortly that he would not do it under any circumstances, and he was greatly incensed and declared that he would like to have it explained to him how it was that he could resign the crown and to whom. Later, however, after various additional arguments had been put forward and explained to him there by the aforesaid lords, he said, "Bring my dear cousin Lancaster here, for I am willing, upon certain conditions which I shall explain to him, to make my resignation to him."

Whereupon, after dinner on that same day, the duke of Lancaster, the earls of Northumberland and Westmorland, and a large number of other

---

[20]   September 28.
[21]   Thomas le Despenser, earl of Gloucester 1385–97.

barons, knights, and esquires rode through Cheap to the Tower, where the archbishops of Canterbury and York, the bishop of Hereford, the abbot of Westminster, the prior of Christchurch Canterbury, and various other spiritual clerks were at that time waiting. And there the king was asked if he was willing to resign all the right that he had to the crown of England and its appurtenances as set out in the bill of resignation handed to him. To which the king replied that he would do it willingly in the interests of his dear cousin the duke of Lancaster upon certain conditions which he would state. He was told by them, however, that there was no way in which this could be done; he must do it simply, without any conditions. Whereupon the king picked up the aforesaid bill himself and read it out with good cheer, loudly and clearly, thus resigning to the duke of Lancaster all the right that he had to the crown of England and its appurtenances, together with all other lands apart from the lands and tenements which he had bought from Roger Walden and from Sir William Scrope, the former treasurer of England, with which to endow a yearly anniversary for his soul at Westminster abbey, the latter having been allowed to him in presence of all the aforesaid lords. And upon this the names of certain witnesses were entered as of record.

Adam of Usk, British Library MS Additional 10104, fols. 162r–162v. In C. Given-Wilson (ed. and trans.) (1997) *The Chronicle, 1377–1421*. Oxford: Clarendon Press, 61–5.
Language: Latin
Manuscript date: 1401

He debased the nobles. It was in this King Richard's nature to debase the noble and to exalt the ignoble – as he did with . . . Sir William,[22] for example, and with other such low-born men whom he elevated to great positions, or the numerous simpletons whom he raised to bishoprics and who were later brought to ruin because of such unwarranted promotion. Thus might it truly be said that this Richard was like Arthgallus, former king of the Britons, for this Arthgallus also debased the noble and exalted the ignoble, seizing the goods of the wealthy and amassing indescribable treasures.

The king deposed. As a result of this, the heroes of the realm, unable to bear such evils any longer, rose up against him, deposed him, and set up his brother as king in his place.[23] Precisely the same things happened with this Richard, concerning whose birth many unsavoury things were commonly said, namely

[22]   Sir William Bagot, one of the Richard's appointed counselors.
[23]   Usk uses Geoffrey of Monmouth (ca. 1100–55), *Historia regum Britanniae*.

that he was not born of a father of the royal line but of a mother[24] given to slippery ways – to say nothing of many other things I have heard.

Reasons for deposing the king. Following this, the question of deposing King Richard and replacing him as king with Henry, duke of Lancaster, and of how and for what reasons this might lawfully be done, was committed for debate to a number of doctors, bishops, and others, one of whom was the writer of this present work; and they decided that perjuries, sacrileges, sodomitical acts, dispossession of his subjects, the reduction of this people to servitude, lack of reason, and incapacity to rule, to all of which King Richard was notoriously prone, were sufficient reasons – according to the chapter "*Ad Apostolice*" taken from "*Re Judicata*" in the *Sextus*, and the other things noted there – for deposing him.[25] Moreover, although he was prepared to abdicate, it was nevertheless decided that, as a further precaution, he should be deposed by authority of the clergy and people for the reasons already stated, for which purpose they were therefore summoned.

On the feast of St. Matthew[26] the second anniversary of the beheading of the earl of Arundel, the writer of this present work was conducted by Sir William Beauchamp to the aforesaid Tower where King Richard was imprisoned, for the specific purpose of ascertaining his mood and behaviour, and I was present there while he dined. And there and then, during dinner, the king began to discourse dolefully as follows: "My God, this is a strange and fickle land, which has exiled, slain, destroyed, and ruined so many kings, so many rulers, so many great men, and which never ceases to be riven and worn down by dissensions and strife and internecine hatreds." And he recounted the names and the histories of those who had suffered such fates, from the time when the realm was first inhabited. Seeing therefore the troubles of his soul, and seeing that none of those who had been deputed to wait upon him were in any way bound to him, or used to serving him, but were strangers who had been sent there simply to spy upon him, I departed much moved at heart, reflecting to myself on the glories of his former state and on the fickle fortune of this world.

Thomas Walsingham, *Annales Ricardi Secundi. Johannis de Trokelowe et Henrici de Blaneforde: Chronica et Annales*, ed. H. T. Riley. London, 1866, 282, 286–7. In C. Given-Wilson (ed.

[24]   Joan of Kent (ca. 1328–85).
[25]   Usk quotes from Pope Innocent IV's 1245 sentence of deposition of Frederick II for sacrilege, heresy, and dispossession and tyranny over his subjects. Both Usk and Walsingham (*Historia Anglicana*) accuse Richard of being sodomitical.
[26]   September 21.

and trans.) (1993) *Chronicles of the Revolution, 1397–1400: The Reign of Richard II*. Manchester: Manchester University Press, 186–7, 188–9.
Language: Latin
Manuscript date: ca. 1420   30

[Henry] had proposed to claim the kingdom by conquest, but Lord William Thirning, justice, said that this was quite impossible, for by doing so he would arouse the anger of the entire population against him. This was because if he claimed the kingdom in this way, it would appear to the people that he had the power to disinherit anybody at will and to change the laws, establishing new ones and revoking old ones, as a result of which no one would be secure in his possessions . . .

[W]hen Lord William Thirning said to him that he had renounced all the honours and dignity pertaining to a king, he replied that he did not wish to renounce those special dignities of a spiritual nature which had been bestowed upon him, nor indeed his anointment; he was in fact unable to renounce them, nor could he cease to retain them. And when William Thirning replied to this that he had himself admitted, in his own Renunciation and Cession, that he was not worthy, or adequate, or able enough to govern, he said that this was not true; it was simply that his government had not been acceptable to the people. But William replied by telling him that this had clearly been stated in the aforesaid Cession and Renunciation, and reminding him of the form in which this confession of his had been written down there. Hearing this, the king simply smiled and asked to be treated accordingly, and not to be deprived of the means with which to sustain himself honourably.

3

Gender, Sexuality, and Difference

Amazons

Christine de Pisan, Boccaccio, and many medieval Troy stories told and retold the ancient tales about Amazons. In them the land of "Femynye" is said to be located (to the modern mind in typically inconsistent fashion) beyond China and near the Caspian Sea. Though similar to many other marvels in romances and travel narratives (see "The Far East," p. 99), Amazons are distinguished in some accounts because they guard the ten lost tribes of Israel, Gog and Magog, from escaping the high hills that enclose them, and they refuse Alexander the Great (356–323 BCE) entry to their land.

According to the extant manuscripts of Sir John Mandeville's *Book* and several other fifteenth-century sources, Mandeville was an English knight who left his native St. Albans to travel to the East in 1322 and returned near the time of writing his account, 1356 or 1357. However, it seems more likely that the text originated in France about this time, its author making extensive use of available pilgrimage narratives, romances, and encyclopedias. The *Book* was quickly translated into English, Latin, and several other languages; its popularity enormous, it survives in approximately two hundred and fifty manuscripts and many early printed versions. About forty English manuscripts and fragments survive as well as several early printings.

The Prose Life of Alexander is primarily based on the pseudo-Callisthenic *Historia de preliis Alexandri Magni*, written by Leo, archpope of Naples, in the tenth century. It is one of several versions of the popular story of Alexander to survive in English. A kind of mirror for princes, romance, and epic, Alexander narratives attracted medieval writers and audiences because of Alexander's heroic and human qualities: his wisdom, his success in defeating eastern kings, and his spectacular feats, but also his rise and premature death, a confirmation of the fleeting presence of worldly glory and enjoyment of sensuality.

Primary documents and further reading

Bunt, G. (1990) "An Exemplary Hero: Alexander the Great." In H. Aersten and A. A. MacDonald (eds.) *Companion to Middle English Romance*. Amsterdam: VU University Press, 29–55.

Duggan, H. N. and T. Turville-Petre (eds.) (1989) *The Wars of Alexander*. EETS, s.s. 10. Oxford: Oxford University Press.

Higgins, I. M. (1997) *Writing East: The "Travels" of Sir John Mandeville*. Philadelphia: University of Pennsylvania Press.

Kleinbaum, A. W. (1983) *The War Against the Amazons*. New York: New Press.

Mandeville, Sir John (1983) *The Travels of Sir John Mandeville*, trans. and intro. C. W. R. D. Moseley. London: Penguin Books.

—— (2001) *The Book of John Mandeville: An Edition of the Pynson Text with Commentary on the Defective Version*, ed. T. Kohanski. Tempe, AZ: Arizona Center for Medieval and Renaissance Studies.

Martin, P. (1996) *Chaucer's Women: Nuns, Wives, and Amazons*. Basingstroke, Hampshire: Macmillan.

Seymour, M. C. (1993) *Sir John Mandeville*. Authors of the Middle Ages 1. Aldershot, Hampshire: Variorum.

Weinbaum, B. (1999) *Islands of Women and Amazons: Representations and Realities*. Austin: University of Texas Press.

Weisl, A. J. (1995) *Conquering the Reign of Femeny: Gender and Genre in Chaucer's Romance*. Rochester, NY: D. S. Brewer.

Sir John Mandeville. British Library MS Cotton Titus C.xvi, fols. 64v–65v. In M. C. Seymour (ed.) (1967) *Mandeville's Travels*. Oxford: Clarendon Press, 113–14.
Language: English (Southeast Midland)
Manuscript date: ca. 1400

Besyde the lond of Caldee[1] is the lond of Amazoyne, that is the lond of Femynye. And in that reme[2] is alle wommen and no man, noght as summe men seyn that men mowe not lyve there but for because that the wommen

[1]   Chaldea in Southwest Asia; along with Mesopotamia and Arabia, Chaldea is said to lie between two of the rivers flowing from paradise, the Tigris and Euphrates.
[2]   realm.

wil not suffre no men amonges hem to ben here sovereynes. For sumtyme ther was a kyng in that contrey, and men maryed as in other contreyes. And so befelle that the kyng had werre with hem of Sichie,[3] the whiche kyng highte Colepeus[4] that was slayn in bataylle and alle the gode blood of his reme. And whan the queen and alle the othere noble ladyes sawen that thei weren alle wydewes and that alle the rialle blood was lost, thei armed hem and as creatures out of wytt thei slowen all the men of the contrey that weren laft, for thei wolden that alle the wommen weren wydewes as the queen and thei weren.

And fro that tyme hiderwardes thei nevere wolden suffren man to dwelle amonges hem lenger than seven dayes and seven nyghtes, ne that no child that were male scholde duelle amonges hem lenger than he were noryscht and thanne sente to his fader. And whan thei wil have ony companye of man, than thei drawen hem towardes the londes marchynge next[5] to hem. And than thei [have] here loves that usen hem, and thei duellen with hem an eight dayes or ten, and thanne gon hom ayen. And yif thei have ony knave child, thei kepen it a certeyn tyme and than senden it to the fadir whan he can gon allone and eten be himself or elles thei sleen it. And yif it be a femele, thei don awey that on pappe[6] with an hote iren. And yif it be a womman of gret lynage, thei don awey the left pappe that thei may the better beren a scheeld. And yif it be a womman on fote, thei don awey the [right] pappe for to scheten with bowe Turkeys, for they schote wel with bowes.

In that lond thei have a queen that governeth alle that lond, and alle thei ben obeyssant to hire. And alweys thei maken here queen by electoun that is most worthy in armes, for thei ben right gode werryoures and orped[7] and wyse, noble, and worthi. And thei gon often tyme in sowd[8] to help of other kynges in here werres for gold and sylver as othere sowdyoures[9] don, and thei meyntenen hemself right vygourely. This lond of Amazoyne is an ile alle envirouned with the see saf in two places where ben two entrees. And beyonde that water duellen the men that ben here paramoures and hire loves, where thei gon to solacen hem whan thei wole.

[3]   Ancient Scythia, north of the Black Sea and east of the Aral Sea.
[4]   Colopeus, King Scolopitus from Vincent of Beauvais, *Speculum historiale.*
[5]   adjacent.
[6]   breast.
[7]   courageous.
[8]   as soldiers.
[9]   soldiers.

Lincoln Cathedral Library MS 91, fols. 26r–27r. In J. S. Westlake (ed.) (1913 for 1911) *The Prose Life of Alexander (Thornton Ms)*. EETS, o.s. 143. The Text. London: Kegan Paul, Trench, Trübner, 65–7.
Language: English (Northeast Midland)
Manuscript date: ca. 1440

Fra theine Alexander sent a lettre till Talifride,[10] quene of Amazon, of this tenour: "Kyng of kynges, and lorde of lordes, Alexander, the son of Godd Amon and the Quene Olympias, un-to Talifride, the quene of Amazon, joy. The grete bataylles that we hafe hadd wit Kyng Darius, and how we hafe conquered all his rewme and his lordchipes, we trowe be noghte unknawen un-to yow.[11] And also how we hafe foghten with Porus, the kyng of Inde, and his cheeffe citee wonnen. And also wit many other folkes, and thay ware never of powere to agaynestande us, the whilke we suppose be noghte unknawen un-to yowe. Whare-fore, we sende yow worde and commandeth yow that ye sende us tribute if ye will that wee com noghte to yow to do yow disesse."

And un-to this lettre Talifride made ansuere by lettre one this wyse: "Talyfride, quene of Amazon, wit other grete ladys of oure rewme, un-tille Alexander, kynge of Macedoyne, joy. We hafe wel herde telle of the hye witt that es in the, thurgh whilke thou hase in mynde thynges that ere passede, and disposeth thynges that ere present, and knaweth thynges that ere to come. Avyse the wele tharefore are thou come till us, what trebulacionnes and disesse may falle the in thi commynge. For thare was never nane yit that werreyed agaynes us that ne he had schame thare-offe at the ende. And thare-fore take hede to thi last ende. For grete schame it es till a wyse man thurgh indiscrecion to falle in mescheffe.

"Bot if it be lykynge to the to knawe our conversacyon and oure habitacion, we declare it un-to the be oure present lettres that oure habitacion es in ane ile that es closede aboute wit a grete rever that nother hase bygynnynge nor endynnge. Bot on a syde we hafe a strayte entree. And the nowmer of women that duelleth ther-in es 214,000 that ere noghte filed wit[12] men. For oure husbandes duelleth noghte amangeth us ne no nother man, bot on the tother syde of the rever. And ilke a yere we make a solempne feste in the wirchipe of Jubiter thirty days. And than we go till oure husbandes and duelleth wit tham other thirty dayes, and hase oure luste and oure disporte to-gedir as kynde askes. And if any of us consayfe and bere a childe, if it be

---

[10]   to Thalestris.
[11]   Alexander defeated Darius III (d. 330 BCE), emperor of Persia.
[12]   raped by, having sex with.

a male, the modere kepis it seven yere and than sendes it to the fadere. And if scho bere a mayden childe, the moder haldes it with hir and teches it oure maners.

"When we goo to werre agayne youre enemys, we ere one hundred thousand rydand one horse wele armede. And sum of us hase bowes and arowes, and sum speres, and other diverse wapyne. And the remanent kepeth oure ile. And when we come wit the victorye, oure husbandes does us grete wirchipe.

"And thare-fore if thou come agaynes us, we late the witt that we will feghte wit the at all oure myghte. And if it happen that thou hafe the victory of us, wirchipe sall it nane be to the bi-cause thou hase discomfit[13] women. And if we discomfit the, it sall be an heghe wirchippe till us that we may discomfit so wirchipfull an emperour, and to the it sall be a hye reprove. Where-fore, we sygnifie un-to the by oure lettres that thou come noghte agaynes us for sekerly thare may grete dysese come thare-offe, that peraventure thou knaweth noghte now offe at this tymme."

When Alexander hadd redd this lettre, he began to lawghe. And onane he garte[14] writte another lettre and sent it to Talyfride, whare-offe the tenour was this: "Alexander, kyng of kynges and of lordes, the son of Godd Amon and the Qwene Olympias, to Talyfride, quene of Amazon, and the other ladys of the same rewme: joy. We late yow weite that thre parties of the werld – that es to say, Asye, Affric, and Europe – we hafe conquered and made subjects un-till us, and thare was never nane of tham that myghte agaynstande oure powere. And if we now suld noghte be of powere to feghte with yowe, it ware ane heghe schame till us. Never-the-lesse, for als mekill als we lufe your conversacion, we consell that ye co[m]e forthe of your ile and your husbondes wit yow, and appere in oure presence. For we swere yow bi God Amon oure Fader and by all oure goddes, that ye sall hafe na disesse of us. Bot gyffeth us sumwhat in name of tribute, and we schall fynd yow and youre Amazonns that come wit yow horse ynowe. And when you listees for to wende hame agayne, ye schall hafe gude leve."

And when the Amazons hadd redd this lettre, thay went to consell and thoghte it was beste for to ascent un-till hym. And than thay sent hym ten stedes, the beste that myghte be funden in any cuntree, and ten other horse, the beste that myghte be geten, and a grete sum of golde. And Talifride hir selfe and other ladys wit hir went un-till hym and accorded wit hym, and went hame agayne wonder glade and blythe.

---

[13] overcome.
[14] had.

Chastity, Marriage, Widowhood, and Virginity

Discussions of chastity went to the core of discourses about sex and marriage in the Middle Ages, in particular as all three topics related to women. The connections begin with St. Paul, who stated that while marital sex was the only kind of sex allowed, chastity was the preferable state. According to medieval thinking, sexuality itself was uncorrupted and directed towards procreation before the Fall, but concupiscence entered the human realm after it. Marriage was one way for the Church to recognize sexuality while regulating it, with writers such as Augustine, Gregory the Great, and Gratian elaborating the prescriptions and guidance. Combined with Jerome's commentary on the three states available to women – virginity, widowhood, and marriage – religious writings about chastity, sex, and marriage reinforced broader societal stereotypes of women as more closely tied with physicality, weakness, and vanity (see also "Marriage," p. 21).

The Book of Vices and Virtues is a late fourteenth-century translation of the thirteenth-century *Somme le Roi* by Lorens d'Orléans, a Dominican friar. Both the French and the English texts are mirrors for princes, manuals for lay instruction which, in scholastic fashion, divide and subdivide topics to explicate the articles of faith, the seven deadly sins and seven virtues, and the seven gifts of the Holy Ghost: wisdom, understanding, counsel, strength, knowledge, pity, and dread of God. Chastity is the remedy against the sin of lechery and arises out of understanding. Chastity itself concerns seven "branches" of people: virgins not dedicated to a religious life, those who are unmarried who have had sex and are repentant, married individuals, widows, dedicated virgins, clerks in orders, and other religious people.

Primary documents and further reading

Brundage, J. A. (1987) *Law, Sex, and Christian Society in Medieval Europe.* Chicago, IL: University of Chicago Press.

Bullough, V. L. and J. A. Brundage (eds.) (2000) *Handbook of Medieval Sexuality.* New York: Garland.

Fuchs, E. (1983) *Sexual Desire and Love: Origins and History of the Christian Ethic of Sexuality and Marriage,* trans. M. Daigle. Cambridge: James Clarke,.

Michel, D. (1866) *Ayenbite of Inwyt, or Remorse of Conscience,* ed. R. Morris. EETS, o.s. 23. London: Trübner.

Nelson, V. (ed.) (1981) *A Myrour to Lewde Men and Wymmen: A Prose Version of the Speculum Vitae.* Heidelberg: Carl Winter.

Salisbury, J. E. (1990) *Medieval Sexuality: A Research Guide.* New York: Garland.
Walker, S. S. (ed.) (1993) *Wife and Widow in Medieval England.* Ann Arbor: University of Michigan Press.

Huntington Library MS HM 147, fols. 95r–98r. In W. N. Francis (ed.) (1942) *The Book of Vices and Virtues: A Fourteenth Century English Translation of the Somme le Roi of Lorens d'Orléans.* EETS, o.s. 217. London: Oxford University Press, 245–52.
Manuscript date: ca. 1400
Language: English (Southeast Midland)

The thridde braunche [of chastity] is the staate and the bonde of mariage, for thei schulle kepe hem everiche for other, clenliche and truliche, with-out any wrong doynge that on to that other, and that asketh the lawe of mariage that that on hold trewthe and feith to that other of his body. For after that thei ben knytte to-gidre flescheliche, thei ben al on body and on soule, as holi writ seith, and therfore schul everiche of hem love other as hymself. For as thei ben on bodi, thei schulde ben of on herte bi trwe love, ne nevere-more to departe of herte ne of body while thei lyven;[1] wherfore, thei scholde kepe here bodies clenliche and chastliche, with-out here owen harme, and therfore seith Seynt Poule that wommen schulde love here hosebondes and honoure, and kepe hem chaste and sobre:[2] chaste, to kepe here bodies from alle othere than from here lordes; sobre in etyng and drynkyng, for of to moche etyng and drynkynge cometh moche quekenyng of the fier of lecherie. And also scholde men kepe here bodies chast that thei ne geve nought to a-nother womman than to here owen.

Mariage is a staate that men schulde wel clenliche and hoiliche kepe for many skilles. For it is a staate of grete autorite. God sett it and made it [in] paradis terrestre in the state of innocence to-fore that ever any man dide synne. And therfore schulde men kepe it hoiliche for God that ordeyned it and for the stede that it was made ynne. After, it is a staate of grete worthinesse. For God hymself wolde be bore of a wif that was of the maide Marie, wherfore the maide Marie made a mantel of mariage wher-under Goddes sone was conceyved and borne. Under that mantel was hiled[3] from the devel the pryvete and the counseil of oure raunsom and of oure helthe, and therfore than scholde men worschipe it moche and clenliche, and honestliche kepe it for the holynesse ther-of. After, men schulde kepe it

---

[1]   Matthew 19.5–6; Mark 10.8–9.
[2]   Titus 2.4–5.
[3]   protected.

holiliche, for it is a sacrament of holy chirche and betokeneth the mariage that is bitwexe Jhesu Crist and holi chirche, and bitwex God and the soule; wherfore, the staate of mariage is so holi and so honest that the dede that was erst dedly synne with-out mariage is with-oute synne in mariage, and not onliche with-out synne but in many caas grete thanke-worthi of God to wynne bi the lif with-outen ende, and it is wel to wite that in thre manere wises ye mowe do the dede of wedeloke with-out synne and have grete merite to the soule.

The first is whan men don that werke in hope to have fruyt of kynde to serve with God, and to suche understondyng was first mariage made and ordeined principalliche. The secunde caas is whan that on yeldeth to that other his dette whan it is asked, and therto schal rightwisnesse move a man that yeldeth every wight that is his owen; wherfore, if that on werneth that other and wole not suffre to have his right whan it is asked or praied, or bi mouth or bi signe, as many wommen don that ben schamefast to aske such thinges, he or sche that werneth to that other that biddeth, doth synne. For he doth hym or hire wrong of thing that is his by right, for that on hath right of that otheres body. But he that yeldeth that he oweth doth wel and rightfulliche whan he doth it in that entente and deserveth thanke of God, for rightwisnesse dryveth hym ther-to and not lecherie. The thridde caas is whan a man biddeth of his wif suche thing to kepe hire fro synne, and nameliche whan he seeth that sche is so ful of schame that sche wolde nevere bidde here lord of suche thing and therfore dredeth that sche myght falle lightliche in synne but he bede hire ther-of. Who-so praieth in that entente and yeldeth his dette, he ne synneth not but deserveth grete thanke of God, for rewthe moveth hym to do that. In thes thre thinges is no synne in the werke of wedloke, but in othere caas mowe men or wommen synne other dedliche or venialliche, and specialliche in thre caas.

The first is whan men or wommen wolneth[4] nothing in suche workes but onliche for delite and likyng and lecherie, and in suche caas may a man or a womman synne dedliche or venialliche, venyaliche, whan the delite passeth not the bondes of mariage, that is to seie whan the delite is suget to right and resoun, that he that doth that ne wolde not do suche thing but to his wif. But whan the delite and the lecherie is so grete in his wif that resoun and right is blent,[5] that he wolde do as moche to hire theigh sche were not his wif, in that caas it is dedly synne. For suche lecheries passen the bondes of mariage. Wher-fore, God is ofte wroth with suche folke and geveth ofte

---

[4] desires.
[5] blinded.

grete power to the devel to do hem scathe,[6] as men reden of Sarre, Ragueles doughter, that was yong Tobies wif and hadde y-had sevene hosebondes, and alle weren slawen with the devel the first nyght that thei wolden ligge bi hire. Wherfore, the aungel seide to Tobie he scholde have hire to his wif. "And I schal the telle," seid the aungel, "in which men that the devel hath power ynne," – in hem that putten God so oute of here hertes and oute of here thoughtes that thei entenden to no thing but to here lecheries, as doth an hors or a mule or an other best, and therfore God bynemeth hem other while fruyt that th[ei] mowe have none children.[7]

And yit mowe men and wommen synne dedliche in a-nother manere, that is to seie whan that on draweth that other to do thing agens kynde and in other wise than kynde of man asketh or lawe of mariage graunteth. Such folke synnen more grevousliche than any of the other to-fore seid, but thilke that in here mariage kepen the drede of oure lord and [k]epen clenliche here mariage as it is ordeyned and sette, such folke ben likyng to God.

The secunde caas wher men and wommen synnen in mariage is whan a man goth to his wif whan he scholde not, that is whan sche is seke, as wommen be comuneliche. He that ne spareth not whan he wot that his wif is in suche poynt, synneth gretliche, and God defendeth that a man come nought nyghe his wif in that poynt for the perel of the children that comen bitwexe hem. For, as Seynt Jerome seith, in that tyme ben ofte begete the maymed folk, that is the blynde, the halte and lame, and the messeles.[8] Wherfore, the womman schal telle hire hosebonde that sche is in that plyt, in that staate, wherfore that he forbere hire to do any thing, and he is holde to suffre hire. Also scholde folke spare of the dedes of wedloke in holy tymes, as at the highe festes that ben solempne in holi chirche for to be more the besy and entendaunt to serve God and praie goode praiers; also in fastynge tymes that ben in holi chirche scholde alle men and wommen forbere suche thinges, not for the synne that it is to do suche thing in suche tyme – in suche entent may a man do it – but otherwhile schal a man forbere thing that he may do with-oute synne for to purchase of God the bettre that a man wolde, as Seynt Austen seith.[9] Also, in the tyme that a womman lith in childebed scholde every man kepe hym from suche worke for schame and for perel that may come ther-of. Men fynden in the boke

---

6   harm.
7   Tobias 6.11–17.
8   Jerome (ca. 350–420).
9   Augustine (354–430).

that speketh of kynde of bestes that the olifaunt wole nevere touche the femele after sche hath conceyved,[10] and a man schulde bi resoun be more attempre than a best, and therfore schulde he in suche tyme suffre, not for than I ne seie that he synneth if he doth that dede bi goode cause in suche tyme, but ther-of God is justice and mote be.

The thridde caas wher-ynne men mowen grevousliche synne in mariage is in holy places, as in holy chirche. For in holy places that ben properliche ordeyned to serve God ynne and praien ynne, ne scholde no wight do the werk of mariage for reverence of God and of the holi place, and who-so ne kepeth hym not to do suche dedes in holi places, he synneth bi cause of the place. For suche thing may be synne in suche stede and suche tymes that is no synne elles-where . . .

The ferthe staate of chastite is of hem that han ben in mariage and deth hath departed hem. He that is left in the lif schal kepe chastite as longe as thei ben in widowhode. For that is an staate that Seynt Poule preiseth moche and seith to widowes that good is to kepe and hold that estate and, if hem like not, thei mowe marye hem agen. For bettre is hem to marye hem than brenne hem.[11] For he brenneth hymself that assenteth to synne, for he putteth his herte bi wille and desire in-to the fier of lecherie, and bettre were hym to be maried than to be besette al a-boute with fier. And this is to understonde of hem that ben in the staate of symple widowhode, not in hem that ben bounden to a vowe to suche estaat that thei ne mowe marye hem with-oute dedly synne after that avowe, but algate if the avowe be symple as that is made pryveliche and with-oute solempnite, al be it that thei synnen dedliche that after suche avowe maryen hem, yit mowe thei dwelle stille in mariage but ther be any other lette,[12] but hem behoveth to do here penaunce for the avowe broken. But whan the avowe is solempne, or bi the hond or bi the bisschop or bi the prelate or bi profession of religion or bi holi ordre that any wight hath take, as subdekne, dekne, or prest, than is the mariage nought but nedes behoveth for to departe such that in suche wise comen to-gidre, for they mowe not be saved in that estate. To widow-hode schulde move the ensaumple of the turtle. For, as the bok seith of kyndes of bestes, after that the turtle hath loste here make, never after wole he holde felawschep with non other but ever-more is alone and fleth the companie of othere.[13]

---

[10] Bartholomeus Anglicus (mid-thirteenth century), *De proprietatibus rerum.*
[11] 1 Corinthains 7.9.
[12] hindrance.
[13] Bartholomeus Anglicus, *De proprietatibus rerum.*

Thre thinges longen to the estate of widowhode. The first is to hide hire and be priveliche dwellyng in hire place and nought for to folewe suspecious felawschep, and ther-of have we ensaumple of Judith, that was widowe and was wonder fair and comeliche, wher-of men reden in holy writt that sche hilde hire in hire chaumbre y-schut with hire maidenes;[14] wherfore, Seynt Poule undertaketh thes yonge wommen widowes that weren idel and besy to go alday hider and thider and jangelode and speke to moche, but thei schulde schut hem with-ynne houses and entende and be besy to do goode dedes, as Seynt Poule techeth.[15] The secunde thing is to entende to bidde God goode praiers and goodliche to be at chirche in devocion and in teeres weping, as men redeth in the gospel of Seynt Luke that thilke good widowe that hight Anne yede nevere out of the temple and served God bothe nyght and day in bidd-ynges and wepynge and fastynge.[16] The thridde thing in scharpe metes and drynkes. For as Seynt Poule seith, "The womman that is widowe and ledeth hire lif in delite is ded in synne."[17] For, as Seynt Bernard seith, chastite is loste in delices, right as he that is under the water is loste, for he may nought drawe his breth.[18] Non may have his heved ne his herte longe in the delite of this world that hym ne behoveth to lese his breth, that is the grace of the Holy Gost wher-bi the soule lyveth in God. To suche staate belongeth also meke clothes, that is, no grete arraye ne riche robes ne queynte, as bi the ensaumple of Judith that lefte hire riche robes and noble atire whan hire lord was ded and toke clothinge of widowhode, meke and symple, that was more tokenyng of wepyng and sorwe than of joye or of veyne glorie and, for sche toke chastite and wolde kepe it al hire lif, sche dide upon hire flesche the hayre and faste every day but the highe holi daies, and yit sche was wonder fair and yong and wise and riche, but goodnesse of herte and love to be chaste made hire do this.[19] Thus schulde thei lyve that wolde kepe chastite in that estate . . .

The fifthe braunche of chastite is virginite and is the fifthe estate of hem that kepen hem and alwey han kepte hem and alwey thenken to kepe al here lyves here bodies hole, with-oute corrupcion, for the love of God. This estate is moche to preise for his worthinesse. For suche estate maketh hem that wole kepe it like to the aungeles of hevene, as the holy men

[14] Judith 8.5.
[15] 1 Timothy 5.13–14.
[16] Luke 2.36–7.
[17] 1 Timothy 5.6.
[18] Bernard of Clairvaux (1090–1153).
[19] Judith 8.6–8.

seien;[20] but as moche han the virgines above the aungeles, that the aungeles lyve with-oute flesche, but thes virgines overcomen hire flesche, and that is grete mervaile, for thei kepen a wel feble castel, that is here body, agens so stronge enemys as the devel is that secheth alle the sleightes that he may take with that castel for to robbe the tresore of virginite; that is the tresore that oure lord speketh of in the gospel whan he seith, "The kyngdom of hevene is liche to tresore that is hid in a feld,"[21] that is virginite y-hidde in the body that is as a felde that men scholde eeren[22] bi penaunce and sowen with grete travaile of good dedes. That tresore is like to the kyngdom of hevene, for the lif of virgines is like to the lif of hevene, that is to seie to the lif of aungeles, wher of oure lord seith in the gospel that in the arisynge ther schal be no mariage as ther is here, but [thei] schul be alle as aungeles of hevene.[23]

The Far East

Accounts of the Far East appealed to medieval people's pleasure in wonder and their desire for political, moral, historical, and geographical intelligence. According to medieval Christian geography, the Orient is the top of the *mappa mundi*. It is the East, farther away but also the natural extension of a spiritual line from Europe at the bottom of the map, up by way of Rome and through Jerusalem, the center of the world. At the top center of the great continent of Asia is earthly paradise, and marvelous and diverse lands, peoples, and creatures fan out below it.

The first half of Mandeville's *Travels* contains depictions of the Holy Land derived from travel guides (for the Mandeville author and the *Book*'s composition, see "Amazons," p. 88). Descriptions of the lands beyond Jerusalem occupy the second half and are based on Friar Odoric of Pordenone's fourteenth-century *Relatio* as well as encyclopedias such as Vincent of Beauvais' *Speculum historiale* and romances.

Primary documents and further reading

Deluz, C. (1988) *Le livre de Jehan de Mandeville: Une "géographie" au XIVe siècle.* Louvain-la-Neuve: Institut d'etudes médiévales de l'Université catholique de Louvain.

[20] Luke 20.34–6.
[21] Matthew 13.44.
[22] plow, cultivate.
[23] Mark 12.25.

Howard, D. R. (1971) "The World of Mandeville's Travels." *Yearbook of English Studies* 1: 1–17.

Odoric of Pordenone (1913) *The Eastern Parts of the World Described. Vol. 2: Cathay and the Way Thither, Being a Collection of Medieval Notices of China*, ed. and trans. H. Yule. Revd. edn. H. Cordier. London: Cambridge University Press.

Sir John Mandeville. British Library MS Cotton Titus C.xvi, fols. 78r–129r. In M. C. Seymour (ed.) (1967) *Mandeville's Travels*. Oxford: Clarendon Press, 138–222 (selections).
Language: English (Southeast Midland)
Manuscript date: ca. 1400

But fast besyde that yle[1] for to passe be see is a gret yle and a gret contree that men clepen *Java*, and it is nygh two thousand myle in circuyt. And the kyng of that contree is a fulle gret lord and a riche and a myghty, and hath under him seven other kynges of seven other yles abouten hym. This yle is fulle wel enhabyted and fulle wel manned. There growen alle maner of spicerie more plentyfouslich than in ony other contree, as of gyngevere, clowe gylofres, canelle, zedewalle,[2] notemuges, and maces. And wyteth wel that the notemuge bereth the maces. For right as the note of the haselle hath an husk withouten that the note is closed in til it be ripe and after falleth out, right so it is of the notemuge and of the maces. Manye other spices and many other godes growen in that yle, for of alle thing is there plentee saf only of wyn. But there is gold and silver gret plentee.

And the kyng of that contre hath a paleys fulle noble and fulle merveyllous and more riche than ony in the world. For alle the degrez to gon up into halles and chambres ben on of gold, another of sylver, and also the pavmentes of halles and chambres ben alle square, on of gold and another of sylver. And alle the walles withinne ben covered with gold and sylver in fyn plates, and in tho plates ben stories and batayles of knyghtes enleved,[3] and the crounes and the cercles abouten here hedes ben made of precious stones and riche perles and grete. And the halles and the chambres of the palays ben alle covered withinne with gold and sylver so that no man wolde trowe the richess of that palays but he had seen it.

And witeth wel that the kyng of that yle is so myghty that he hath many tymes overcomen the Grete Cane of Cathay in bataylle,[4] that is the most

---

[1]   "Betemga," an unidentified island near or part of Sumatra.
[2]   ginger, cloves, cinnamon, zedoary.
[3]   carved.
[4]   Kublai Khan unsuccessfully tried to conquer Java in 1293.

gret emperour that is under the firmament, outher beyonde the see or on this half. For thei han had often tyme werre betwene hem because that the Grete Cane wolde constreynen him to holden his lond of him but that other at alle tymes defendeth him well ayenst him.

After that yle in goynge be see men fynden another yle gode and gret that men clepen *Pathen*,[5] that is a gret kyngdom fulle of faire cytees and fulle of townes. In that lond growen trees that beren mele wherof men maken gode bred and white and of gode savour, and it semeth as it were of whete but it is not allynges[6] of such savour. And there ben other trees that beren hony gode and swete.

And other trees that beren venym ayenst the whiche there is no medicyne but [on], and that is to taken here propre leves and stampe hem and tempere him with water and than drynke it, and elles he schalle dye, for triacle wil not avaylle ne non other medicyne. Of this venym the Jewes had let seche of on of here frendes for to enpoysone alle Cristiantee, as I have herd hem seye in here confessioun before here dyenge. But, thanked be allemyghty God, thei fayleden of hire purpos, but alleweys thei maken gret mortalitee of poeple. And other trees ther ben also that beren wyn of noble sentement.[7]

And yif you lyke to here how the mele cometh out of the trees, I schalle seye you. Men hewen the trees with an hachet alle aboute the fote of the tree tille that the bark be perced in many parties. And than cometh out therof a thikke lykour, the whiche thei resceyven in vesselles and dryen it at the hete of the sonne. And than thei han it to a mylle to grynde, and it becometh faire mele and white. And the hony and the wyn and the venym ben drawen out of other trees in the same manere and put in vesselles for to kepe.

In that yle is a ded see that is a lake that hath no ground. And yif ony thing falle into that lake it schalle never comen up ayen. In that lake growen reedes that ben cannes[8] that thei clepen *thaby*,[9] that ben thirty fadme[10] long, and of theise cannes men maken faire houses. And ther ben other cannes that ben not so longe that growen nere the lond and han so longe rotes that duren[11] wel a four quarteres of a furlong ore more. And at the knottes

---

[5]   Also referred to as "Thalamass" or "Salamasse" in other versions, possibly part of Borneo.

[6]   in all.

[7]   Starting in the thirteenth century, Christians regularly accused Jews of poisoning wells and causing the pestilence (see the image "Miracle of the Boy Singer," p. 147).

[8]   I.e., bamboo.

[9]   Solinus (third century) calls the lake *Tabi*.

[10]   fathom.

[11]   extend.

of tho rotes men fynden precious stones that han gret vertues.[12] And he that bereth ony of hem upon him, yren ne steel ne may not hurt him ne drawe no blod upon him. And therfore thei that han tho stones upon hem fighten fulle hardyly bothe on see and lond, for men may not harmen [hem] on no partye. And therfore thei that knowen the manere and schulle fighte with hem, thei schoten to hem arwes and quarelles withouten yren or steel, and so thei hurten hem and sleen hem. And also of tho cannes thei maken houses and schippes and other thinges, as wee han here makynge houses and schippes of oke or of ony other trees. And deme no man that I seye it but for a truffulle, for I have seen of tho cannes with myn owne eyyen fulle many tymes lyggynge upon the ryvere of that lake, of the whiche twenty of oure felowes ne myghten not liften up ne beren on to the erthe.

After this yle, men gon be see to another yle that is clept *Calonok*,[13] and it is a fair lond and a plentifous of godes. And the kyng of that contrey hath als many wyfes as he wole, for he makth serche alle the contree to geten him the fairest maydens that may ben founde and maketh hem to ben brought before him. And he taketh on o nyght and another another nyght, and so forth contynuelly sewyng,[14] so that he hath a thousand wyfes or mo. And he liggeth never but o nyght with on of hem and another nyght with another but yif that on happene to ben more lusty to his plesance than another. And therfore the kyng geteth fulle many children, sumtyme an hundred, sumtyme an two hundred, and sumtyme mo.

And he hath also into a fourteen thousand olifauntz or mo that he maketh for to ben brought up amonges his vileynes be alle his townes. For in cas that he had ony werre ayenst ony other kyng aboute him, thanne maketh [he] certeyn men of armes for to gon up into the castelles of tree made for the werre that craftylly ben sett upon the olifantes bakkes for to fyghten ayen hire enemyes. And so don other kynges thereaboute. For the maner of werre is not there as it is here or in other contrees, ne the ordynance of werre nouther. And men clepen the olifantes *warkes*.

And in that yle there is a gret mervayle more to speke of than in ony other partie of the world. For alle manere of fissches that ben there in the see abouten hem comen ones in the yeer, eche manere of dyverse fissches, on maner of kynde after other, and thei casten hemself to the see banke of that yle so gret plentee and multitude that no man may unnethe see but fissch. And there thei abyden three dayes, and every man of the contree

---

[12]   Concretions of silica form at bamboo's joints.
[13]   Cam Pha, off the coast from present-day northeastern Vietnam.
[14]   following.

taketh of hem als many as him lyketh. And after that maner of fissch after the thridde day departeth and goth into the see. And after hem comen another multitude of fyssch of another kynde and don in the same maner as the firste diden other three dayes. And after hem another tille alle the dyverse maner of fisshes han ben there and that men han taken of hem that hem lyketh.

And no man knoweth the cause wherfore it may ben. But thei of the contree seyn that it is for to do reverence to here kyng that is the most worthi kyng that is in the world, as thei seyn, because that he fulfilleth the commandement that God bad to Adam and Eve whan God seyde, "*Crescite et multiplicamini et replete terram.*"[15] And for because that he multiplieth so the world with children, therfore God sendeth him so the fissches of dyverse kyndes of alle that ben in the see to taken at his wille for him and alle his peple. And therfore alle the fissches of the see comen to maken him homage as the most noble and excellent kyng of the world and that is best beloved with God, als thei seyn.

I knowe not the resoun whi it is, but God knoweth. But this, me semeth, is the moste merveylle that evere I saugh. For this mervaylle is ayenst kynde and not with kynde, that the fisshes that han fredom to enviroun alle the costes of the see at here owne list comen of hire owne wille to profren hem to the deth withouten constreynynge of man. And therfore I am syker that this may not ben withouten a gret tokene.

There ben also in that contree a kynde of snayles that ben so grete[16] that many persones may loggen hem in hire schelles, as men wolde don in a litylle hous. And other snayles there ben that ben fulle grete but not so huge as the other. And of theise snayles and of gret white wormes that han blake hedes, that ben als grete as a mannes thigh and somme lesse as grete wormes that men fynden there in wodes, men maken vyaunde rialle[17] for the kyng and for other grete lordes. And yif a man that is maryed dye in that contree, men buryen his wif with him alle quyk, for men seyn there that it is resoun that sche make him companye in that other world as sche did in this.

From that contree men gon be the See Occean be an yle that is clept *Caffolos.*[18] Men of that contree, whan here frendes ben seke, thei hangen

---

[15] "Increase and multiply, and fill the earth," Genesis 1.28.
[16] I.e., tortoises.
[17] A sweetened jellied dish.
[18] Kafa, or Feodosiya, in the Crimea; if this interpretation is correct, it is unclear why this region is described here.

hem upon trees and seyn that it is better that briddes that ben angeles of God eten hem than the foule wormes of the erthe.

From that yle men gon to another yle where the folk ben of fulle cursed kynde, for thei norysschen grete dogges and techen hem to strangle here frendes whan thei ben syke. For thei wil nought that thei dyen of kyndely deth, for thei seyn that thei scholde suffren to gret payne yif thei abyden to dyen be hemself as nature wolde. And whan thei ben thus enstrangled, thei eten here flesch instede of venysoun.

Afterward men gon be many yles be see unto an yle that men clepen *Milke*.[19] And there is a fulle cursed peple, for thei delyten in nothing more than for to fighten and to sle men. And thei drynken gladlyest mannes blood, the whiche thei clepen *dieu*. And the mo men that a man may slee, the more worschipe he hath amonges hem. And yif two persones ben at debate and peraventure ben accorded be here frendes or be sum of here alliance, it behoveth that every of hem that schulle ben accorded drynke of otheres blood. And elles the accord ne the alliance is noght worth, ne it schalle not be no repref to him to breke the alliance and the acord but yif every of hem drynke of otheres blood.

And from that yle men gon be see from yle to yle unto an yle that is clept *Tracoda*,[20] where the folk of that contree ben as bestes and unresonable and duellen in caves that thei maken in the erthe, for thei have no wytt to maken hem houses. And whan thei seen ony men passynge thorgh here contrees, thei hyden hem in here caves. And thei eten flessch of serpentes, and thei eten but litille, and thei speken nought but thei hissen as serpentes don. And thei sette no prys be non aveer[21] ne ricchess but only of a precyous ston that is amonges hem that is of sixty coloures. And for the name of the yle thei clepen it *Tracodoun*, and thei loven more that ston than ony thing elles. And yit thei knowe not the vertue thereof, but thei coveyten it and loven it only for the beautee.

After that yle men gon be the See Occean be many yles unto an yle that is clept *Nacumera*,[22] that is a gret yle and good and fayr, and it is in kompas aboute more than a thousand myle. And alle the men and wommen of that yle han houndes hedes, and thei ben clept *canopholos*.[23] And thei ben fulle resonable and of gode understondynge saf that thei worschipen an ox for

---

[19]   Probably Malacca or Malaya.
[20]   A fictional island, probably named after *draconitis*, a mythical precious stone.
[21]   possession.
[22]   Probably the Nicobar Islands in the eastern Indian Ocean.
[23]   The Greek *cynocephali*.

here god. And also everych of hem bereth an ox of gold or of sylver in his forhed in tokene that thei loven wel here god. And thei gon alle naked saf a litylle clout that thei coveren with here knees and hire membres. Thei ben grete folk and wel fyghtynge, and thei han a gret targe[24] that covereth alle the body and a spere in here hond to fighte with. And yif thei taken ony man in bataylle, anon thei eten him.

The kyng of that yle is fulle riche and fulle myghty and right devout after his lawe. And he hath abouten his nekke three hundred perles oryent, gode and grete and knotted as Pater Nostres here of amber. And in maner as wee seyn oure Pater Nostre and oure Ave Maria, cowntynge the Pater Nostres, right so this kyng seyth every day devoutly three hundred preyeres to his god or that he ete. And he bereth also aboute his nekke a rubye oryent, noble and fyn, that is a fote of lengthe and fyve fyngres large. And whan thei chesen here kyng, thei taken him that rubye to beren in his hond, and so thei leden him rydynge alle abouten the cytee. And from thensfromward thei ben alle obeyssant to him. And that rubye he schalle bere allewey aboute his nekke for, yif he hadde not that rubye upon him, men wolde not holden him for kyng. The Grete Cane of Cathay hath gretly coveyted that rubye, but he myghte never han it for werre ne for no maner of godes. This kyng is so rightfulle and of equytee in his doomes that men may go sykerlych thorgh-out alle his contree and bere with him what him list, that no man schalle ben hardy to robben him but, yif he were, the kyng wolde justifye anon.

Fro this lond men gon to another yle that is clept *Silha*,[25] and it is welle a eight hundred myles aboute. In that lond is fulle mochelle wast, for it is fulle of serpentes, of dragouns, and of cokadrilles, that no man dar duelle there. Theise cocodrilles ben serpentes yalowe and rayed aboven and han four feet and schorte thyes and grete nayles as clees or talouns. And there ben somme that han five fadme in lengthe, and somme of six and of eight and of ten. And whan thei gon be places that ben gravelly, it semeth as though men hadde drawen a gret tree thorgh the gravelly place. And there ben also many wylde bestes and namelych of olyfauntes.

In that yle is a gret mountayne,[26] and in mydd place of the mount is a gret lake in a fulle faire pleyn, and there is gret plentee of water. And thei of the contree seyn that Adam and Eve wepten upon that mount an hundred yeer whan thei weren dryven out of paradys. And that water thei seyn is of here teres, for so moche water thei wepten that made the forseyd lake. And

---

[24] shield.
[25] Ceylon, Sri Lanka.
[26] Sri Pada.

in the botme of that lake men fynden many precious stones and grete perles. In that lake growen many reedes and grete cannes, and there withinne ben many cocodrilles and serpentes and grete waterleches.

And the kyng of that contree ones every yeer yeveth leve to pore men to gon into the lake to gadre hem precyous stones and perles be weye of almess for the love of God that made Adam. And alle the yeer men fynde ynowe. And for the vermyn that is withinne thei anoynte here armes and here thyes and legges with an oynement made of a thing that is clept *lymons*, that is a manere of fruyt lych smale pesen,[27] and thanne have thei no drede of no cocodrilles ne of non other venymous vermyn.

This water renneth flowynge and ebbynge be a syde of the mountayne, and in that ryver men fynden precious stones and perles gret plentee. And men of that yle seyn comounly that the serpentes and the wilde bestes of that contree ne wil not don non harm ne touchen with evylle no strange man that entreth into that contree but only to men that ben born of the same contree.

In that contree and othere therabouten there ben wylde gees that han two hedes.[28] And there ben lyouns alle white and als grete as oxen, and many othere dyverse bestes and foules also that be not seyn amounges us. And witeth wel that in that contree and in other yles thereabouten the see is so high that it semeth as though it henge at the clowdes and that it wolde coveren alle the world. And that is gret mervaylle that it myghte be so, saf only the wille of God that the eyr susteyneth it. And therfore seyth David in the Psautere, "*Mirabiles elaciones maris.*" . . .[29]

[Mandeville continues to describe the lands of the Far East, coming to present-day Korea.] In that same regioun ben the mountaynes of Caspye that men clepen *Uber*[30] in the contree. Betwene tho mountaynes the Jewes of ten lynages ben enclosed, that men clepen *Goth* and *Magoth*, and thei mowe not gon out on no syde. There weren enclosed twenty-two kynges with hire peple that dwelleden betwene the mountaynes of Sychye,[31] there Kyng Alisandre chacede hem betwene tho mountaynes, and there he thoughte for to enclose hem thorgh werk of his men. But whan he saugh that he myghte not don it ne bryng it to an ende, he preyed to god of nature that he wolde parforme that that he had begonne. And alle were it so that he

---

[27] peas.
[28] hornbills*:*
[29] "The floods have lifted up their waves," Psalms 92.4.
[30] The classical *Ubera Aquilonis*, "the breasts of the North Wind," the Caucasian Mountains.
[31] Scythia, Caucasus.

was a payneme[32] and not worthi to ben herd, yit God of his grace closed the mountaynes togydre so that thei dwellen there alle faste ylokked and enclosed with high mountaynes all aboute, saf only on o syde, and on that syde is the see of Caspye.

Now may sum men asken, "Sith that the see is on that o syde, wherfore go thei not out on the see syde for to go where that hem lyketh?" But to this questioun I schal answere: that see of Caspye goth out be londe under the mountaynes and renneth be the desert at o syde of the contree and after it streccheth unto the endes of Persie. And alle though it be clept a see, it is no see ne it toucheth to non other see, but it is a lake, the grettest of the world. And though thei wolden putten hem into that see, thei ne wysten never where that thei scholde arryven. And also thei conen no langage but only hire owne, that no man knoweth but thei. And therfore mowe thei not gon out.

And also yee schulle understonde that the Jewes han no propre lond of hire owne for to dwellen inne in alle the world but only that lond betwene the mountaynes. And yit thei yelden tribute for that lond to the queen of Amazoine, the whiche that maketh hem to ben kept in cloos fulle diligently that thei schulle not gon out on no syde but be the cost of hire lond. For hire lond marcheth to tho mountaynes.

And often it hath befallen that summe of the Jewes han gon up the mountaynes and avaled[33] down to the valeyes. But gret nombre of folk ne may not do so, for the mountaynes ben so hye and so streght up that thei moste abyde there maugree[34] hire myght. For thei mowe not gon out but be a litille issue that was made be strengthe of men, and it lasteth wel a four grete myle. And after is there yit a lond alle desert where men may fynde no water ne for dyggynge ne for non other thing. Wherfore, men may not dwellen in that place, so is it fulle of dragounes, of serpentes, and of other venymous bestes that no man dar not passe, but yif it be strong wynter. And that streyt passage men clepen in that contree *Clyron*.[35] And that is the passage that the queen of Amazoine maketh to ben kept. And thogh it happene sum of hem be fortune to gon out, thei conen no maner of langage but Ebrew so that thei can not speke to the peple.

And yit natheles men seyn thei schulle gon out in the tyme of Antecrist and that thei schulle maken gret slaughter of Chistene men. And therfore

---

[32] pagan.
[33] descended.
[34] in spite of.
[35] Direu, a region on the Caspian shore.

alle the Jewes that dwellen in alle londes lernen alleweys to speken Ebrew in hope that whan the other Jewes schulle gon out, that thei may understonden hire speche and to leden hem into Cristendom for to destroye the Cristene peple. For the Jewes seyn that thei knowen wel be hire prophecyes that thei of Caspye schulle gon out and spreden thorghout alle the world and that the Cristene men schulle ben under hire subjeccoun als longe as thei han ben in subjeccoun of hem.

And yif that yee wil wyte how that thei schulle fynden hire weye, after that I have herd seye, I schalle telle you. In the tyme of Antecrist a fox schalle make there his trayne[36] and mynen an hole where Kyng Alisandre leet make the gates, and so longe he schalle mynen and percen the erthe til that he schalle passe thorgh towardes that folk. And whan thei seen the fox, they schulle have gret merveylle of him because that thei saugh never such a best. For of alle othere bestes thei han enclosed amonges hem, saf only the fox. And thanne thei schullen chacen him and pursuen him so streyte tille that he come to the same place that he cam fro. And thanne thei schullen dyggen and mynen so strongly tille that thei fynden the gates that Kyng Alisandre leet make of grete stones and passynge huge, wel symented and made stronge for the maystrie. And tho gates thei schulle breken and so gon out be fyndynge of that issue . . .

And beyonde the lond and the yles and the desertes of Prestre Johnes lordschipe[37] in goynge streight towardes the est, men fynde nothing but montaynes and roches fulle grete. And there is the derke regyoun where no man may see nouther be day ne nyghte, as thei of the contree seyn. And that desert and that place of derknesse duren fro this cost unto paradys terrestre, where that Adam oure formest fader and Eve weren putt that dwelleden there but lytylle while, and that is towardes the est at the begynnynge of the erthe. But that is not that est that we clepe oure est on this half where the sonne riseth to us. For whanne the sonne is est in tho partyes toward paradys terrestre, it is thanne mydnyght in oure parties o this half for the roundeness of the erthe, of the whiche I have towched to you of before.[38] For oure lord God made the erthe alle rownd in the mydde place of the firmament. And there as mountaynes and hilles ben and valeyes, that is not but only of Noes flode that wasted the softe ground and the tendre, and felle doun into valeyes. And the harde erthe and the roche abyden

[36]   burrow.
[37]   Prester John was the name given to an alleged twelfth-century Christian priest and king of the Far East, fictional author of the *Littera Presbyteris Johannis*.
[38]   Chapter 20.

mountaynes whan the soft erthe and tendre wax nessche thorgh the water, and felle, and becamen valeyes.

Of paradys ne can I not speken propurly, for I was not there. It is fer beyonde, and that forthinketh me, and also I was not worthi. But as I have herd seye of wyse men beyonde, I schalle telle you with gode wille. Paradys terrestre, as wise men seyn, is the highest place of erthe that is in alle the world, and it is so high that it toucheth nygh to the cercle of the mone, there as the mone makith hire torn. For sche is so high that the flode of Noe ne myght not come to hire that wolde have covered alle the erthe of the world alle abowte and aboven and benethen, saf paradys only allone. And this paradys is enclosed alle aboute with a walle, and men wyte not wherof it is, for the walles ben covered alle over with mosse, as it semeth. And it semeth not that the walle is ston of nature ne of non other thing that the walle is. And that walle streccheth fro the south to the north, and it hath not but on entree that is closed with fyre brennynge so that no man mortalle ne dar not entren.

And in the most high place of paradys, evene in the myddel place, is a welle that casteth out the four flodes that rennen be dyverse londes,[39] of the whiche the firste is clept *Phison* or *Ganges* (that is alle on) and it renneth thorghout Ynde or Emlak,[40] in the whiche ryvere ben manye preciouse stones and mochel of *lignum aloes* and moche gravelle of gold. And that other ryvere is clept *Nilus* or *Gyson* that goth be Ethiope and after be Egypt. And that other is clept *Tigris* that renneth be Assirye[41] and be Armenye the Grete.[42] And that other is clept *Eufrate* that renneth also be Medee[43] and be Armonye and be Persye. And men there beyonde seyn that all the swete watres of the world aboven and benethen taken hire begynnynge of that welle of paradys, and out of that welle watres comen and gon . . .

And yee schulle understonde that no man that is mortelle ne may not approchen to that paradys. For be londe no man may go for wylde bestes that ben in the desertes and for the high mountaynes and grete huge roches that no man may passe by for the derke places that ben there and that manye. And be the ryveres may no man go, for the water renneth so rudely and so scharply because that it cometh doun so outrageously from the high places aboven that it renneth in so grete wawes that no schipp may not

[39] Genesis 2.10–14.
[40] Southern Asia.
[41] Asia Minor.
[42] Armenia.
[43] The kingdom of Media in Southwest Asia.

rowe ne seyle agenes it. And the water roreth so and maketh so huge noyse and so gret tempest that no man may here other in the schipp though he cryede with alle the craft that he cowde in the hieste voys that he myghte. Many grete lordes han assayed with gret wille many tymes for to passen be tho ryveres toward paradys with fulle grete companyes, but thei myght not speden in hire viage. And manye dyeden for weryness of rowynge ayenst tho stronge wawes. And many of hem becamen blynde and mane deve for the noyse of the water. And summe weren perisscht and loste withinne the wawes so that no mortelle man may approche to that place withouten specyalle grace of God, so that of that place I can sey you no more. And therfore I schalle holde me stille and retornen to that that I have seen.

God's Unknowability

Original compositions of contemplative, or mystical, writings in English as well as translations of continental works into the vernacular flourished in the late-fourteenth and fifteenth centuries. From Richard Rolle in the 1340s and even during the persecutions of Lollards in the 1400s (see "Lollardy Trials," p. 59), English writers and translators explored modes of spirituality that centered around ways of approaching God and composed descriptions of union with Jesus. Remarkably popular, religious and lay people comprised the audiences for these texts, many, like Julian of Norwich and Margery Kempe, developing novel and emotionally vivid narratives.

The author of *The Cloud of Unknowing* is unknown but is thought to have been active in the last quarter of the fourteenth century, also writing a paraphrase of the fifth-century pseudo-Dionysian *Deonise Hid Divinite* and a sequel to the *Cloud*, *The Book of Privy Counselling*, as well as translations. Seventeen manuscripts of the *Cloud* survive, the majority from the mid-fifteenth century. The *Cloud* is addressed explicitly to people living the contemplative life and not to tellers of tales or the idle curious. It proposes the *via negativa*, a negative way to God, based on the teachings of pseudo-Dionysius and thirteenth-century commentators such as Thomas Gallus, the abbot of St. Andrew's at Vercelli. As opposed to affective piety, which involves a conscious and deliberate striving to reach the Godhead often through physical representations, negative theology has its basis in human-kind's radical separation from God. God is incomprehensible by human means, including the senses, intellectual capacities, and desire.

Primary documents and further reading

Burrow, J. A. (1997) "Fantasy and Language in *The Cloud of Unknowing.*" *Essays in Criticism* 27: 283–98.

Ellis, R. (1980) "A Literary Approach to the Middle English Mystics." In M. Glasscoe (ed.) *The Medieval Mystical Tradition in England: Papers Read at The Exeter Symposium, July 1980.* Exeter: University of Exeter Press, 99–119.

Gerson, J. (1969) *Selections from A Deo exivit, Contra curiositatem studentium, and De mystica theologia speculativa,* ed. and trans. S. E. Ozment. Leiden: E. J. Brill.

Hilton, W. (2000) *The Scale of Perfection,* ed. T. H. Bestul. Kalamazoo, MI: Medieval Institute.

Hodgson, P. (ed.) (1955) *"Deonise Hid diuinite" and Other Treatises on Contemplative Prayer Related to "The Cloud of Unknowing."* EETS, o.s. 231. London: Oxford University Press.

Knowles, D. (1961) *The English Mystical Tradition.* New York: Harper.

Robertson, E. A. (1990) *Early English Devotional Prose and the Female Audience.* Knoxville: University of Tennessee Press.

Rolle, R. (1996) [1896] *The Fire of Love and The Mending of Life or The Rule of Living,* ed. R. Harvey. EETS, o.s. 106. Woodbridge, Suffolk: Boydell and Brewer.

British Library MS Harley 674, fols. 24v–62r. In P. Hodgson (ed.) (1985) *The Cloud of Unknowing and The Book of Privy Counselling.* EETS, o.s. 218. 1944. London: Oxford University Press, 16–83 (selections).
Language: English (East Midland)
Manuscript date: ca. 1425

Lette not therfore, bot travayle ther-in[1] tyl thou fele lyst. For at the first tyme when thou dost it, thou fyndest bot a derknes and as it were a cloude of unknowyng;[2] thou wost never what, savyng that thou felist in thi will a nakid entent unto God. This derknes and this cloude is, how-so-ever thou dost, bitwix thee and thi God, and letteth thee that thou maist not see him cleerly by light of understonding in thi reson ne fele him in swetnes of love in thin affeccion. And therfore schap thee to bide in this derknes as longe as thou maist, evermore criing after him that thou lovest for, if ever schalt thou fele him or see him, as it may be here, it behoveth alweis be in this cloude and in this derknes. And if thou wilte besily travayle as I bid thee, I triste in his mercy that thou schalt come ther-to . . .

---

[1]   I.e., thinking on God himself.
[2]   See Exodus 24.15–18.

And wene not, for I clepe it a derknes or a cloude, that it be any cloude congelid of the humours that fleen in the ayre ne yit any derknes soche as is in thin house on nightes when thi candel is oute. For soche a derknes and soche a cloude maist thou ymagin with coriouste of witte, for to bere before thin iyen in the lightest day of somer, and also agenswarde in the derkist night of wynter thou mayst ymagin a clere schinyng light. Lat be soche falsheed. I mene not thus. For when I sey derknes, I mene a lackyng of knowyng; as alle that thing that thou knowest not, or elles that thou hast forgetyn, it is derk to thee, for thou seest it not with thi goostly iye. And for this skile it is not clepid a cloude of the eire, bot a cloude of unknowyng that is bitwix thee and thi God . . .

And if ever thou schalt come to this cloude and wone and worche ther-in as I bid thee, thee byhoveth, as this cloude of unknowyng is aboven thee, bitwix thee and thi God, right so put a cloude of forgetyng bineth thee, bitwix thee and alle the cretures that ever ben maad.[3] Thee thinketh, para-venture, that thou arte ful fer fro God, forthi that this cloude of unknowing is bitwix thee and thi God, bot sekirly, and it be wel conseyved, thou arte wel ferther fro hym when thou hast no cloude of forgetyng bitwix thee and all the creatures that ever ben maad. As ofte as I sey "Alle the creatures that ever ben maad," as ofte I mene not only the self creatures bot also alle the werkes and the condicions of the same creatures. I oute-take[4] not o creature, whether thei ben bodily creatures or goostly, ne yit any condicion or werk of any creature, whether thei be good or ivel, bot schortly to sey, alle schuld be hid under the cloude of forgetyng in this caas.

For thof al it be ful profitable sumtyme to think of certeyne condicions and dedes of sum certein special creatures, nevertheles yit in this werke it profiteth lityl or nought. For why mynde or thinkyng of any creature that ever God maad, or of any of theire dedes outher, it is a maner of goostly light; for the iye of thi soule is openid on it and even ficchid[5] ther-apon as the iye of a schoter is apon the prik[6] that he schoteth to. And o thing I telle thee, that alle thing that thou thinkest apon, it is aboven thee for the tyme and bitwix thee and thi God, and in so mochel thou arte the ferther fro God that ought is in thi mynde bot only God.

Ye, and if it be cortesye and semely to sey, in this werk it profiteth litil or nought to think of the kyndenes or the worthines of God, ne on oure Lady, ne on the seintes or aungelles in heven, ne yit on the joies in heven, that is

[3]   Richard of St. Victor (d. 1173), *Benjamin major.*
[4]   exclude.
[5]   fixed.
[6]   target.

to say, with a special beholding to hem, as thou woldest bi that beholding fede and encrees thi purpos. I trowe that on no wise it schuld be so in this caas and in this werk. For thof al it be good to think [a]pon the kindenes of God, and to love hym and preise him for hem, yit it is fer betyr to think apon the nakid beyng of him, and to love him and preise him for him-self . . .

But now thou askest me and seiest: "How schal I think on him-self, and what is hee?" And to this I cannot answere thee bot thus: "I wote never." For thou hast brought me with thi question into that same derknes and into that same cloude of unknowyng that I wolde thou were in thi-self. For of alle other creatures and theire werkes – ye, and of the werkes of God self – may a man thorou grace have fulheed[7] of knowing and wel to kon thinke on hem, bot of God him self can no man thinke. And therfore I wole leve al that thing that I can think and chese to my love that thing that I can-not think. For whi, he may wel be loved bot not thought. By love may he be getyn and holden bot bi thought neither. And therfore, thof al it be good sumtyme to think of the kyndnes and the worthines of God in special, and thof al it be a light and a party of contemplacion, nevertheles in this werk it schal be casten down and keverid with a cloude of forgetyng. And thou schalt step aboven it stalworthly, bot listely,[8] with a devoute and a plesing stering[9] of love, and fonde[10] for to peerse that derknes aboven thee and smyte apon that thicke cloude of unknowyng with a scharp darte of longing love, and go not thens for thing that befalleth . . .

I bid thee put doun soche a scharp sotil thought, and kever him with a thicke cloude of forgetyng, be he never so holy, ne hote he thee never so weel for to help thee in thi purpos. For whi love may reche to God in this liif bot not knowing. And al the whiles that the soule wonith in this deedly body, evermore is the scharpnes of oure understonding in beholding of alle goostly thinges, bot most specialy of God, medelid with sum maner of fantasie for the whiche oure werk schuld be unclene, and bot if more wonder were, it schuld lede us into moche errour . . .

And thou schalt understonde that thou schalt not only in this werk forgete alle other creatures then thi-self, or theire deddes or thine, bot also thou schalt in this werk forgete bothe thi-self and also thi dedes for God as wel as alle other creatures and theire dedes. For it is the condicion of a parfite lover not only to love that thing that he loveth more then him-self, bot also in maner for to hate him-self for that thing that he lovith.

[7]   plenitude.
[8]   readily, cautiously.
[9]   stirring.
[10]   strive.

Thus schalt thou do with thi-self: thou schalt lothe and be wery with alle that thing that worcheth in thi witte and in thi wil, bot if it be only God. For whi sekirly elles what-so-ever that it be, it is bitwix thee and thi God. And no wonder thof thou lothe and hate for to think on thi-self; when thou schalt alweis fele synne a foule stynkyng lumpe, thou wost never what, bitwix thee and thi God, the whiche lumpe is none other thing than thi-self. For thee schal think it onyd[11] and congelid with the substaunce of thi beyng, ye, as it were with-outyn departyng.

And therfore breek doun alle wetyng and felyng of alle maner of creatures bot most besily of thi-self. For on the wetyng and the felyng of thi-self hangith wetyng and felyng of alle other creatures, for in rewarde of it, alle other creatures ben lightly forgetyn. For, and thou wilt besily set thee to the preof, thou schalt fynde, when thou hast forgeten alle other creatures and alle theire werkes, ye, and therto alle thin owne werkes, that ther schal leve yit after, bitwix thee and thi God, a nakid weting and a felyng of thin owne beyng, the whiche wetyng and felyng behovith alweis be distroied er the tyme be that thou fele sothfastly the perfeccyon of this werk.

Lechers and Sodomites

After the Fourth Lateran Council in 1215, the classification of sins into groups and degrees of severity had even more pragmatic consequences. Drawing on earlier canon law, a principal focus of the pastoral function became the redemption of sinners through sermon and confession, and new compendia of writings on the priest's role in confession as well as practical instructional manuals for administering confession appeared. Discussions of sexuality in *The Book of Vices and Virtues* draw on this categorizing impulse (see "Chastity, Marriage, Widowhood, and Virginity," p. 93). Invariably, sins "against nature," sodomitical acts, are named as the most severe form of *luxuria*, and they encompass bestiality, same-sex practices, and any other act that does not lead to procreation, such as oral sex and masturbation.

Primary documents and further reading

Boswell, J. (1980) *Christianity, Social Tolerance, and Homosexuality: Gay People in Western Europe from the Beginning of the Christian Era to the Fourteenth Century.* Chicago: University of Chicago Press.

[11] united.

Bullough, V. L., and J. A. Brundage (eds.) (2000) *Handbook of Medieval Sexuality.* New York: Garland.

Burger, G. (2002) *Chaucer's Queer Nation.* Minneapolis: University of Minnesota Press.

Dinshaw, C. (1999) "Eunuch Hermeneutics." In D. Pearsall (ed.) *Chaucer to Spenser: A Critical Reader.* Oxford: Blackwell, 65–106.

Jordan, M. D. (1997) *The Invention of Sodomy in Christian Theology.* Chicago: University of Chicago Press.

Mannyng, R. (1997) [1901, 1903] *Robert of Brunne's "Handlyng Synne,"* ed. F. J. Furnivall. 2 parts. EETS, o.s. 119, 123. Woodbridge, Suffolk: Boydell and Brewer.

Michel, D. (1866) *Ayenbite of Inwyt, or Remorse of Conscience,* ed. R. Morris. EETS, o.s. 23. London: Trübner.

Huntington Library MS HM 147, fols. 16v–17v. In W. N. Francis (ed.) (1942) *The Book of Vices and Virtues: A Fourteenth Century English Translation of the Somme le Roi of Lorens d'Orléans.* EETS, o.s. 217. London: Oxford University Press, 43–6.

Manuscript date: ca. 1400

Language: English (Southeast Midland)

The sixte heved of this best [of deadly sin] is lecherie, that is outrajeous love and yvel ordeyned in lykyng of reyns[1] or in delyt of fleschely lustes. And in this synne tempteth the devel a man in fyve maneres, as Seynt Gregory seith: First in folily lokes. And after in foule wordes. And after in foule touchynges. And after in foule kissynges. And after cometh a man to do the dede.[2] For thurgh the folily lokes cometh a man to speke, and fro speche to touchynge, and fro touchynge to kissynge, and fro the kissynge to the foule dede of synne. And thus slyghly bryngeth the devel fro on in-to a-nother. This synne is departed first in two maneres, for ther is lecherie in herte and lecherie in body.

Lecherie of herte hath foure degres, for ther is a spirit that is cleped a spirit of fornicacioun that serveth for the synne of lecherie. First he maketh thoughtes come and the figures and liknesses of that synne in a mannes or a wommannes herte, and maketh hym thenke ther-on. And after the hirte abideth and dwelleth stille and deliteth, and natheles thei ne wolde not do the dede for no thing. That ilke dwellyng and the delyt that is the secunde degre may be dedly synne, ye, so gret may be the delit. The thridde degre is the acord of the herte and of the resoun and of the wille, and suche acord is evere-more dedly synne. After assyntynge cometh desire and the grete

---

[1]   loins, sexual gratification.

[2]   Gregory the Great (ca. 540–604), *Moralia in Job.*

brennynge wille that thei haveth to synne, and doth mo than twelve synnes on the thridde day; that is to beholde thes ladies and thes maidenes and dameseles araied and apparailed that ofte sithe apparailen hem more queyntely and gaily for to make nyse lokers to loken on hem, and weneth not to do gret synne, for thei have no wille to do the synne the more in dede. But certeynly thei synneth wel grevously, for thei maken and beth cause of losse of many soules, and wher-thurgh many man is ded and falleth in-to gret synne, for men seyn in olde proverbes, "Ladies of riche and gay apparail is arwblast of tour." For sche hath no membre on hire body that nys a grynne of the devel, as Salamon seith,[3] wherfore thei mote yelde acountes at the day of dom of alle the soules that by enchesoun of[4] hem are dampned, that is to seye, whan a womman gyveth enchesoun[5] and cause to synnen, here wytynge.

Lecherie of body is departed in lecherous biholdyng, and heryng, spekynge, and handlynge, and in alle the fyve wittes, and namely in the foule dede. To that synne longen alle thinges that a mannes flesch is meved to, and desireth fleschly lustes, as ben outrageous etynges and drynkynges and esy beddynges, and delicious and softe schertes and smokkes and swote[6] robes of scarlet, and alle othere eses of the body that is more than nede is.

The synne of lecherie is departed in many braunches as after the staates of persones that doth it, and evere it clymbeth upper and upper, and alwey wors and wors. The first is of man and womman that beth not bounde bi a vow, ne bi mariage, ne bi ordre, ne bi religioun, ne bi othere weies. Yit is this the first dedly synne of lecherie, who-so doth it. The secounde is with a comune womman. That synne is wel more, for it is fouler. And for suche ben ofte of religioun and forsaketh no man, that is to seye brother, ne cosyn, ne fadre. The thridde is a man unbounde with a womman bounde bi a vow. The ferthe is with a mayde. The fifthe is with a womman maried, that is cleped in holy writ avoutrie; that is a wel grevous synne, for ther is brekyng of oure bileve and trewthe that that on schal bere to that other, also ther is the synne of sacrilege, whan a man breketh the sacrament of holi chirche, that is of mariage. And ther-of cometh ofte disheritynges, and false heires, and wrongful mariages. And this synne doubleth otherwhile, as a man maried with a-nother mannes wif, and also a womman maried with a-nother man y-maried that is nought hire owne husbonde. The sixte is whan a man

---

[3]   Ecclesiastes 7.27.
[4]   I.e., because of.
[5]   occasion.
[6]   beautiful.

with his owne wif doth thing forboden and defended, agens kynde and agens the ordre of wedloke, for a man may slen hymself with his owne swerd, and also a man may do dedly synne with his owne wif, and therfore smot God Ozam, Jacobes cosyn.[7] And the devel that height Asmodeus strangelede sevene husbondes of the holy womman Sare that afterward was yong Tobies wif.[8] For alle the sacramentes of holy chirche scholde men fare clenly with and holde hem in gret reverence and worschipe. The sevene is a man with his modre or with his doughter, or with the children of his godfadre or of his godmodre, for suche folke mowe not come to-gidre with-out dedly synne, not in mariage. The eighthe, a man with his kynnes womman, and this synne is grettere and smallere after that the kyn is nygh or feer. The nynthe is a man with his wyves kyn or the womman with hire housbondes kyn. This synne is wel perilous, for whan a man taketh a womman, he may not after that wedde noon of hire coseynes and, yif he take any of hem, the mariage is as noon; and yif he take a womman and after taketh a-nother of hire kyn, he leseth the right that he had to his wif, in as moche that he may not dele with hire but if sche bidde hym bifore-hond. The tenthe, a womman with a clerke with-ynne holi ordre. That synne is grettere or smallere as the ordres beth gretter or smaller. The eleventhe is with a womman of religioun or a womman of the world with a man of religioun. The twelfthe is a man of religioun with a womman of religion, and this synne is more or lasse after that the staat is of hem that doth it. The threttenthe is of prelates of holi chirche that scholde be techers bi ensaumple of hemself and to al the world of alle clennesses and of alle holynesses. The last is so foule and so hidous that [it] scholde not be nempned,[9] that is synne agens kynde that the devel techeth to a man or to a womman in many wises that mowe not be spoken, for the matere is so foul that it is abhomynacioun to speke it; but nathelès, be it man or woman that be gilty ther-of, he mote telle it openly in his schrifte to the prest as it was y-don. For in that that the synne is fouler and schamfuller, in so moche is the schrift more worth, for the schame that he hath that schryveth hym ther-of, for that is gret part of his penaunce. This synne is so myslykyng to God that he made reyne fier and stynkynge brymston upon the citees of Sodom and Gomorre, and sunke in-to helle fyve citees.[10] The devel hymself, that purchaseth that synne, is squeymous ther-of whan any doth it.

[7] 2 Samuel 6–7.
[8] Tobias 6.14.
[9] named.
[10] Genesis 18–19.

Saracens

Medieval Christians' views of Islam developed throughout the Middle Ages, beginning with concerns about easterners' military and political conquests and developing into a greater understanding of some of the tenets of Islam. This second phase began due to contact with Muslims during the crusades (1096, 1146, 1189, 1228) and the arrival of Arab philosophy and science in the West via Spain in the twelfth and thirteenth centuries. This familiarity with the life of Muhammad and the Koran came mixed with Orientalist fabrications. Christian traders, crusaders, and clerics understood that Muslims thought of themselves as following the religion of the prophets and of the Koran as the third and ultimate revelation. However, they also saw the Koran simply as corroborating biblical scripture, the prophet as human and fallible, and Islam as a violent, depraved, and irrational religion.

In Mandeville's exordium to his *Book*, the author pleads for Christians to take back the Holy Land, "oure right heritage, and chacen out alle the mysbeleevynge men." If the West could unite, he says, it would be a short time before this Christian "heritage" was restored (on the *Book*'s composition, see "Amazons," p. 88). However, when Mandeville is in the Near East, he states amiably that he received favors from the Sultan of Egypt, including an offer to marry a prince's daughter. These contradictory approaches to the Muslim world reflect earlier Christian inconsistencies and also arise out of his sources for the following passage, which include William of Boldensele's *Un traictie de lestat de la terre sainte*... (1336), whose hostility to the Saracens he tends to omit, and William of Tripoli's more informed *Tractatus de statu Saracenorum* (1273).

Primary documents and further reading

Daniel, N. (1958) *Islam and the West: The Making of an Image.* Edinburgh: Edinburgh University Press.

—— (1975) *The Arabs and Mediaeval Europe.* London: Longman.

Dawson, C. (ed.) (1987) [1955] *Mission to Asia.* Toronto: Toronto University Press.

Grady, F. (1996) "'Machomete' and *Mandeville's Travels.*" In J. V. Tolan (ed.) *Medieval Christian Perceptions of Islam: A Book of Essays.* New York: Garland, 271–88.

Kedar, B. Z. (1988) *Crusade and Mission: European Approaches toward the Muslims.* Princeton, NJ: Princeton University Press.

Tolan, J. V. (2002) *Saracens: Islam in the Medieval European Imagination.* New York: Columbia University Press.

William of Boldensale (1972) *Liber de quibusdam ultramarinis partibus et praecipue de Terra Sancta*, ed. C. Deluz. Unpublished dissertation, Sorbonne.
William of Tripoli (1992) *Notitia de Machometo; De statu Sarracenorum*, ed. P. Engels. Würzburg: Echter.

Sir John Mandeville. British Library MS Cotton Titus C.xvi, fols. 55v–60v. In M. C. Seymour (ed.) (1967) *Mandeville's Travels*. Oxford: Clarendon Press, 96–104.
Language: English (Southeast Midland)
Manuscript date: ca. 1400

Of the customes of Sarasines and of hire lawe, and how the Soudan arresond[1] me, auctour of this book, and of the begynnynge of Machomete
Now because that I have spoken of Sarazines and of here contre, now yif yee wil knowe a partye of here lawe and of here beleve, I schalle telle you after that here book that is clept *Alkaron* telleth. And sum men clepen that book *Meshaf*, and summe clepen it *Harme* after the dyverse langages of the contree, the whiche book Machamete toke hem,[2] in the whiche boke among other thinges is writen, as I have often tyme seen and radd, that the gode schulle gon to paradys and the evele to helle. And that beleeven alle Sarazines.

And yif a man aske hem what paradys thei menen, thei seyn to paradys that is a place of delytes where men schulle fynde alle maner of frutes in alle cesouns and ryveres rennynge of mylk and hony, and of wyn and of swete water, and that thei schulle have faire houses and noble, every man after his dissert, made of precyous stones and of gold and of sylver, and that every man schalle have eighty wyfes, alle maydenes, and he schalle have ado every day with hem, and yit he schalle fynden hem alleweys maydenes.[3]

Also thei beleeven and speken gladly of the Virgine Marie and of the incarnacoun. And thei seyn that Marie was taught of the angel, and that Gabrielle seyde to hire that sche was forchosen from the begynnynge of the world, and that he schewed to hire the incarnacoun of Jhesu Crist, and that sche conceyved and bare child mayden. And that wytnesseth here boke. And thei seyn also that Jhesu Crist spak als sone as he was born, and that he was an holy prophete and a trewe in woord and dede, and meke and pytous and rightfulle and withouten ony vyce.

And thei seyn also that whan the angel schewed the incarnacoun of Crist unto Marie, sche was yong and had gret drede. For there was thanne an

[1] rebuked.
[2] The Koran, also called *mashaf* (book) and *horme* (holy).
[3] The number of maidens is not in the Koran. Paradise is described in many places. See 56 and 47.15.

enchantour in the contree that deled with wycchecraft that men clepten *Takina*, that be his enchauntementes cowde make him in lykness of an angel and wente often tymes and lay with maydenes. And therfore Marie dredde lest it hadde ben Takina that cam for to desceyve the maydenes, and therfore sche conjured the angel that he scholde telle hire yif it were he or non. And the angel answerde and seyde that sche sholde have no drede of him, for he was verry messager of Jhesu Crist. Also, here book seyth that whan that sche had childed under a palme tre, sche had gret schame that sche hadde a child, and she grette[4] and seyde that sche wolde that sche hadde ben ded. And anon the child spak to hire and comforted hire and seyde, "Moder, ne dysmaye the nought, for God hath hidd in the his prevytees[5] for the salvacoun of the world."[6]

And in othere many places seyth here Alkaron that Jhesu Crist spak als sone as he was born. And that book seyth also that Jhesu was sent from God Allemyghty for to ben myrour and ensample and tokne to alle men.[7] And the Alkaron seyth also of the Day of Doom, how God schal come to deme alle maner of folk, and the gode he schalle drawen on his syde and putte hem into blisse, and the wykkede he schal condempne to the peynes of helle.[8] And amonges alle prophetes Jhesu was the most excellent and the moste worthi next God, and that he made the gospelles, in the whiche is gode doctryne and helefulle, fulle of claritee and sothfastness and trewe prechinge to hem that beleeven in God, and that he was a verry prophete and more than a prophete and lyved withouten synne and yaf syght to the blynde and helede the lepers and reysede dede men and steygh to hevene.[9]

And whan thei mowe holden the boke of the gospelles of oure Lord writen, and namely *Missus est angelus Gabriel*,[10] that gospelle thei seyn, tho that ben lettred, often tymes in here orisouns, and thei kissen it and worschipen it with gret devocoun. Thei fasten an hool moneth in the yeer and eten nought but be nyghte, and thei kepen hem from here wyfes alle that moneth. But the seke men be not constreyned to that fast.

Also this book spekth of Jewes and seyth that thei ben cursed for thei wolde not beleven that Jhesu Crist was comen of God, and that thei lyeden

---

[4]   wept.
[5]   divine secrets.
[6]   See 19.16–34 on birth, dates, and speaking, but the preceding passage is not all from "here boke."
[7]   3.55–63.
[8]   56.1–56.
[9]   3.49–51, 5.110.
[10]   "The angel Gabriel was sent," Luke 1.26.

falsely on Marie and on hire sone Jhesu Crist, seyenge that thei hadden crucyfyed Jhesu, the sone of Marie. For he was nevere crucyfyed, as thei seyn, but that God made him to stye up to him withouten deth and withouten anoye.[11] But he transfigured his lyknesse into Judas Scarioth, and him crucifyeden the Jewes and wenden that it had ben Jhesu Crist, but Jhesu steygh to hevene alle quyk. And therfore thei seyn that the Cristene men erren and han no gode knouleche of this, and that thei beleeven folyly and falsly that Jhesu Crist was crucyfyed. And thei seyn yit that, and he had been crucyfyed, that God had don ayen his rightwisnes for to suffre Jhesu Crist that was innocent to ben put upon the cros withouten gylt. And in this article thei seyn that wee faylen and that the gret rightwisnes of God ne myghte not suffre so gret a wrong.[12]

And in this fayleth here feyth. For thei knoulechen wel that the werkes of Jhesu Crist ben gode and his wordes and his dedes and his doctryne be his gospelles weren trewe and his meracles also trewe; and the blessede Virgine Marie is good and holy mayden before and after the birthe of Jhesu Crist; and alle tho that beleven perfitely in God schul ben saved. And because that thei gon so ny oure feyth, thei ben lyghtly converted to Cristene lawe whan men preche hem and schewen hem distynctly the lawe of Jhesu Crist and tellen hem of the prophecyes.

And also thei seyn that thei knowen wel be the prophecyes that the lawe of Machomete schalle faylen as the lawe of the Jewes dide, and that the lawe of Cristene peple schalle laste to the Day of Doom. And yif ony man aske hem what is here beleeve, thei answeren thus and in this forme: "Wee beleven God formyour of hevene and of erthe and of alle othere thinges that he made and withouten him is no thing made. And we beleven of th[e D]ay of Doom, and that every man schalle have his meryte after he hath disserved. And we beleve it for soth alle that God hath seyd be the mouthes of his prophetes."

Also, Machomet commanded in his Alkaron that every man scholde have two wyfes or three or four,[13] but now thei taken unto nine and of lemmannes[14] als manye as he may susteyne. And yif ony of here wifes mysberen hem ayenst hire husbonde, he may caste hire out of his hous and departe fro hir and take another, but he schalle departe with hire of his godes.[15]

---

[11] suffering.
[12] 4.157.
[13] 4.3.
[14] lovers.
[15] 2.229, 2.236–7, 2.241, 65.1–7.

Also, whan men speken to hem of the Fader and of the Sone and of the
Holy Gost, thei seyn that thei ben three persones but not o God, for here
Alkaron speketh not of the Trynyte. But thei seyn wel that God hath speche
and elles were he dowmb. And God hath also a spirit thei knowen wel, for
elles thei seyn he were not on lyve. And whan men speken to hem of the
incarnacoun, how that be the word of the angel God sente his wysdom into
erthe and enumbred[16] him in the Virgyne Marie and be the woord of God
schulle the dede ben reysed at the Day of Doom, thei seyn that it is soth
and that the woord of God hath gret strengthe. And thei seyn that whoso
knew not the woord of God, he scholde not knowe God. And thei seyn also
that Jhesu Crist is the woord of God, and so seyth hire Alkaron where it
seyth that the angel spak to Marie and seyde, "Marie, God schalle preche
the the gospelle be the woord of his mowth, and his name schalle be clept
Jhesu Crist." And thei seyn also that Abraham was frend to God, and that
Moyses was familier spekere with God, and Jhesu Crist was the woord and
the spirit of God, and that Machomete was right messager of God. And thei
seyn that of theise four Jhesu was the most worthi and the most excellent
and the most gret so that thei han many gode articles of oure feyth, alle be
it that thei have no parfite lawe and feyth as Cristene men han.[17] And
therfore ben thei lightly converted, and namely tho that understonden the
Scriptures and the prophecyes, for they han the gospelles and the prophecyes
and the Byble writen in here langage; wherfor, thei conen meche of Holy
Wrytt, but thei understonde it not but after the lettre. And so don the
Jewes, for thei undirstonde not the lettre gostly but bodyly, and therfore
ben thei repreved of the wise that gostly understonden it. And therfore
seyth Seynt Poul, "*Litera occidit, spiritus autem vivificat.*"[18] Also the Sarazines
seyn that the Jewes ben cursed for thei han defouled the lawe that God
sente hem be Moyses. And the Cristene ben cursed also, as thei seyn, for
thei kepen not the commandementes and the preceptes of the gospelle that
Jhesu Crist taughte hem.[19]

And therfore I schalle telle you what the Soudan tolde me upon a day in
his chambre. He leet voyden out of his chambre alle maner of men, lordes
and othere, for he wolde speke with me in conseille. And there he asked me
how the Cristene men governed hem in oure contree, and I seyde him,
"Right wel, thonked be God." And he seyde me: "Treulych nay. For yee

[16]   concealed.
[17]   19.16–65.
[18]   "The letter killeth, but the spirit quickeneth," 2 Corinthians 3.6.
[19]   5.14.

Cristene men ne recche right noght how untrewly ye serven God. Yee scholde yeven ensample to the lewed peple for to do wel, and yee yeven hem ensample to don evylle. For the comownes upon festyfulle dayes whan thei scholden gon to chirche to serve God, than gon thei to tavernes and ben there in glotony alle the day and alle nyght, and eten and drynken as bestes that have no resoun and wite not whan thei have ynow.

"And also the Cristene men enforcen hem in alle maneres that thei mowen for to fighten and for to desceyven that on that other. And therewithalle thei ben so proude that thei knowen not how to ben clothed, now long, now schort, now streyt, now large, now swerded, now daggered, and in alle manere gyses. Thei scholden ben symple, meke, and trewe, and fulle of almesdede as Jhesu was, in whom thei trowe, but thei ben alle the contrarie and evere enclyned to the evylle and to don evylle. And thei ben so coveytous that for a lytylle sylver thei sellen here doughtres, here sustres, and here owne wyfes to putten hem to leccherie. And on withdraweth the wif of another. And non of hem holdeth feyth to another, but thei defoulen here lawe that Jhesu Crist betook hem to kepe for here salvacoun.

"And thus for here synnes han thei lost alle this lond that wee holden. For, for hire synnes, here God hath taken hem into oure hondes, noght only be strengthe of oureself but for here synnes. For wee knowen wel in verry soth that whan yee serven God, God wil helpe you, and whan he is with you, no man may ben ayenst you. And that knowe we wel be oure prophecyes that Cristene men schulle wynnen ayen this lond out of oure hondes whan thei serven God more devoutly. But als longe as thei ben of foul and of unclene lyvynge as thei ben now, wee have no drede of hem in no kynde, for here God will not helpen hem in no wise."

And than I asked him how he knew the state of Cristene men. And he answerde me that he knew alle the state of alle contres of Cristene kynges and princes, and the state of the comounes also be his messangeres that he sente to alle londes in manere as thei weren marchauntes of precyous stones, of clothes of gold, and of othere thinges for to knowen the manere of every contree amonges Cristene men. And than he leet clepe in alle the lordes that he made voyden first out of his chambre, and there he schewed me four that weren grete lordes in the contree, that tolden me of my contree and of manye other Cristene contrees als wel as thei had ben of the same contree, and thei spak Frensch right wel and the Sowdan also, wherof I had gret mervaylle.

Allas, that it is gret sclaundre to oure feith and to oure lawe whan folk that ben withouten lawe, schulle repreven us and undernemen[20] us of oure

---

[20]   rebuke, censure, mock.

synnes. And thei that scholden ben converted to Crist and to the lawe of Jhesu be oure gode ensamples and be oure acceptable lif to God, and so converted to the lawe of Jhesu Crist ben, thorgh oure wykkednesse and evylle lyvynge, fer fro us and straungeres fro the holy and verry beleeve, schulle thus appelen[21] us and holden us for wykkede lyveres and cursede. And treuly thei sey soth. For the Sarazines ben gode and feythfulle, for thei kepen entierly the commandement of the holy book Alkaron that God sente hem be his messager Machomet, to the whiche, as thei seyn, Seynt Gabrielle the aungel often tym tolde the wille of God.

And yee schulle understonde that Machamote was born in Arabye, that was first a pore knave that kepte cameles that wenten with marchantes for marchandise. And so befelle that he wente with the marchandes into Egipt, and thei weren thanne Cristene in tho partyes. And at the desertes of Arabye he wente into a chapelle where a eremyte duelte. And whan he entred into the chapelle that was but a lytille and a low thing and had but a lityl dore and a low, than the entree began to wexe so gret and so large and so high as though it had ben of gret mynstre or the gate of a paleys. And this was the firste myracle the Sarazins seyn that Machomete did in his youthe.

After began he for to wexe wyse and riche. And he was a gret astronomer, and after he was governour and prince of the lond of Corrodane.[22] And he governed it fulle wisely in such manere that whan the prince was ded he toke the lady to wyfe, that highte Gadrige.[23] And Machomete felle often in the grete sikeness that men callen the fallynge evylle,[24] wherfor the lady was fulle sory that evere sche toke him to husbonde. But Machomete made hire to beleeve that alle tymes whan he felle so, Gabriel the angel cam for to speke with him and for the gret light and brightness of the angelle he myghte not susteyne him fro fallynge. And therfore the Sarazines seyn that Gabriel cam often to speke with him.

This Machomete regned in Arabye the yeer of oure lord Jhesu Chist six hundred and ten, and was of the generacoun of Ysmael, that was Abrahames sone that he gat upon Agar his chamberere.[25] And therfore ther ben Sarazines that ben clept *Ismaelytenes* and summe *Agarynes of Agar*, and the othere propurly ben clept *Sarrazines of Sarra*,[26] and summe ben clept *Moabytes*,

[21]   accuse.
[22]   Possibly Kharesm, the lowland between the Aral and Caspian seas, but Mohammed was neither a governor nor prince at this time.
[23]   Khadija.
[24]   epilepsy.
[25]   Hagar, Ishmael's "chamberere" or concubine.
[26]   Possibly the city of Shiraz in southwestern Persia.

and summe *Amonytes*, for the two sones of Loth, Moab and Amon, that he begatt on his doughtres that weren aftirward grete erthely princes.

And also Machomete loved wel a gode heremyte that duelled in the desertes a myle fro Mount Synay in the weye that men gon fro Arabye toward Caldee and toward Ynde, o day journey fro the see, where the marchauntes of Venyse comen often for marchandise. And so often wente Machomete to this heremyte that alle his men weren wrothe, for he wolde gladly here this heremyte preche and make his men wake alle nyght. And therfore his men thoughten to putte the heremyte to deth. And so befelle upon a nyght that Machomete was dronken of gode wyn and he felle on slepe. And his men toke Machometes swerd out of his schethe whils he slepte, and therewith thei slowgh this heremyte and putten his swerd al blody in his schethe ayen. And at morwe whan he fond the heremyte ded, he was fulle sory and wroth and wolde have don his men to deth. But thei alle with on accord [and oon assent seide] that he himself had slayn him whan he was dronken, and schewed him his swerd alle blody. And he trowed that thei hadden seyd soth. And than he cursed the wyn and alle tho that drynken it.[27]

And therfore Sarrazines that ben devout drynken nevere no wyn. But summe drynken it prevyly for, yif thei dronken it openly, thei scholde ben repreved. But thei drynken gode beverage and swete and norysshynge that is made of galamelle,[28] and that is that men maken sugre of, that is of right gode savour, and it is gode for the breest.

Also it befalleth sumtyme that Cristene men becomen Sarazines outher for povertee or for sympleness or elles for here owne wykkedness. And therfore the archiflamyn or the flamyn,[29] as oure e[r]chebisshopp or bisshop, whan he resceyveth hem scyth thus, "*Lu ellet ollu sylu Machomet rores alla*," that is to seye, "There is no god but on, and Machomete his messager."

Now I have told you a party of here lawe and of here customes, I schal seye you of here lettres that thei have, with here names and the manere of hire figures what thei ben: [the alphabet follows in the manuscript]. And four lettres thei have more than othere for dyversitee of hire langage and speche, for als moche as thei speken in here throtes. And wee in Englond have in oure langage and speche two lettres mo than thei have in hire abc, and that is þ and 3, the whiche ben clept *thorn* and *yogh*.

[27] This story does not appear in the Koran.
[28] sugar cane.
[29] imam.

Women: Margaret Paston

Women in the fourteenth and fifteenth centuries had greatly varied lives not only because of class differences but also because of geographical location, marital status, religious involvement, and individual experience. Even within the smaller group of aristocratic and middle-class women, one needs to remain aware of differences, especially given the nature of writings about women from clerical, literary, legal, and historical sources. Many women of the nobility and the middle strata legally held land, were admitted to guilds and city franchises to make crafts or sell goods (see "Guilds," p. 156), and ran estates and households. However, options for these women tended to be limited, their existence centering around one or more marriages and subordinating their lives in many ways to their husbands.

The first records of the Paston family concern Clement Paston, a plowman who owned some hundred acres of land in the immediate vicinity of Paston on the northeastern coast of Norfolk. His son, William, was educated at the Inner Temple and eventually became a judge, purchasing many lands and buildings. William's son, John, also bought and administered lands, some of which he acquired through his marriage to Margaret Mautby, the daughter of an esquire, in 1440. The majority of the collection of Paston letters survives because John was away on business so frequently, and John and Margaret's children maintained their own collections. These letters, which begin in 1425 and end soon after 1500, are remarkable for their quantity and depth in comparison to the few other collections of letters that have survived from the period even though certain details are undiscoverable.

Margaret Paston is similar to many women of her status but, because of the Pastons' substantial local properties and her husband's business in London and elsewhere for the bulk of the time they were married, she confidently and boldly handled their affairs in eastern England. Her letters reveal various concerns. In the first she is pregnant with John Paston II, who was born some time before April 15, 1442. The second, about a number of relations, is while her husband John is sick in London. The third concerns her flight from Robert Hungerford, Lord Moleyns, and his men. The issue concerned a disputed manor at Gresham, which John Paston I inherited from his father William. However, Moleyns claimed it and on February 17, 1448, occupied it, eventually completely evicting Margaret on January 29, 1449, and sacking the place. Margaret fled to the neighboring town of Sustead but then moved on at the beginning of February to Norwich because of threats that she would be kidnapped. Late that year John took possession of another manor owned by Moleyns and again Margaret occupied it until in January, 1450, Moleyns sent what is claimed to be a thousand armed men, forcibly turning her out with her twelve companions.

Primary documents and further reading

Barratt, A. (ed.) (1992) *Women's Writing in Middle English*. London: Longman.

Goldberg, P. J. P. (ed.) (1995) *Women in England, c. 1275–1525: Documentary Sources*. Manchester: Manchester University Press.

Jewell, H. M. (1996) *Women in Medieval England*. Manchester: Manchester University Press.

Mate, M. E. (1999) *Women in Medieval English Society*. Cambridge: Cambridge University Press.

Richmond, C. (1990) *The Paston Family in the Fifteenth Century: The First Phase*. Cambridge: Cambridge University Press.

—— (2000) *The Paston Family in the Fifteenth Century: Endings*. Manchester: Manchester University Press.

British Library MS Additional 43490, fol. 34, and Additional 34888, fols. 8, 24. In N. Davis (ed.) (1971) *Paston Letters and Papers of the Fifteenth Century*, 2 vols. Oxford: Clarendon Press, I: 216–19, 230–3.

Language: English (Southeast Midland)

Manuscript date: 1441–9

To my ryth reverent and worscheful husbond John Paston:

Ryth reverent and worscheful husbond, I recomau[n]de me to yow, desyryng hertyly to here of yowre wylfare, thankyng yow for the tokyn that ye sent me be Edmunde Perys, preyng yow to wete that my modyr sent to my fadyr[1] to London for a goune cloth of mustyrddevyllers[2] to make of a goune for me, and he tolde my modyr and me wanne he was comme hom that he cargeyt[3] yow to bey[4] it aftyr that he were come oute of London. I pre yow, yf it be not bowt, that ye wyl wechesaf to by it and send yt hom as sone as ye may, for I have no goune to werre this wyntyr but my blake and my grene a Lyere,[5] and that ys so comerus that I ham wery to wer yt.

---

[1]   Margaret's mother, Margery, and her second husband Ralph Garneys of Gelderstone ("Gerlyston").

[2]   Muster-de-vilers, a gray woolen cloth, originally from Montivilliers in Normandy.

[3]   charged.

[4]   send.

[5]   cloth of Lierre (Brabant).

As for the gyrdyl that my fadyr be-hestyt[6] me, I spake to hym ther-of a lytyl be-fore he yede to London last, and he seyde to me that the faute was in yow that ye wolde not thynke ther-uppe-on to do mak yt, but I sopose that ys not so. He seyd yt but for a skeusacion. I pre yow, yf ye dor tak yt uppe-on yow, that ye wyl weche-safe to do mak yt a-yens[7] ye come hom, for I hadde never more nede ther-of than I have now, for I ham waxse so fetys[8] that I may not be gyrte in no barre[9] of no gyrdyl that I have but of on.

Elysabet Peverel hath leye seke fifteen or sixteen wekys of the seyetyka,[10] but sche sent my modyr word be Kate that sche xuld come hedyr wanne God sent tyme, thoou sche xuld be crod[11] in a barwe.

Jon of Dam was here, and my modyr dyskevwyrd me[12] to hym, and he seyde be hys trouth that he was not gladder of no thyng that he harde thys towlmonyth than he was ther-of.[13] I may no le[n]ger leve be my crafte; I am dysscevwyrd of alle men that se me. Of alle odyr thyngys that ye deseyreyd that I xuld sende yow word of, I have sent yow word of in a letter that I dede wryte on Ouwyr Ladyis Day laste was.[14]

The Holy Trenyté have yow in hese kepyng. Wretyn at Oxnede in ryth gret hast on the Thrusday next be-fore Seynt Tomas Day.[15]

I pre yow that ye wyl were the reyng wyth the emage of Seynt Margrete that I sent yow for a rememrau[n]se tyl ye come hom. Ye have lefte me sweche a rememrau[n]se that makyth me to thynke uppe-on yow bothe day and nyth wanne I wold sclepe.

Yowre ys, M. P.[16]

To my rygth worchepful husbond Jhon Paston, dwellyng in the Innere Temple at London, in hast: Ryth worchipful hosbon, I recomande me to yow, desyryng hertely to here of your wilfare, thanckyng God of your a-mendyng of the grete dysese that ye have hade, and I thancke yow for the

---

[6]   promised.
[7]   before.
[8]   shapely.
[9]   ornamental bar.
[10]   sciatica.
[11]   conveyed.
[12]   made me known.
[13]   John Damme was a friend of John Paston's and assisted the Pastons in legal matters.
[14]   Probably the Conception, December 8, 1441.
[15]   The Pastons had a manor at Oxnead; probably the Day of St. Thomas Apostle, December 21, 1441.
[16]   Margaret Paston.

letter that ye sent me, for be my trowthe my moder[17] and I were nowth[18] in hertys es fro the tyme that we woste of your sekenesse tyl we woste verely of your a-mendyng. My moder hat be-hestyd a-nodyr ymmage of wax of the weytte[19] of yow to Oyur Lady of Walsyngham, and sche sent four nobelys to the four orderys of frerys at Norweche to pray for yow, and I have be-hestyd to gon on pylgreymmays to Walsyngham and to Sent Levenardys for yow.[20] Be my trowth, I had never so hevy a sesyn as I had fro the tyme that I woste of your sekenesse tyl I woste of your a-mendyng, and yth[21] myn hert is in no grete esse, ne nowth xal be tyl I wott that ye ben very hol.

Your fader and myn[22] was dys day sevenyth at Bekelys[23] for a matyr of the Pryor of Bromholme, and he lay at Gerlyston that nyth and was ther tyl it was nine of the cloke and the toder day. And I sentte thedyr for a gounne, and my moder seyde that I xulde non have dens tyl I had be ther a-gen, and so thei cowde non gete. My fader Garneyss sentte me worde that he xulde ben here the nexth weke, and myn emme[24] also, and pleyn hem here wyth herre hawkys, and thei xulde have me hom wyth hem. And, so God help me, I xal exscusse me of myn goyng dedyr yf I may, for I sopose that I xal redelyer have tydyngys from yow herre dan I xulde have ther.

I xal sende my moder[25] a tokyn that sche toke me, for I sopose the tyme is cum that I xulde sendeth here yf I kepe the be-hest that I have made. I sopose I have tolde yow wat it was. I pray yow hertely that [ye] wol wochesaf to sende me a letter as hastely as ye may, yf wrytyn be non dysesse to yow, and that ye wollen wochesaf to sende me worde quowe your sor dott.[26] Yf I mythe have hade my wylle, I xulde a seyne yow er dys tyme. I wolde ye wern at hom, yf it were your ese, and your sor myth ben as wyl lokyth to here as it tys ther ye ben now, lever[27] dan a new gounne, thow it were of scarlette. I pray yow, yf your sor be hol and so that ye may indure to ryde, wan my fader com to London, that ye wol askyn leve and com hom

---

[17] I.e., her mother-in-law, Agnes Paston (d. 1479).
[18] not.
[19] weight.
[20] Walsingham was the site of a shrine to the Virgin (see "Lollardy Trials," p. 59). St. Leonard's Priory was also in Norfolk.
[21] yet.
[22] William Paston (1378–1444) and her stepfather, Garneys.
[23] Beccles, Suffolk.
[24] uncle.
[25] Margery.
[26] how your sore does.
[27] rather.

wan the hors xul be sentte hom a-geyn, for I hope ye xulde be kepte as tenderly herre as ye ben at London.

I may non leyser have to do wrytyn half a quarter so meche as I xulde seyn to yow yf I myth speke wyth yow. I xal sende yow a-nothyr letter as hastely as I may. I thanke yow that ye wolde wochesaffe to remember my gyrdyl, and that ye wolde wryte to me at this tyme, for I sopose the wrytyng was non esse to yow. All-myth God have yow in hys kepyn and sende yow helth. Wretyn at Oxenede in ryth grete hast on Sent Mihyllys Evyn.[28]

Yourrys, M. Paston

My modyr gretit yow wel and sendyt yow Goddys blyssyng and here, and sche prayith yow, and I pray yow also, that ye be wel dyetyd of mete and dryngke, for that is the grettest helpe that ye may have now to your helthe ward. Your sone[29] faryth wel, blyssyd be God.

litere pertinentes manerio de Gresh:[30]

Ryt wurchypful hosbond, I recommawnd me to you, desyryng hertyly to heryn of yowr wele-fare, be-seching you that ye be not displesyd thow I be com fro that place that ye left me in for, be my trowth, ther were browth me seche tydyngys be dyverys personys qhiche ben yowre wele-willerys and myn that I durst no lengere abyd there, of qhyche personys I xall late you have wetyng qhan ye com hom. It was done me to wete that dyverys of the Lord Moleynys men saydyn if thei myt gete me, they xuld stele me and kepe me wyth-inne the kastell, and than they seyd thei wold that ye xuld feche me owth. An thei seydyn it xuld ben but a lytyll hert-brenny[n]g to you. And after that I herd these tydyngys, I kowd no rest have in myn hert tyl I was here, nere I durst nowt owt of the place that I was in tyll that I was redy to ryden; nere ther was non in the place wist that I xul com thens save the godewyf not an owre be-fore that I kam thens. And I told here that I xuld com hedder to don maken seche gere as I wold have made for me and for the childer and seyd I sopposyd that I xuld be here a fowrtennythe or three wekys. I pray you that the caws of my komyng away may ben kownsell tyl I speke wyth you, for thei that lete me have warnyng ther-of wold not for no good that it were diskuryd.[31]

I spac wyth yowr modyr as I kam hidderwardys, and sche profyrd me, if ye wold, that I xuld abydyn in this town. Sche wold wyth rytgh a good will

---

28   September 28, probably 1443.
29   John Paston II.
30   "letter pertaining to the manor at Gresham," 10 miles northwest of Paston in Norfolk.
31   disclosed.

that we xul abyde in here place and delyveryn me seche gere as sche myt for-bere to kepen wyth hwsold tyl ye mytgh ben purvayd of a place and stuff of yowr owyn to kepe wyth howsold. I pray you send me word be the brynger of this how ye wil that I be demenyd.[32] I wol ben rytgh sory to dwel so nere Gressam as I dede tyl the mater were fully determynyd be twix the Lord Moleynis and you.

Barow[33] told me that ther ware no better evydens in I[n]glond than the Lord Moleynys hathe of the maner of Gressam. I told hym I sopposyd that thei were seche evydens as Willyam Hasard[34] seyd that yowr were. He seyd the sellys[35] of hem were not yett kold. I seyd I sopposyd his lordys evydens were seche. I seyd I wost wele, as for yowr evydens, ther mytgh no man have non better than ye have, and I seyd the selys of hem were to hundred yere elder than he is. The seyd Barow sayd to me if he com to London qhil ye were there, he wold drynk wyth you for any angyr that was be-twyx yow. He seyd he dede but as a servaw[n]t and as he was commawndyd to don. Purry[36] xall tell you qhat langage was be-twyx Barow and me qhan I kam fro Walsy[n]gham. I pray you hertyly, at the reverens of God, be ware of the Lord Moleynys and his men; thow thei speke never so fayr to you, trost hem not, ne ete not, nere drynk wyth hem, for thei ben so fals it is not for to trost in hem. And also I pray you be ware qhat ye eten ar drynk wyth any othere felaschep, for the pepyll is ful on-trosty.

I pray you hertylye that ye wil vowche-save to send me word how ye don and how ye speden in yowr materis be the brynger of this. I merveyl meche that ye send me nomore tydyngys than ye have sent.

Rogere Foke of Sparham[37] sent to me and seythe that he dare nott gon owt of his hows for be kawse of the sewte that Heydon[38] and Wymdam[39] have agens hem, for he is thrett that if he may be gette, he xal be ladde to preson. Heydon sent Spendlove and other to wayte qhere he were and to arest hym to the kastell, and the forseyd Roger is so aferd that his drede makyth hym so seke that but if he have sokowr sone, it is lyke to ben his dethe. Qhere-for I pray you, and he bothyn, that ye wil purvay a remedy for hym that he may gon at large, for it hurtit bothen yowr katel and hym.

---

[32] ruled.
[33] Walter Barrow, one of Lord Moleyns's men.
[34] Another of the lord's men.
[35] seals.
[36] One of the Pastons' men.
[37] The Pastons' man at Sparham, one of their manors.
[38] John Heydon of Baconsthorpe, a lawyer for Lord Moleyns.
[39] John Wyndham of Felbrigg.

Yowr closys and yowr pastowr lythe all opyn be-kawse he may not gon abrodde to don hem amendyn, and yowr schep ar not lokyd at as they xuld ben for ther is no schepeherd but Hodgis sonys, for other schepherd dare non abyd ther ner com up-on the comown be-kause that Wichyngham men thretyn hem to bete if thei comen on here komon. And but if yowr bestys mown comown ther, it xall ben grette hurt to hem but if the have more pasture than thei have be-syd thatt.

Watkyn Schipdam recommawndyth hym to you and prayt you that ye woll speke to Sere Jon Fastolf for the harneys that ye hadden of hym and tellyn hym how it is that som ther-of is gon and speke to hym that thei that arn bownd ther-for nere thei that delyveryd it ben no hurt.[40]

I have yove Purry a gown. I pray you take heed qhat it is and send me word if ye wil that I purway all yowr leverés[41] of the same. The pris of a yerd ther-of is thirteen and a half pence, and so me semyt it is wele worth.

The parson of Sparrammys dowter and other talkedyn largely and seydyn that ye have hadde on schote and, but if ye ben ware, ye xall have more or Estern. Ye xall for-bere[42] Sporyl and Sweynysthorp[43] also but if ye bere you wele er ye have do wyth the mater of Gressam. It is told me as for Gressam, the Lord Moleynys xuld not cleym it now nother be tayl[44] nere be evydens but be infefment of on of his anseteris, qhiche dyid sesynnyd,[45] and in the same wise it is seyd that Sweynysthorp xul be cleymyd. In qhat wyse Sporyl xuld ben cleymyd I wote not but, if ther be any seche thing to-ward, I send you wor[d] here-of that ye may taken hede the . . .[46] Thomas Skipping seyd qhan he kam fro London to a man that he wend xuld not a dis[kuryd] it that th . . . yke to for-gon the maner of Sporyll wyth-in rytgh schort tym. As for the pleyntys in the hundred . . . Purry xall tell . . . you qhat is don and of other thingys more.

The Holy Trynyté have you in his keping. W[retyn at] Norwyche on the Fryday nexst after Puver Weddenysday.[47]

---

[40]   Margaret knew Sir John Falstof through her family. John, her husband, came to act for Falstof in business matters which, after Falstof's death in 1459, embroiled him in complicated legal matters.

[41]   clothes.

[42]   forego.

[43]   Two Paston properties.

[44]   entail (to heirs).

[45]   confer legal possession of.

[46]   The manuscript page starts to deteriorate here.

[47]   February 28, 1449.

4

Images

Lovell Lectionary

British Library MS Harley 7026, fol. 4v
Language: Latin
Manuscript date: ca. 1408

The Lovell Lectionary image is outstanding in the history of English portraits, the history of presentation scenes, size, and composition. The only
other contemporary portraits executed in such a realistic style are of Chaucer
(see "Thomas Hoccleve, *Regiment of Princes*," p. 141). Book presentation
images much more commonly show an author or patron kneeling before
an authority figure (see "Anne of Burgundy, duchess of Bedford, before St.
Anne," p. 135). Such illuminations usually contain full-length figures in small
miniatures, not this large composition where the figures are dramatically
close up, one framed by the window.

It is unclear whether Lovell presents the book to the monk or is receiving
the book from him, but the scroll on the left identifies the context of the
donation of the lectionary: "Orate pro anima domini iohannis louell qui hunc
librum ordinauit ecclesie cathedrali Sarum pro speciali memoria sui & uxoris"
("Pray for the soul of Lord John Lovell, who bequeathed this book for
Sarum Cathedral in special memory of him and his wife"). The faint inscrip-
tion in the lower frame, "ffrater Johes SiferWas," provides further clues about
the book. It seems that John Holand, Lord Lovell (d. 1408), of Titmarsh,
Northamptonshire, commissioned the book from John Siferwas, a Dominican
identified as the illuminator of other books (including the Sherborne Missal),
and then donated it to the cathedral presumably before his death. His wife,

Maud de Holand, died in 1423. The lectionary was probably made at the Benedictine Abbey of the Blessed Virgin Mary, Glastonbury, Somerset.

Primary documents and further reading

Backhouse, J. (1999) *The Sherborne Missal.* London: British Library.
Herbert, J. A. (Intro.) (1920) *The Sherborne Missal.* Oxford: Roxburghe Club.
Mathew, G. (1968) *The Court of Richard II.* London: John Murray.
Millar, E. G. (1928) *English Illuminated Manuscripts of the XIVth and XVth Centuries.* Paris: G. Van Oest.

Anne of Burgundy, duchess of Bedford, before St. Anne

British Library MS Additional 18850, fol. 257v (Bedford Hours)
Language: Latin and French
Manuscript date: ca. 1423

Medieval illuminated manuscripts and paintings frequently include portraits of secular and religious donors (see also "Royal Benefactors," p. 154). The sumptuous full-page illumination from the Bedford Hours depicts Anne of Burgundy (1403–32) kneeling over a book before her patron, St. Anne, the mother of the Virgin Mary (behind St. Anne), and the infant Jesus. The man on the right of the duchess may be Joseph; on the left side are St. Anne's husbands; at bottom are St. Anne's other daughters and their husbands separated by the armorial of the duke and duchess. Anne of Burgundy's motto, "Jen suis contente," repeats throughout the background. The Bedford Hours was probably commissioned by both Anne and John of Lancaster (1389–1435), duke of Bedford, possibly to celebrate their marriage in 1423. The duchess and duke, and their families, owned several other major illuminated manuscripts, including the analogously sumptuous Bedford Hours and Psalter (see also "Books," p. 235). The principal artist, the Master of the Duke of Bedford, completed the book in his Paris workshop before 1430 when the duchess presented it to their nephew, the 9-year-old Henry VI, who had just been crowned king. The Hours includes on the preceding page an illumination showing John, duke of Bedford, with St. George, and the volume as a whole contains many other large miniatures, historiated initials, and roundels. The traditional ideas that St. Anne taught Mary to read and that the Virgin was reading at the time of the Annunciation, common images in late medieval art, were important archetypes for women's literacy.

Primary documents and further reading

Backhouse, J. (1990) *Medieval Manuscripts in the British Library: The Bedford Hours*. New York: New Amsterdam.

Meale, C. M. (ed.) (1993) *Women and Literature in Britain, 1150–1500*. Cambridge: Cambridge University Press.

Scott, K. L. (1996) "Introduction: The Production of Illustrated Books in the Fifteenth Century in England." In *Later Gothic Manuscripts, 1390–1490*, 2 vols. London: Harvey Miller.

Stratford, J. (1993) *The Bedford Inventories: The Worldly Goods of John, Duke of Bedford, Regent of France (1389–1435)*. London: Society of Antiquaries of London.

Sutton, A. F. and L. Visser-Fuchs (1997) *Richard III's Books: Ideals and Reality in the Life and Library of a Medieval Prince*. Stroud, Gloucestershire: Sutton.

Williams, E. C. (1963) *My Lord of Bedford, 1389–1435*. London: Longmans, Green.

Geoffrey Chaucer, *Canterbury Tales*

Henry E. Huntington Library MS 26 C 9, fol. 1r (Ellesmere)
Language: English (Southeast Midland)
Manuscript date: ca. 1405

The *Canterbury Tales* survives in 82 manuscripts, 55 of which are complete or near complete. Chaucer wrote the *Tales* between 1387 and 1400, but no manuscript survives from his lifetime (ca. 1343–1400). Only about a third of the manuscripts is illuminated, and the Ellesmere manuscript of the *Canterbury Tales* is the most elaborately decorated. It is the version modern editors of the *Tales* use most frequently for the order of the tales, but its text is inferior compared with the Hengwrt manuscript (for which, see the Hengwrt image, p. 139). Most probably produced in London, over a third of Ellesmere's vellum pages are decorated with pink and blue foliated initials on a gold ground with demi-vinet borders, such as this opening page. Marginal glosses in the General Prologue distinguish the pilgrim descriptions. Twenty-three portraits of the pilgrims appear opposite the first line of each of their tales in the manuscript, including a Chaucer portrait (see also the image "Thomas Hoccleve, *Regiment of Princes*," p. 141).

Primary documents and further reading

Benson, L. D. (ed.) (1987) *The Riverside Chaucer*, 3rd edn. Boston, MA: Houghton Mifflin.

Hanna, R., III (Intro.) (1989) *The Ellesmere Manuscript of Chaucer's Canterbury Tales: A Working Facsimile*. Cambridge: D. S. Brewer.

Manly, J. M. and E. Rickert (1940) *The Text of the Canterbury Tales Studied on the Basis of All Known Manuscripts*, 8 vols. Chicago, IL: University of Chicago Press.

Stevens, M. and D. Woodward (eds.) (1995) *The Ellesmere Chaucer: Essays in Interpretation*. San Marino, CA: Huntington Library.

Woodward, D. and M. Stevens (eds.) (1995) *The Canterbury Tales: The New Ellesmere Chaucer Facsimile (of Huntington Library MS EL 26 C 9)*. San Marino, CA: Huntington Library.

Whan that Aprill with his shoures soote
The droghte of March hath perced to the roote
And bathed euery veyne in swich licour
Of which vertu engendred is the flour
Whan zephirus eek with his swete breeth
Inspired hath in euery holt and heeth
The tendre croppes and the yonge sonne
Hath in the Ram his half cours yronne
And smale foweles maken melodye
That slepen al the nyght with open eye
So priketh hem nature in hir corages
Thanne longen folk to goon on pilgrimages
And palmers for to seken straunge strondes
To ferne halwes kowthe in sondry londes
And specially fram euery shires ende
Of Engelond to Caunterbury they wende
The hooly blisful martir for to seke
That hem hath holpen whan that they were seeke
Bifil that in that seson on a day
In Southwerk at the Tabard as I lay
Redy to wenden on my pilgrymage
To Caunterbury with ful deuout corage
At nyght was come in to that hostelrye
Wel nyne and twenty in a compaignye
Of sondry folk by auenture y falle
In felaweshipe and pilgrimes were they alle
That toward Caunterbury wolden ryde
The chambres and the stables weren wyde
And wel we weren esed atte beste
And shortly whan the sonne was to reste
So hadde I spoken with hem euerichon
That I was of hir felaweshipe anon
And made forward erly for to ryse
To take oure wey ther as I yow deuyse
But nathelees whil I haue tyme and space
Er that I ferther in this tale pace
Me thynketh it acordaunt to resoun
To telle yow al the condicioun
Of ech of hem so as it semed me
And whiche they were and of what degree
And eek in what array that they were inne
And at a knyght than wol I first bigynne
A knyght ther was and that a worthy man
That fro the tyme that he first bigan
To riden out he loued chiualrie
Trouthe and honour fredom and curteisie
Ful worthy was he in his lordes werre
And therto hadde he riden no man ferre

¶ Knyght

Geoffrey Chaucer, *Canterbury Tales*

National Library of Wales, Peniarth 392D, fol. 2r (Hengwrt)
Language: English (Southeast Midland)
Manuscript date: ca. 1405

The Hengwrt manuscript of the *Canterbury Tales* is less complete than the Ellesmere manuscript, and its tales are in a different and unique order (see the Ellesmere image, p. 137). Its vellum manuscript is in poorer condition; it is stained, and vermin have eaten about 9 cm from the outer corners of leaves. However, its text, probably written in London, is very regular and is therefore used by most modern editors. Its dialect, spelling, and paleography are similar to Ellesmere, which has led some scholars to conjecture that the same scribe wrote both. Only this first page of Hengwrt has a pink and blue full vinet border, also like Ellesmere; the remainder of the pages are undecorated.

Primary documents and further reading

Blake, N. F. (ed.) (1980) *The Canterbury Tales, Edited from the Hengwrt Manuscript*. London: Edward Arnold.

Ramsey, R. V. (1982) "The Hengwrt and Ellesmere Manuscripts of the *Canterbury Tales*: Different Scribes." *Studies in Bibliography* 35: 133–54.

——— (1986) "Paleography and Scribes of Shared Training." *Studies in the Age of Chaucer* 8: 107–44.

Ruggiers, P. G. (ed.) (1979) *The Canterbury Tales: A Facsimile and Transcription of the Hengwrt Manuscript, with Variants from the Ellesmere Manuscript*. Norman: University of Oklahoma Press.

Smith, J. J. (ed.) (1988) *The English of Chaucer and His Contemporaries: Essays by M. L. Samuels and J. J. Smith*. Aberdeen: Aberdeen University Press.

Stubbs, E. (ed.) (2000) *The Hengwrt Chaucer Digital Facsimile*. Leicester: Scholarly Digital Editions.

Here bygynneth the book of the tales of canterbury

Whan that Aueryll wt his shoures soote
The droghte of march hath perced to the roote
And bathed euery veyne in swich lycour
Of which vertu engendred is the flour
Whan zephirus eek wt his sweete breeth
Inspired hath in euery holt and heeth
The tendre croppes and the yonge sonne
Hath in the ram his half cours yronne
And smale foweles maken melodye
That slepen al the nyght with open Iye
So priketh hem nature in hir corages
Thanne longen folk to goon on pilgrimages
And palmeres for to seeken straunge strondes
To ferne halwes kowthe in sondry londes
And specially from euery shires ende
Of Engelond to Caunterbury they wende
The hooly blisful martir for to seke
That hem hath holpen whan þt they weere seeke
Bifil þt in that seson on a day
In southwerk at the tabard as I lay
Redy to wenden on my pilgrimage
To Caunterbury with ful deuout corage
At nyght was come in to that hostelrye
Wel nyne and twenty in a compaignye
Of sondry folk by auenture yfalle
In felaweshipe and pilgrymes weere they alle
That toward Caunterbury wolden ryde
The chambres and the stables weeren wyde
And wel we weeren esed atte beste
And shortly whan the sonne was to reste
So hadde I spoken with hem euerichon
That I was of hir felaweshipe anon

Chaucer portrait: Thomas Hoccleve, *Regiment of Princes*

British Library MS Harley 4866, fol. 88r
Language: English (Southeast Midland)
Manuscript date: ca. 1411

Portraits of Geoffrey Chaucer appear in the Ellesmere *Canterbury Tales* and in a few other Thomas Hoccleve *Regiment* manuscripts (see the image of an Ellesmere page, "Geoffrey Chaucer, *Canterbury Tales*," p. 137). Hoccleve wrote the *Regiment of Princes* for Henry, Prince of Wales, in the years preceding 1413, the date of his accession as Henry V. A mirror for princes and begging poem, it survives in over forty manuscripts. Hoccleve asserts that he knew Chaucer, and he states in these lines (4990–5017 in printed editions) that he is afraid others will forget his "worthy maistir." He also compares the mnemonic function of his portrait to why saints are depicted in churches, which has resonances for Lollardy (see "Plays and Representations," p. 262).

Primary documents and further reading

Carlson, D. R. (1991) "Thomas Hoccleve and the Chaucer Portrait." *Huntington Library Quarterly* 54: 283–300.
Hoccleve, T. (1999) *The Regiment of Princes*, ed. C. R. Blyth. Kalamazoo, MI: Medieval Institute.
Knapp, E. (2001) *The Bureaucratic Muse: Thomas Hoccleve and the Literature of Late Medieval England*. University Park: Pennsylvania State University Press.
Krochalis, J. (1986) "Hoccleve's Chaucer Portrait." *Chaucer Review* 21: 234–45.
Seymour, M. C. (ed.) (1981) *Selections from Hoccleve*. Oxford: Clarendon Press.
Spielmann, M. H. (1900) *The Portraits of Geoffrey Chaucer*. London: Kegan Paul, Trench, Trübner.
Spurgeon, C. F. E. (1960) [1908–17] *Five Hundred Years of Chaucer Criticism and Allusion, 1357–1900*, 7 vols. Repr. 3 vols. New York: Russell and Russell.

Howe he þ[at] sauiur was mayden marie
And sir his loue floure and fructifie

¶ Al þogh his lyfe be queynt þe resemblaunce
Of him hap in me so fressh lyflynesse
þat to putte othir men in remembraunce
Of his p[er]sone ȝ haue heere his liknesse
Do make to þis ende in soothfastnesse
þat þei þ[at] haue of him left þoght & mynde
By þis peynture may aȝeyn him fynde

¶ The ymages þ[at] in þe chirche been
maken folk þenke on god & on his seyntes
Whan þe ymages þei be holden & seen
Were oft vnsyte of hem caussth restreyntes
Of þoughtes good whan a þing depeynt is
Or entayled if men take of it heede
Thoght of þe liknesse it wil in hym breede

¶ Yit some holden oppynyon and sey
þat none ymages schuld ȝ maked be
þei erren foule & goon out of þe wey
Of trouth haue þei scant sensibilite
Passe ou[er] þt now blessid trinite
vpon my maistres soule mercy haue
ffor him lady eke þ[at] mercy ȝ craue

¶ The othir þing wolde ȝ fayne speke & touche
Heere in þis booke but such is my dulnesse
ffor þat al voyde and empty is my pouche
þat al my lust is queynt w[i]t[h] heuynesse
And heuy spirit co[m]maundeth stilnesse

Geoffrey Chaucer, *Troilus and Criseyde*

Cambridge, Corpus Christi College MS 61, fol. 1v
Language: English (Southeast Midland)
Manuscript date: ca. 1420

Chaucer wrote his "book of Troilus" about 1381–6; it survives in 16 manuscripts and the same number of fragments; Corpus Christi College, Cambridge, MS 61 is one of the earliest manuscripts. Only two others and an early Caxton print of the poem have illuminations, but the Corpus Christi College manuscript's full-page illumination is much more ambitious (see also the images of the *Canterbury Tales* manuscripts, above). The intense blues, pinks, reds, oranges, and greens, and the stippled gold make for a vibrant prefatory page. The border, figures, and setting suggest French and Italian influences on what was perhaps more than one English illuminator. The manuscript's decoration is otherwise incomplete, approximately ninety spaces existing for other images, several of which would also have been full page.

Interpretations of the content of the two scenes (divided by rocks) are as specific as stating that the foreground shows Chaucer reciting the poem to an audience of identifiable nobles and the background as a particular scene in *Troilus and Criseyde*. However, other explications point to the generic and non-specific aspects of the oral performance in the foreground and probably a fifteenth-century interpretation of the poem in the background.

Primary documents and further reading

McGregor, J. H. (1977) "The Iconography of Chaucer in Hoccleve's *De Regimine Principum* and in the *Troilus* Frontispiece." *Chaucer Review* 11: 338–50.

Parkes, M. B. and E. Salter (Intro.) (1978) *Troilus and Criseyde: A Facsimile of Corpus Christi College Cambridge MS 61.* Cambridge: D. S. Brewer.

Pearsall, D. (1977) "The *Troilus* Frontispiece and Chaucer's Audience." *Yearbook of English Studies* 7: 68–74.

Salter, E. and D. Pearsall (1980) "Pictorial Illustration of Late Medieval Poetic Texts: The Role of the Frontispiece or Prefatory Picture." In F. G. Andersen et al. (eds.) *Medieval Iconography and Narrative: A Symposium.* Odense: Odense University Press, 100–23.

Scott, K. L. (2000) "Limner-Power: A Book Artist in England, c. 1420." In F. Riddy (ed.) *Prestige, Authority, and Power in Late Medieval Manuscripts and Texts.* Woodbridge, Suffolk: York Medieval Press, 55–75.

Windeatt, B. A. (ed.) (1984) *Troilus and Criseyde: A New Edition of "The Book of Troilus."* New York: Longman.

Court of King's Bench

Library of the Inner Temple, Miscellaneous MS 188, Court of King's Bench
Manuscript date: ca. 1470
Language: French

By the fourteenth and fifteenth centuries, England's secular court system was highly developed and extensively centralized. Three main branches administered justice: the Court of King's Bench was the highest court of appeals and also the court that dealt with matters relating to the king's person and property; the Court of Exchequer principally handled financial cases; and the Court of Common Pleas adjudicated the matters of private free individuals. The Chancery was the central royal governmental secretarial office. Centered in London, these courts also administered itinerant justices, who traveled around the country to adjudicate local trials and disputes, advising, working with, and superseding the many local courts around the country (see "The Revolt," p. 175). The principal forms of justice were writ and jury.

The Inner Temple Library manuscript survives only as four manuscript leaves that show the four courts, each in vivid colors. Presumably they belonged originally to a law treatise. The Court of King's Bench image shows five presiding judges, below them court officials, two ushers on the table, and a jury to the left. A marshal guards the prisoner, and two sergeants-of-law stand on either side in front of other shackled prisoners.

Primary documents and further reading

Alford, J. A. (1977) "Literature and Law in Medieval England." *PMLA* 92: 941–51.
Alford, J. A. and D. P. Seniff (1984) *Literature and Law in the Middle Ages: A Bibliography of Scholarship.* New York: Garland.
Baildon, W. P. (ed.) (1896) *Select Cases in Chancery, A. D. 1364 to 1471.* London: Seldon Society.
Fortescue, Sir John (1997) *On the Laws and Governance of England*, ed. S. Lockwood. Cambridge: Cambridge University Press.
Green, R. F. (1999) "Medieval Literature and the Law." In D. Wallace (ed.) *The Cambridge History of Medieval English Literature.* Cambridge: Cambridge University Press, 407–31.
Plucknett, T. F. T. (ed.) (1929) *Year Books of Richard II: 13 Richard II, 1389–1390.* London: Ames Foundation.
Pollock, F. and F. W. Maitland (1968) [1895] *The History of English Law Before the Time of Edward I*, 2 vols. London: Cambridge University Press.
Sayles, G. O. (ed.) (1971) *Select Cases in the Court of King's Bench under Richard II, Henry IV, and Henry V*, vol. 7. London: Seldon Society.

"Miracle of the Boy Singer"

Bodleian Library MS English Poetry a.1, fol. 124v (Vernon)
Language: English (Southwestern)
Manuscript date: ca. 1390

The Vernon manuscript is the longest and largest surviving volume of Middle English writings; it was originally over 420 vellum leaves long, the pages ruled in 2 or 3 columns with over 80 lines of text each. The contents include passages from the *South English Legendary*, *Northern Homilies*, miracles of our Lady, poems, and prose pieces generally of vernacular theology. Of the original 41 Virgin miracles in the manuscript (compilations of which were popular among men and women in the later Middle Ages), 9 survive. The second poem's narrative is "Hou the Jewes in despit of ore Lady threwe a chyld in a gonge," one of three extant poems containing Jewish characters. Anti-semitic stories were common in the later Middle Ages, particularly in Marian legends, and stories of the murder of Christian children by Jews in England first appeared in Norwich after 1144 and in Lincoln in 1255. Even though the Jews were officially expelled from England in 1290, the stories remained popular.

The five-part story is depicted in compact form in muted greens, browns, and reds, with the bishop's clothing illuminated with gold: the old Jew invites the boy who has been singing the *Alma redemptoris mater* into his house, cuts his throat, and then pitches him down the "gonge," or toilet. On the lower right, the mother pleads before the mayor and bailiff, and on the left the bishop holds the lily found in the boy's throat which, the poem states, had "Alma redemptoris mater" inscribed on it in gold letters. In the poem also the boy's corpse rises during his funeral and sings "Salve, sancta parens" ("Hail, holy mother"). The poem's version of the child's hymn reads: "Godus Moder, mylde and clene / Hevene gate and sterre of se, / Save thi peple from synne and we [woe]."

Primary documents and further reading

Brown, C. (1910) *A Study of the Miracle of Our Lady Told by Chaucer's Prioress*. London: Chaucer Society.

Doyle, A. I. (Intro.) (1987) *The Vernon Manuscript: A Facsimile of Bodleian Library, Oxford, MS. Eng. Poet. a.1*. Cambridge: D. S. Brewer.

Horstmann, C. and F. J. Furnivall (eds.) (1892, 1901) *The Minor Poems of the Vernon Manuscript*, 2 vols. EETS, o.s. 98, 117. London: Kegan Paul, Trench, Trübner.

Kruger, S. F. (1998) "The Spectral Jew." *New Medieval Literatures* 2: 9–35.

Langmuir, G. I. (1972) "The Knight's Tale of Young Hugh of Lincoln." *Speculum* 47: 459–82.

Pearsall, D. (ed.) (1990) *Studies in The Vernon Manuscript*. Woodbridge, Suffolk: D. S. Brewer.

Roth, C. (1964) [1941] *A History of the Jews in England*. Oxford: Clarendon Press.

Whiteford, P. (ed.) (1990) *The Myracles of Oure Lady edited from Wynkyn de Worde's Edition*. Heidelberg: Carl Winter.

New College, Oxford University

Oxford, New College MS C.288, fol. 3v
Language: Latin
Manuscript date: ca. 1465

Oxford and Cambridge were England's only medieval universities, and they began about 1170 and 1210 respectively. Numbers fluctuated around 1,500 at each university, where students generally studied theology but also law, medicine, and other arts and sciences. The individual colleges, such as New College which began in 1379, were initially founded to house and fund scholars going on to these higher degrees. Agriculture and rents usually supplied the revenue for the colleges, which paid for supporting the students, several of whom came from poorer backgrounds. Students at New College had already completed study in Latin grammar and rhetoric at Winchester College before entering on the BA and then MA (see "*Enarratio* (Analysis and Exposition of Texts)," p. 249). College members could be elected as fellows of the college after two years.

Oxford, New College MS C.288 is a memorial to William of Wykham, bishop of Winchester (1367–1404), who was responsible for the construction of Winchester College, the nave of Winchester Cathedral, and New College, Oxford. Thomas Chaundler (ca. 1418–90), chancellor of Oxford and warden of New College, donated the book to Thomas Bekyngton, Bishop of Bath and Wells (1443–65) some 60 years after Wykham's death. The manuscript also contains three other prefatory images: of Winchester College, of bishops and academics (including Wykham), and of Wells. The high angle of folio 3v and the symmetrical layout of the picture display the important aspects of the image clearly: the buildings and grounds in color with figures in the background, and in the foreground the hundred members of the New College – warden, fellows, and students – the number set by Bishop Wykham.

Primary documents and further reading

Anstey, H. (ed.) (1868) *Munimenta Academica, or Documents Illustrative of Academical Life and Studies at Oxford*, 2 vols. London: Longmans, Green, Reader, and Dyer.

Bennett, J. A. W. (1974) *Chaucer at Oxford and at Cambridge*. Oxford: Clarendon Press.

Courtenay, W. (1987) *Schools and Scholars in Fourteenth-century England*. Princeton, NJ: Princeton University Press.

Moran, J. A. H. (1985) *The Growth of English Schooling, 1340–1548: Learning, Literacy, and Laicization in Pre-Reformation York Diocese*. Princeton, NJ: Princeton University Press.

Myers, A. R. (ed.) (1969) *English Historical Documents, 1327–1485*, vol. 4. London: Eyre and Spottiswoode.

Rashdall, H. (1997) [1895] *The Universities of Europe in the Middle Ages*, vol. 3. Oxford: Oxford University Press.

Storey, R. L. (1979) "The Foundation and the Medieval College, 1379–1530." In J. Buxton and P. Williams (eds.) *New College, Oxford, 1379–1979*. Oxford: Warden and Fellows of New College, 3–43.

Weisheipl, J. A. (1964) "Curriculum of the Faculty of Arts at Oxford in the Early Fourteenth Century." *Mediaeval Studies* 26: 143–85.

Revolt: Jean Froissart, *Chroniques*

London, British Library, MS Royal 18 E.1, fol. 175r
Language: French
Manuscript date: 1460–80

Jean Froissart's narrative of the revolt is valuable for several details it provides of the revolt, including, for instance, a sermon by John Ball, the priest from Kent and rebel leader. Manuscript Royal 18 E.1 was made in Flanders for William Hastings, Baron Hastings. It contains 48 richly colorful illuminations of events in France and England in the years 1377–85, including three images of the revolt. The large illumination on folio 175r represents two moments from the meeting of Richard II, William Walworth (mayor of London), and Wat Tyler with the rebels at Smithfield on June 15, 1381, which are recounted in the *Anonimalle Chronicle*.

See "The Revolt" (p. 175) and "Tournaments" (p. 224) for information and bibliographies on the revolt and Froissart.

Richard II presented to the Virgin and Christ

London, National Gallery (Wilton Diptych)
Date: ca. 1395
570 × 292 mm ($22\frac{1}{4}$ × $11\frac{3}{8}$ in.)

Although few medieval English paintings survived Oliver Cromwell's iconoclasm, paintings on wooden backgrounds once adorned church retables, altars, and furniture as well as religious and secular tombs, walls, ceilings, and screens. By the fourteenth century, the "International Gothic style" from French and Italian sources dominated English painting, illumination, textile work, and architecture. Rich decorative patterns, an interest in nature, and detailed colored figures and faces appear in works that were often made in monasteries but came more and more to be made by artisans residing in London.

The Wilton Diptych is an outstanding example of such a style, with rich embellishment and an interest in nature. It is thought to be a portable altarpiece made for Richard II some time after 1395, and its vibrant colors in egg tempera and rich gilding have survived well (on Richard II, see "Usurpation," p. 69). On the exterior wings of the hinged oak diptych are Richard II's arms and a large recumbent white hart (his personal emblem). The interior shown here depicts two royal English saints, Edmund and Edward the Confessor, and Richard's patron saint John the Baptist, who present the king to the Virgin and Christ Child. Despite the king's posture, the gestures of these figures make him central within the composition. The banner signals Christ's resurrection, and the orb at the top encloses a tiny island naval kingdom.

Primary documents and further reading

Gordon, D. (1993) *Making and Meaning: The Wilton Diptych*. London: National Gallery.

Gordon, D., L. Monnas, and C. Elam (eds.) (1997) *The Regal Image of Richard II and the Wilton Diptych*. Coventry: Harvey Miller.

Rickert, M. (1954) *Painting in Britain: The Middle Ages*. London: Penguin Books.

Saul, N. (1997) *Richard II*. New Haven, CT: Yale University Press.

Royal Benefactors

London, British Library, MS Cotton Nero D.vii, fols. 6v–7r (Golden Book of St. Albans)
Language: Latin
Manuscript date: 1380

The Golden Book of St. Albans (also known as the *Liber Benefactorum, Book of Benefactors*) is a record of the names of benefactors and their con- tributions to the Benedictine abbey of St. Albans (for more on donors, see the image "Anne of Burgundy, duchess of Bedford, before St. Anne," p. 135). The monk and historian Thomas Walsingham began the record in 1380, and it was continued to the end of the fifteenth century (on Walsingham, see "Usurpation," p. 69). Over 230 illuminations of bene- factors and their donations appear in the Golden Book's 157 folio pages, many like this one in reds, purples, greens, and blues. The illuminator's name was Alan Strayler, who included a self-portrait on another page. Folios 6v–7r show Edward II (1284–1327), Edward III (1312–77), Edward, Prince of Wales, the Black Prince (1330–76), Richard II (1367–1400), John of Gaunt (1340–99), and Queen Matilda (1102–67).

Primary documents and further reading

Galbraith, V. H. (1932) "Thomas Walsingham and the Saint Albans Chronicle, 1272–1422." *English Historical Review* 47: 12–30.
—— (ed.) (1937) *The St. Albans Chronicle, 1406–1420*. Oxford: Clarendon Press.
Walsingham, T. (1866) *Annales Ricardi Secundi. Johannis de Trokelowe et Henrici de Blaneforde: Chronica et Annales*, ed. H. T. Riley. London: Longmans, Green, Reader, and Dyer.

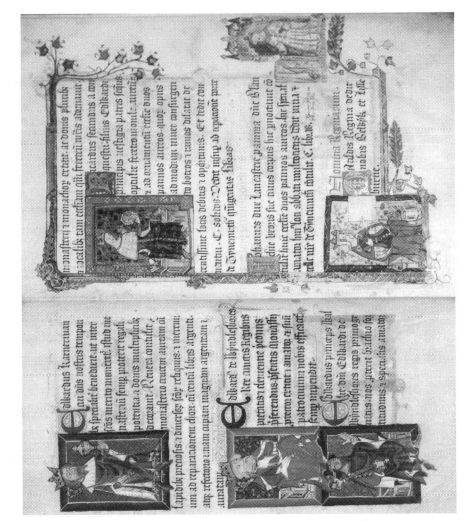

5

Labor and Capital

Guilds

Guilds were associations of men and sometimes women that performed a combination of social, religious, and economic activities. More prevalent in urban areas, they tended to be either parish organizations created to perform religious devotions, or craft or trade fellowships designed to regulate their organizations (membership, craft standards, and other activities), protect their business from local and overseas competition, and expand trade in national and foreign markets. With the wool staples, which began in the early fourteenth century and which favored English rather than alien traders, English and particularly London trade guilds became very wealthy and powerful, often influencing royal policies because they were a principal source of income for the crown.

   Guild records of organizational structure, activities, and membership tended to be kept in French until the fifteenth century, when they begin frequently to appear in English. In 1388 King Richard II gave additional impetus to record keeping when he requested from towns and guilds descriptions of the make-up of the guilds. The Grocers' Company, as the most powerful guild in London in the fourteenth century, has the greatest number of London records to survive. It shows an annual membership of between 70 and 130 senior members in the late-fourteenth to mid-fifteenth centuries who were involved in importing spices, fruit, and chemical products, and exporting primarily wool.

   Over twenty-five guilds existed in Bristol, a principal English craft and trade town, in the fifteenth century. The Weavers in the second excerpt express concerns first raised earlier in the century about workers not from the city. The specific interest in women guild members is a new feature in their records. Women in England generally had been able to become guild members, but they were a distinct minority and were usually accorded fewer rights, privileges, and advantages than their male counterparts. Traditional women's work in households and in seasonal work also tended to exclude them from forming or partaking in guilds.

Primary documents and further reading

Kowaleski, M. and J. M. Bennett (1989) "Crafts, Gilds, and Women in the Middle Ages: Fifty Years after Marian K. Dale." In J. M. Bennett et al. (eds.) *Sisters and Workers in the Middle Ages.* Chicago, IL: University of Chicago Press, 11–38.

McRee, B. R. (1993) "Charity and Gild Solidarity in Late Medieval England." *Journal of British Studies* 32: 195–225.

Nightingale, P. (1995) *A Medieval Mercantile Community: The Grocers' Company and the Politics and Trade of London, 1000–1485.* New Haven, CT: Yale University Press.

Smith, T. and L. Brentano (eds.) (1963) [1870] *English Gilds: The Original Ordinances of More than One Hundred Early English Gilds.* EETS, o.s. 40. London: Oxford University Press.

Thrupp, S. L. (1948) *The Merchant Class of Medieval London, 1300–1500.* Ann Arbor: University of Michigan Press.

—— (1963) "The Gilds." In M. M. Postan, E. E. Rich, and E. Miller (eds.) *The Cambridge Economic History of Europe.* Vol. 3: *Organization and Policies in the Middle Ages.* Cambridge: Cambridge University Press, 230–80.

Unwin, G. (1908) *The Gilds and Companies of London.* London: Methuen.

Manuscript Archives, Company of Grocers, fols. 117–22. "Ordenances of the Grocers' Company." In J. A. Kingdon (ed.) (1886) *Facsimile of First Volume of MS Archives of the Worshipful Company of Grocers of the City of London, A.D. 1345–1463*, vol. 1. London: Company of Grocers, 117–22.
Language: English (Southeast Midland)
Manuscript date: 1418

Theis ordynaunces ar be gonne in the worchyp of God in the yer of owr Lord 1345, of the fraternite of St. Antonyn off the grocers for hem to maynteyn and susteyn in the best maner, to the wiche we praye God help, hys modyr Seynt Marye, and all the holy cumpanye off heven. And the same ordynaunce turnyd in to Englysche be the avyce of the fraternite in the yer of owr Lord 1418, Robert Chechele, alderman, that tyme governour,[1] Esmond Twyn and Thomas Catworth, maysteres.

---

[1]   Also mayor 1421–2.

The acord is made be comun assent that every man of the brothyr hood the day of Seynt Antonyn in the moneth off May schall comen to chirch of Seynt Antonyn fornseid,[2] yf they bien in London, for to hyer the hye messe, and ther for to abyde from the begynnyng in to endyng of the messe. And iche of hem schall ofyr a peny in the worchyp of God, and of hys blessyd moder Marye, and of Seynt Antonyn, and all seynts, and who so faileth schall paye twelve pence. And the same day, ethyr in eight dayes next folowyng, the whiche day schall be assygnyd be the maistres, schall comen to gedres all that ben in London off this fraternite for to speke to gedirs and, as they accordyn, to gedyr etyn and, aftir the ordenaunce of the maystres, thay schullyn be servyd. And all tho that beyn in the clothing schull paye two shillings, six pence. And he that is owt of towun shall paye als moche as hit is be fornseid for the fornseid mete and for to susteyn the prest.[3] And all tho that bien owte of the clotyng, and he hold shop, schall paye twelve pence,[4] com he or com he nought. And that every brothir of the same fela-shepe holdynge ocupacion up on himself shal quarterly paye to ther prest seven pence.

And the same daye of the assemble the maystres, whan the mangerye[5] is endyd, shullen comen with three chapeletts,[6] and they schull chesyn othyr three wardeyns for the yer folowyng, apon whom the forseid chapelletts schullen be sette, and to hem delyvered, yf they be ther present.

And than to hem delivered in presence of hem ensosyyd[7] to hem, the whiche be chosin be all the compaignie, all the monye, all the avoyr,[8] and the paper, and all that langith to the fornseyd fraternite in payne of losse of ten pounds and so forth from yer to yer. And who so refusith to be maystre, he is bounden to paye to the forseyd brothirhed ten pounds sterlynges and than to be put owt of the brothirhed for all dayes.

And yf eny of the compaignie be put owt of the compaignie for any trespasse that he hath doon ageins the fraternite, he schalle nowght be take in to the clotyng ageyn witowten the comun assent of the same fraternite.

Also, hyt is ordeyned that at the first congregacioun off the newe maystres that there bie chosyn an alderman of the same craft to be governour ovyr

---

[2]   May 24; the church of St. Anthony at the intersection of (formerly) Soper's Lane with Watling Street and Budge Row.
[3]   The last phrase deleted in manuscript.
[4]   Amount deleted in manuscript.
[5]   feast.
[6]   head bands.
[7]   associated or united (in authority).
[8]   owned items.

the maystres, that ben for the yer. Also, at devyse of the maystres and the feleshyp, ther beien chosyn six or ten of the compaignie in helpyng and counseylyng of the same maystres that bien for the yer, and they schullen be redy at alle tymes whan they bien assygnyd, and they that faylle pay twelve pence. And yf eny of the maystres faylle, paye two shillings but they hafe resonable excusacion. And at the same ferst congregacioun alle these poyntes to be rehersyd to forn the fraternyte or ellys the maystres at that tyme lese ten pounds.

Also, hyt is ordeyned that they schull have a bedyl to warne and somune the feleschyp als oft tymes as he is boden be the wardeyns, and he that is than warnyd by the bedel and comyth nought shall been amersyd for that defaut als wel as he were preyed, othyr warned, by the wardeyns. And the bedel schall have for hys travayle of the commoun good five marc a yer, a gown, mete, and drynk of the maystres that ben for the yer.

The same day is ordeyned that the wardeyns schull nought aventour over the see, neyther leve the comun good, bot at her owen aventur.

Also, it is accorded in the same yer that every yer ageyns[9] Crystemas they schull ben clothyd in sewt, the same clothyng to be kepte two hole yer; that clothyng and all othyr that perteneth to the comun of the craft shall be bought be the avyse of the wardeyns forn seyd.

Also that they resseyve no man in to her clothyng bot he have servyd his termes as aprentice, and than, be counseyle of the maystres and the felawship that is ensosyed to hem, enquer that he be of good name and ellys resseyve hym nowght. And yf any othyr man that is freman of othyr craft, or ellys be redempcioun freyd of the same craft, he shall nought be resseyvyd in to the forseyd fraternite lesse than he paye at the lest for hys entre ten pounds sterlynges, and yt nought resseyvyd wit owten hem that bien to the maystres ensosyed for the yer. And yf they don the contrarye, paye to the fornseyd fraternite twenty pounds. And whan eny man hath servyd hys prentyshod in the same fraternite that, be the avyse and discrescioun of the maystres and hem be fornseyd, shal be resseyvyd and sworn, payynge three shillings, four pence for his entre.

Also that the newe maystres be boundon to the old jointely in the som that they delyver hem. And that they make rekenyng and acompt, and delyver the monye, with all othir thynges that ben longyng to the craft, be amoneth after that they han chosyn newe maistres, or ellys lese ten pounds to the box.

---

[9]   in preparation for.

Also that non of the same fraternite hold in hys schop but apprentices or elles alowes[10] that hath servyd hys termes as apprentice in the craft; but yf it so be that eny of the same fraternite dye or ellys fall in to povert wher for that he may nowght maygten hym ne lerne hym as apprentyse schuld be and be accord depart fram hys maystre, than it is leful to eny of the fraternite, with owte fraude or mal engyn, to hold hym as apprentice for the terme that he is be hynde with hys maystre forseyd. And yf eny of the fraternite hold eny man in hys schop or in othyr place ocupyith in any othyr maner than it is to forn ordeyned, he schall paye forty shillings within eight dayes aftyr that he is warnyd to voyd hym, and every woke after twenty shillings to he be voyded.

Also that the maystres onys in the yer at the leste, or as ofte as they have any man suspecte, goon and asseyen weyghtys, powdres, confescions,[11] plasters, oynements, and all othyr thynges that longyth to the same craft, they takyng in every schope that they fyndyn defectyve, the same defawt to be redressid be hem and her felischyp, they takyng of everi man, as well that be nought defectif as othyr, for ther labour of the forseyd serch, four pence.

Also, what man comyth nought at dew tyme warnyd be the bedel, that is to seyn to rydyng ageins the kyng, qwien, or othyr lordes with mayr, shereff, or goyng on prossession wit ther mayr, as comun cours is at Cristemas and othir tymes, congregacions, or any othir thynges that they ben warnyd, to pay the payn to the bedel, or ellys, yf they abyde tyl the maystres comen, to paye the dowble.

Also, it is be comun assent of the fraternite that no man of the fraternite take ne be frawde do take hys neighbours hows that is of the same fraternite or hawns[12] the rent ageyns the wille of thyn forseyde neyghbour; he that is found in thys defawt schall paye at iche tyme ten pounds, that is to wetyn, five pounds to the fraternite and five pounds to hym that is thus put owght of ys hous.

And yf eny debate be be twix eny of the fraternite for mys governaunce of wordys, or askyng of dette, or eny othyr thynges, that anon the partye plentyff come to the maystres that ben for the yer and tel hys grevaunce, and they to maken an ende ther of, and yf the maystres mowe nowght, by leve of the maystres go to the lawe and, yf they don wit owght leve, paye forty shillings to the maystres in helpyng of the same brothyrhode.

[10]   allows.
[11]   compound medicines.
[12]   raise.

And whan eny of the brothyhode dyen in London, the maystres that ben
for the yer shul don her bedel to warn hem in what clotyng they schull
comyn to the dirige and the morwe to the messe, and tho that fayle paye
twelve pence. And yf any of the same brethyrhode die and is nought of
power to paye for the costes of the berying, than the same brothyrhod
grauntyth that it be don of the comyn good, and they to be ther in her
clotyng as they schuld for the richest man of the same bretherhode apon the
payn fornseyde.

And whane eny man of the same bretherhode take apprentice wit any
summe of goods or monye wit hym, he schall paye six shillings, eight pence
to the maystres in help of the same brothyrhode and, yf he take non monye
wit the apprentice, than paye three shillings, four pence wit in eight dayes
aftyr, upon peyne of the dowble.

And yf any man of the same fraternite be aventur of the see, or borowhode,
or eny othyr meschyef have lost hys good, than that the maystres with the
fraternite ordeyne that he may be holpyn and susteyned of the comun good
or ellis of her almes and whan eny of the brothyrhod makyth hys testament
that aftyr hys owen fre ville he devise that is likyng to hym to the forseyd
fraternite in helpyng and performyng of the almes of hem that have nede in
the same fraternite.

Also, an ordinaunce was made in the yer of owr Lord 1346 be comun
assent of the same fraternite: a bonde to the maystres that bien for the yer,
the wiche bonde schall bien asselyd of every brothyr of the same fraternite,
and a byd in the maystres handys for the yer, be the wiche they schull
constreyn, and the stresse hold in here kepynge with owten eny othyr
officer. And he that is ageyns here ordenaunce of eny thyng that is devysyd
to forn or be better avyse here aftyr, he to paye that the wardeyns wit here
felawschyp ensocyed to hem wollen award apon hym, and this to be kepte
at all dayes. Amen.

Bickley, F. B. (ed.) (1900) *The Little Red Book of Bristol*, fols. 130r–131r, vol. 2. Bristol:
Council of the City and County of Bristol, 127–9.
Language: English (West Midland)
Book date: ca. 1344–1574

Item, hit is aggreed, ordeigned, and assented by William Canynges, maire
of the towne of Bristowe;[13] Thomas Kempson, sherif of the same; and all

---

[13]   Mayor 1450–1, 1461–2, 1466–7.

the comune councell of the seid towne of Bristowe holde in the guyldhalle there the twenty-ninth day of Septembre in the yere of the reigne of Kyng Edward the fourth after the conquest the first,[14] that for asmuche as divers persons of wevers crafte of the seid towne of Bristowe puttyn, occupien, and hiren ther wyfes, doughtours, and maidens, some to weve in ther owne lombes and some to hire them to wirche with othour persons of the seid crafte, by the whiche many and divers of the kynges liege people likkely men to do the kyng servis in his warris and in the defence of this his lond, and sufficiently lorned in the seid crafte, gothe vagaraunt and unoccupied and may not have ther labour to ther levyng, therefor that no person of the seid crafte of wevers within this seid towne of Bristowe fro this day foreward sett, putt, or hire his seid wyfe, doughter, or maide to no suche occupacion of wevyng in the lombe with hymselfe or with any othour person of the seid crafte within the seid towne of Bristowe and that upon payn of lesyng at every tyme that any person found defective of the seid crafte, and hit justly and truly presented by the maisters of the seid crafte to the maire for the tyme beyng and tofore the seid maire so proved, of seven shillings, eight pence to be leveide, half to the use of the chambour of Bristowe aforseid and half to the contribucion of the seid crafte, provide alwey and excepte that thes acte strecche not to any mannes wyfe of the crafte of wevers nowe levyng at the makyng of thes acte but that they may occupy ther seid wyfes duryng ther naturall lyfe of the seid women in maner and fourme as thei didden tofore the makyng of thes seide acte, etc.

Item, hit is aggreed, ordeigned, and assented by Philip Meede, maire of Bristowe;[15] William Spencer, Sherif; and all the comyn councell of the seid towne at the councell of Bristowe hold in the guyldhall of the seid towne the laste day of May, in the yere of the reigne of Kyng Edward the fourth after the conquest the second,[16] that for asmuche that divers and many of the crafte and occupacion of wevers daily receyven and put in occupacion of the seid crafte straungiers, allions, and othour not born under the kynges obeisaunce, and for ther singuler profit, provokyn and stere divers marchauntz and othour to bryng in to this towne of Bristowe people of divers countrees not born undir the kynges obeisaunce but rebellious, which been sold to theyme as hit were hethen people, and through the contynuance thereof in defaute of correccion hit hath caused that suche straungiers and allions beth gretely multeplied and encreased within the towne of Bristowe and that the

[14] March 4, 1461–March 3, 1462.
[15] Mayor 1459–60, 1462–3.
[16] March 4, 1462–March 3, 1463.

kynges liege people born within this seid towne and othour parties of this his realme bene vagarauntz and unoccupied, and may not have ther labour for ther levyng, that therefor fro this day foreward no maner person of the seid crafte of wevers within this towne of Bristowe set or put any suche estraungier or allion to witche in the occupacion of the seid crafte of wevers, nor in any thyng therto belongyng or perteynyng; and yf by due cerche made by the maisters of the seid crafte to the maire of Bristowe for the tyme beyng be presented, and tofore the seid maire, truly, justly, and lawfully proved that any suche person or persones bith so occupieng and excercisyng suche straungiers and allions in wevers crafte or any thyng belongyng or perteynyng therto hereafter contrary to this seid ordnaunce, that he or they and every of theyme lese, forfeite, and pay as oftyn tymes as he or they be founden defective of the premisses for every suche defaute six shillings, eight pence, half to the use of the comyn chambour of Bristowe and the othour half to the contribucion of the seid craft, provyd alwey and excepte that thes acte strecche not to any person or persons that was or were made prentice to any burgeise within this seid towne of Bristowe tofore the feste of Cristmas last passed and at that tyme they beyng in theyre prentiswyke. In witnes of the whiche premisses and ordnaunces aboveseid, we Philip Mede, maire of Bristowe, by the assent and concent of all the comune councell of Bristowe aforseid, have putto oure seall of Office of Mairalte of Bristowe the day and yere aboveseid, etc.

Ordinance and Statute of Laborers

Legislation to enforce labor as well as fix wages and prices was aimed at serfs bound to serve a lord, at free laborers who worked in agriculture, at specific crafts such as masonry or brewing, and at mendicant beggars. The king's council, which published the 1349 Ordinance on June 18, sought to lower workers' wages to pre-plague levels (which had doubled in some cases, see "Pestilence," p. 169), curb the laborers' abilities to move around for work as they saw advantages, and press free people who refused to work into service. The 1351 Statute in the first parliament (February 9–March 1) extended the list of occupations the legislation covered and specified how and when the justices appointed in a district were obliged to enforce the law. Convictions and sentences of fines, the stocks, and forced service exist from the many commissions and local bodies who prosecuted the cases. Very few convictions against the enforcers for corruption or abuse exist, of which many people complained. Coupled with high and repeated taxation, the laws aimed against laborers contributed to the causes of the 1381 revolt (see "The Revolt," p. 175).

Primary documents and further reading

Dyer, C. (2000) "Wages and Earnings in Late Medieval England: Evidence from the Enforcement of the Labour Laws." In C. Dyer (ed.) *Everyday Life in Medieval England*. London: Hambeldon Press, 167–89.

Hilton, R. H., and T. H. Aston (eds.) (1984) *The English Rising of 1381*. Cambridge: Cambridge University Press.

Knighton, H. (1995) *Knighton's Chronicle, 1337–1396*, ed. and trans. G. H. Martin. Oxford: Oxford University Press.

Putnam, B. H. (1908) *The Enforcement of the Statute of Labourers During the First Decade of the Statute of Labourers, 1349–1359*. New York: Columbia University Press.

—— (ed.) (1938) *Proceedings before the Justices of the Peace in the Fourteenth and Fifteenth Centuries*. London: Spottiswoode, Ballantyne.

Ritchie, N. (1962) [1934] "Labour Conditions in Essex in the Reign of Richard II." In E. M. Carus-Wilson (ed.) *Essays in Economic History*, vol 2. London: Arnold, 91–111.

Sillem, R. (ed.) (1936) *Records of Some Sessions of the Peace in Lincolnshire, 1360–1375*. Hereford: Lincoln Record Society.

The Statutes of the Realm (1810) vol. 1. London: Eyre and Strahan, 23. Edward 3, stat. 1, cc. 1–6, 307–8.
Language: Latin
Date: 1349

Edward,[1] by the grace of God, etc., to the reverend father in Christ William, by the same grace archbishop of Canterbury, primate of all England, greeting. Because a great part of the people and especially of the labourers and servants recently died of the pestilence, some, seeing the needs of masters and scarcity of servants, are unwilling to serve unless they receive excessive wages while others prefer to beg idly rather than labour to get their living. We, considering the grave inconveniences which might come especially from the lack of ploughmen and such labourers, through deliberation and discussion with prelates and nobles, and with assistance from other learned men concerning this and with their unanimous counsel, do hereby ordain:

---

[1] Edward III (r. 1327–77).

[1.] That every man and woman of our realm of England, of whatever condition, free or bonded, who is able bodied and younger than sixty years old, not living by trade, carrying on a determinate craft, owning enough by which to live, or else having his own land to cultivate and occupy himself, nor serving another, if he, his estate considered, be required to serve in a suitable role, he shall be bound to serve the man who needs him, and he shall take only the wages, livery, recompense, or salary which was customary in the places where he ought to serve in the twentieth year of our reign of England or five or six common years ago.[2] This with the proviso that the lords are preferred before others in retaining the service of their bondsmen or their landed tenants so long as the lords only retain as many as are necessary and not more. If any such man or woman, being sought after to serve, will not do this, and this is proven by two or three true men before the sheriff, bailiffs of our lord the king, or constables of the community where this happens to take place, immediately they or someone else shall arrest the person and send him to the nearest jail, and there he shall remain in secure custody until he find surety to serve in the aforesaid form.

[2.] If any reaper, mower, or other labourer or servant, of whatever degree or condition he be, is retained in anyone's service but departs from the service before the end of the agreed term without reasonable cause or permission, he shall undergo the punishment of imprisonment. Moreover, no one, under the same penalty, shall presume to receive or retain such a person in his service.

[3.] That no one shall pay or allow to be paid to anyone more wages, livery, recompense, or salary than was customary as stated before, nor shall any in another manner ask for or receive it under penalty of paying double the amount paid, promised, demanded, or received to him who feels himself aggrieved. And if no such person is willing to proceed, the sum shall be devoted to any of the people who will prosecute, and such prosecution shall be in the court of the lord of the place wherever this case shall happen.

[4.] Also, if the lords of the towns or manors presume in any way by themselves or through their servants to act contrary to the present ordinance, then they shall be prosecuted in the counties, wapentakes, trithings,[3] or some such other courts for treble the penalty paid or promised by them or their servants in the aforesaid manner. And if, by any chance, prior to the present ordinance the employer has agreed with anyone else that the worker will serve for a higher salary, the employer shall not be bound because of the agreement to pay more than was customarily paid at the previous time

[2]   January 25, 1346–January 24, 1347.
[3]   Wapentakes are parts of counties and similar to hundreds; trithings are third parts of shires.

to such a person; indeed, upon the aforesaid penalty, he shall not presume to pay more.

[5.] Item, that saddlers, skinners, leather preparers, cordwainers, tailors, smiths, carpenters, masons, tilers, shipwrights, carters, and all other craftsmen and labourers shall not take for their labour and handiwork more than was customarily paid to them in the said twentieth year and other common years preceding, as said previously, in the places where they happen to work and, if any man take more, he shall be committed to the nearest jail in the aforesaid manner.

[6.] Item, that butchers, fishmongers, hostlers, brewers, bakers, pullers, and all other vendors of whatever kind of victuals shall be bound to sell such victuals for a reasonable price, having consideration for the price at which such victuals are sold in the adjoining places so that these vendors have moderate, not excessive, profits, which depend upon how much the distance of the places from where the victuals have to be carried seems to require. And if anyone sells these victuals in another manner and therefore is convicted in the aforesaid way, he shall pay double of that which he received from him whom he caused the loss to or, in default of him, to any other person who will prosecute on his behalf. Also, the mayors and bailiffs of the cities and boroughs, merchant and other towns, and of sea ports and other maritime places shall have the power to inquire whether anyone in any way offend against this and to levy the stated penalty to go to those who bring a suit against such who are convicted. In cases where the same mayors and bailiffs are negligent in executing the aforesaid and because of this are convicted before the justices to be assigned by us, then these mayors and bailiffs shall be compelled by the same justices to pay treble the price of the item sold to the wronged person or to him who will prosecute in his place, and moreover, they shall be grievously punished by us.

[7.] Because many healthy beggars refuse to labour as long as they are able to live by begging alms, giving themselves to idleness and sins, and sometimes to larceny and other shameful acts, no one shall give anything to those who are able to work under colour of mercy or alms or presume to nurse them in their laziness so that they may thus be compelled to labour for the necessities of life.

The Statutes of the Realm (1810), vol. 1. London: Eyre and Strahan, 25 Edward 3, stat. 2, cc. 1–7, 311–13 (selections).
Language: French
Date: 1351

Against the malice of servants, who were idle and unwilling to serve after the pestilence without taking excessive wages, it was recently ordained by our lord the king, and with the assent of the prelates, nobles, and others of his council, that such kinds of servants, men as well as women, should be made to serve and receive the salaries and wages that were customary in the places where they ought to serve in the twentieth year of the reign of our present king, or five or six years ago, and that these servants, who refused in this way, should be punished with bodily imprisonment, as is more fully stated in the said ordinance. Whereupon commissions were given to various people in every county to inquire about and punish those who offended against the said ordinance. However, now our lord the king has been given to understand in this present parliament, by the petition of the commons, that these servants have no regard for the said ordinance but instead for their ease and singular greed they withdraw their service from great men and others unless they have livery and wages that are double or treble those they used to take in the said twentieth year and before to the huge damage of the great men and the impoverishment of all the members of the said commons; accordingly, the commons request a remedy. Therefore, in the same parliament with the assent of the prelates, earls, barons, and other great men as well as that of the assembled commons, the following things were ordained and established in order to stop the malice of the said servants:

[Four items follow that detail agricultural and other laborers who must only receive wages equal to those received five to six years previously.]

[5.] Item: that the said stewards, bailiffs, and constables of the said communities shall be sworn before the same justices to inquire diligently by all the good ways they can of all those who infringe against this ordinance and to certify to the justices all their names when the justices come to the district to hold their sessions. These same justices, having received certification as to the names of the rebels from these stewards, bailiffs, and constables, shall have them arrested to appear before them in order to answer for such contempts and to pay fines and ransoms to the king if they are convicted. Moreover, the rebels shall be ordered to prison, there to remain until they have found surety to serve, take their wages, do their work, and to sell their saleable goods in the manner prescribed. And in cases where any of them breaks his oath and is therefore convicted, he shall be imprisoned for forty days and, if convicted again, he shall be imprisoned for a quarter of a year, so that each time he offends and is convicted, his punishment will be doubled.

Also, each time the justices come they shall inquire of the said stewards, bailiffs, and constables whether they have made good and lawful certification or whether any conceals anything because of a gift, procurement, or affinity, and the justices shall punish him by fine and ransom if he is found culpable. Also, the same justices shall have the power to inquire and punish the said administrators, workers, labourers, and all other servants, and also hostlers, innkeepers, and those who sell victuals and other things not specified here either because of the suit of a party or because of a formal statement presented to them. The justices are to hear, determine, and carry out the items by means of an *exigend* after the first *capias* if need be,[4] and to depute as many others and of the sort they think best under them for the keeping of the same ordinance. And those who wish to sue such servants, workers, and labourers for excess taken from them shall have this excess back if the servants are convicted because of their suit. In the case where no one will sue to recover such excesses, then it shall be levied on the said servants, workers, labourers, and artificers, and delivered to the collectors of the fifteenth[5] to alleviate the communities where the excess is taken.

[6.] Item: that no sheriffs, constables, bailiffs, jailers, clerks of justices or sheriffs, nor other administrators whatsoever shall receive anything from the same servants for the sake of their offices, neither fees, suits of prison, nor in any other manner. If they have taken or take anything in such manner in the past or in the future, they shall deliver it to the collectors of tenths and fifteenths to help the commons during the time of levying of the tenths and fifteenths. Also, the justices shall inquire in their sessions whether these administrators have received anything from the same servants and, if they find by means of such inquests that the administrators have received anything, the justices shall impose a levy on each of the said administrators and deliver to the collectors what they received together with excesses, fines, and ransom, as well as the amercements of all those who are amerced before these justices for the alleviation of the communities as stated before. And in the case where the excess found in a community exceeds the amount of the fifteenth for the same community, the remainder of that excess shall be levied and paid by the said collectors to the nearest poor communities in order to assist their fifteenths upon the advice of the justices. Also, the servants' and labourers' fines, ransoms, excesses, and amercements, during the time when the said fifteenths are being levied, shall be delivered to the said collectors in the aforesaid form, via indentures made between the collectors and the justices so that the collectors will be charged on their

---

[4]   An *exigend* is a summons to appear; a *capias* is a writ of arrest.
[5]   Taxation based on a fraction of the value of possessions.

account by means of the same indentures in cases where the fines, ransoms, amercements, and excesses are not paid to assist the said fifteenth. And when the said fifteenth ceases, the income shall be levied for the king's use with the sheriffs of the counties answering to him.

[7.] Item: that the said justices shall make their sessions in all the counties of England at least four times a year, namely at the feasts of the annunciation of our lady, Saint Margaret, Saint Michael, Saint Nicholas, and also at all times that the justices decide are necessary.[6] Those who speak in the presence of the justices or do anything else in their absence or presence to encourage or maintain the said servants and labourers against this ordinance shall be severely punished at the discretion of the justices. Also, if any of the said labourers, artificers, or servants flees from one county to another because of this ordinance, the sheriffs of the counties where the fugitives are found shall apprehend them, according to the mandate of the justices of the counties from which they have fled, and bring them to the principal jail of this same county. They are to remain there until the next session of the same justices, and the sheriffs shall return the mandates they received before these justices at their next sessions. Also, this ordinance shall be held and kept in the city of London as in the other cities, boroughs, and other places throughout the land, both within and outside franchises.

Pestilence

The pestilence (not called the Black Death until the sixteenth century) arrived on England's southwestern shores in the summer of 1348 and quickly spread so that by the following summer it had reached London and beyond. It recurred in 1361–2, 1368–9, and 1375, then at irregular intervals thereafter, but the first outbreak was the most severe. Between one third and one half of England's population died as a result of what was probably a combination of bubonic, pulmonary, and septicemic plagues, a figure slightly higher than most of Europe, where the diseases first appeared in 1347. More of the young and the old, and more clergy, died, but similar numbers of men and women, and urban and rural people of all classes succumbed to the pestilence's devastating effects. The reduction in the population began seriously to affect the nation's economy in the 1370s, with prices for goods and land dropping while wages remained high; direct governmental intervention soon became ineffective in the face of labor shortages (see "Ordinance and Statute of Laborers," p. 163).

[6] Respectively, March 25, July 20, September 29, and December 6.

Henry Knighton (d. ca. 1396) was an Augustinian canon at St. Mary of the Meadows in Leicester. His *Chronicle* of English history begins in the tenth century and ends in 1396, his principal source for the early years up to 1337 being Ranulf Higden's *Polychronicon* (see "The English and England," p. 50). Knighton's *Chronicle* is especially valuable for his descriptions of local Wycliffite activities of late fourteenth-century Lancastrians (who were the patrons of St. Mary's abbey) and of the revolt of 1381 (see "The Revolt," p. 175). His depiction of the pestilence is the most comprehensive in English historical narratives, the best continental description appearing in Boccaccio's preface to his *Decameron*.

Further reading

Biraben, J.-N. (1975–6) *Les Hommes et la peste en France et dans les pays européens et méditerranéens*, 2 vols. Paris: Mouton.

Hatcher, J. (1977) *Plague, Population, and the English Economy, 1348–1530*. London: Macmillan.

Platt, C. (1996) *King Death: The Black Death and Its Aftermath in Late-medieval England*. London: University College of London Press.

Ziegler, P. (1971) *The Black Death*. New York: Harper.

Henry Knighton. British Library MS Cotton Tiberius C.vii, fols. 155v–157r. In G. H. Martin (ed. and trans.) (1995) *Knighton's Chronicle, 1337–1396*. Oxford: Oxford University Press, 94–105.
Language: Latin
Manuscript date: ca. 1396

A universal mortality. In this year and the next there was a general plague upon mankind throughout the world. It began in India, then spread to Tartary, and then to the Saracens, and finally to the Christians and the Jews, so that in the space of a single year, from one Easter to the next as the report ran in the papal court, some eight thousand legions of people died suddenly in those distant parts, besides Christians.

The king of Tartary proposes to turn Christian. The king of Tartary,[1] seeing the sudden and unparalleled slaughter of his subjects, made his way with a great number of his nobles towards Avignon, proposing to turn Christian and be baptized by the pope[2] as he thought that God's judgement

---

[1] I.e., central Asia and eastward to the Caspian Sea.
[2] Clement VI (pope 1342–52).

had been visited upon his people for their unbelief. Therefore, when he had travelled for twenty days and heard that the plague was as fatal to Christians as to other people, he shrewdly turned about, abandoned his journey, and hastened to his own country, but the Christians pursued him and slew some two thousand of his people.

There died at Avignon in one day, according to a reckoning made before the pope, 1,312, and on another day four hundred and more. Of the Dominicans in Provence 358 died during Lent,[3] and of 140 friars at Montpellier[4] only seven survived. At Magdelaine[5] only seven friars remained out of eight score (which was enough). At Marseilles of seven score and ten Minorites, truly, only one remained to tell the tale (and just as well). Of the Carmelites sixty-six perished at Avignon before the citizens knew what was happening, for they were believed to have slain one another. Not one of the Augustinian friars, nor yet their order, survived in Avignon. At the same time the pestilence raged in England, beginning at several places in the autumn and running through the country to end at the same time the next year.

Earthquakes. Meanwhile at Corinth and in Achaea[6] several towns were destroyed, and the earth covered them. Castles and towns were rent and shattered, and swallowed up. Mountains in Cyprus were levelled so that the courses of rivers were blocked, and many cities were flooded and villages washed away. Similarly, when a certain friar was preaching at Naples, the whole city was destroyed by earthquake and tempest, and the earth opened suddenly as though a stone were thrown into water, and everyone perished with the friar who was preaching except one other friar, who fled and escaped into a garden outside the town. And all that was the work of the earthquake.[7]

Then the pope sent letters seeking to restore peace between the kingdoms, that they might escape the vengeance of God's right hand, asserting that all those misfortunes had come upon mankind because of their sins. Whereupon the king sent the earl of Lancaster[8] and the earl of Suffolk[9] to Calais, with other magnates, to negotiate a peace. The French nobles lodged at Saint-Omer.[10]

---

[3]   March–April, 1348.
[4]   Southeast France.
[5]   Magdelaine-sur-Tarn, southern France.
[6]   Greece.
[7]   The Naples earthquake was in September 1349.
[8]   Henry de Grosmont, earl 1337–61.
[9]   Robert de Ufford, earl 1337–69.
[10]   (Pas-de-Calais), southeast of Calais.

However, in the mean time the commons of Flanders with French and certain other Flemings gained Bruges by deceit, and beheaded and hanged those Flemings whom they found to have supported the king of England. King Edward[11] assembled his army, wishing to go to Flanders and destroy those who had turned against him, and took to the road. But the earl of Lancaster intercepted him to say that all the Flemings had been brought over to the king, on certain terms, as will appear below. Also, it was agreed that representatives of England and of France should negotiate a peace between the kingdoms from that time to September when, if they could not agree, the crown of France should be taken to some place within the kingdom of France with consent of both parties and there awarded by formal battle without further contention.

Then a lamentable plague travelled by sea to Southampton and on to Bristol, where almost the whole population of the town perished, snatched away, as it were, by sudden death, for there were few who kept their beds for more than two or three days, or even half a day. And thence cruel death spread everywhere with the passage of the sun. There died in Leicester, in the little parish of St. Leonard's, more than nineteen score, four hundred in the parish of Holy Cross,[12] and in St. Margaret's parish seven hundred, and so on in every parish, in great numbers.

The bishop of Lincoln gives chaplains power to absolve. Then the bishop of Lincoln[13] sent word throughout the diocese and gave a general power to all priests, both regular and secular, to hear confessions and full episcopal authority to absolve, excepting only in matters of debt, in which the debtor should make restitution, if he were able, while he lived, or others should be appointed to do so, with his goods, after his death.

The pope grants a general remission. In the same way the pope granted full remission of all sins to any in danger of death, upon a single occasion, a power which was to last until the following Easter,[14] and everyone could choose his or her own confessors at will.

Disease amongst sheep. In the same year there was a great plague amongst sheep everywhere in the realm so that in one place more than five thousand died in one pasture, and they so rotted that neither beast nor bird would touch them.

A fall in the price of goods. The fear of death caused the price of every-thing to fall, for there were very few who cared either for wealth or for

---

[11]   Edward III (r. 1327–77).
[12]   St. Martin's.
[13]   John Gynwell (bishop 1347–62).
[14]   March 28, 1350.

possessions. A man might have a good horse, which previously would have cost forty shillings, for half a mark, a heavy, fat ox for four shillings, a cow for twelve pence, a heifer for six pence, a fat sheep for four pence, a ewe for three pence, a lamb for two pence, a great pig for five pence, a stone of wool for nine pence. And sheep and cattle wandered through the fields and amongst the crops, and there was none to seek them or round them up, and they perished in out-of-the-way places amongst the furrows and under hedges for want of a keeper in numbers beyond reckoning throughout the land, for there was such a shortage of hands and servants that no one knew what ought to be done.

For there was no memory of so unsparing and savage a plague since the days of Vortigern, king of the Britons, in whose time, as Bede records in his history of the English, there were not enough left alive to bury the dead.[15] In the following autumn no one could hire a mower for less than eight pence with his keep or a reaper for less than twelve pence with his keep. So many crops rotted in the fields for want of harvesting, but in the year of the plague, as has been said already in another connection, there was such an abundance of grain that almost no one cared for it.

The Scots mock the English over the plague. The Scots, hearing of the cruel plague amongst the English, attributed it to the avenging hand of God, and took it up as an oath, as a common report came to ears, and when they wished to swear they would say, "By the filthy death of England" (or in English, "Be the foul deth of Engelond"). And thus the Scots, believing God's dreadful judgement to have descended upon the English, gathered in the forest of Selkirk ready to over run the whole kingdom of England. And a fierce pestilence arose, and blew a sudden and monstrous death upon the Scots, and some five thousand of them died in a short time, and the rest of them, some fit and some enfeebled, prepared to make their way home, but the English pursued them and fell upon them, and slew a great many of them.

Master Thomas Bradwardine was consecrated archbishop of Canterbury by the pope and, when he returned to England, he came to London and within two days he was dead.[16] He was celebrated beyond all the scholars of Christendom, in theology pre-eminently but also in all other liberal learning.

At that time there was such a shortage of priests everywhere that many churches were bereft of the divine office: of masses, matins, and vespers, of sacraments and observances. A man could scarcely retain a chaplain to serve

[15] I.e., ca. 450, Bede (672–735), *Ecclesiastical History.*
[16] Bradwardine was consecrated archbishop on July 19, 1349, and died August 26.

a church for less than ten pounds, or perhaps ten marks, and where one might have had a chaplain for four or five marks, or two marks and his keep, with such numbers of priests as there were about before the plague, now in those times there was almost no one willing to take a vicarage for twenty pounds or perhaps twenty marks. But within a short time there came into holy orders a great multitude of those whose wives had died in the plague, many of them illiterate, the merest laymen, who if they were able to read at all were unable to understand what they read.

Ox hides fell to a wretched price, namely twelve pence, and yet a pair of gloves would cost ten pence, twelve pence, or fourteen pence, and a pair of breeches three or four shillings. In the mean time the king sent word into every shire that mowers and other workmen should take no more than they had before, under the penalties laid down in the order, and thereupon made a statute.[17] Nevertheless, the workmen were so puffed up and contrary-minded that they did not heed the king's decree and, if anyone wanted to hire them, he had to pay what they asked: either his fruit and crops rotted or he had to give in to the workmen's arrogant and greedy demands.

When it came to the king's notice that they had not obeyed his order and had given their employees higher wages, he inflicted heavy fines upon abbots and priors, and upon greater and lesser knights, and upon the others, great and small, of the land: from some one hundred shillings, from some twenty shillings, and from each according to what he could pay. And he took twenty shillings from every ploughland in the kingdom, and received not less than a fifteenth would yield.

Then the king caused many labourers to be arrested and put them in prison. Many ran away and took to the woods and forests for a time, but those who were caught were grievously fined. And most were sworn that they would not take more than the old established daily rate and so were freed from prison. And artisans in the boroughs and townships were treated in the same way.

Translation of St. Thomas of Hereford. In the same year the translation of St. Thomas of Hereford took place, on October 25, 1349.[18] After the plague, many buildings, both large and small, in all cities, boroughs, and townships decayed and were utterly razed to the ground for want of occupants, and similarly many villages and hamlets were deserted with not a house left in them, for all who had lived there were dead, and it is likely that many of those villages will never be inhabited again.

[17]   See "Ordinance and Statute of Laborers," p. 163.
[18]   St. Thomas Cantelupe (ca. 1218–82).

In the following winter there was such a want of hands for every kind of work that people believed that the like shortage had never been known at any time in the past, for cattle and such livestock as a man might have wandered about without a keeper, and there was no one to look after people's possessions. And thus the necessities of life became so dear that what in previous times was worth one penny now cost four pence or five pence.

Lords remit their tenants' rent. Whereupon both the magnates of the realm and also lesser lords who had tenants remitted the payment of rents lest their tenants should quit for want of labour and the high cost of living: some half the rent, some more or less, some for two years, some for three, some for one, according to what they could agree.

The Revolt

In May 1381 people in Essex gathered together and refused to pay poll taxes to a local steward, eventually forcing him and other officials who attempted to support him to leave the area. In the next few weeks villagers and rural workers in Kent, Hertfordshire, Cambridgeshire, Suffolk, Norfolk, and elsewhere, not only in an eastern arc around London, but farther away in Leicestershire, Northampton, Yorkshire, and Hampshire, collectively resisted local powers and special royal commissions sent to suppress the new uprisings. Their actions in the countryside and towns included beheading minor officials and those who tried to enforce legal actions against them as well as clerks and lawyers who were part of intended proceedings, attacking the houses of local oligarchs, freeing prisoners from jails, looting and burning especially records of villeinage and land holdings, and destroying the property of oppressive secular and religious lords.

On June 11–14 thousands of men and women from these areas met up with others in London, burning John of Gaunt's Savoy Palace and St. John's Hospital, Clerkenwell, and killing most notably Simon Sudbury, Archbishop of Canterbury, and Sir Robert Hales, master of St. John's and Treasurer for the crown. Richard II, still in his minority and 14 years old, made his first serious foray into national politics when he tried to calm matters in the city and throughout the realm by agreeing to some of the rebel demands and finally meeting with one of their leaders, Wat Tyler, at Smithfeld, about which the *Anonimalle Chronicle* excerpt tells below.

The causes of the uprisings throughout England that reached a highpoint in May–July 1381 were many. In several areas free tenants were more numerous than serfs, yet even the free were made subject to a variety of fees and were obliged to perform labor for their ecclesiastical and secular land-lords. Landowners had also recently renewed a variety of measures to put the relatively better-off laborers and craftspeople back in what was thought of as their natural places, out of which they had been breaking free at least since the first outbreak of the pestilence in 1348 (see "Ordinance and Statute of Laborers," p. 163, and "Sumptuary," p. 215). Local and probably corrupt or at least arrogant officials enforced repeated national taxes, including the inequitable and much-resisted poll taxes. The rebels demanded an end to serfdom, the heads of those who tried to enforce the recent discriminatory taxes, and an end to local corruption by means of greater participation in local governments.

Accounts of large and small rebellions and their suppression exist in chronicles, and parliamentary and local records (see the image "Froissart, *Chroniques,*" p. 151). Historians credit the "anonimalle" (that is, anonymous) author's account in the *Anonimalle Chronicle* with accuracy, perhaps even eye-witness reporting in places, impressions which the attention to detail and less-distinct expressions of opinion reinforce. The chronicle survives in a unique manuscript from St. Mary's Abbey in York, the Benedictine abbey of central importance in Yorkshire. It is over 350 folios long and contains versions of the French *Brut* and Latin Lanercost chronicles as well as other miscellaneous records. The scribes of the manuscript copied from chronicles and records now lost to continue from where the *Brut* finishes its narrative at 1333, the St. Mary's compilers ending their account with events in 1382.

Further reading

Dobson, R. B. (ed.) (1983) *The Peasants' Revolt of 1381.* London: Macmillan.

Hilton, R. H. (1973) *Bond Men Made Free: Medieval Peasant Movements and the English Rising of 1381.* New York: Viking.

Hilton, R. H. and T. H. Aston (eds.) (1984) *The English Rising of 1381.* Cambridge: Cambridge University Press.

Justice, S. (1994) *Writing and Rebellion: England in 1381.* Berkeley: University of California Press.

Oman, C. (1969) [1906] *The Great Revolt of 1381.* Oxford: Clarendon Press.

British Library MS Stowe 1047, fols. 340r–350r. In V. H. Galbraith (ed.) (1927) *The Anonimalle Chronicle, 1333 to 1381.* Manchester: Manchester University Press, 133–50 (selections).
Language: French
Manuscript date: ca. 1396

At this time[1] the commons of southern England suddenly rose in two groups, one in Essex and the other in Kent, to do evil against the duke of Lancaster and the other lords of the realm because of the very grievous tenths, fifteenths, and other subsidies lightly conceded in parliaments and levied by extortion from the poor people. These subsidies did nothing for the kingdom's profit but were spent badly and deceitfully to the great impoverishment of the commons, who therefore rose, as you will now hear.

Because in the year 1380 subsidies had been granted lightly at the parliament of Northampton[2] and because it seemed to various lords and the commons that the said subsidies had not been properly nor honestly collected but were commonly taken from the poor and not the rich – to the great profit and advantage of the collectors and the deception of the king and the commons – the king's council appointed certain commissions[3] to inquire in every township how they had been levied. Among these commissions, one for Essex was sent to one Thomas de Bamptoun,[4] seneschal of one lord, who was considered a king or great lord in that country because of his large state. One day before Whit-Sunday[5] he sat in the town of Brentwood in Essex in order to make an inquisition, and he showed the commission that had been sent to him to raise the money that was in default and to inquire how the collectors had levied the aforesaid subsidy. He had summoned before him the townships of a neighbouring hundred and wanted to have from them a new subsidy, commanding the people of those townships to make a diligent inquiry, give their replies, and make their payment. Among these townships was Fobbing, where people responded that they would not pay anything because they already had an acquittance from him for the said subsidy, at which the said Thomas strongly threatened them, and he had with him two of our lord king's sergeants-at-arms. Out of fear of his malice, the people of Fobbing took counsel with those of Corringham, and the people of the two towns rose and assembled, sending instructions to the people of Stanford-le-Hope to rise with them for the common profit of all. Then the people of these three townships came together to the number of a hundred or more and, with one assent, went to the said Thomas de Bamptoun and openly gave him the answer that they would not deal with him nor give him any money. At this the said Thomas commanded the

[1] June 1381.
[2] The first poll tax in 1377 was one grant, the second in 1379 was graduated according to status, but this third poll tax was a flat rate of 1 shilling (three grants).
[3] On March 16.
[4] Bamptoun's name was correctly John.
[5] The day before Whit-Sunday was Saturday, June 1.

sergeants-at-arms to arrest the people and put them in prison, but the commons rose against them and would not be arrested but made ready with the purpose to kill the said Thomas and the two sergeants. So Thomas fled towards London to the king's council, and the commons went into the woods because of their fear of his malice, hiding there for some time until they were almost famished and afterwards went from town to town, rousing other people to rise against the great lords and the good men of the country.

Because of these things that happened to the said Thomas, Sir Robert Bealknap, Chief Justice of the Common Bench of our lord the king, was sent into the country on a commission of trailbaston,[6] and indictments against various persons were laid before him. The people of the country had such fear that they intended to abandon their holdings. So the commons rose against him, came before him, and told him that he was a traitor to the king and the kingdom, and that he malevolently and maliciously wanted to show them as in default by means of the false inquests presented before him. They made him swear on the Bible that never again would he hold such sessions nor act as a justice in such inquests, and they made him tell them all the names of the jurors. They took all the jurors that they could, beheaded them, and threw their houses to the ground. The said Sir Robert hastily went home without any delay. Afterwards, the said commons assembled before the Whit-Sunday to the number of fifty thousand, and they went to the various manors and townships of those who would not rise with them and threw their buildings to the ground and set them on fire. At this time they captured three of Thomas de Bamptoun's clerks, cut off their heads, and carried them about with them for seven days on poles as an example to others. And they wanted to kill all the lawyers, all the jurors, and the king's servants they could find. Meanwhile, all the great lords of that country and other nobles fled towards London or to other counties where they might be safe.

Now, at that time the high master of the Hospital of St. John of Clerkenwell in London[7] had a very fine and pleasant manor in Essex, which he had ordered to have victuals and other necessities for the holding of his general chapter, so it was stuffed full with wines and nicely stocked for such a lord and his brothers. The commons came to the said manor, ate the food, drank three casks of good wine, and razed the building and burned it to the great damage and loss of the said master. Then the commons sent

---

[6]   Warrants against anyone who harmed the king's lieges.
[7]   Sir Robert Hales, the Treasurer.

various letters to Kent, Suffolk, and Norfolk, so people would rise with them and, when they were assembled, they left in a number of companies, doing great harm in the surrounding countryside.

Afterwards, on Whit-Monday[8] a knight of our lord the king's household, Sir Simon de Burley by name, came to Gravesend in the company of two of the king's sergeants-at-arms, and there he charged a man with being his own serf. The good men of the town came to the knight to make an agreement because of their respect for the king, but the said Sir Simon would not take less than three hundred pounds in silver, a huge amount for the said man. At this the good men prayed that he mitigate his demand, but they could not come to terms nor get him to lower the sum even though they said to Sir Simon that the man was a Christian and of good repute, and so ought not to be ruined forever. Wherefore, the said Sir Simon became irritable and angry, and he greatly despised these good townsfolk and, out of the haughtiness of his heart, he made the sergeants bind the said man and take him to Rochester castle for safe-keeping, from which came great evil and mischief. After his departure, the commons began to rise, embracing the men of many townships in Kent.

And at this time a justice was assigned by the king and his council to go into Kent on a commission of trailbaston in the same manner as in Essex. With him went a sergeant-at-arms of our lord the king named Master John Legge, carrying with him a great number of indictments against various people of that area to make the king rich. They wanted to hold their sessions at Canterbury, but they were turned back by the commons.

After this, the commons of Kent, without a leader or a chief, gathered together in great numbers day by day. On the Friday [after] Whit-Sunday[9] they came to Dartford, took counsel together, and ordained that no one who lived anywhere within twelve leagues of the sea should come with them but should guard the coasts from enemies. They said among themselves that there were more kings than one and that they would neither suffer nor have any king except King Richard. At this same time the commons of Kent came to Maidstone, cut off the head of one of the best men of the town, and cast to the ground various houses and tenements of people who would not rise with them, as they had done before in Essex. On the Friday after that, they came to Rochester[10] and there met a great number of the Essex commons, and because of the case of the Gravesend man, they

---

[8] June 3.
[9] I.e., June 7, but probably June 5.
[10] The events at Rochester actually occurred Thursday, June 6.

besieged Rochester castle in order to free their companion from Gravesend whom the aforesaid Sir Simon had imprisoned. They made a strong assault on the castle and, although the constable defended it vigorously for half a day, he at last delivered the castle to them because of the fear he had of the great multitude of people without reason from Essex and Kent. The commons entered the castle and took their companion and all the other prisoners out of the prison. Then the men of Gravesend returned home with their companion in great joy and without doing anything more, but the others from Maidstone took their way with the rest of the commons through the surrounding countryside, and there they made their chief one Wat Tyler of Maidstone to maintain them and counsel them.

On the following Monday, after Trinity Sunday,[11] they came to Canterbury before the hour of noon, and four thousand of them entered the mother-church of St. Thomas at the time of high mass and, kneeling, all cried with one voice to the monks to elect a monk to be archbishop of Canterbury, "For he who is archbishop now is a traitor and will be beheaded for his iniquity," and so he was within five days.[12] And when they had done this, they went into the town to their companions, and with one assent they summoned the mayor, bailiffs, and commons of the said town and examined them as to whether they would swear with good will to be faithful and loyal to King Richard and to the loyal commons of England or not. The mayor replied that they would willingly do so, and they swore their oaths. Then the rebels asked them if there were any traitors among them, and the townsfolk said there were three and named them. These the commons immediately dragged out of their houses and cut off their heads. Afterwards, the commons took five hundred people of the town with them towards London, but the others they left to guard the town.

At this time the commons had as their counsellor a chaplain of evil disposition named Sir John Ball, and that Sir John advised them to get rid of all the lords, archbishops, bishops, abbots, priors, and most of the monks and canons so that there should be no bishop in England except for one archbishop, who would be himself. He also said that there should be no more than two monks or canons in each religious house and their possessions should be divided among the laity, for which he was considered a prophet by the commons. He worked with them day by day to strengthen them in their malice, and he got a good reward later: he was drawn, disemboweled, hanged, and beheaded as a traitor.

---

[11]   June 10.
[12]   Simon Sudbury became archbishop in 1375 and was beheaded June 14.

After this, the said commons went to various towns and raised the people, some willingly and others against their will, until they had gathered a good sixty thousand. And as they went towards London, they met several men of law and twelve of the king's knights of that country; they captured them and made them swear that they would support them or else they would be beheaded. They did much damage in Kent, notably to Thomas de Heselden, a servant of the duke of Lancaster,[13] because of the hatred they had for the said duke, and they cast his manors and houses to the ground and sold his livestock – horses, oxen, cows, sheep and pigs – and all sorts of meal at a cheap price. Every day they desired to have his head and the head of Sir Thomas Orgrave, Clerk of the Receipt and Sub-Treasurer of England.

When the king heard of their doings, he sent messengers to them on the Tuesday after Trinity Sunday,[14] asking why they were doing these things in this manner and why they had risen in his land. And they replied by the said messengers that they had risen to save him and to destroy traitors to him and to the kingdom. The king again sent messengers to them, wanting them to cease their activity out of reverence to him until he could speak with them, and that he would make reasonable amends for the evil done to them according to their will. The commons sent through his messengers that they desired to meet and speak with him at Blackheath. The king sent back a third time saying that he would willingly come to them the next day at the hour of prime,[15] in order to hear their intentions. Then the king, who was at this time at Windsor, moved as hastily as he could to London. At that moment the mayor and the good men of London came to meet him and to bring him safely to the Tower of London. And all the council as well as all the lords of the surrounding area assembled there, namely the archbishop of Canterbury and Chancellor of England; the bishop of London;[16] the master of the Hospital of St. John of Clerkenwell (who was Treasurer of England); the earls of Buckingham, Kent, Arundel, Warwick, Suffolk, Oxford, and Salisbury; and others to the number of six hundred.

On the eve of Corpus Christi Day[17] the commons of Kent came to Blackheath, three leagues from London, to the number of fifty thousand to await the king, and they displayed two banners of St. George and sixty pennons; and the commons of Essex came to the other side of the water to

---

[13] Controller of John of Gaunt's household.
[14] Tuesday, June 11.
[15] 6 a.m.
[16] William Courtenay, bishop 1375–81.
[17] Wednesday, June 12.

the number of sixty thousand in order to help them and have the king's reply. On this Wednesday, the king being in the Tower of London and thinking how to handle the affair, had his barges made ready, took with him in his barge the archbishop, treasurer, and others of his council, and four other barges for his men, and travelled to Greenwich, three leagues from London. There the said chancellor and treasurer informed the king that it would be too great a folly to go to the commons, for they were men lacking in reason and did not have it in them to behave well.

Because of the chancellor's and treasurer's persuasion, the king would not come to them, so the said commons of Kent sent a petition to him, calling for him to grant them the heads of the duke of Lancaster and fifteen other lords, of whom fourteen were bishops present with him in the Tower of London. And these were their names: Master Simon of Sudbury, archbishop of Canterbury and Chancellor of England; Sir Robert Hales, prior of the Hospital of St. John, Treasurer of England; the bishop of London; Sir John Fordham, clerk of the Privy Seal and bishop-elect of Durham;[18] Sir Robert Belknap, Chief Justice of the Common Bench; Sir Ralph Ferrers; Sir Robert Plessington, Chief Baron of the Exchequer; John Legge, sergeant-at-arms of our lord the king; Thomas de Bamptoun already mentioned, and others. To this the king would not assent, whereupon the commons sent to him again a yeoman, praying that he would come and speak with them. He replied that he would do so willingly, but the said chancellor and treasurer counselled him to do the opposite and to tell them that if they would come to Windsor on the following Monday, they would have a suitable response there. And the said commons had among themselves a "wache worde" in English: "With whom haldes yow?" And the response was, "Wyth Kynge Richarde and wyth the trew communes," and those who did not know how or would not reply were beheaded and put to death.

And at this time there came a knight in all the haste he could, crying to the king to wait, and the king was startled and waited for his arrival and to hear what he wished to say. The said knight came to the king and notified him that he had heard from a servant, who had been held by the rebels for the day, that if the king went to them, all the land would be lost, for they would never allow him to leave them for any reason, but that they wanted to take him with them around all of England, and they would force him to grant them all their wishes and that their purpose was to kill all the lords and ladies of great renown as well as all the archbishops and bishops, abbots and priors, monks and canons, parsons and vicars on the advice and counsel

[18]   Bishop 1382–8.

of the aforementioned Sir John Ball. Therefore, the king returned to London as quickly as he could, and he was at the Tower at the hour of tierce.[19] At that time the man, called before the yeoman, hastened to Blackheath, crying out to his companions that the king had left and that it would be good for them to go on to London to pursue their purpose.

[The chronicle goes on to describe how the commons of Kent and Essex forced prisoners from various jails, burned ecclesiastical and legal records, beheaded 18 people, and destroyed buildings, including John of Gaunt's Savoy manor, an action which the chronicle attributes to Londoners.]

At this time a great body of the commons went to the Tower of London to speak with the king and, as they could not get to speak with him, they laid siege to the Tower from the side of St. Katherine's, towards the south. And another part of the commons, who were in the city, went to the Hospital of St. John, Clerkenwell, and on their way they burnt the place and houses of Roger Legett, questmonger, who had been beheaded in Cheapside, and all the rented properties and tenements of the Hospital of St. John they could find. Afterwards, they came to the beautiful priory of the said hospital and set on fire many fine and delightful buildings within the same, great damage and horrible actions for all time to come. Then they returned to London to rest or for more mischief.

At this time the king was in a turret of the great Tower of London, and he saw the manor of the Savoy, the Hospital of Clerkenwell, the houses of Simon Hosteler near Newgate, and John Butterwick's place burning all at once. He summoned all the lords about him in a chamber and asked the counsel what should be done in such a necessity. None of them could or would give him counsel, so the young king said that he would order the mayor of the city to command the sheriffs and aldermen to have it cried within their wards that all people between the age of fifteen and sixty years, on pain of life and limb, should go next morning (which was Friday) to Mile End, and meet him there at seven of the bell. He did this in order that all the commons, who were there around the Tower, might be made to abandon the siege and come to Mile End to see and hear him so that all those who were in the Tower could leave safely at their desire and save themselves as they wished. But it came to nothing, for some of them did not have the good fortune to be saved.

Later on that same Thursday, the said feast of Corpus Christi, the king was in the Tower, thoughtful and sad, and he climbed onto a little turret

[19]   9 a.m.

near St. Katherine's where a large number of the commons were lying. And
he had it proclaimed to them that they should all go peacefully to their
homes, and he would pardon them of all their kinds of offences. But they
all cried with one voice that they did not want to go before they had the
traitors within the Tower and had charters to free them from all manner of
serfdom and they had certain other kinds of things, which they wished to
demand. The king benevolently granted all and made a clerk write a bill in
their presence in this manner: "Richard, king of England and France, gives
great thanks to his good commons for that they have so great a desire to see
and keep their king, and grants them pardon for all manner of trespasses,
and misprisions, and felonies done up to this hour and wills and commands
that every one should now immediately return to his own home, and wills
and commands that everyone put his grievances in writing and have them
sent to him, and he will provide, with the aid of his loyal lords and his
good council, such remedy as shall be profitable both to him and to them as
well as to the kingdom." He put his signet seal to this document in their
presence and then sent the said bill by the hands of two of his knights to
those around St. Katherine's. And he caused it to be read to them, and the
man who read it stood on an old chair above the others so that all could
hear. All this time the king was in the Tower in great distress of mind. And
when the commons had heard the bill, they said that it was nothing but
trifles and mockery. Therefore, they returned to London and had it cried
around the city that all lawyers, all those men of the chancery and the
exchequer, and everyone who knew how to write a brief or a letter should
be beheaded wherever they could be found. At this time they burnt several
more houses in the city, and the king himself ascended a high garret of the
Tower in order to watch the fires. Then he descended again and sent for
the lords to have their counsel, but they did not know how they should
counsel him and were surprisingly abashed.

On the next day, Friday,[20] the commons of the country and the commons
of London assembled in fearful strength to the number of a hundred thousand or more, besides some four score who remained on Tower Hill to
watch those who were in the Tower. Some went to Mile End, on the way
to Brentwood, to wait for the king's arrival because of the proclamation
that he had made. Others came to Tower Hill and, when the king learned
that they were there, he sent them orders by a messenger to join their
companions at Mile End, saying that he would come to them very soon. And
at this time in the morning he counselled the archbishop of Canterbury

[20]   June 14.

and the others who were in the Tower to go down to the little water-gate and take a boat and save themselves. And the archbishop did it in this manner, but a wicked woman raised a cry against him, and he had to return to the Tower to his confusion.

By seven o'clock the king himself came to Mile End and with him his mother in a carriage, and the earls of Buckingham, Kent, Warwick, and Oxford, as well as Sir Thomas Percy, Sir Robert Knolles, the mayor of London, and many knights and squires, and Sir Aubrey de Vere carried the royal sword. And when the king arrived and the commons saw him, they all knelt down to him, saying, "Welcome, our lord King Richard, if it pleases you; we will not have any other king but you." And Wat Tyler, their master and leader, prayed on behalf of the commons that the king would suffer them to take and deal with all the traitors against him and the law. And the king granted that they should have to do as they liked with all who were traitors and who could be proved to be traitors by the law. The said Walter and the commons were carrying two banners as well as pennons and smaller pennons while they made their petition to the king. And they required that from then on no man should be a serf nor make homage or any type of service to any lord but should give four pence for an acre of land. They asked also that no one should serve any man except at his own will and by means of regular covenant. And at this time the king made the commons array themselves in two lines, and had it proclaimed before them that he would confirm and grant to them that they should be free, and generally should have their will, and that they could travel through all the realm of England and take all the traitors and bring them safely to him, and then he would deal with them as the law demanded. Under this grant, the said Wat Tyler and commons took their way to the Tower to seize the archbishop and the others while the king remained at Mile End.

At this time, the archbishop had sung his mass devoutly in the Tower and confessed the prior of the Hospital of Clerkenwell and others, and then he heard two or three masses and chanted the *Commendatio*, the *Placebo* and *Dirige*, the Seven Psalms, and the Litany and, when he was at the words "*Omnes sancti orate pro nobis*,"[21] the commons entered and dragged him out of the chapel of the Tower and struck and hustled him roughly, as they did to the others who were with him, and conducted them to Tower Hill. There they cut off the heads of Master Simon of Sudbury, archbishop of Canterbury; of Sir Robert Hales, High Prior of the Hospital of St. John's of Clerkenwell, Treasurer of England; and of Brother William of Appleton,

---

[21]   "To all saints, pray for us."

a great physician and surgeon, and one who had much influence with the king and the duke of Lancaster. And some time after they beheaded John Legge, the king's sergeant-at-arms, and with him a juror. At the same time the commons had it proclaimed that whoever could catch any Fleming or other aliens of any nation should cut off their heads, and so they did after this. Then they took the heads of the archbishop and of the others, put them on wooden poles, and carried them before them in procession through all the city as far as the shrine of Westminster Abbey, to the contempt of themselves, of God, and of holy church, for which vengeance descended on them very soon afterwards. Then they returned to London Bridge and set the head of the archbishop above the gate and eight other heads of those they had beheaded so that all who passed over the bridge could see them. This done, they went to the church of St. Martin's in the Vintry, and found therein thirty-five Flemings, whom they dragged outside and beheaded in the street. On that day there were beheaded 140 or 160 persons. Then they took their way to the places of Lombards and other aliens, broke into their houses, and robbed them of all their goods that they could find. This went on for all that day and the night following, with hideous cries and horrible tumult.

At this time, because the Chancellor had been beheaded, the king made the earl of Arundel Chancellor for the day, and entrusted him with the Great Seal, and all that day he caused various clerks to write charters, patents, and letters of protection, granted to the commons and touching the matters before mentioned without taking any fines for the sealing or writing . . .

Then the king caused a proclamation to be made that all the commons of the country who were still in the city should come to Smithfield to meet him there, and so they did. And when the king with his people arrived there, he turned to the east to in front of St. Bartholomew's, a house of canons, and the commons arrayed themselves to the west in a great number of formations. At this moment the mayor of London, William of Walworth, came up, and the king ordered that he approach the commons and make their chieftain come to him. And when he was called by the mayor, Wat Tyler of Maidstone by name came to the king with great confidence, mounted on a little horse so that the commons might see him. And he dismounted, holding a dagger in his hand, which he had taken from another man and, when he had dismounted, he half bent his knee and took the king by the hand and shook his arm forcefully and roughly, saying to him, "Brother, be of good comfort and joyful, for you shall have, in the coming two weeks, forty thousand more commons than you have at present, and we shall be good companions." And the king said to Walter, "Why will you not go back to your own country?" But the other answered with a great oath that neither he nor his companions would leave until they had got their charter as they wished to have it with certain points written out in this charter that they wished to demand, threatening that the lords of the realm would repent bitterly if the commons did not have these points settled as they wished. Then the king asked him what were the points that he wished to have, and he should have them freely and without contradiction written out and sealed. Thereupon the said Wat rehearsed the points which were to be demanded: he asked that there should be no law except for the law of Winchester,[22] that from then on there should be no outlawry in any process of law, and that no lord should have lordship in future, but that it should be divided among all men, except for the king's own lordship. He also asked that the goods of Holy Church should not remain in the hands of the religious, nor of parsons and vicars and other churchmen but that clergy already in possession should have a sufficient sustenance, and the rest of their goods should be divided among parishioners. And he demanded that there should be only one bishop in England and only one prelate, and all the lands and tenements of the possessioners should be taken from them and divided among the commons, only reserving for them a reasonable sustenance. And he demanded that there should be no more villeins in England, and no serfdom nor villeinage but that all men should be free and of one condition. To this the king gave an easy answer and said that Wat should have all that he could fairly grant, reserving only for himself the regality of his crown, and he commanded him to go back to his home without delay. During all the time that the king was speaking, no lord or counsellor dared or wished to give a response to the commons in any place except for the king himself.

Presently, Wat Tyler in the presence of the king sent for a tankard of water to rinse his mouth because of the great heat that he felt and, as soon as the water was brought, he rudely and coarsely rinsed out his mouth in front of the king. And then he made them bring him a tankard of ale, and drank a great draught, and then in the presence of the king climbed on his horse again. At the same moment a valet from Kent, who was among the king's retinue, asked to see the said Wat, chieftain of the commons, and when he saw him, he said aloud that he was the greatest thief and robber in all Kent. Wat heard these words, and asked the man to come out to him, shaking his head at him in a sign of malice, but Wat refused to go over to him because of his fear of the others there. At last the lords made the valet

---

[22] That local communities should judge laws rather than centralized royal judges who traveled on circuit.

go out to Wat to see what the latter would do before the king. And when Wat saw him, he ordered one of his followers, who was mounted on horseback and carrying a banner displayed, to dismount and behead the said valet. But the valet answered that he had done nothing to deserve death, for what he had said was true, and he would not deny it but that he could not lawfully have a debate in the presence of his liege lord, without leave, except in his own defense, but that he could do without reproof because whoever struck him he would strike back. And for these words, Wat wanted to strike him with his dagger and would have slain him in the king's presence but, because he tried to do so, the mayor of London, William of Walworth, reasoned with the said Wat for his violent behaviour and contempt done in the king's presence and arrested him. And because he arrested him, the said Wat in great anger stabbed the mayor with his dagger in the body. But, as it pleased God, the mayor had armor and received no harm, but like a hardy and vigorous man drew his baselard and struck back at Wat's neck, giving him a deep wound and then a huge cut on the head. And during this scuffle, a valet of the king's household drew his sword and ran Wat two or three times through the body, mortally wounding him. Wat spurred his horse, crying to the commons to avenge him, and the horse carried him some four score paces, and then he fell to the ground half dead. And when the commons saw him fall and did not know for certain how it happened, they began to bend their bows and to shoot. Therefore, the king himself spurred his horse and went to them, commanding them that they should all come to him at the field of St. John of Clerkenwell.[23]

Meanwhile, the mayor of London rode as hastily as he could back in to London and commanded those who were in charge of the twenty-four wards to have it cried around their wards that everyone should arm himself as quickly as he could and come to the king in St. John's Fields where the commons were, to help the king for he was in great trouble and necessity. But at this time almost all of the knights and squires of the king's household and many others, because of the fear they had of this affray, left their liege lord and went each his own way.

Afterwards, when the king had reached the open fields, he made the commons array themselves on the west side. And presently the aldermen came to him in a body, bringing with them the keepers of the wards arrayed in a number of bands, a fine company of well-armed men in great strength. And they enveloped the commons like sheep in a pen. Meanwhile, after the mayor had sent the keepers of the city on their way to the king, he returned

---

[23]   A few hundred yards north of Smithfield.

with a good company of lances to Smithfield in order to make an end of the captain of the commons. And when he came to Smithfield, he did not find the said captain Wat Tyler there, at which he marvelled a lot and asked what had become of the traitor. And he was told that Wat had been carried by a some of the commons to the hospital for the poor near St. Bartholomew's and put to bed in the chamber of the master of the said hospital. And the mayor went there and found him, and had him carried out to the middle of Smithfield in the presence of his companions and had him beheaded. And so ended his wretched life. But the mayor had his head set on a pole and carried before him to the king, who had remained in the field. And when the king saw the head, he had it brought near him in order to subdue the commons and thanked the mayor greatly for what he had done. And when the commons saw that their chieftain, Wat Tyler, was dead in such a manner, they fell to the ground there among the wheat, like beaten people, imploring the king for mercy for their misdeeds. And the king benevolently granted them mercy, and most of them took to flight. But the king appointed two knights to lead the other men from Kent through London and over London Bridge without doing them harm so that each of them could go in peace to his own home. Then the king ordered the mayor, William Walworth, to put a basinet on his head because of what was to happen, and the mayor asked for what reason he was to do so, and the king told him that he was much beholden to him and that for this reason he was to receive the order of knighthood. The mayor answered that he was not worthy nor able to have or to meet the costs of a knight's estate, for he was nothing but a merchant and had to live by commerce, but finally the king made him put on the basinet and took a sword in both his hands and firmly dubbed him knight with great good will. The same day he made three other citizens of London knights for the same reason and in the same place, and these are their names: John Philipot, Nicholas Brembre, and [Robert Launde,] and the king gave Sir William Walworth one hundred pounds in land and each of the others forty pounds in land for them and their heirs. And after this the king took his way to London to his Wardrobe to ease him of his great toils.

6

Style and Spectacle

Feasts

Noble households were large socioeconomic enterprises, and meals were an integral part of their owners' desire to display their status both at home and as they traveled around the countryside. Royal households employed anywhere from 300–800 indentured and other servants, while the households of lords and clergy employed an average of between 20 and 150 servants to perform the duties for the immediate family and its guests. In terms of meals, breakfasts were not common until the fifteenth century, so the first meal was usually lunch and then supper later in the day. These two meals could occupy between four and six hours of the day in noble households. Elaborate rituals accompanied each meal, from the sequence of entrance and seating, the layout of the table, and the courses (usually three by the fifteenth century), to the order and rites of service, entertainment, and conversation.

British Library MS Harley 5086 is one of a number of anonymous treatises on food and table manners to survive from the later Middle Ages. These texts were in general aimed at younger men and women from noble families (the meaning of "babee" here) and form a sub-genre of a larger group of courtesy texts. They therefore share characteristics with and have similar intentions as *Fürstenspiegel*, advice to princes, and even romances, and many are French in origin. That several such tracts are written in verse suggests a mnemonic function.

Primary documents and further reading

Austin, T. (ed.) (1964) [1888] *Two Fifteenth-century Cookery-books*. EETS, o.s. 91. London: Oxford University Press.

Caxton, W. (1998) [1868] *Book of Curtesye*, ed. F. J. Furnivall. EETS, e.s. 3. Woodbridge, Suffolk: Boydell and Brewer.

Chambers, R. W. and W. W. Seton (eds.) (1914) *A Fifteenth-century Courtesy Book and Two Fifteenth-century Franciscan Rules*. EETS, o.s. 148. London: Kegan Paul, Trench, Trübner.

Dyer, C. (1989) *Standards of Living in the Later Middle Ages: Social Change in England, c. 1200–1520*. Cambridge: Cambridge University Press.

Heal, F. (1990) *Hospitality in Early Modern England*. Oxford: Clarendon Press.

Hieatt, C. B. and S. Butler (eds.) (1985) *Curye on Inglysch: English Culinary Manuscripts of the Fourteenth-century (including the Forme of Cury)*. EETS, s.s. 8. London: Oxford University Press.

Manzalaoui, M. A. (ed.) (1977) *Secretum Secretorum: Nine English Versions*. EETS, o.s. 276. Oxford: Oxford University Press.

Rickert, E. and L. J. Naylor (trans.) (2002) [1908] *The Babees' Book: Medieval Manners for the Young*. Woodbridge, Suffolk: Boydell and Brewer.

Woolgar, C. M. (1999) *The Great Household in Late Medieval England*. New Haven, CT: Yale University Press.

British Library MS Harley 5086, fols. 86r–90r. "The Babees Book." In F. J. Furnivall (ed.) (1868) *The Babees Book, etc.* EETS, o.s. 32. London: N. Trübner, 1–9.
Language: English (West Midland)
Manuscript date: ca. 1475

In this tretys, the whiche I thenke to wryte
Out of Latyn in-to my comune langage,
He me supporte (sen I kan nat endyte),
The whiche only after his owne ymage
5   Fourmyd man-kynde. For alle of tendre age
In curtesye resseyve shulle document
And vertues knowe by this lytil coment.

And Facett[1] seythe the book of curtesye
Vertues to knowe, thaym forto have and use,
10   Is thing moste heelfulle in this worlde treuly.
Therfore, in feythe I wole me nat excuse

[1] *Facetus de moribus*, attributed to John of Garland (fl. 1230), a conduct book used in schools.

From this labour ywys, nor hit refuse,
For myn owne lernynge wole I say summe thing
That touchis vertues and curtesye havyng.

15   But, O yonge babees, whome bloode royalle
Withe grace, feture, and hyhe habylite   *great ability*
Hathe enourmyd, on yow ys that I calle   *endowed, exalted*
To knowe this book, for it were grete pyte,
Syn that in yow ys sette sovereyne beaute,
20   But yf vertue and nurture were withe alle;
To yow therfore I speke in specyalle

And nouhte to hem of elde that bene experte
In governanunce, nurture, and honeste,
For what nedys to yeve helle peynes smerte,
25   Joye unto hevene, or water unto the see,
Heete to the fyre that kan nat but hoote be?
It nedys nouhte; therfore, O babees yynge,   *young*
My book only is made for youre lernynge.

Therfore, I pray that no man reprehende
30   This lytyl book, the whiche for yow I make,
But where defaute ys, latte ylke man amende
And nouhte deme yt; [I] pray thaym for youre sake.
For other mede, ywys, I kepe noone take
But that God wolde this book myhte yche man plese
35   And in lernynge unto yow donne somme ese.

Eke, swete children, yf there be eny worde
That yee kenne nouhte, spyrre whils yee yt ken.   *ask*
Whanne yee yt knowe, yee mowe holde yt in horde,
Thus thurhe spyrryng yee mowe lerne at wyse men.
40   Also, thenke nouhte to straungely at my penne,
In this metre for yow lyste to procede,
Men usen yt; therfore, on hit take hede.

But amonge alle that I thenke of to telle
My purpos ys first only forto trete
45   How yee babees in housholde that done duelle
Shulde have youre sylf whenne yee be sette at mete   *behave*

And how yee shulde, whenne men lyste yow rehete,   *show good will*
Have wordes lovly, swete, bleste, and benyngne.   *towards*
In this helpe me O Marie, modir dyngne!

50 And eke, O lady myn, Facecia,   *Cleverness, Wit*
My penne thow guyde, and helpe unto me shewe,
For as the firste off alle lettres ys the A,
So artow firste modir of alle vertue.
Off myn unkunnynge, swete lady, now rewe,
55 And thouhe untauhte I speke of governaunce,
Withe thy swete helpe supporte myn ygnoraunce.

A, bele babees, herkne now to my lore!
Whenne yee entre into your lordis place,
Say first, "God spede," and alle that ben byfore
60 Yow in this stede, salue withe humble face.   *greet*
Stert nat rudely, komme inne an esy pace,
Holde up youre heede, and knele but on oone kne
To youre sovereyne or lorde, whedir he be.

And yf they speke withe yow at youre komynge,
65 Withe stable eye loke upone them rihte,
To theyre tales and yeve yee goode herynge
Whils they have seyde; loke eke withe alle your myhte
Yee jangle nouhte; also caste nouhte your syhte
Aboute the hous, but take to them entent
70 Withe blythe vysage and spiryt diligent.

Whenne yee answere or speke, yee shulle be purveyde
What yee shalle say; speke eke thing fructuous.
On esy wyse latte thy resone be sayde
In wordes gentylle and also compendious,
75 For many wordes ben rihte tedious
To ylke wyseman that shalle yeve audience.
Thaym to eschewe therfore doo diligence.

Take eke noo seete but to stonde be yee preste;
Whils forto sytte, ye have in komaundement
80 Your heede, youre hande, your feet, holde yee in reste.
Nor thurhe clowyng your flesshe loke yee nat rent.
Lene to no poste whils that ye stande present

Byfore your lorde, nor handylle ye no thyng
Als for that tyme unto the hous touching.

85   At every tyme obeye unto youre lorde
Whenne yee answere, ellis stonde yee styl as stone
But yf he speke; loke withe oon accorde
That yf yee se komme inne eny persone
Better thanne yee, that yee goo bak anoone
90   And gyff him place; youre bak eke in no way
Turne on no wihte, as ferforthe as ye may.   *far*

Yiff that youre lorde also yee se drynkynge,
Looke that ye be in rihte stable sylence
Withe-oute lowde lauhtere or jangelynge,
95   Rounynge, japynge, or other insolence.
Yiff he komaunde also in his presence
Yow forto sytte, fulfille his wylle belyve,   *quickly*
And for youre seete, looke nat withe other stryve.

Whenne yee er sette, take noone unhoneste tale;
100   Eke forto skorne eschewe withe alle your myhte.
Latte ay youre chere be lowly, blythe, and hale,
Withe-oute chidynge as that yee wolde fyhte.
Yiff yee perceyve also that eny wihte
Lyst yow kommende that better be thanne yee,
105   Ryse up anoone and thanke him withe herte free.

Yif that yee se youre lorde or youre lady,
Touching the housholde, speke of eny thinge,
Latt theym alloone, for that is curtesy,
And entremete yow nouhte of theyre doynge,   *interfere*
110   But be ay redy withe-oute feynynge
At hable tyme to done your lorde service.   *suitable*
So shalle yee gete anoone a name of price.   *renown*

Also to brynge drynke, holde lihte whanne tyme ys
Or, to doo that whiche ouhte forte be done,
115   Looke yee be preste, for so yee shalle ywys
In nurture gete a gentyl name ful sone.
And yif ye shulde at God aske yow a bone,

Als to the worlde better in noo degre
Mihte yee desire thanne nurtred forto be.

120   Yif that youre lorde his owne coppe lyste commende
To yow to drynke, ryse up whanne yee it take
And resseyve it goodly withe boothe youre hende.
Of yt also to noone other profre ye make,
But unto him that brouhte yt yee, hit take
125   Whenne yee have done, for yt in no kyn wyse
Auhte comune be, as techis us the wyse.

Now must I telle in shorte, for I muste so,
Youre observaunce that ye shalle done at none.
Whenne that ye se youre lorde to mete shalle goo,
130   Be redy to fecche him water sone,
Summe helle water; summe holde to he hathe done   *healthy*
The clothe to him, and from him yee nat pace
Whils he be sette and have herde sayde the grace.

Byfore him stonde whils he komaunde yo sytte
135   Withe clene handes ay redy him to serve.
Whenne yee be sette, your knyf withe alle your wytte
Unto youre sylf bothe clene and sharpe conserve
That honestly yee mowe your owne mete kerve.
Latte curtesye and sylence withe yow duelle,
140   And foule tales looke noone to other telle.

Kutte withe your knyf your brede and breke yt nouhte.
A clene trenchour byfore yow eke ye lay   *cutting dish*
And, whenne your potage to yow shalle be brouhte,   *thick soup, stew*
Take yow sponys and soupe by no way,
145   And in youre dysshe leve nat your spone, I pray,
Nor on the borde lenynge be yee nat sene,
But from embrowyng the clothe yee kepe clene.   *dirtying*

Oute overe youre dysshe your heede yee nat hynge,
And withe fulle mouthe drynke in no wyse.
150   Youre nose, your teethe, your naylles, from pykynge
Kepe at your mete, for so techis the wyse.
Eke or ye take in youre mouthe, yow avyse,

So mekyl mete but that yee rihte welle mowe
Answere and speke whenne men speke to yow.

155   Whanne ye shalle drynke, your mouthe clence withe a clothe,
Youre handes eke that they in no manere
Imbrowe the cuppe, for thanne shulle noone be lothe   *dirty*
Withe yow to drynke that ben withe yow yfere.
The salte also touche nat in his salere
160   Withe nokyns mete, but lay it honestly   *no kinds of*
On youre trenchoure, for that is curtesy.

Youre knyf withe mete to your mouthe nat bere,
And in youre hande not holde yee yt no way;
Eke, yf to yow be brouhte goode metys sere,   *diverse*
165   Luke curteysly of ylke mete yee assay,
And yf your dysshe withe mete be tane away
And better brouhte, curtesye wole certeyne
Yee late yt passe and calle it nat ageyne.

And yf straungers withe yow be sette at mete
170   And unto yow goode mete be brouhte or sente,
Withe parte of hit goodely yee theym rehete,
For yt ys nouhte ywys convenyent,
Withe yow at mete whanne other ben present,
Alle forto holde that unto yow ys brouhte,
175   And as wrecches on other vouchesauf nouhte.

Kutte nouhte youre mete eke as it were felde men
That to theyre mete have suche an appetyte
That they ne rekke in what wyse, where ne when,
Nor how ungoodly they on theyre mete twyte,   *tear*
180   But, swete children, have al-wey your delyte
In curtesye, and in verrey gentylnesse,
And at youre myhte eschewe boystousnesse.

Whanne chese ys brouhte, a trenchoure ha ye clene,
On whiche withe clene knyf [ye] your chese mowe kerve.
185   In youre fedynge luke goodly yee be sene,
And from jangelyng your tunge al-wey conserve,
For so ywys yee shalle a name deserve

Off gentylnesse and of goode governaunce,
And in vertue al-wey youre silf avaunce.

190   Whanne that so ys that ende shalle kome of mete,
Youre knyffes clene where they ouhte to be,
Luke yee putte uppe and holde eke yee your seete
Whils yee have wasshe, for so wole honeste.
Whenne yee have done, looke thanne goodly that yee
195   Withe-oute lauhtere, japynge, or boystous worde,
Ryse uppe and goo unto youre lordis borde,

And stonde yee there, and passe yee him nat fro
Whils grace ys sayde and brouhte unto an ende.
Thanne somme of yow for water owe to goo,
200   Somme holde the clothe, somme poure upon his hende.
Other service thanne this I myhte comende
To yow to done but, for the tyme is shorte,
I putte theym nouhte in this lytyl reporte,

But overe I passe, prayying withe spyrit gladde
205   Of this labour that no wihte me detray,   *belittle*
But where to lytyl ys, latte him more adde,
And whenne to myche ys, latte him take away;
For thouhe I wolde, tyme wole that I no moresay.
I leve therfore, and this book I directe
210   To every wihte that lyste yt to correcte.

And, swete children, for whos love now I write,
I yow beseche withe verrey lovande herte
To knowe this book that yee sette your delyte
And myhtefulle God, that suffred peynes smerte,
215   In curtesye he make yow so experte
That, thurhe your nurture and youre governaunce,
In lastynge blysse yee mowe your self avaunce.

The Hunt

Even though hunting was a widespread practice and important source of
food for the majority rural population in the Middle Ages, various laws

attempted to exclude unpropertied and unconnected people from game areas, including the specific game law of 1390. The nobility saw the hunt, especially of large game such as deer, as an important occasion for the exhibition of wealth, not only because of the servants and beasts required, but also because of the elaborate accommodations, clothing, and feasts that accompanied their gatherings. Medieval reserves for gaming were themselves also expensive investments in which to perform courtly power.

Edward of Norwich, duke of Aumale and second duke of York (ca. 1373–1415), was the son of the marriage of Edmund of Langley, earl of Cambridge, and Isabella of Castile, and was the grandson of Edward III. One of the intimates of Richard II's court, he was in and out of favor with Henry IV and Henry V before dying on the battlefield at Agincourt. As master of game for his cousin Henry IV, in the Prologue Edward dedicates his book to Henry's son, Henry, prince of Wales. Edward wrote *The Master of Game* in 1406–13. It survives in some twenty-five manuscripts and is a translation and expansion of the late fourteenth-century *Livre de chasse* by Gaston de Foix (Gaston Phoebus).

Primary documents and further reading

Berners, J. (1964) *Boke of Huntyng*, ed. G. Tilander. Karlshamn: E. G. Johanssons.

Cummins, J. (1988) *The Hound and the Hawk: The Art of Medieval Hunting*. London: Weidenfeld and Nicolson.

Marvin, W. P. (1999) "Slaughter and Romance: Hunting Reserves in Late Medieval England." In B. A. Hanawalt and D. Wallace (eds.) *Medieval Crime and Social Control*. Minneapolis: University of Minnesota Press, 224–52.

Rooney, A. (1993) *Hunting in Middle English Literature*. Woodbridge, Suffolk: Boydell.

Twiti, W. (1977) *The Art of Hunting, 1327*, ed. B. Danielsson. Stockholm: Almqvist and Wiksell.

Warner, Sir George (ed.) (1912) *Queen Mary's Psalter: Miniatures and Drawings by an English Artist of the 14th Century*. London: British Museum.

Edward, Second Duke of York. British Library MS Cotton Vespasian B.xii. In W. A. Baillie-Groham and F. Baillie-Groham (eds.) (1904) *The Master of Game: The Oldest English Book on Hunting*. London: Ballantyne, Hanson, 93–111 (selections).
Language: English (Southeast Midland)
Manuscript date: ca. 1420

How the assemble that men clepen gaderyng shuld be makyd both wynter and somyre aftir the gise of biyonde the see.

The assemble that men clepyn *gaderyng* shuld be makyd in this manere. The nyght bifore that the lord or the maystir of the game wil go to wode, he must make come bifore hym alle the hunters, her helpes, the gromes, and the pages, and shuld assigne to everych one of hem her questes[1] in a certayn place, and soner the oon fro the other, and the oon shuld not come upon the quest of that other ne do hym non noyaunce ne lett. And everichon shuld quest in her best wise in the maner that I have said and shuld assigne hem the place where the gaderyng shuld be makyd at moost eese of hem alle and at nyghest of her questes and the place where the gaderyng shuld be makyd in a faire mede wel grene where faire trees welex[2] alle about, the on f[a]r from that other, and a clere wel or some rennyng breke besides. And it is cleped *gaderyng* bicause that alle men and houndes for the huntyng gadren hem thider, for thei that goon in the quest shuld alle come agen in a certayn place that I have spoke of, and also thci that partyn from home and alle the officers that parten from home shuld bryng thider al that hem neden, overychon in his office wel and plenteuously, and shuld lay the towailes and boordclothes al about upon the grene gras and sette divers metis upon a grete plater after the lordis pouere. And some shuld ete sittyng and some standynge, some lenyng upon hcr clbowes, some shuld drynk and some laugh, some jangle, some borde, som play, and shortly do alle manere disportis of gladnesse. And whan men shuld be sette at tables or thei ete, than shuld come the lynmers,[3] and her gromes with the lymers, the whiche han be in the quest, and evrychon shal say his report to the lord of that thei han don and yfounde, and lay the fumes[4] bifore the lord, he that hath eny founde, and than the lord or the maistere of the huntyng, bi the counsel of hem alle, shall chese to the whiche thei wil mene[5] and renne to, and which shalle be the grettest hert and hiest deer. And whan thei shul have ete, the lord shal devyse where the relaies shal go and other thing whiche y shal say more playnly, and than every mane spede hym to his place, and thei also hast hem that shullen go to the fyndeng.

---

[1]   Particular searchings after game.
[2]   grow.
[3]   Limers were leashed tracking dogs, limerers their handlers.
[4]   excrements.
[5]   move.

How the hert shuld be mevyd with the lymer and ronne to and slayn wth strengthe.

...[F]or to wit whedir it be the hunted deer or noon, the tokenys ben rehersid bifore, and he hath be so wel ronne to and enchased and entreved,[6] and so oft relayed and vannlaied to,[7] and that he seeth that bi betyng up the ryvers or brokes, nor foillyng hem doun, ne goyng soile,[8] nor rusyng to or fro upon hymself, whiche is to say in his owne fues,[9] ne may not helpe hym, than turne he his lede and standeth at a bay, and than, as fere as it may be herd, every man draweth thider, and the knowyng therof is that what hunter that commeth first and so hunter aftir other, as thei halowe all togedir and blowen a moot and rechace[10] alle at onys, and that do thei never but whan he is at a bay, or whan a bay is made for the houndes aftir he is dede whan that thei shuld be rewardid or enquerreyde.[11] And whan the hunters that holden relaies ben ther either that thei ben nye the abay, thei shuld pulle of the couples fro the houndes nekys and late hem draweth thider, and the hunters breke[12] the abaye as oft as the myght for two causes, that oon lest the hert houndes if he stonde and rest longe in a place, another that the relaies that stondeth fer may come with her houndes the whiles he is alyve and be at his ende, and it is to wete that if eny of the hunters have be eny tyme, while the deer hath be ronne to, out of heryng of hounde and horn, he shuld have blowe the forloyne[13] but if he were in a par[k]e, for ther shuld it never be iblowe. And who so that first herd hym soo blow shulde blowe agein to hym the perfit[14] if it so be that he were in the ryghtes and ellis not, for bi that he be brought to redynesse and comfort that er ne wist where the game ne noon of his felawes were. And it so is that hym thought that the abay hath lastid long ynowe, than shuld who so were most maistir ther bidde some of the hunters go spay[15] hym even behynde the shulder forthward to the hert. But the hunter shuld lat slippe the rope while he stood on his fete and lat the lymer go to, for bi ryght the lymer ne

---

[6]   discovered.
[7]   Chased by relays of dogs, and dogs held in reserve and released before the other dogs have passed.
[8]   Traveling downstream to hide the scent, and wallowing in soil.
[9]   tracks.
[10]   A single note, and three short notes followed by a long note.
[11]   compensated.
[12]   I.e., break up.
[13]   A distinct set of notes.
[14]   A distinct set of notes to signal that the hunter is on the right path of the prey.
[15]   stab.

shuld never out of the roope thougthe he shippe[16] fro never so fer. And
whan the deer is boun and lieth on that oon syde, that at herst[17] is tyme for
to blow the deer, for it shuld never be iblowe at the hert huntyng to the
deer be on that on side. And than shuld the hundes ben coupled up and,
fast as a man may, oon if the beerners[18] shuld encore hym, that is to say
turne his hornes to the erthward and the throte upward and slitte the skynn
of the throte alenonlong the neke and kytte labelles[19] on either side of the
skyn, which shuld honge fulle upon the hede, for this longeth to an herte
slayne with strengthe and ellis nought. And than shuld the hunter flene
doun the skynne as fer as he may and than with a trenchour[20] kitte as thik
as he can the flesshe doun to the nek bone and, this doon, every man
stonde abrode[21] and blowe the deth and make a short [a]bay for to reward
the houndes. And every man have a smal rodde in his honde to holde the
houndes that thei shuld the better abay, and every blowe the deeth that
blowe may . . .

Of the ordinaunce of the maner of hundyng whan the kyng wil hunt in foreste
or in parke for the herte with bowes, grey-houndes, and stable.[22]
The maister of the game shuld be accorded with the maistir forster or
parker wheder that it be where the kyng shal huntt soche a day and, if the
sette[23] be wide, the forsaid forster or parker shuld warne the shiref of the
shire that the huntyng shuld be inne for to ordeyne stable suffisaunt and
cartis eke for to brynge the deer that shuld be slayn to the place where as
quyrreis[24] at huntyngges have ben acustomed to be, and than he shuld
warne the hunters and feutreres[25] whider thei shuld commen. And the
forster shuld have men redely there to mete with hem that the gon no
ferther ne strangle[26] not about for drede lest thei fray[27] the game or the

---

[16]   be let slip.
[17]   for the first time.
[18]   Attendants in charge of hounds.
[19]   small flaps.
[20]   knife.
[21]   apart.
[22]   Greyhounds were several breeds of dogs used for hunting; stable were stations of hunters and
hounds around the park for relaying after the prey and to serve as a perimeter to turn it back.
[23]   Area in a forest around which stables or stations of men and hounds have been placed.
[24]   Curées, the rituals of giving the hounds their rewards, named after the parts of the deer
given to the dogs and the collection of game killed.
[25]   Handlers who care for and manage the hounds.
[26]   straggle.
[27]   frighten.

kyng come. And if the huntyng shal be in a park, alle men shuld abide atte park gate sauf the stable that oweth to be sette or the kyng come, and thei shuld be sett bi the parkers or forsteres. And the mornyng erly the mayster of the game shuld be at wode to se that alle be redy, and he or his lieuetenaunte or which of the hunters that hym lust, oweth to sette the greihound and ho so be tesours[28] to the kyng or to the quene or to ther lesshes.[29] As oft as eny hert commeth, he shal, whan he passed, blow a moot and rechace, and lette hem after to teise it forth. And if it be a stag, he shalle late passe as I saide and relie[30] for to make the fowtreres avised what commeth out. And to lasse deer ne shud no wight renne . . . And than the maister forstere or parker oweth to shewe hym the kyngges stond and if the kyng wold stonde with his bowe and where al the remenaunt of the bowes shuld stond, and the yemen for the kynges bowe owen to be ther to kepe and make the kyngges stondyng and abide ther without noyse to the kyng come. And the gromys that kepyn the kynges dogges and chastised greihoundes[31] shuld be ther with hym for thei longen to the yemens office. And also the mayster of the game shuld be enfourmed by the forster or parker what game the kyng fyndeth with inne the sette and, whan alle this is do, than shuld the maister of the game worthe[32] upon hors and mete with the kyng and brynge hym to his stondyng and telle hym what game is with inne the sett and how the greihoundes ben sett and eke the stable and also to telle hym wheder he be bettir to stond with his bow or with the greihoundes, for it is wit that the les[33] of his chamber and of the quenes shuld be best sette. And ther twey fewtreres owyn to make faire logges of grene bowes at her trestes[34] for to kepe the kyng and the quene and the ladies and gentil women and eke the greyhoundes fro the sonne and fro evil wedir. And whan the kyng is at his stondyng or at his trist, wheder that hym be levir, and that the maister of his game or his lieftenaunt have sette the bowys and assigned who shal lede the quene to hur trist, than he shal blow three long moote to the uncouplyng . . . And than shuld the eirere[35] uncou-ple his houndes and blow three moot, and seke forth, saying loude and longely, "Ho sto, ho sto, moun amy, ho sto." And if thei drawe fer from

[28]   Small dogs that tease out game.
[29]   Sets of three hounds.
[30]   rally.
[31]   Trained hounds.
[32]   mount.
[33]   A set of three hounds.
[34]   Stations where hunters await the game.
[35]   Harrier, a handler of smaller dogs also for hunting deer.

hym rebelly,[36] he shuld say to hem in that caas as whan he seketh for the
hare . . . [A]nd if it be an hert and eny of the hert houndes mete withal, thei
shul blow a moot and rechase, and relay and go forthe therwith, al rechasyng
among and, if it come to bowes or to greihoundes and be dede, he shuld
blow the deeth whan he is commen thider and reward his houndes a litel
and couple hem up and go agein to his place . . . And whan the rascaile[37] is
thus voided, than ben the hert houndes uncoupled, and thei fynde the grete
olde wily deer that wil not lightly voide, and thei enchace hem wel and
lustely, and make hem voide both to bowes and to grei-houndes so that
thei do here devoire[38] at fulle. And alle the while that the huntyng lasteth
shal cartis go about fro place to place to bryng the deer to the quyrre and
ther lay it on a rewe, all the hedes oo way and every deres fete to other bak
And the hertes shuld be laide on a rowe or two or three after that thei be
many or fewe, and the rascaile in the same wise bi hemself, and thei shuld
kepe that no man come with inne the quyrre to the kyng come, save the
maister of the game. And whan the coverte is wele sought and voided that
was ther inne, than shuld the maister of the game come to the kyng to wit
if he will eny more hunt . . . And if the kyng wil hunt no more, than shuld
the maister of his game, if the kyng wil not blow, blow a moot and strake[39]
with a mote in the myddel, and the sergeaunt or who so bloweth next hym,
ne non man ellis, shuld blow the first moot – the myddel – and so every
man as oft as hym lust to strake if thei have had that thei hunted fore, and
ellis the myddel moot shuld not be blowe save of hym that blowethe next
the maister, and therbi may a man wit as thei here men strake homward
wher thei han wel-spedde or none. And this maner of strakyng shuld serve
in wise as I have rehersed for alle huntynges save whan the hert is slayn with
strength. And whan the mote is blow and strake, than shuld the maister of
the game lede the kyng to the quirre and shewe it hym, and no man as is
said aboven shuld come with inne it but every man with out it. And than
shuld the kyng telle the maister of the game what dere he wold were then[40]
and to whom and, if the kyng list abide, he may. Natheless, he is wouned[41]
whan that he thus hath don to go home.

36   rebelliously.
37   Younger deer or other animal that is not the principal object of the chase.
38   duty.
39   A distinct set of notes.
40   thence, i.e., given.
41   accustomed.

Pageants

As the growing quantity of records in the *Records of Early English Drama* series attests, medieval moralities and cycle plays were not only the occasion for many different kinds of play but were also economically significant enterprises. Morality plays often required large place and scaffold structures, costuming, and sometimes large casts while, most notably, town guilds and other civic and religious bodies created elaborate wagons, sets, props, and costumes for the enormous cycles staged in the streets of cities and villages.

The majority of the records that survive concerning medieval drama are accounts for expenses and income generated from the more formal annual plays and the sporadic performances of indoor and street theater of many kinds. Many are guild ordinances (see "Guilds," p. 155). In York the municipal authorities and the guilds collaborated for the prestige of the city and the individual crafts and trades involved. The plays were quite a financial burden for guilds, and negotiations and adjustments of costs between the town council and the guilds, and among the guilds themselves, are a prominent part of the records.

Primary documents and further reading

Beadle, R. (ed.) (1994) *The Cambridge Companion to Medieval English Theatre.* Cambridge: Cambridge University Press.

Beckwith, S. (2001) *Signifying God: Social Relation and Symbolic Act in the York Corpus Christi Plays.* Chicago, IL: University of Chicago Press.

Centre for Research in Early English Drama. *Records of Early English Drama (REED).* Toronto: University of Toronto Press.

Sponsler, C. (1997) *Drama and Resistance: Bodies, Goods, and Theatricality in Late Medieval England.* Minneapolis: University of Minnesota Press.

Swanson, H. (1989) *Medieval Artisans: An Urban Class in Late Medieval England.* Oxford: Blackwell.

A/Y Memorandum Book, fols. 19v, 187v–188r, 60v, 247r–247v. In A. F. Johnston and M. Rogerson (eds. and trans.) (1979) *Records of Early English Drama: York*, 2 vols. Toronto: University of Toronto Press, II: 697–724 (selections).
Language: French and Latin
Manuscript date: 1399–1422

1399

To the honourable men, the mayor, and aldermen of the city of York, the commons of the same city beg that, inasmuch as they incur great expense and costs in connection with the pageants and plays of Corpus Christi day,[1] the which cannot be played or performed on the same day as they ought to be because the aforesaid pageants are played in so many places at considerable hardship and deprivation to the said commons and strangers who have travelled to the said city on the same day for the same purpose, that it please you to consider that the said pageants are maintained and supported by the commons and the craftsmen of the same city in honour and reverence of our Lord Jesus Christ and for the glory and benefit of the same city, that you decree that the aforesaid pageants be played in the places to which they were limited and assigned by you and by the aforesaid commons previously, the which places are annexed to this bill in a schedule, or in other places from year to year, according to the disposition and will of the mayor and the council of the chamber, and that anyone who acts in contravention of the aforesaid ordinances and regulations shall incur a fine of forty shillings to be paid to the council chamber of the said city, and that if any of the aforesaid pageants be delayed or held back through fault or negligence on the part of the players, that they shall incur a penalty of six shillings, eight pence to the same chamber. And they (the commons) beg that these aforesaid matters be performed, or otherwise the said play shall not be played by the aforesaid commons. And they (the commons) ask these things for the sake of God and as a work of charity for the benefit of the said commons and of the strangers who have travelled to the said city for the honour [of] God and the promotion of charity among the same commons.

Places where the play of Corpus Christi will have been played: first at the gates of Holy Trinity in Micklegate; second at Robert Harpham's door; third at John de Gyseburne's door; fourth at Skeldergate and North Street; fifth at the end of Coney Street opposite the Castlegate; sixth at the end of Jubbergate; seventh [at] Henry Wyman's door in Coney Street; eighth at the end of Coney Street next to the Common Hall; ninth at Adam del Brigg's door; tenth at the gates of the Minster of Blessed Peter; eleventh at the end of Girdlergate in Petergate; twelfth on the Pavement.

And it has been ordained that the banners of the play with the arms of the city be delivered by the mayor on the eve of Corpus Christi to be set in the places where the play of the pageants will be, and that each year on the day after Corpus Christi, the banners be returned to the chamber to the hands of the mayor and chamberlains of the city and kept there for the entire year following, under penalty of six shillings, eight pence to be paid to the needs of the commons by anyone who shall have kept the banners beyond the next day and shall not have given them up in the manner which is stated.

---

[1]   The first Thursday after Trinity Sunday, i.e., during the last week in May or first week in June.

June 7, 1417

[T]he mayor, the honourable men, and the whole said commons, by their unanimous consent and assent, order [that] all those who receive money for scaffolds, which they may build in the aforesaid places before their doors on public property at the aforesaid sites, from those sitting on them shall pay the third penny of the money so received to the chamberlains of the city to be applied to the use of the same commons. And if they have refused to pay or agree upon a third penny of this kind or other monies with the chamber decently, that then the play be transferred to other places at the will and disposition of the mayor holding office at the time and of the council of the chamber of the city. No one spoke against this kind of ordinance except only a few holders of scaffolds in Micklegate . . .

And, indeed, because of the closeness of the said feast of Corpus Christi and the shortness of time, the said matter was not able to be committed to the aforesaid execution fully. Therefore, those assembled in the chamber of the council on the twelfth day of June in the abovesaid year of the lord and the king, considering that it would be improper and not to the profit of the commons that the said play be performed in the same certain places and in no other yearly, since everyone bear his charge towards the upholding of this play according to his estate, it was therefore unanimously ordained that for the benefit of the commons the places for the performance of the aforesaid play would be changed unless those before whose places the play used to be performed have paid whatever was enjoined yearly to the commons for having this, his individual profit, thus. And it was ordained that in all the years following while this play is played, it must be played before the doors and holdings of those who have paid better and more generously to the chamber and who have been willing to do more for the benefit of the whole commons for having this play there, not giving favour to anyone for his individual benefit but rather that the public utility of the whole of the commons of York ought to be considered. And the abovesaid reverend gentleman John Moreton, in the matter of his buildings, submitted himself completely to the disposition and ruling of the mayor and the council of the chamber as to how much he should pay towards the abovesaid play for having the play before the gate of his house in the quarter of Micklegate and at other buildings of his in the city.

1417–1418

There follows the agreement of the saucemakers and sellers of Paris candles.

And because a serious complaint had been made here in the council chamber by the saucemakers, craftsmen of the city, namely, by those whom we commonly call *salsemakers*, that although by the hitherto usual custom the members of the saucemakers' craft as well as all candlemakers outside the flesh shambles who used to sell Paris candles in their houses and windows, have sustained that pageant in the feast and play of Corpus Christi in this city, both in its costs and its expenses, in which it is shown that Judas Iscariot hung himself and cried out in the midst; further, although the skinners and other craftsmen of this city of York in great number, who are not saucemakers, make and presume to sell, through themselves and their wives, Paris candles in their homes and windows; nevertheless, they, having been asked, refuse to be contributors to the support of the said pageant. And unless a remedy be quite speedily imposed so that from now on they be contributors of this kind with the saucemakers, the saucemakers them selves will be unable to support that pageant any longer. Wherefore, in the year of our Lord 1417 and in the fifth year of the reign of King Henry the sixth after the conquest of England, it was decided by the mayor, William Bowes,[2] and the council of the chamber, that each and every craftsman of the city, of whatever kind they be, who are not butchers or wives of butchers and who, through themselves or through their wives, sell Paris candles by retail within the city of York and the suburbs of the same, shall from now on contribute every third penny along with the saucemakers of this city to maintaining the aforesaid pageant in the feast and play of Corpus Christi. Afterwards, when John Moreton was mayor,[3] the aforesaid ordinance notwithstanding, it was agreed between the Saucemakers and makers of Paris candles that anyone making or selling such Paris candles would pay two pence per annum for the presentations of the aforesaid play and no more, with the exception of butchers or their wives, as mentioned previously.

January 31, 1422

He who is ignorant of nothing knows, and the whole people lament, that the play on the day of Corpus Christi in this city, the institution of which was made of old for the important cause of devotion and for the extirpation of vice and the reformation of customs, alas, is impeded more than usual because of the multitude of pageants, and unless a better and more speedy device be provided, it is to be feared that it will be impeded much further in a very brief passage of time. And the craftsmen of the painters, stainers, pinners, and latteners[4] of the aforesaid city, formerly appointed separately to

[2] Mayor 1417, 1418.
[3] Mayor 1418
[4] Makers of and workers in latten, brass, and similar yellow-colored mixed metals.

two pageants which must be performed in the aforesaid play, viz., one on the stretching out and nailing of Christ on the cross, and the other, indeed, on the raising up of the crucified upon the mount, knowing that the matter of both pageants could be shown together in one pageant for the shortening of the play rather profitably for the people hearing the holy words of the players, consented for themselves and their other colleagues in the future that one of their pageants should be left out from now on and the other maintained, following what the mayor and the council of the chamber wished to arrange. And upon this business the searchers and craftsmen of the aforesaid crafts came before Richard Russell, the mayor of York,[5] the aldermen, and other honourable men in the council chamber situated here on Ouse Bridge on the last day of January in the ninth year of the reign of King Henry the fifth after the conquest of England and presented to them their desire and intention as stated above . . . Wherefore, the aforesaid mayor, aldermen, and honourable men, receiving this kindly and commending the aforesaid craftsmen for their laudable proposal, ordered and ordained, on their own counsel and that of all the aforesaid craftsmen, that from this day forward the pageant of the painters and stainers should be thoroughly removed from the aforesaid play, and that the craftsmen of the pinners and latteners should take upon themselves the burden of performing in their pageant the matter of the speeches, which were previously performed in their pageant and in the pageant of the painters and stainers, and that the painters and stainers each year should collect among themselves from the men of their craft five shillings sterling yearly and pay them yearly to those who are the masters of the pageant of the pinners and latteners [at the time], yearly on the eve of Corpus Christi. And if at any time they default in this payment, then they wish and agree that they and all their successors be distrained and strictly compelled in their homes and places of habitation or elsewhere, where they can be better and [more easily] distrained by the mayor and those who are chamberlains of this city at the time, to pay forty shillings of good English money to those who were masters of the pageant of the pinners and latteners at the time, on the next Sunday following the said feast without further delay. And that the punishments levied in this case shall remain in their power until satisfaction has been made fully to the aforesaid pageant masters concerning the aforesaid forty shillings together with the costs and expenses borne in their recovery, thus always, so that he who is mayor at the time may receive and have one half of the aforesaid

---

[5]   Mayor 1421, 1430.

forty shillings for the use of the commons, and those who shall have been pageant masters of the pinners and latteners at the time shall have the other half for the use and maintenance of their said pageant. For making which payments well and faithfully, indeed, in the manner and form written above, and for holding to and fulfilling the present ordinance in everything, the aforesaid . . . [guildsmen] for their part pledge themselves and their successors of their crafts, provided only that the said craftsmen of the painters and stainers do not meddle in the pageant of the pinners or in their accounts hereafter in any way.

Processions

London quickly received news of Henry V's October 25, 1415, victory at Agincourt. Three days later, on October 28, the newly elected mayor, Nicholas Wotton, and many of London's citizens processed on foot to Westminster to give thanks to God and praise for Henry before the queen and lords of the realm. In the month before the king arrived back in London on Saturday, November 23 (via Calais), the city prepared elaborate architectural sceneries, *tableaux vivants*, and other acts. Combined royal and civic ceremonies were common in the later Middle Ages, and this royal entry is in particular similar to Henry VI's entry into Paris in 1431 and his return to London in 1432.

For information on Agincourt and *Gesta Henrici Quinti*, see "Battle of Agincourt," p. 46.

Primary documents and further reading

Brie, F. W. D. (ed.) (1960) [1906, 1908] *The Brut, or the Chronicle of England*, 2 vols. EETS, o.s. 131, 136. London: Oxford University Press.
Curry, A. (ed.) (2000) *The Battle of Agincourt: Sources and Interpretations*. Woodbridge, Suffolk: Boydell.
DeVries, D. N. (1996) "And Away Go Troubles Down the Drain: Late Medieval London and the Poetics of Urban Renewal." *Exemplaria* 8: 401–18.
Fabyan, R. (1811) *The New Chronicles of England and of France*, ed. H. Ellis. London: Rivington et al.
Kingsford, C. L. (ed.) (1905) *Chronicles of London*. Oxford: Clarendon Press.
Kipling, G. (ed.) (1990) *The Receyt of Ladie Kateryne*. EETS, o.s. 296. Oxford: Oxford University Press.
—— (1998) *Enter the King: Theatre, Liturgy, and Ritual in the Medieval Civic Triumph*. Oxford: Clarendon Press.

Strohm, P. (1998) *England's Empty Throne: Usurpation and the Language of Legiti-mation, 1399–1422*. New Haven, CT: Yale University Press.
Walsingham, T. (1937) *The St. Albans Chronicle, 1406–1420*, ed. V. H. Galbraith. Oxford: Clarendon Press.
Withington, R. (1963) [1918, 1920] *English Pageantry: An Historical Outline*, 2 vols. New York: Blom.

British Library MS Cotton Julius E. iv, fols. 120v–122r. In F. Taylor and J. S. Roskell (eds. and trans.) (1975) *Gesta Henrici Quinti (The Deeds of Henry the Fifth)*. Oxford: Clarendon Press, 101–13.
Language: Latin
Manuscript date: 1416–17

[H]aving taken a day's rest in the port [of Dover], the king resumed his journey by way of the sacred thresholds of Canterbury Cathedral and the church of St. Augustine to his manor of Eltham, it being his intention to honour his city of London on the following Saturday with his personal presence. And the citizens, having heard the greatly longed-for, nay indeed most joyful, news of his arrival, had in the meantime made ready themselves and their city, as far as the time available allowed, for the reception of the most loving and most beloved prince whom God of his mercy had so gloriously and marvellously brought back home in triumph from a rebellious and stubborn people. And as soon as it was light on that eagerly awaited Saturday,[1] the citizens went out to meet the king as far as the heights of Blackheath, that is, the mayor and the twenty-four aldermen in scarlet and other citizens of lower degree in red gowns with parti-coloured hoods of red and white to the number of about twenty thousand on horses. All of them, according to their crafts, wore some particular richly fashioned badge, which conspicuously distinguished the crafts one from another. And when, about ten o'clock, the king came through their midst and the citizens had given to God glory and honour, and to the king congratulations and thanks for the victory he had gained and for his efforts on behalf of the common weal, the citizens hastened on ahead towards the city, and the king followed with his own, though only quite modest, retinue.

And now to let my pen interpose amid these glorious deeds, some account of what the city and so many of its noble citizens had done to express its praise and to embellish itself. When the tower at the entrance to the bridge was reached, there was seen placed high on top of it and representing as it

---

[1]   November 23.

were the entrance into the city's jurisdiction, an image of a giant of aston-
ishing size who, looking down upon the king's face, held like a champion a
great axe in his right hand and like a warder the keys of the city hanging
from a baton in his left. At his right side stood a figure of a woman, not
much smaller in size, wearing a scarlet mantle and adornments appropriate
to her sex, and they were like a man and his wife, who in their richest attire
were bent upon seeing the eagerly awaited face of their lord and welcoming
him with abundant praise. And, all around them, projecting from the ramparts, staffs bearing the royal arms and trumpets, clarions, and horns ringing
out in multiple harmony embellished the tower, and the face of it bore this
choice and appropriate legend inscribed on the wall: *Civitas Regis Justicie.*[2]

And, proceeding farther as far as the little drawbridge, in front of this on
each side there was found a lofty pillar resembling a turret which, constructed
of timberwork with no less skill than artistry, was covered with linen cloth
painted the colour of white marble and green jasper as if made of stones
squared and dressed by the handiwork of masons. And the top of the pillar
to the right bore the figure of an antelope, standing erect, with a shield of
the royal arms resplendent hanging from its neck, and in its extended right
forefoot it held a royal sceptre. And the top of the other pillar supported
the figure of a lion, also standing erect, which in the claws of its right paw
held aloft a staff with a royal standard unfurled. And over the foot of the
bridge and spanning the route had been raised a tower, constructed and
painted like the said pillars, and half-way up it, in a canopied niche richly
fashioned, there stood a most beautiful statue of St. George in armour save
for his head, which was adorned with laurel studded with gems sparking like
precious stones, and behind the statue was a crimson tapestry all aglow with
his heraldic arms on a large number of shields. And to its right hung his
triumphal helm and to its left a shield of his arms of matching size. With his
right hand he held the hilt of the sword with which he was girded and with
his left a scroll which extended over the ramparts, containing these words:
Soli deo honor et gloria.[3] And the tower was distinguished by this prophetic
message of congratulation on the front: *Fluminis impetus letificat civitatem
dei,*[4] and at the top it was embellished by spears bearing the royal arms
unfurled, standing above the canopies and the ramparts. And in a house
next to and behind the tower were innumerable boys representing the

[2] "City of the Just King."
[3] "Honour and glory to God alone," 1 Timothy 17.
[4] "The stream of the river maketh the city of God joyful," Psalms 45.5.

hierarchy of angels, clad in pure white, their faces glowing with gold, their wings gleaming, and their youthful locks entwined with costly sprays of laurel, who, at the king's approach, sang together in sweetly sounding chant accompanied by organs, following their texts, this angelic anthem: [*Benedictus qui venit in nomine Domini*].[5]

And when, further on, the tower of the conduit in Cornhill was reached, that tower was found to be covered over with crimson cloth stretched out like a tent on staffs wrapped in similar cloth. Lower down, in four prominent places, the arms of St. George, St. Edward, St. Edmund, and of England encircled the middle of the tower with, in between them, escutcheons of the royal arms, amongst which was set this legend of pious import: *Quoniam Rex sperat in domino et in misericordia altissimi non commovebitur.*[6] And higher up on the ramparts and serving for their adornment were the arms of the royal house borne aloft on staffs. And under an awning was a company of prophets with venerable white hair in tunicles and golden copes, their heads wrapped and turbaned with gold and crimson, who, when the king came by, released in a great flock, as an acceptable sacrifice to God for the victory he had conferred, sparrows and other tiny birds, of which some descended on to the king's breast, some settled upon his shoulders, and some circled around in twisting flight. And the prophets sang in sweetly sounding chant, following their texts, this psalm of approbation: *Cantate domino canticum novum, Alleluia. Quia miribilia fecit, Alleluia. Salvavit, etc.*[7]

From there they proceeded to the tower of the conduit at the entrance to Cheapside which, to make it look like a building, had had spread over it a green cover strewn and inwoven with escutcheons of the city's arms in gay profusion on poles draped in the same colour. And there adorned the tower higher up on the ramparts, staffs with coats of arms, borne aloft as elsewhere, and the middle of it, all round . . . And under an awning were men of venerable old age in the garb and of the number of the apostles, having the names of the twelve apostles written in front of them, together with twelve kings of the English succession, martyrs and confessors, girt about the loins with golden belts with sceptres in their hands, crowns upon their heads, and their emblems of sanctity plain to see, who, at the kings' approach, in perfect time and in sweetly sounding chant, following their texts, sang the

---

[5]   "Blessed is he that cometh in the name of the Lord."
[6]   "For the king hopeth in the Lord and, through the mercy of the most high, he shall not be moved," Psalms 20.8.
[7]   "Sing ye to the Lord a new canticle because he hath done wonderful things . . . The Lord hath made known his salvation, etc.," Psalms 97.

psalm [*Salvasti enim nos de affligentibus nos, et odientes nos confudisti*].[8] And they delivered to him round leaves of silver intermingled with wafers of bread, equally thin and of the same size and shape, and wine from the pipes and spouts of the conduit, that they might receive him with bread and wine just as Melchizedek did Abraham when he returned with victory from the slaughter of the four kings.[9]

And when they had proceeded farther, to the cross in Cheapside, that cross was not to be seen. Instead, built round it was what resembled a very fine castle which, constructed of timberwork with no less ingenuity than decorative effect, was adorned with graceful towers, pillars, and ramparts in rich profusion, having on both sides of it, to a good height of almost a spear's length and a half, vaulted arches, one end of each of which had, with considerable skill, been made to rest on the castle itself, and, reaching out over the street, the other end rose up from among the adjacent buildings as if originally built when they had been, and under these arches, through a space that was wide enough and to spare, being as broad as a spear's length, people rode as if through two gateways. And there was written on the front of the gateways on each side: *Gloriosa dicta sunt de te, civitas dei.*[10] And the covering of the castle was of linen fabric painted in colours to look like white marble, and green and crimson jasper as if the whole work had been made by the art of masonry from squared and well-polished stones of great price. There adorned the top of the castle and a very high tower the arms of St. George with, on one side, the king's arms and, on the other, those of the emperor, borne aloft on spears, and the arms of members of the royal house and of the great nobles of the realm adorned the lower turrets. And from the middle of the castle there projected out towards the king a gatehouse, very fine indeed and no less ingeniously constructed, from which extended a wooden bridge with about fifteen steps, and it was of a fair width and waist-high from the ground, and the gatehouse, covered and elegantly furnished with hangings on the posts and pales on either side to enhance its appearance, was constructed elaborately and yet securely enough to prevent anyone from forcing a way in. Over this bridge there went out from the castle to meet the king a choir of most beautiful young maidens very chastely adorned in pure white raiment and virgin attire, singing together with timbrel and dance as if to another David coming from the

[8] "Thou hast saved us from them that afflict us, and hast put them to shame that hate us," Psalms 43.8.
[9] Genesis 14.18.
[10] "Glorious things are said of thee, O city of God," Psalms 86.3.

slaying of Goliath[11] (who might appropriately be represented by the arrogant French) this song of congratulation, following their texts: "Welcome Henry ye fifte, kynge of Englond and of Fraunce." And from the very top of the castle to the bottom, on the towers, ramparts, arches, and pillars, were innumerable boys like a host of archangels and angels, beautiful in heavenly splendour, in pure white raiment with gleaming wings, their youthful locks entwined with jewels and other resplendent and exquisite ornaments, and they let fall upon the king's head as he passed beneath golden coins and leaves of laurel, singing together in perfect time and in sweetly sounding chant accompanied by organs, to the honour of Almighty God and as a token of victory, this angelic hymn, following their texts: *Te deum laudamus, te dominum confitemur, etc.*[12]

And when, further on, they had come to the tower of the conduit in the way out from Cheapside towards St. Paul's, they saw encircling that tower about half-way up many canopied niches skilfully contrived, and in each one was a most exquisite young maiden like a statue decked out with emblems of chastity richly fashioned, and all of them, crowned with laurels and girt about with golden belts, held in their hands chalices of gold from which, with gentlest breath scarcely perceptible, they puffed out round leaves of gold upon the king's head as he passed by. And higher up the tower was covered by a canopy, sky-blue in colour with clouds inwoven, massed with great artistry. There adorned the very top of it the figure of an archangel seemingly made of the brightest gold and with other vivid colours resplendently intermingled, and the four poles on which the canopy was borne were themselves upheld by four angels of a design no less artistic. And underneath the canopy was enthroned a figure of majesty in the form of a sun and, emitting dazzling rays, it shone more brightly than all else. Around it, in heavenly splendour, archangels moved rhythmically together, psalming sweetly and accompanied by every kind of musical instrument, following their texts . . . And there adorned the ramparts of the tower . . . borne aloft on posts. And in order that that tower should with its legend seem to conclude, in the same strain as the preceding legends, the tributes of praise to the honour and glory not of men but of God, it presented to the gaze of those passing by this culmination of praise: *Deo gracias.*

And apart from the dense crowd of men standing still or hurrying along the streets, and the great number of those, men and women together, gazing from windows and openings however small along the route from

---

[11]   1 Samuel 18.6.
[12]   "You are God; we praise you, etc."

the bridge, so great was the throng of people in Cheapside from one end to the other that the horsemen were only just able, although not without difficulty, to ride through. And the upper rooms and windows on both sides were packed with some of the noblest ladies and womenfolk of the kingdom and men of honour and renown, who had assembled for this pleasing spectacle and who were so very becomingly and elegantly decked out in cloth of gold, fine linen, and scarlet, and other rich apparel of various kinds, that no one could recall there ever having previously been in London a greater assemblage or a more noble array.

Amid these public expressions of praise and the display made by the citizens however, the king himself, wearing a gown of purple, proceeded, not in exalted pride and with an imposing escort or impressively large retinue, but with an impassive countenance and at a dignified pace, and with only a few of the most trusted members of his household in attendance there following him, under a guard of knights, the dukes, counts, and marshal, his prisoners. Indeed, from his quiet demeanour, gentle pace, and sober progress, it might have been gathered that the king, silently pondering the matter in his heart, was rendering thanks and glory to God alone, not to man. And then, after he had visited the thresholds of the apostles Peter and Paul,[13] he departed to his palace of Westminster, the citizens escorting him.

Sumptuary

Church writers, national and local administrations, and interested observers of society regularly condemned their contemporaries' extravagant behavior and appearance. Manners, carriage, gestures, diet, drink, clothing, makeup, and hairstyles all formed a complex aggregation thought to be specific to particular estates, classes, genders, sexualities, and occupations (see "Feasts," p. 190). The pestilences of the later fourteenth century stimulated anxieties about social movement and personal transgressions, as evidenced in the legislation to control labor (see "Pestilence," p. 169, and "Ordinance and Statute of Laborers," p. 163). An additional sign of this concern may be found in national and local legislation to restrict how people spent their money on personal items.

The sumptuary legislation of 1363 followed closely the second outbreak of the pestilence. It was the third such general law passed during Edward III's reign (the previous two were in 1336 and 1337), and it was repealed in

---

[13]   At Westminster Abbey and St. Paul's Cathedral.

the following year. Nevertheless, various other attempts to institute laws occurred in the Lancastrian era, but it was not until 1463–4 that parliament passed another similar act, which was soon followed by two more in 1477 and 1483. Despite little evidence of enforcement, the laws signal attempts to compel visible signs of class distinctions, curb practices that were believed to have deleterious moral effects, and change people's spending habits, particularly to favor local industries during the Hundred Years' War.

Geoffrey de la Tour-Landry, in his instructions to his daughters, is characteristically very concerned about women's appearances, and his vituperative tone is also typical. The passage from *Dives and Pauper* is from chapter 13 on adultery, the subject of the seventh commandment. For introductions to Geoffrey's *Book* and *Dives and Pauper*, see "Marriage," p. 21.

Primary documents and further reading

Baldwin, F. E. (1926) *Sumptuary Legislation and Personal Regulation in England.* Baltimore, MD: Johns Hopkins University Press.
Hodges, L. F. (2000) *Chaucer and Costume: The Secular Pilgrims in the General Prologue.* Cambridge: D. S. Brewer.
Riley, H. T. (ed. and trans.) (1868) *Memorials of London and London Life in the XIIIth, XIVth, and XVth Centuries.* London: Longmans, Green.
Scattergood, J. (1987) "Fashion and Morality in the Late Middle Ages." In D. Williams (ed.) *England in the Fifteenth Century: Proceedings of the 1986 Harlaxton Symposium.* Woodbridge, Suffolk: Boydell. 255–72.
Strohm, P. (1992) *Hochon's Arrow: The Social Imagination of Fourteenth-Century Texts.* Princeton, NJ: Princeton University Press.

The Statutes of the Realm, vol. 1 (1810). London: Eyre and Strahan. 37 Edward 3, stat. 10, cc. 1–6, 380–2.
Language: Latin
Date: 1363

Item: for the outrageous and excessive apparel of diverse people against their estate and degree, to the great destruction and impoverishment of all the land, it is ordained that grooms, servants of lords, as well as those of mysteries and artificers, shall be served to eat and drink once a day of flesh or of fish, and the remnant of other victuals, as of milk, butter, and cheese, and other such victuals, according to their estate; and that they have clothes for their vesture, or hosing, whereof the whole cloth shall not exceed two marks, and that they wear no cloth of higher price of their buying nor otherwise, nor anything of gold nor of silver embroidered, enameled, nor of silk, nor anything pertaining to the said things; and their wives, daughters, and children of the same condition in their clothing and apparel, and they shall wear no veils passing twelve pence a veil.

Item: that people of handicraft and yeomen shall neither take nor wear cloth of a higher price for their vesture or hosing than within forty shillings the whole cloth by way of buying nor otherwise, nor stone, nor cloth of silk nor of silver, nor girdle, knife, button, ring, garter, nor ouche,[1] ribbon, chain, nor any such other things of gold or of silver, nor any manner of apparel embroidered, enameled, nor of silk in any way; and that their wives, daughters, and children be of the same condition in their vesture and apparel, and that they wear no veil of silk but only of yarn made within the realm, nor any manner of fur nor of budge but only lamb, coney, cat, and fox.

Item: that esquires and all manner of gentlemen under the estate of a knight who have not land or rent to the value of one hundred pounds a year shall not take nor wear cloth for their clothing or hose of a higher price than within the price of four and a half marks the whole cloth, by way of buying or otherwise, and that they wear no cloth of gold, nor silk, nor silver, nor any manner of clothing embroidered, ring, buttons, nor ouche of gold, ribbon, girdle, nor any other apparel, nor harness of gold nor of silver, nor anything of stone, nor any manner of fur; and that their wives, daughters, and children be of the same condition as to their vesture and apparel, without any turning up or purple; and that they wear no manner of apparel of gold, nor silver, nor of stone. But that esquires who have land or rent to the value of two hundred marks a year and above may take and wear cloths of the price of five marks the whole cloth, and cloth of silk and of silver, ribbon, girdle, and other apparel reasonably garnished of silver; and that their wives, daughters, and children may wear fur turned up of miniver, without ermine or lettice,[2] or any manner of stone but for their heads.

Item: that merchants, citizens, and burgesses, artificers, people of handicraft, as well within the city of London as elsewhere, who have clearly goods and chattels to the value of five hundred pounds, and their wives and children, may take and wear in the same manner as the esquires and gentlemen who have land and rent to the value of one hundred pounds a year; and that the same merchants, citizens, and burgesses, who have clearly goods and chattels to the value of one thousand pounds, and their wives and children, may take and wear in the same manner as esquires and gentlemen

---

[1]   A clasp, buckle, or brooch for holding together two sides of a garment.
[2]   A kind of light gray fur.

who have land and rent to the value of two hundred pounds a year; and no groom, yeoman, or servant of merchant, artificer, or handicraftmen shall wear otherwise in apparel than is above-ordained of yeomen of lords.

Item: that knights, who have land or rent within the value of two hundred pounds shall take and wear cloth of six marks the whole cloth for their vesture and of no higher price; and that they wear neither cloth of gold nor cloaks, mantle, nor gown furred with miniver nor of ermins, nor any apparel embroidered with stone, nor otherwise; and that their wives, daughters, and children be of the same condition, and that they wear no turning up of ermins, nor of lettices, nor any manner of stone but only for their heads; but that all knights and ladies, who have land or rent over the value of four hundred marks a year to the sum of one thousand pounds, shall wear at their pleasure, except ermins and lettices, and apparel of pearls and stone, but only for their heads.

Item: that clerks who have a degree in any church, cathedral, college, or schools, or clerk of the king, that have such estate that requires fur, shall do and use according to the constitution of the same, and all other clerks, who have two hundred marks of land per year, shall wear and do as knights of the same rent; and other clerks within the same rent shall wear as the esquires of one hundred pounds of rent; and that all those, knights as well as clerks, who by this ordinance may wear fur in winter in the same manner shall wear linure[3] in the summer.

Item: that carters, ploughmen, drivers of the plough, oxherds, cowherds, shepherds, swineherds, dairymen, and all other keepers of beasts, threshers of corn, and all manner of people of the estate of a groom attending to husbandry and other people that have not forty shillings of goods nor of chattels, shall not take nor wear any manner of cloth but blanket and russet, of wool, worth not more than twelve pence, and shall wear girdles of linen according to their estate; and that they come to eat and drink in the same manner that pertains to them and not excessively. And it is ordained that if any wear or do contrary to any of the points aforesaid, that he shall forfeit to the king all the apparel that he has so worn against the form of this ordinance.

Item: to the intent that this ordinance for the taking and wearing of cloths be maintained and kept in all points without blemish, it is ordained that all the makers of cloths within the realm, men as well as women, shall conform them to make their cloths according to the price limited by this

---

[3]   lawn.

ordinance, and that all the drapers shall buy and purvey their items according to the same price so that so great plenty of such cloths be made and set to sale in every city, borough, and merchant town, and elsewhere in the realm, that for default of such cloths the said ordinance be in no point broken; and to that shall the said clothmakers and drapers be constrained by any manner or way that seems best to the king and his council. And this ordinance of new apparel shall begin at Candlemas next coming.[4]

Offord, M. Y. (ed.) (1971) Geoffrey de la Tour Landry, *The Book of the Knight of the Tower*, trans. W. Caxton. EETS, s.s. 2. London: Oxford University Press, 70–3.
Language: English (Southeast Midland)
Book date: 1484

How a hooly bisshop reprysed and taught many ladyes.
I shalle telle yow how a hooly man late dide preche, and was a bisshop, a right good clerke. At his prechynge and sermon were many ladyes and damoisellys, of which som were dressid and clothed after the newe manere. The remenaunt of their heedes was lyke two hornes and their gownes made after the newe gyse. Wherof, the good holy man had merveyle and began to repreve them, gyvynge and rehercynge to fore them many a fair ensample, and told them how the deluge or gaderyng of waters in the dayes of Noe was bycause of the pryde and desguysynge of men and specially of wymmen that counterfeted them self of newe and dishonest rayments. And thenne when thenemye sawe their grete pryde and their desguysynge, he made them to falle in the fylthe of the stynkyng synne of lecherye, whiche thynge was so moche displesynge to God that he dyde made to rayne fourty dayes and fourty nyghtes withoute cessynge in so moche that the waters were above the erthe and surmounted by heyght of ten cubites upon the hyhest montayn. Thenne was all the world drowned and perysshed, and none abode on lyve sauf only Noe, his wyf, his thre sones, and his thre doughters. And alle this grete meschyef cam bycause of that synne. And thenne as the bisshop had shewed to them this fayte[5] and many other, he said that the wymmen that were so horned were like the snayle[s] that ben horned. He said more. "I doute,"[6] said he, "that betwyxt their hornes thenemye hath made his mancion and dwellynge. For as they take hooly water, they cast dounward theyr faces, and that maketh the devylle syttynge upon their

---

[4] February 2.
[5] action.
[6] believe.

heede by nature and strengthe of the hooly water." He tolde and reherced to them many merveyles in so moche that at the ende of his predicacion he made to be mowrnynge and full of thought, for he hadde repreved them so sore that they had so grete shame that they ne durst lyfte up their hedes and helde them mocked and diffamed of their vyce. And after, many of them caste awey their braunches and hornes, and held them lowe and went symply, for he saide that suche coyntyses,[7] and suche countre-faytyng, and suche wantonnesse were to compare to the copspyn[8] that maketh his nette to take the flyes. Ryght soo dothe the devylle by his temptacion the desguysyng in men and wymmen to the ende they may be enamoured one of other and for to take and brynge them to the delyte of lechery. He taketh them and byndeth them as the copspyn doth the flees in her nette, as a holy heremyte telleth in the booke of the faders of lyf, to whome was shewed by tonge as ye may fynde playnly in the said book.[9] And yet he saith that the coulpe[10] of the synne was in them that first tooke and brought up suche desguysynge, and that every good womman and wyse ought wel to drede the takynge and werynge of suche raymentes unto the tyme she seeth that every one comynly took and went in hem. For after the word of God, the first shall be the most blamed and the last shal syt on the hyhe syege.[11] The bisshop, that a good man, was sayd an ensample upon the fait of them that hasted them to be the fyrst in takynge and bryngynge up suche novelteees, and said thus.

How the yong ladyes were scorned and mocked of the olde and auncyent.
It befelle that many ladyes and damoysels were come at the weddyng of a maide. As they were goyng to ward the place where as the dyner sholde be, they found a passynge fowle wey within a medowe. Thenne said the yong ladye[s], "We shalle wel go thorugh this medowe and leve the hyhe waye." The auncyent and wyse said they shold go the hyhe way, for it was the best and more sure goynge and moost drye. The yonge ladyes, that ful were of their wylle, wolde not folowe them and thought they shold be bifore them at the said place. And soo they tooke their weye thorugh the medowe where were old cloodes[12] all roten. As they were upon them, they brake under theyr feet, and soo they felle in the myere and dyrte unto the knees,

---

[7]   vanities, fineries.
[8]   spider.
[9]   The thirteenth-century poem, *Vie des Peres* or *Vie des Anciens Peres*, a compilation of devout tales, some of which draw on the much earlier *Vitae Patrum*.
[10] culpability.
[11] seat.
[12] clothes.

and with grete peyne cam they oute ageyne and took the hyghe weye. They
made clene their hosen and gownes with theyr knyves the best they couthe.
So long they were in wasshyng of their hoses and gownes that they myght
not come to the begynnyng of the dyner. Every one demaunded and asked
after them, but no body couth tell of them. At the last they cam as the fyrst
mes or cours was eten, and after they had taken their refection and wel
dronken, they beganne to telle and recounte how they were falle in the
myre unto the knees to. "Ye," said thenne a good auncyent and wyse lady
that was come by the hyghe weye. "Ye wend to take the shortest way to
thende ye myght be the sonner and fyrst at the place and wold not folowe
us. Hit is wel bestowed. For I telle yow for certayne that some wene to
avaunce them self that hyndreth them, and suche one is that weneth to be
the first and formest that ofte fyndeth her the last of all." She gaf them
these two notables to thende they shold know their faute. For as saith the
said holy man, "Thus is hit of this worlde. They that first may have noveltees
of the world wene to doo wel and be therfore enhaunced and tofore other
ben holden and wysshed, but as for one that holdeth hit wel done, ther ben
ten that m[o]ken of hit. For suche one preyseth their doynge before them
that behynde their back putteth out his tonge, scorynynge and mockyn
them."

Yet of the same.
She holdeth her self the best welcome that firste bryngeth upon her ony
noveltees, but as the good and hooly man saith, "They that firste take suche
newe raymentis be lyke to the yong ladyes that fylle in the myere wherof
they were mocked by the wyse ladyes that tooke the best and ryght wey, for
men may not mocke them that kepe suche wey and that use their lyf after
reason and not after theyr owne wylle. I say not but that whan that manere
of newe raymentis is taken and comynly wered of every one and in every
towne, it may be thenne worne and taken, but yet the wyse woman shal leve
and forbere it yf she can. And suche wymmen shalle not be lyke ne compared
to them that fylle in the myere by cause they wold be first in the place, and
they were the last." Ther-fore, my faire doughters, hit is good that none
hast her not, but good is to holde the myddel estate. The lesse is the moost
certayne and seurest, but as now is a cursed and shrewed world for, yf
somme folysshe woman full of her wylle taketh and bryngeth upon her ony
noveltee and newe estate, every other one shalle soone saye to her lorde,
"Syre it is told to me that suche one hath suche a thynge that over faire is,
and that so wel becometh her, I pray yow good syre that I may have suche
one, for I am as good and as gentyll of blood. And, ye, as gentyl a man as

she and her lord ben and have as wel for to paye as she hath." And thus she shalle fynde soo many reasons that she shalle have her wylle or els ryote and noyse shalle all day be at home and never shalle be ther pees tylle she have her parte, be it right or wronge. She shalle not loke yf ony of hir neyghbours have that thynge that she wylle have. Also, she shalle not abyde till every one have it, but the hastlyest that she may, she shalle doo shape and make it, and forth-with shalle were it. It is merveyle of suche coyntyse and noveltees wherof the grete clerkes say that, seynge the men and wymmen so desguysed and takyng every day newe raiments, they doute that the world shalle perysshe as it dyd in tyme of Noe that the wymmen desguysed them and also the men, whiche displeysed God. And herupon I shalle reherce yow [a] merveil whiche a good lady dyde recounte to me in this same yere. She tolde and saide to me that she, with many other ladyes, were come to a feeste of Seynt Margrete, where as every yere was grete assemble made. There cam a lady moche coynt[13] and joly, and dyversly disguysed and arraid more than ony other there. And by cause of her straunge and newe array, everychone of them cam to beholde and loke on her, as it had be a wylde beest, for her clothyng and araye was different and no thyng lyke to theyr, and therfore she had wel her part beholdyng and lokyng. Thenne said the good ladyes to her, "My frende, telle ye us yf it please yow how ye name that aray that he have on youre heed?" She answerde and saide, "The galhows aray." "God bless us said the good lady, the name of hit is not faire, and I ne wote how suche aray may plese yow." The tydyng of this aray and of his name were borne al aboute hyghe and lowe, wherof every one s[c]orned and mocked her. And as mockyng and scornynge cam there she was to beholde and loke upon her, I dyde aske of the good lady the manere and facion of the same araye, and she tolde me the manere of it, but evylle I witheld it. But as ferre as I me remembre of it, hit was hyghe enlewed[14] with longe pynnes of sylver uppon her hede after the makynge and maner of a gybet or galhows, right straunge and merveylous to se. And in good feyth after that tyme, the yonge and folysshe lady that had that araye on her heede was ever mocked and scorned and nought set by. Here shal I leve to speke of the newe and desguysed ray-mentis and of the good bisshop that so repreved them that hadde and wered suche araye. And that dede shewe to them by ensamples and hooly scripture how that suche noveltees that specially wymmen took on them was token and signe of somme gret meschyef to come as is were, famyne, and pestylence.

---

13   well-dressed.
14   inlaid.

Glasgow University Library MS Hunterian 270, fols. 173r–173v. In P. H. Barnum (ed.) (1976, 1980) *Dives and Pauper*, 2 parts. EETS, o.s. 275, 280. Oxford: Oxford University Press, II: 90–2.
Language: English (Southwestern)
Manuscript date: ca. 1450

DIVES: Womanys aray steryt[15] mychil folc to lecherye. PAUPER: And though in cas the aray and the tyr[16] is nout to blamyn no mor than is hyr bewte to blamyn. Be comon cours of kende, bothin man and woman sekyn to ben onestlyche adyth aftir her stat and aftir the maner of the contre that thei dwellyn in, nout to temptyn folc to lecherye, ne for pride, ne for non other synne, but for honeste of mankende and to the worchepe of God, to wose lyknesse man and woman is mad, and he is our brothir. In dyvers contres ben divers maners of aray, but if thei don it for pryde, or to temptyn folc to lecherye, or for ony other synne, or that thei take on hem atyre that is not acardyng to hem – yf it be to costful, or to straunge in schap, or to wyde, or to syde,[17] not reulyd be reson – be it man be it woman, he synnyth wol grevouslyche in the syght of God, and namely tho men that clothin hem so schorte that man and woman may sen the forme and the schap of her pryve menbrys, whyche it is a schame to schewyn, and the syghte is gret cause of temptacioun and of wyckyd thoughtis. Sent Powil byddith that women schuldyn adyghtyn hem in honest aray with schamfastnesse and sobyrnesse, nout in broydyng of her heyre, nout in gold and in sylver, ne in perre,[18] ne in ovyrdon precious cloth, 1 Timothy 2.[19] And that same seith Sent Petyr in hys fyrste pystyl 3,[20] wher he byddith that men schul-dyn han her wyfys in worchepe and kepyn hem honestlyche. DIVES: Women these dayys arayyn hem wol mychil agenys the techyng of Petyr and Powyl, and therfor Y drede me that they synnyn wol grevously. PAUPER: Petir and Powyl defendedyn nout uttyrlyche swyche aray, but thei defendedyn women swyche aray to usyn in pryde or to provokyn folc to lecherye and to usyn swyche aray pasyng her astat, for we fyndyn that Sent Cecilie and many othir holy women wentyn adyth in clothis of gold and in ryche perre and weredyn the heyre undir that solempne atyr. Also, Petir and Powil seydyn tho wordis pryncipaly for tyme of preyere, as for

[15] stirs.
[16] attire.
[17] long.
[18] jewels.
[19] 1 Timothy 2.9–10.
[20] 1 Peter 3.3–5.

Lentyn, embyrdayys,[21] gangdayys,[22] Frydayys, vygilyys and in tyme of general processioun mad for nede. In swyche tyme man and woman schuldyn levyn al pompe and pryde in aray, for, as the glose seyth there, proud clothinge getyth no good of God and makyth folc to demyn omys, namely if it pase mesure and good manere. The principal intencion of Sent Powil ther he seith tho wordis is to enformyn men and women in preyere, for whom thei schul preyyn, why and how and wher thei schul preyyn, as seith the glose, and he enformyth hem to preyyn in lownesse withoutyn pompe of clothinge and of gret aray, for I am sekyr that the foule stynkyng pompe and pride of aray that is now usyd in this lond in al the thre partyes of the chyrche, that is to sey, in the defendourys and in the clergy and in the commonerys, wyl not bene unvengyd but it be sone amendyd be very repentaunce and forsakyng of this synne, for fro the heyest unto the loweste in every state and in every degre and neyhand in every persone is now aray passyng to[23] mannys body and wommans agens al reson and the lawe of God.

Tournaments

Tournaments were part of a knight's training for war, and they became the ritualistic occasion for demonstrations of military prowess and the development of male social status. More mock battles than jousts in lists, tournaments began to flourish in the twelfth century and tended more and more towards theatrical and elaborately decorated ceremonies as the centuries progressed. Descriptions of chivalric criteria and tournaments appear in legal, historical, instructional, biographical, and of course poetic texts. Often lavish in presentation, chivalric texts appealed to the seemingly unlimited taste for courtly ideals and the examination of violence in relation to these mores. The following excerpt adds to the tournament the complication of international alliances during the Hundred Years' War (see "Battle of Agincourt," p. 46).

Jean Froissart (ca. 1338–ca. 1410) wrote his *Chroniques* in several redactions from 1369 to after 1400; they contain information on the wars

[21]   Ember days, i.e., any of four groups of three prayer and fasting days (Wednesday, Friday, and Saturday) after Pentecost, the first Sunday in Lent, the feast of St. Lucy, and the feast of the Holy Cross.
[22]   Procession days, Rogation Days.
[23]   close to.

on the Continent as well as valuable narratives about Richard II (see "Jean Froissart, *Chroniques*," p. 151, for an image from it). He was a clerk of Queen Philippa of Hainault (d. 1369), wife of Edward III, and he spent several years in England, presenting Richard II with a book of love poems in 1395. Froissart's writings are more romantically inflected than other chroniclers, and his versions of his chronicles become more and more complimentary towards the French and critical of the English. His chivalric material in particular appealed to Sir John Bourchier, Lord Berners (ca. 1467–1533), a deputy of Calais who published English translations of Froissart's work in 1523 and 1525.

Primary documents and further reading

Barber, R. W. and J. R. V. Barker (1989) *Tournaments: Jousts, Chivalry, and Pageants in the Middle Ages*. Woodbridge, Suffolk: Boydell.
Bentley, S. (ed.) (1831) "Tournament between Lord Scales and the Bastard of Burgundy, A.D. 1467." *Excerpta Historica, or Illustrations of English History*. London: Richard Bentley, 171–212.
Charny, G. de (1996) *The Book of Chivalry of Geoffroi de Charni*, ed. and trans. R. W. Kaeuper and E. Kennedy. Philadelphia: University of Pennsylvania Press
Fradenburg, L. O. (1991) *City, Marriage, Tournament: Arts of Rule in Late Medieval Scotland*. Madison: University of Wisconsin Press.
Froissart, J. (1869–1975) *Chroniques de J. Froissart*, 15 vols., ed. S. Luce, G. Raynaud, and L. Mirot. Paris: Société de l'histoire de France.
Jones, T. (1994) *Chaucer's Knight: The Portrait of a Medieval Mercenary*, revd. edn. London: Methuen.
Kaeuper, R. W. (1999) *Chivalry and Violence in Medieval Europe*. Oxford: Oxford University Press.
Keen, M. H. (1984) *Chivalry*. New Haven, CT: Yale University Press.
——(1996) *Nobles, Knights, and Men-at-Arms in the Middle Ages*. London: Hambledon Press.
Marshal, W. (1891–1901) *L'Histoire de Guillaume le maréchal*, 3 vols., ed. P. Meyer. Paris: Librarie Renouard.

J. Froissart (1967) *The Chronicle*, trans. Sir John Bourchier, intro. W. P. Ker. New York: AMS Press, 419–26 (selections).
Language: French

Of a feest and justes made by the kyng of Englande in London whyle the Christen knyghtes and squyers were at the sege before the towne of Aufryke agaynst the Sarazyns,[1] and howe this feest was publisshed in dyvers countreis and landes.

Ye have herde before in this hystorie what a feest was holden at Paris whan Quene Isabell of Fraunce[2] made there her first entre, of the whiche feest tidynges sprede abrode into every countre. Than Kynge Richarde of Englande and his thre uncles, heryng of this goodly fest at Paris by the reportes of suche knyghtes and squyers of their owne as had ben at the same fest, ordayned a great fest to be holden at the cyte of London where there shulde be justes and sixty knyghtes to abyde all commers and with them sixty ladyes fresshely apparelled to kepe them company, and these knightes to just two dayes besyde Sonday, and the chalenge to begyn the next Sonday after the fest of Saint Michaell,[3] as than in the yere of oure Lorde God one thousand, three hundred, fourscore, and ten, whiche Sonday the said sixty knightes and sixty ladyes at two of the clocke at afternoon shuld issue oute of the towre of London, and so to come along the cytie through Chepe, and so to Smythfelde, and that day twelve knightes to be there redy to abyde all knyghtes straungers suche as wolde just. This Sonday was called the Sonday of the fest of chalenge; and on the Monday next after, the sayd sixty knightes to be in the same place redy to juste and to abyde all commers curtesly to ron with rokettes,[4] and to the best doer of the out syde shulde be gyven hym for a price a riche crowne of golde and the best doer of the in syde, duely examyned by the ladyes in the quenes chambre, shulde have for a price a riche gyrdell of golde. And the Tuesday folowynge the knightes shulde be agayne in the same place and to abyde all maner of squyers straungers and other suche as wolde just with rokettes, and the best juster on the out syde shulde have for his price a courser sadled, and the chiefe doer of the in syde shulde have a faucon.

The maner of this fest was thus ordayned and devised, and herauldes were charged to crye and publysshe this feest in Englande, in Scotlande, in Almayne, in Flaunders, in Brabant, in Heynalt, and in Fraunce. The heraldes departed, some hider and some thider; these tidynges sprede abrode into dyvers countreys; the herauldes had daye and tyme suffycient. Knightes and squiers in dyvers countreys apparelled themselfes to be at this feest, some to se the maner of Englande and some to juste. Whan these tidynges came

[1] Louis II, duke of Bourbon, led a "crusade" against Mahdiya in North Africa in 1390.
[2] Isabella (1389–1409), daughter of Charles VI, king of France, would marry Richard II in 1396.
[3] I.e., October 2.
[4] Blunt lanceheads.

into Heynalt, Sir Wyllyam of Heynalt, erle of Ostrevaunt, who was yonge and lyberall, and desyrous to juste, purposed in hymselfe to go to the feest in Englande to se and to honour his cosyns, Kyng Rycharde of Englande and his uncles, whome he had never sene before.[5] He hadde great desyre to be aquaynted with them and desyred other knightes and squyers to kepe hym company, and specially the lorde of Gomegynes bycause he was well acquaynted with Englysshemen, for he had ben dyvers tymes amonge them. Thanne Sir Wyllyam of Haynaulte purposed whyle he made his provisyon to go into Hollande to se his father Auberte, erle of Heynaulte, Hollande, and Zelande, to the entente to speke with hym and to take leave to go into Englande. He departed fro Quesnoy in Heynault and rode tyll he came to Haye in Hollande, where the erle his father was at that tyme, and there he shewed his father his purpose that he was to go into Englande to se the countrey and his cosyns, whom he had never sene. Than theerle his father answered and sayd, "Wyllyam my fayre son, ye have nothyng to do in Englande, for nowe ye be by covenaunt of maryage alyed to the realme of Fraunce and your suster to be maryed to the duke of Burgoyne;[6] wherfore, ye nede nat to seke none other alyaunce." "Dere father," quod he, "I wyll nat go into Englande to make any alyaunce; I do it but to feest and make myrthe with my cosins there, whom as yet I never sawe, and bycause the feest whiche shal be holden at London is publisshed abrode; wherfore, syth I am signifyed therof and shulde nat go thyder, it shulde be sayd I were proude and presumptuous; wherfore, in the savynge of myne honoure I wyll go thider; therfore, dere father, I requyre you agree therto." "Sonne," quod he, "do as ye lyste, but I thynke surely it were better that ye taryed at home." Whan the erle of Ostrevaunt sawe that his wordes contented nat his father, he wolde speke no more therof but fell in other communicacion, but he thought well ynough what he wolde do and so dayly sent his provisyon towardes Calais. Gomegynes the heraulde was sente into Englande fro therle of Ostrevaunt to gyve knowlege to Kynge Rycharde and to his uncles howe that he wolde come honorably to his fesst at London. Of those tidynges the kynge and his uncles were ryght joyouse . . .

[The earl of Ostrevaunt travels to London.] On the Sonday nexte after the feest of Saynt Michaell, this feest and triumphe shulde begyn, and that daye to be done in Smythfelde justes called the chalenge. So the same

---

[5] William of Bavaria or Hainault, count of Ostrevant (d. 1417), eldest son of Albert of Bavaria (d. 1405).
[6] In 1385 William had married Margaret of Burgundy and John (the Fearless) of Burgundy had married Margaret of Bavaria, William's sister.

Sonday, about thre of the clocke at afternoone, there issued out of the towre of London, first, threscore coursers apparelled for the justes and on every one a squier of honour ridyng a softe pase.[7] Than issued out threscore ladyes of honour mounted on fayre palfreys, ridyng on the one syde, richely apparelled, and every lady ledde a knight with a cheyne of sylver, which knightes were apparelled to just. Thus they cam ridynge alonge the stretes of London with great nombre of trumpettes and other mynstrelles, and so came to Smythfelde where the quene of Englande and other ladies and damoselles were redy in chambres richely adorned to se the justes, and the king was with the quene. And whan the ladyes that ledde the knyghtes were come to the place, they were taken downe fro their palfreys, and they mounted up into chambres redy aparelled for them. Than the squiers of honour alighted fro the coursers and the knightes in good order mounted on them; than their helmes were sette on and made redy at all poyntes. Than thyder came the erle of Saynt Poule, nobly accompanyed with knyghtes and squyers all armed with harnesse for the justes to begynne the feest, whiche incontynent[8] beganne, and there justed all knyghtes straungers, suche as wolde and hadde leysar and space, for the nyght came on. Thus these justes of chaleng began and contynued tyll it was night; than knyghtes and ladyes withdrue themselfes, and the quene was lodged besyde Poules in the bysshoppes palace, and there was the supper prepared. The same evennynge came therle of Ostrevaunt to the kyng, who was nobly receyved . . .

On the nexte day, whiche was Mondaye, ye myght have sene in dyvers places of the cytie of London, squyers and varlettes goynge aboute with harnesse and doynge of other busynesse of their maisters. After noon, Kynge Richarde came to the place all armed, richely apparelled, accompanyed with dukes, erles, lordes, and knyghtes; he was one of the inner partie. Than the quene, well accompanyed with ladyes and damosels, came to the place where the justes shulde be and mounted into chambres and scaffoldes ordayned for them. Than came into the felde the erle of Ostrevaunte well accompanyed with knyghtes of his countrey, and all were redy to juste; than came the erle of Saynt Poule and other knyghtes of Fraunce, suche as wolde juste. Than began the justes; every man payned hymselfe to gette honour. Some were stryken down fro their horses. These justes contynued tyll it was nere nyght, than every person drewe to their lodgynges, knyghtes and ladyes, and at the hour of supper every man drewe to the courte; there was

[7]   at an easy or moderate pace.
[8]   immediately.

a goodly supper and well ordayned. And as that day the price was gyven to the erle of Ostrevaunt for the best juster of the utter partie, and well he deserved it, the price was gyven hym by the ladyes, lordes, and herauldes, who were ordained to be judges. And of the inner partie a knyght of Englande, called Sir Hughe Spenser, had the price . . .

[Jousts and feast continued through the week.] And on the Saturdaye the kyng and all the lordes departed fro London to Wyndsore, and therele of Ostrevaunt and the erle of Saynt Poule, with all other knightes and squyers straungers were desyred to acompany the kyng to Wyndsore; every man rode as it was reason to the castell of Wyndsore. Than there began agayne great feestes with dyners and suppers gyven by the king, and specially the kyng dyde great honour to the erle of Ostrevaunt his cosyn, whiche erle was desyred by the kyng and his uncles that he wolde be content to take on hym the order of the garter. The erle aunswered howe he wolde take counsayle in that mater. Than he counsayled with lorde of Gomegines and with Fierabras of Vertan bastarde, who in no wyse wolde discorage nor counsayle hym to refuce the order of the garter. So he toke it on hym, wherof the knightes and squyers of Fraunce suche as were there had great marveyle and murmured sore therat among themselfe, sayeng, "The erle of Ostrevaunt sheweth well that his courage enclyneth rather to be Englysshe than Frenche whan he taketh on hym the order of the garter and weareth the kynge of Englandes devyse. He sheweth well he regardeth nat the house of Fraunce nor the house of Burgoyne. The tyme wyll come he shall repent hymselfe; all thynges consydred, he knoweth nat what he hath done, for he was wel beloved with the Frenche kynge and with the duke of Thourayne his brother, and with all the blode royall in suche wyse that whan he came to Parys or into any other place to any of them, they ever made hym more honour than any other of their cosyns." Thus these Frenchemen evyll accused hym without cause for that he had done was nothyng contrary nor hurtfull to the realme of Fraunce nor to his cosyns nor frendes in Fraunce, for he thought none otherwyse but honour and love, and to pleace his cosyns in Englande and to be therby the rather a good meane bytwene Fraunce and Englande if nede were, nor the daye that he toke on hym the order of the garter and his othe every man maye well understande that he made none alyaunce to do any prejudyce to the realme of Fraunce. For that he dyde was but for love and good company, howebeit no man canne let the envyous to speke yvell.

When they had daunced and sported them a certayne space in the castell of Wynsore and that the kyng hadde gyven many fayre gyftes to the knightes and squyers of honour of the realme of Fraunce and Heynaulte, and specially

to the yonge erle of Ostrevaunt, than every man toke leave of the kynge and
of the quene, and of other ladyes and damoselles, and of the kynges uncles.
Thane the erle of Saynt Poule and the Frenchemen, and the Henowayes
and Almaygnes departed. Thus ended this great feest in the cytie of London, and every man went to their owne. Than it fortuned, as anone brute[9]
ronneth farre of, the Frenche kynge,[10] his brother, and his uncles were
enfourmed, by suche as hadde ben in Englande at the sayde feest, of every
thyng that hadde been done and sayd; nothynge was forgotten but rather
more putte to in the exaltyng of yvell dedes than fortheryng of good
dedes. It was shewed the kynge playnly how the erle of Ostrevaunt had ben
in Englande and taken great payne to exalte and to do honoure to the
Englysshemen and in helpynge forwarde the feest holden at London, and
howe he hadde the chiefe prise and honoure of the justes above all other
straungers, and how he had spoken so fayre to the Englysshmen that he was
become the kynge of Englands man and had made servyce and alyaunce
with hym, and taken on hym the order of the garter in the chapell of Saynt
George in Wyndsore, whiche order was fyrste stablysshed by Kynge Edwarde
the Thirde and his sonne Prince of Wales, and howe that no man myght
entre into that confrary or company without he make servyaunt or othe
never to beare armoure agaynste the crowne of Englande, whiche promyse
they sayd the erle of Ostrevaunt had made without any reservacyon. With
these tydynges the Frenche kynge, his brother, and his uncles were sore
troubled and grevously displeased with the erle of Ostrevaunt. Than the
Frenche kyng sayde, "Lo, sirs, ye maye se what it is to do for hym. It is nat
yet a yere paste sythe he desyred me that his brother myght be bysshoppe of
Cambray and, by these tidynges, that gyfte were rather prejudycial to the
realme of Fraunce than avauncement; it hadde been better we had gyven it
to our cosyn of Saynt Poule; the Heynoways dyd never good to us, nor
never wyll, for they be proude, presumptuous, and to fierse; alwayes they
have owed better good wyll to the Englysshemen than to us, but a daye
shall come they shall repent them; we wyll sende to the erle of Ostrevaunt,
commaundynge hym to come to us to do us homage for the countie of
Ostrevaunt, or els we shall put hym fro it and annexe it to oure realme."
They of his counsayle answered and sayde, "Sir, ye have well devysed; lette
it be done as ye have sayde." It maye well be thought that the duke of
Burgoyne, whose doughter the erle of Ostrevaunt had to his wyfe, was

[9]   fame, renown.
[10]   Charles VI (r. 1380–1422).

nothynge content with those tidynges, for alwayes he had avaunsed his
sonne of Ostrevaunt towardes the kyng and his counsaile. This mater was
nat forgotten, but incontinent the Frenche kyng wrote sharpe letters to
therle of Ostrevaunt, who was at Quesnoy in Heynaulte, commaundyng
hym to come to Parys to do his homage before the kynge and the other
peeres of Fraunce for the countie of Ostrevaunt or els the kyng wolde take
it fro hym and make hym warre . . . [William sought counsel from his own
men and then from his father the king, who was not surprised that things
had turned out this way. In the end William had to pay homage to King
Charles in Paris.]

7

Textualities

Audience Reactions to Sermons

Medieval theoreticians and practitioners adapted the Classical arts of rhetoric – the *artes dictaminis* (letter-writing), *artes poetriae* (poetry), and *artes praedicandi* (speaking) – to their specific needs. The focus of the *artes* or *ars praedicandi* became the province of preachers, lawyers, and rulers, who learned the art of composing and delivering their sermons, arguments, and speeches. Very little, however, is known about the reception of any of these oral performances, including sermons, the principal source of religious knowledge for the laity, but information can be gleaned from the various manuals and other writings.

John Mirk, whose birth and death dates are unknown, became prior of the Augustinian abbey of Lilleshall in Shropshire and is the author of three works: *Festial* (ca. 1382–90), a collection of sermons on feasts indebted to Jacobus de Voragine's *Legenda aurea, Manuale sacerdotis* (ca. 1414), also a work belonging to the *artes praedicandi*, and the *Instructions for Parish Priests* of about 1400, which draws on William of Pagula's *Oculus sacerdotis*. The *Instructions* survive in seven manuscripts. Its 1,934 lines of generally octosyllabic couplets suggest a practical aim for priests: to remember the religious instruction their lay audiences need throughout their Christian lives. The following excerpt is from a discussion of the role of communion.

Primary documents and further reading

Hudson, A. and P. Gradon (eds.) (1983–96) *English Wycliffite Sermons*, 5 vols. Oxford: Clarendon Press.

Krul, L. (trans.) (2001) Robert of Basevorn, "The Form of Preaching." In J. J. Murphy (ed.) *Three Medieval Rhetorical Arts*. Tempe: Arizona Center for Medieval and Renaissance Studies, 114–215.

Murphy, J. J. (2001) *Rhetoric in the Middle Ages: A History of Rhetorical Theory from Saint Augustine to the Renaissance*. Tempe: Arizona Center for Medieval and Renaissance Studies.

Owst, G. R. (1961) *Literature and Pulpit in Medieval England: A Neglected Chapter in the History of English Letters and of the English People*, 2nd edn. Oxford: Blackwell.

—— (1965) *Preaching in Medieval England: An Introduction to Sermon Manuscripts of the Period c. 1350–1450*. New York: Russell and Russell.

Powell, S. (ed.) (1981) *The Advent and Nativity Sermons from a Fifteenth-century Revision of John Mirk's Festial*. Heidelberg: C. Winter.

Ross, W. O. (ed.) (1998) *Middle English Sermons*. EETS, o.s. 209. Woodbridge, Suffolk: Boydell and Brewer.

Spencer, H. L. (1993) *English Preaching in the Late Middle Ages*. Oxford: Clarendon Press.

John Mirk. British Library MS Cotton Claudius A.ii, fols. 132r–133r. In G. Kristenson (ed.) (1974) *Instructions for Parish Priests*. Lund: Gleerup, 82–6.
Language: English (West Midland)
Manuscript date: ca. 1425

	Yet thow moste teche hem mare,	*more*
265	That whenne they doth to chyrche fare,	
	Thenne bydde hem leve here mony wordes,	
	Here ydel speche, and nyce bordes,	
	And put a-way alle vanyte,	
	And say here Pater Noster and here Ave.	
270	No mon in chyrche stonde schal,	
	Ny lene to pyler ny to wal,	
	But fayre on kneus they schule hem sette,	
	Knelynge doun up-on the flette,	*paved floor*
	And pray to God wyth herte meke	
275	To geve hem grace and mercy eke.	
	Soffere hem to make no bere,	*commotion*
	But ay to be in here prayere;	
	And whenne the gospelle i-red be schalle,	
	Teche hem thenne to stonde up alle,	
280	And blesse [hem] feyre as they conne	
	Whenne *gloria tibi* ys by-gonne,	

And whenne the gospel ys i-done,
Teche hem eft to knele downe sone;
And whenne they here the belle rynge
285   To that holy sakerynge,[1]
Teche hem knele downe, bothe yonge and olde,
And bothe here hondes up to holde
And say thenne in thys manere,
Feyre and softely, wyth-owte bere,
290   "Jhesu, lord, welcome thow be
In forme of bred as I the se.
Jhesu! for thy holy name,
Schelde me to-day fro synne and schame.
Schryfte and howsele, lord, thou graunte me bo
295   Er that I schale hennes go,
And verre contrycyone of my synne,
That I, Lord, never dye there-inne;
And as thow were of a may I-bore,   *maid born*
Sofere me never to be for-lore,
300   But whenne that I schale hennes wende,
Grawnte me the blysse wyth-owten ende. Amen."
Teche hem thus other sum othere thynge
To say at the holy sakerynge.
Teche hem also, I the pray,
305   That whenne they walken in the way
And sene the preste a-gayn hem comynge,
Goddes body wyth hym berynge,
Thenne, wyth grete devocyone,
Teche hem there to knele a-downe.
310   Fayre ne fowle, spare they noghte
To worschype hym that alle hath wroghte,
For glad may that mon be
That ones in the day may hym se,
For so mykyle gode doth that syght –
315   As Seynt Austyn techeth a-ryght –
That day that thow syst Goddes body,
These benefyces schalt thou have sycurly:
Mete and drynke at thy nede,
Non schal the that day be gnede;   *needy*

[1]   I.e., "sacring," the consecration of the bread and wine.

320   Idele othes and wordes also
       God for-geveth the also.
       Soden deth that ylke day
       The dar not drede wythoute nay.
       Also, that day, I the plyghte,   *pledge*
325   Thow schalt not lese thyn ye-syghte,
       And every fote that thou gost thenne,
       That holy syght for to sene,
       They schule be tolde to stonde in stede
       Whenne thow hast [moste] nede.
330   Also, wyth-ynne chyrche and seyntwary,
       Do ryght thus as I the say;
       Songe and cry and suche fare,
       For to stynte thow schalt not spare;
       Castynge of axtre and eke of ston,   *axle*
335   Sofere hem there to use non.
       Bal and bares,² and suche play,
       Out of chyrcheyorde put a way;
       Courte-holdynge and suche maner chost,   *of quarrelling*
       Out of seyntwary put thow most.
340   For Cryst hym-self techeth us
       That holy chyrche ys hys hows.
       That ys made for no thynge elles
       But for to praye in, as the boke telles.
       There the pepulle schale geder with-inne
345   To prayen and to wepen for here synne.

Books

Larger book collections in the Middle English period tended to be eclectic
and restricted to wealthier individuals because of their price, but even less-
moneyed people frequently owned one or more volumes. A newly commissioned luxury book could cost as much as 35 pounds, a simpler missal 20
shillings. Nobility and courtiers often had collections of between five and
fifteen books: Bibles, primers, and other religious writings, historical works,
romances, and books of philosophy (see the image, "Anne of Burgundy,
duchess of Bedford, before St. Anne," p. 135). These tend predominantly

² An outdoor children's game, probably the original of prisoner's base.

to be in Latin or French but increasingly in English. Thomas of Woodstock, duke of Gloucester (1355–97), and Richard II's uncle, has the largest recorded collection for the Middle English period, over 80 items. Richard II inherited 14 books in 1384–5. In the later fifteenth century, an inventory of one of the Johns Pastons lists 17 works, many of them compilations in English, including texts by Geoffrey Chaucer and John Lydgate, romances, and some of William Caxton's printed books.

Richard de Bury (1287–1345) was born near Bury St. Edmunds in Suffolk and went on to study at Oxford University. He became tutor to Edward, earl of Chester, the son of Edward II and Isabella of France. When Edward III assumed personal rule in 1330, Richard was made envoy to Pope John XXII at Avignon where he met Petrarch. He was consecrated bishop of Durham in 1333 and made High Chancellor of England in 1334 and Treasurer in 1336. He was influential in the founding of Durham College at Oxford, and he intended that his large library, which he had developed throughout his life, would supply its basis (see the image, "New College, Oxford University," p. 149). No list of the books he owned survives, although it is possible to piece together the kinds of books he preferred, which are fairly typical of his age: religious works, legal texts, rhetorics and grammars, philosophies, histories, and poetry and drama.

Richard completed his *Philobiblon* in the last year of his life. It survives in 35 manuscripts from the late fourteenth and fifteenth centuries, which the modern editor Ernest Thomas collated for his translation. The *Philobiblon* contains praise for books, criticisms of their mistreatment, his stated preferences for the ancients over the moderns, and his reasons for favoring certain genres; he also extols the benefits of reading and pleads for the careful copying and preservation of manuscripts.

Primary documents and further reading

Boyd, B. (1973) *Chaucer and the Medieval Book*. San Marino, CA: Huntington Library.

Brechka, F. T. (1983) "Richard de Bury: The Books He Cherished." *Libri* 33: 302–15.

Camille, M. (1997) "The Book as Flesh and Fetish in Richard de Bury's *Philobiblon*." In D. W. Frese and K. O. O'Keeffe (eds.) *The Book and the Body*. Notre Dame, IN: University of Notre Dame Press, 34–77.

Krochalis, J. E. (1988) "The Books and Reading of Henry V and His Circle." *Chaucer Review* 23: 50–77.

Scattergood, V. J. and J. W. Sherborne (eds.) (1983) *English Court Culture in the Later Middle Ages*. London: Geral and Duckworth.

Taylor, A. (1999) "Authors, Scribes, Patrons and Books." In J. Wogan-Browne, N. Watson, A. Taylor, and R. Evans *The Idea of the Vernacular: An Anthology of Middle English Literary Theory, 1280–1520.* University Park: Pennsylvania State University Press, 353–65.

Viscount Dillon and W. H. St. John Hope (eds.) (1897) "Inventory of the Goods and Chattels Belonging to Thomas, Duke of Gloucester." *Archaeological Journal* 54: 275–308.

E. C. Thomas (ed. and trans.) (1888) Richard de Bury, *Philobiblon.* London: Kegan Paul, Trench, 161–240 (selections).
Language: Latin
Manuscript dates: 1375–1458

That the treasure of wisdom is chiefly contained in books.

. . . In books I find the dead as if they were alive, in books I foresee things to come, in books warlike affairs are set forth, from books come forth the laws of peace. All things are corrupted and decay in time; Saturn ceases not to devour the children that he generates; all the glory of the world would be buried in oblivion unless God had provided mortals with the remedy of books. Alexander, the conqueror of the earth; Julius, the invader of Rome and of the world who, the first in war and arts, assumed universal empire under his single rule; faithful Fabricius and stern Cato would now have been unknown to fame if the aid of books had been wanting. Towers have been razed to the ground, cities have been overthrown, triumphal arches have perished from decay, nor can either pope or king find any means of more easily conferring the privilege of perpetuity than by books. The book that he has made renders its author this service in return, that so long as the book survives, its author remains immortal and cannot die, as Ptolemy declares in the Prologue to his *Almagest*: "He is not dead," he says, "who has given life to science."

Who, therefore, will limit by anything of another kind the price of the infinite treasure of books, from which the scribe who is instructed bringeth forth things new and old? Truth that triumphs over all things, which overcomes the king, wine, and women, which it is reckoned holy to honour before friendship, which is the way without turning and the life without end, which holy Boethius considers to be threefold in thought, speech, and writing,[1] seems to remain more usefully and to fructify to greater profit in books. For the meaning of the voice perishes with the sound. Truth latent in the mind is wisdom that is hid and treasure that is not seen, but truth

---

[1]   *De interpretione.*

which shines forth in books desires to manifest itself to every impressionable sense. It commends itself to the sight when it is read, to the hearing when it is heard, and moreover in a manner to the touch when it suffers itself to be transcribed, bound, corrected, and preserved. The undisclosed truth of the mind, although it is the possession of the noble soul, yet because it lacks a companion, is not certainly known to be delightful while neither sight nor hearing takes account of it. Further, the truth of the voice is patent only to the ear and eludes the sight, which reveals to us more of the qualities of things and, linked with the subtlest of motions, begins and perishes as it were in a breath. But the written truth of books, not transient but permanent, plainly offers itself to be observed and, by means of the pervious spherules of the eyes, passing through the vestibule of perception and the courts of imagination, enters the chamber of intellect, taking its place in the couch of memory, where it engenders the eternal truth of the mind . . .

The degree of affection that is properly due to books.
. . . Let us next dwell a little on the recital of the wrongs with which they requite us, the contempts and cruelties of which we cannot recite an example in each kind, nay, scarcely the main classes of the several wrongs. In the first place, we are expelled by force and arms from the homes of the clergy, which are ours by hereditary right, who were used to have cells of quietness in the inner chamber, but alas! in these unhappy times we are altogether exiled, suffering poverty without the gates. For our places are seized now by dogs, now by hawks, now by that biped beast whose cohabitation with the clergy was forbidden of old, from which we have always taught our nurslings to flee more than from the asp and cockatrice; wherefore, she, always jealous of the love of us and never to be appeased, at length seeing us in some corner protected only by the web of some dead spider, with a frown abuses and reviles us with bitter words, declaring us alone of all the furniture in the house to be unnecessary and complaining that we are useless for any household purpose, and advises that we should speedily be converted into rich caps, sendal and silk and twice-dyed purple, robes and furs, wool and linen; and, indeed, not without reason if she could see our inmost hearts, if she had listened to our secret counsels, if she had read the book of Theophrastus or Valerius, or only heard the twenty-fifth chapter of Ecclesiasticus with understanding ears.[2]

---

[2]   The book of Theophrastus is the *Aureolus liber Theophrasti de nuptiis,* a text against marriage attributed to him by Jerome in his *Epistola adversus Jovinianum.* In *De nugis curialium* Walter Map claims that Valerius Maximus' *Dissuasio Valerii ad Rufinum Philosophum ne uxorem ducat* is his own composition.

And hence it is that we have to mourn for the homes of which we have been unjustly robbed . . . Now we would pursue a new kind of injury, by which we suffer alike in person and in fame, the dearest thing we have. Our purity of race is diminished every day, while new authors' names are imposed upon us by worthless compilers, translators, and transformers and, losing our ancient nobility while we are reborn in successive generations, we become wholly degenerate; and thus against our will the name of some wretched step-father is affixed to us, and the sons are robbed of the names of their true fathers. The verses of Virgil, while he was yet living, were claimed by an impostor, and a certain Fidentinus mendaciously usurped the works of Martial, whom Martial thus deservedly rebuked:

"The book you read is, Fidentinus! mine,
Though read so badly, 't well may pass for thine!"

What marvel then, if, when our authors are dead, clerical apes use us to make broad their phylacteries since even while they are alive they try to seize us as soon as we are published? Ah! how often ye pretend that we who are ancient are but lately born and try to pass us off as sons who are really fathers, calling us who have made you clerks the production of your studies. Indeed, we derived our origin from Athens, though we are now supposed to be from Rome, for Carmentis was always the pilferer of Cadmus, and we who were but lately born in England will tomorrow be born again in Paris, and thence being carried to Bologna, will obtain an Italian origin based upon no affinity of blood. Alas! how ye commit us to treacherous copyists to be written, how corruptly ye read us and kill us by medication while ye supposed ye were correcting us with pious zeal. Oftentimes we have to endure barbarous interpreters, and those who are ignorant of foreign idioms presume to translate us from one language into another, and thus all propriety of speech is lost and our sense is shamefully mutilated contrary to the meaning of the author! Truly noble would have been the condition of books if it had not been for the presumption of the tower of Babel, if but one kind of speech had been transmitted by the whole human race.

We will add the last clause of our long lament, though far too short for the materials that we have. For in us the natural use is changed to that which is against nature, while we who are the light of faithful souls every-where fall a prey to painters knowing nought of letters and are entrusted to goldsmiths to become, as though we were not sacred vessels of wisdom, repositories of gold-leaf. We fall undeservedly into the power of laymen, which is more bitter to us than any death, since they have sold our people for nought, and our enemies themselves are our judges . . .

Of showing due propriety in the custody of books.
We are not only rendering service to God in preparing volumes of new books but also exercising an office of sacred piety when we treat books carefully and again when we restore them to their proper places and commend them to inviolable custody that they may rejoice in purity while we have them in our hands and rest securely when they are put back in their repositories. And surely next to the vestments and vessels dedicated to the Lord's body, holy books deserve to be rightly treated by the clergy, to which great injury is done so often as they are touched by unclean hands. Wherefore, we deem it expedient to warn our students of various negligences, which might always be easily avoided and do wonderful harm to books.

And in the first place, as to the opening and closing of books, let there be due moderation that they be not unclasped in precipitate haste nor, when we have finished our inspection, be put away without being duly closed. For it behoves us to guard a book much more carefully than a boot.

But the race of scholars is commonly badly brought up and, unless they are bridled in by the rules of their elders, they indulge in infinite puerilities. They behave with petulance and are puffed up with presumption, judging of everything as if they were certain though they are altogether inexperienced.

You may happen to see some headstrong youth lazily lounging over his studies and, when the winter's frost is sharp, his nose running from the nipping cold drips down, nor does he think of wiping it with his pocket-handkerchief until he has bedewed the book before him with the ugly moisture. Would that he had before him no book but a cobbler's apron! His nails are stuffed with fetid filth as black as jet, with which he marks any passage that pleases him. He distributes a multitude of straws, which he inserts to stick out in different places so that the halm may remind him of what his memory cannot retain. These straws, because the book has no stomach to digest them and no one takes them out, first distend the book from its wonted closing and, at length, being carelessly abandoned to oblivion, go to decay. He does not fear to eat fruit or cheese over an open book or carelessly to carry a cup to and from his mouth and, because he has no wallet at hand, he drops into books the fragments that are left. Continually chattering, he is never weary of disputing with his companions and, while he alleges a crowd of senseless arguments, he wets the book lying half open on his lap with sputtering showers. Aye, and then hastily folding his arms, he leans on the book and, by a brief spell of study, invites a long nap; and then, by way of mending the wrinkles, he folds back the margin of the leaves to the no small injury of the book. Now the rain is over and gone, and the flowers have appeared in our land. Then the scholar we are speaking of, a neglecter rather than an inspector of books, will stuff his volume with violets and primroses, with roses and quatrefoil. Then he will use his wet and perspiring hands to turn over the volumes; then he will thump the white vellum with gloves covered with all kinds of dust and, with his finger clad in long-used leather, will hunt line by line through the page; then, at the sting of the biting flea, the sacred book is flung aside and is hardly shut for another month until it is so full of dust that has found its way within that it resists the effort to close it.

But the handling of books is specially to be forbidden to those shameless youths who, as soon as they have learned to form the shapes of letters, straightway, if they have the opportunity, become unhappy commentators and, wherever they find an extra margin about the text, furnish it with monstrous alphabets, or if any other frivolity strikes their fancy, at once their pen begins to write it. There the Latinist and sophister and every unlearned writer tries the fitness of his pen, a practice that we have frequently seen injuring the usefulness and value of the most beautiful books.

Again, there is a class of thieves shamefully mutilating books, who cut away the margins from the sides to use as materials for letters, leaving only the text, or employ the leaves from the end, inserted for the protection of the book, for various uses and abuses – a kind of sacrilege which should be prohibited by the threat of anathema.

Again, it is part of the decency of scholars that whenever they return from meals to their study, washing should invariably precede reading and that no grease-stained finger should unfasten the clasps or turn the leaves of a book. Nor let a crying child admire the pictures in the capital letters lest he soil the parchment with wet fingers, for a child instantly touches whatever he sees. Moreover, the laity, who look at a book turned upside down just as if it were open in the right way, are utterly unworthy of any communion with books. Let the clerk take care also that the smutty scullion reeking from his stewpots does not touch the lily leaves of books, all unwashed, but he who walketh without blemish shall minister to the precious volumes. And, again, the cleanliness of decent hands would be of great benefit to books as well as scholars if it were not that the itch and pimples are characteristic of the clergy.

Whenever defects are noticed in books, they should be promptly repaired, since nothing spreads more quickly than a tear, and a rent which is neglected at the time will have to be repaired afterwards with usury.

Censorship

Beginning in the 1370s and 1380s, debate about writing, translating, and reading in the vernacular grew more intense because of the dissemination of written religious texts and ideas to audiences outside direct Church control. Writings in English posed a particular threat to Church authorities who were concerned about the heresies promulgated by those who followed the ideas of John Wyclif and others (see "Lollardy Trials," p. 59, and "Plays and Representations," p. 262). Lollards insisted that God's word should be available in the most accessible language and that the choice of language did not affect the meaning.

Thomas Arundel (d. 1414) was bishop of Ely (1374–88), archbishop of York (1388–96), and archbishop of Canterbury (1396–7, 1399–1414). He was also Chancellor of England during the Ricardian and Lancastrian eras. Exiled by Richard II in 1397, he returned with Henry Bolingbroke in 1399 to depose the king (see "Usurpation," p. 69). Composed at Oxford in 1407, his *Constitutions* refocused the force of the earlier *De heretico comburendo* (1401), and their publication in 1409 coincides with the Lollard Disendowment Bill. Because of the *Constitutions*, Church authorities subsequently examined books and individuals, trying and condemning both. It has been argued that the *Constitutions* also had a less direct but wider ranging restrictive effect on fifteenth-century vernacular writers, copiers, and readers in general.

Primary documents and further reading

"*Constitutiones domini Thomae Arundel, Cantuariensis archiepiscopi.*" *Concilia Magnae Britanniae et Hiberniae, ab anno MCCCL ad annum MDXLV.* Vol. 3. (1737) London, 314–19.

Hudson, A. (ed.) (1978) *Selections from English Wycliffite Writings.* Cambridge: Cambridge University Press.

—— (1985) "Lollardy: The English Heresy?" In A. Hudson (ed.) *Lollards and Their Books.* London: Hambledon, 141–63.

—— (1988) *The Premature Reformation: Wycliffite Texts and Lollard History.* Oxford: Clarendon Press.

Watson, N. (1995) "Censorship and Cultural Change in Late-medieval England: Vernacular Theology, the Oxford Debate, and Arundel's Constitutions of 1409." *Speculum* 70: 822–64.

Wogan-Browne, J., N. Watson, A. Taylor, and R. Evans (eds.) (1999) *The Idea of the Vernacular: An Anthology of Middle English Literary Theory, 1280–1520.* University Park: Pennsylvania State University Press.

"The Cruel Constitution of Thomas Arundel, Archbishop, against the Gospellers, or Followers of God's Truth." Trans. John Foxe. In *The Acts and Monuments of John Foxe*, 1563. Vol. 3. New York: AMS Press (1965), 243–7.
Language: Latin
Date: 1409

We will and command, ordain and decree that no manner of person, secular or regular, being authorized to preach by the laws now prescribed or licensed by special privilege, shall take upon him the office of preaching the word of God or by any means preach unto the clergy or laity, whether within the church or without, in English, except he first present himself and be examined by the ordinary of the place where he preacheth and, so being found a fit person as well in manners as knowledge, he shall be sent by the said ordinary to some one church or more, as shall be thought expedient by the said ordinary, according to the quality of the person. Nor any person aforesaid shall presume to preach except first he give faithful signification in due form of his sending and authority, that is, that he that is authorized do come in form appointed him in that behalf and that those that affirm they come by special privilege do show their privilege unto the parson or vicar of the place where they preach. And those that pretend themselves to be sent by the ordinary of the place shall likewise show the ordinary's letters made unto him for that purpose under his great seal. Let us always understand, the curate (having the perpetuity) to be sent of right unto the people of his own cure, but if any person aforesaid shall be forbidden by the ordinary of the place or any other superior to preach by reason of his errors or heresies which before, peradventure, he hath preached and taught, that then and from thenceforth he abstain from preaching within our province until he have purged himself and be lawfully admitted again to preach by the just arbitrement of him that suspended and forbade him and shall always, after that, carry with him to all places wheresoever he shall preach the letters testimonial of him that restored him.

Moreover, the parish priests or vicars temporal, not having perpetuities nor being sent in form aforesaid, shall simply preach in the churches where they have charge only those things which are expressly contained in the provincial constitution set forth by John, our predecessor,[1] of good memory, to help the ignorance of the priests, which beginneth, "*Ignorantia sacerdotum*," which book of constitution we would should be had in every parish church in our province of Canterbury within three months next after the publication of these presents and (as therein is required) that it be effectually declared by the priests themselves yearly and at the times appointed. And, lest this wholesome statute might be thought hurtful to some by reason of payment of money or some other difficulty, we therefore will and ordain that the examinations of the persons aforesaid and the making of their letters by the ordinary be done *gratis* and freely, without any exaction of money at all by those to who it shall appertain. And if any man shall willingly presume to violate this our statute grounded upon the old law, after the publication of the same, he shall incur the sentence of greater excommunication, "*ipso facto*," whose absolution we specially reserve by tenor of these presents to us and our successors. But, if any such preacher, despising this wholesome statute and not weighing the sentence of greater excommunication, do the second time take upon him to preach, saying and alleging, and stoutly affirming that the sentence of greater excommunication aforesaid cannot be appointed by the church in the persons of the prelates of the same, that then the superiors of the place do worthily rebuke him and forbid him from the communion of all faithful Christians.

And that the said person hereupon lawfully convicted (except he recant and abjure after the manner of the church) be pronounced a heretic by the ordinary of the place. And that from thenceforth he be reputed and taken for a heretic and schismatic, and that he incur "*ipso facto*" the penalties of heresy and schismacy expressed in the law and, chiefly, that his goods be adjudged confiscate by the law, and apprehended, and kept by them to whom it shall appertain. And that his fautors, receivers, and defenders, being convicted, in all cases be likewise punished if they cease not off within one month, being lawfully warned thereof by their superiors . . .

[Any clergymen who allow anyone to preach in their churches without proof of the person's authorization to do so will have the religious places put under interdict.]

Moreover, like as a good householder casteth wheat into the ground well ordered for that purpose, thereby to get the more increase, even so we will and command that the preacher of God's word, coming in form aforesaid,

---

[1]   John Pecham, archbishop of Canterbury 1279–92.

preaching either unto the clergy or laity, according to his matter proposed, shall be of good behavior, sowing such seed as shall be convenient for his auditory. And, chiefly preaching to the clergy, he shall touch the vices commonly used amongst them, and to the laity he shall declare the vices commonly used amongst them, and not otherwise. But if he preach contrary to this order, then shall he be sharply punished by the ordinary of that place, according to the quality of that offence.

Item, forasmuch as the part is vile that agreeth not with the whole, we do decree and ordain that no preacher aforesaid or any other person whatsoever shall otherwise teach or preach concerning the sacrament of the altar, matrimony, confession of sins, or any other sacrament of the church, or article of the faith, than what already is discussed by the holy mother church; nor shall bring any thing in doubt that is determined by the church, nor shall, to his knowledge, privily or apertly pronounce blasphemous words concerning the same; nor shall teach, preach, or observe any sect or kind of heresy whatsoever contrary to the wholesome doctrine of the church. He that shall wittingly and obstinately attempt the contrary after the publication of these presents, shall incur the sentence of excommunication "*ipso facto*," from which, except in point of death, he shall not be absolved until he have reformed himself by abjuration of his heresy at the discretion of the ordinary in whose territory he so offended and have received wholesome penitence for his offences. But if the second time he shall so offend, being lawfully convicted, he shall be pronounced a heretic, and his goods shall be confiscated and apprehended and kept by them to whom it shall appertain. The penance before-mentioned shall be after this manner: if any man, contrary to the determination of the church, that is, in the decrees, decretals, or our constitutions provincial, do openly or privily teach or preach any kind of heresy or sect, he shall, in the parish church of the same place where he so preached, upon one Sunday or other solemn day, or more, at the discretion of the ordinary and as his offence is more or less, expressly revoke what he so preached, taught, or affirmed, even at the time of the solemnity of the mass when the people are most assembled, and there shall he effectually and without fraud preach and teach the very truth determined by the church and, further, shall be punished after the quality of his offence as shall be thought expedient at the discretion of the ordinary.

Item, forasmuch as a new vessel, being long used, savoureth after the head, we decree and ordain that no schoolmasters and teachers whatsoever, that instruct children in grammar or others whosoever in primitive sciences, shall, in teaching them, intermingle any thing concerning the catholic faith, the sacrament of the altar, or other sacraments of the church contrary to the determination of the church; nor shall suffer their scholars to expound the holy scriptures (except the text, as hath been used in ancient time); nor shall permit them to dispute openly or privily concerning the catholic faith or sacraments of the church. Contrariwise, the offender herein shall be grievously punished by the ordinary of the place as a favorer of errors and schisms.

Item, for that a new way doth more frequently lead astray than an old way, we will and command that no book or treatise made by John Wickliff or others whomsoever about that time, or since, or hereafter to be made, be from henceforth read in schools, halls, hospitals, or other places whatsoever within our province of Canterbury aforesaid, except the same be first examined by the university of Oxford or Cambridge, or, at least, by twelve persons whom the said universities or one of them shall appoint to be chosen at our discretion or the laudable discretion of our successors; and the same, being examined as aforesaid, to be expressly approved and allowed by us or our successors, and in the name and authority of the university to be delivered unto the stationers to be copied out, and the same to be sold at a reasonable price, the original thereof always after to remain in some chest of the university. But if any man shall read any such kind of book in schools or otherwise, as aforesaid, he shall be punished as a sower of schism, and a favorer of heresy, as the quality of the fault shall require.

Item, it is a dangerous thing, as witnesseth blessed St. Jerome, to translate the text of the holy scripture out of the tongue into another, for in the translation the same sense is not always easily kept, as the same St. Jerome confesseth that although he were inspired, yet oftentimes in this he erred.[2] We therefore decree and ordain that no man hereafter by his own authority translate any text of the scripture into English or any other tongue by way of a book, libel, or treatise, and that no man read any such book, libel, or treatise now lately set forth in the time of John Wickliff, or since, or hereafter to be set forth, in part or in whole, privily or apertly, upon pain of greater excommunication, until the said translation be allowed by the ordinary of the place or, if the case so require, by the council provincial. He that shall do contrary to this shall likewise be punished as a favorer of error and heresy.

Item, for that almighty God cannot be expressed by any philosophical terms or otherwise invented of man and St. Augustine saith that he hath oftentimes revoked such conclusions as have been most true because they have been offensive to the ears of the religious,[3] we do ordain and specially

---

[2]   St. Jerome (ca. 347–420), *Epistolae.*
[3]   St. Augustine (354–430), *Retraciones.*

forbid that any manner of person of what state, degree, or condition soever he be, do allege or propone any conclusions or propositions in the catholic faith or repugnant to good manners (except necessary doctrine pertaining to their faculty of teaching or disputing in their schools or otherwise) although they defend the same with ever such curious terms and words. For, as saith blessed St. Hugh of the sacraments, "That which oftentimes is well spoken is not well understood."[4] If any man, therefore, after the publication of these presents, shall be convicted wittingly to have proponed such conclusions or propositions, except (being monished) he reform himself in one month, by virtue of this present constitution, he shall incur the sentence of greater excommunication "*ipso facto*," and shall be openly pronounced an excommunicate until he hath confessed his fault openly in the same place where he offended and hath preached the true meaning of the said conclusion or proposition in one church or more as shall be thought expedient to the ordinary.

Item, no manner of person shall presume to dispute upon the articles determined by the church that are contained in the decrees, decretals, or constitutions provincial, or in the general councils, but only to seek out the true meaning thereof, and that expressly, whether it be openly or in secret, and none shall call in doubt the authority of the said decretals or constitutions, or the authority of him that made them, or teach any thing contrary to the determination thereof and, chiefly, concerning the adoration of the holy cross, the worshipping of images, of saints, going on pilgrimage to certain places or to the relics of saints, or against the oaths in cases accustomed to be given in both common places, that is to say, spiritual and temporal. But by all it shall be commonly taught and preached that the cross and image of the crucifix, and other images of saints, in honor of them whom they represent, are to be worshipped with procession, bowing of knees, offering of frankincense, kissings, oblations, lighting of candles, and pilgrimages, and with all other kind of ceremonies and manners that have been used in the time of our predecessors, and that giving of oaths in cases expressed in the law and used of all men to whom it belongeth, in both common places, ought to be done upon the book of the gospel of Christ. Contrary unto this, whosoever doth preach, teach, or obstinately affirm, except he recant in manner and form aforesaid, shall forthwith incur the penalty of heresy and shall be pronounced a heretic in all effect of law.

Item, we do decree and ordain that no chaplain be admitted to celebrate in any diocese within our province of Canterbury where he was not born or

---

[4]   Hugh of St. Victor (ca. 1096–1141), *De sacramentis.*

received not orders except he bring with him his letters of orders and letters commendatory from his ordinary and also from other bishops in whose diocese of a long time he hath been conversant, whereby his conversation and manners may appear so that it may be known whether he hath been defamed with any new opinions touching the catholic faith or whether he be free from the same; otherwise, as well he that celebrateth as he that suffereth him to celebrate shall be sharply punished at the discretion of the ordinary.

Finally, because those things, which newly and unaccustomably creep up stand in need of new and speedy help, and where more danger is, there ought to be more wary circumspection and stronger resistance, and not without good cause, the less noble ought discreetly to be cut away, that the more noble may the more perfectly be nourished, considering, therefore, and in lamentable wise showing unto you how the ancient university of Oxford, which as a fruitful vine was wont to extend forth her fruitful branches to the honor of God, the great perfection and defense of the church, now partly being become wild, bringeth forth bitter grapes which, being indiscreetly eaten of ancient fathers that thought themselves skilful in the law of God, hath set on edge the teeth of their children, and our province being infected with divers and unfruitful doctrines, and defiled with a new and damnable name of Lollardy to the great reproof and offence of the said university, being known in foreign countries and to the great irksomeness of the students there, and to the great damage and loss of the church of England, which in times past by her virtue, as with a strong wall, was wont to be defended, and now is like to run into ruin not to be recovered; at the supplication, therefore, of the whole clergy of our province of Canterbury, and by the consent and assent of all our brethren and suffragans, and other the prelates in this convocation assembled, and the proctors of them that are absent, lest the river being cleansed, the fountain should remain corrupt and so the water coming form thence should not be pure, intending most wholesomely to provide for the honor and utility of our holy mother the church and the university aforesaid, we do ordain and decree that every warden, provost, or master of every college, or principal of every hall within the university aforesaid shall, once every month at the least, diligently inquire in the said college, hall, or other place where he hath authority, whether any scholar or inhabitant of such college or hall, etc. have holden, alleged, or defended, or by any means proponed any conclusion, proposition, or opinion concerning the catholic faith, or sounding contrary to good manners, or contrary to the determination of the church otherwise than appertaineth to necessary doctrine; and if he shall find any suspected or defamed herein, he shall, according to his office, admonish him to desist. And if, after such monition given, the said party offend again in the same or such like, he shall incur "*ipso facto*" (besides the penalties aforesaid) the sentence of greater excommunication. And, nevertheless, if it be a scholar that so offendeth the second time, whatsoever he shall afterwards do in the said university shall not stand in effect. And if he be a doctor, a master, or bachelor, he shall forthwith be suspended from every scholar's act, and in both cases shall lose the right that he hath in the said college or hall whereof he is, "*ipso facto*" and, by the warden, provost, master, principal, or other to whom it appertaineth, he shall be expelled, and a catholic, by lawful means, forthwith placed in his place . . . [The wardens, provosts, masters, and principals are required to enforce the measures upon pain of losing their positions and, if found to favor or defend ideas and practices against the aforesaid, they will also be excommunicated. Anyone else will be unable to receive a benefice for three years. In order to more easily prosecute the offenders, condemnation can take place without the accused actually being present.]

Enarratio (Analysis and Exposition of Texts)

Enarratio, the analysis and exposition of texts, was part of the discipline of grammar, itself one of the three major areas of study within the *trivium* (grammar, rhetoric, and logic or dialectic). Medieval grammar encompassed reading practices from simple grammar as we know it today to sophisticated literary interpretation. *Enarratio* means literally to lift a linguistic unit – a letter, syllable, word, or a longer passage – out of the narrative of a text and to interpret it according to other received readings or one's own ideas. Medieval England did not differ from the rest of Europe in the Middle Ages, which combined Greek and Classical with Christian ideas of literary interpretation, but the appearance of Lollardy in the late fourteenth century complicated the application of grammatical ideas in vernacular contexts (see "Lollary Trials," p. 59, and "Censorship," p. 242).

Reginald Pecock (ca. 1390–ca. 1460), bishop of St. Asaph (1444–50) and Chichester (1450–8), authored six books on religious and literary matters. Consistently anti-Lollard, he became subject to accusations of heresy himself in 1447 and more seriously in 1457 because he suggested that reason could be a better basis for judgment on religious matters than scriptural or Church authority. Given the choice of being burned or recanting his claims, he publicly abjured his writings, which were themselves burned before a large crowd. He wrote the *Repressor* between 1449 and 1455, which (in typical scholastic style) presents Lollard arguments and then systematically returns to them in order to refute them with multiple arguments and examples.

Primary documents and further reading

Colish, M. L. (1983) *The Mirror of Language: A Study in the Medieval Theory of Knowledge*, revd. edn. Lincoln: University of Nebraska Press.

Copeland, R. (1991) *Rhetoric, Hermeneutics, and Translation in the Middle Ages*. Cambridge: Cambridge University Press.

Irvine, M. (1994) *The Making of Textual Culture: "Grammatica" and Literary Theory, 350–1100*. Cambridge: Cambridge University Press.

Minnis, A. J. and A. B. Scott (1991) *Medieval Literary Theory and Criticism, c.1100–c.1375: The Commentary-Tradition*, revd. edn. Oxford: Clarendon Press.

Morison, J. L. (ed.) (1909) *Reginald Pecock's Book of Faith: A Fifteenth-century Theological Tractate*. Glasgow: J. Maclehose.

Pecock, R. (1924) *The Folewer to the Donet*, ed. E. V. Hitchcock. EETS, o.s. 164. Oxford: Oxford University Press.

Scase, W. (1996) "Reginald Pecock." In M. C. Seymour (ed.) *Authors of the Middle Ages 8. English Writers of the Late Middle Ages*, vol. 3. Aldershot, Hampshire: Variorum, 69–146.

Wogan-Browne, J., N. Watson, A. Taylor, and R. Evans (eds.) (1999) *The Idea of the Vernacular: An Anthology of Middle English Literary Theory, 1280–1520*. University Park: Pennsylvania State University Press.

Reginald Pecock. Cambridge University Library MS Kk.4.26. *The Repressor of Over Much Blaming of the Clergy*. Ed. C. Babington. Vol. 1. London: Longman, Green, Longman, and Roberts (1860), 5–100 (selections).
Language: English (Southeast Midland)
Manuscript date: ca. 1460

The firste of these thre trowingis, holdingis,[1] or opiniouns is this: That no governaunce is to be holde of Cristen men, the service or the lawe of God, save it which is groundid in Holi Scripture of the Newe Testament, as summe of the bifore seid men holden, or namelich save it which is groundid in the Newe Testament or in the Oold and is not bi the Newe Testament revokid, as summe othere of hem holden. In this trowing and holding thei ben so kete[2] and so smert and so wantoun that whanne ever eny clerk

[1] tenets.
[2] stubborn.

affermeth to hem eny governaunce being contrarie to her witt or pleasaunce, though it ligge[3] ful open and ful sureli in doom of resoun, and ther fore sureli in moral lawe of kinde, which is lawe of God forto be doon, yit thei anoon asken, "Where groundist thou it in the Newe Testament?" or "Where groundist thou it in Holi Scripture in such place which is not bi the Newe Testament revokid?" And if thei heere not where so in Holi Scripture it is witnessid, thei it dispisen and not receyven as a governaunce of Goddis service and of Goddis moral lawe . . .

The secunde trowing or opinyoun is this: That what ever Cristen man or womman be meke in spirit and willi forto undirstonde treuli and dewli Holi Scripture, schal without fail and defaut fynde the trewe undirstonding of Holi Scripture in what ever place he or sche schal rede and studie though it be in the Apolcalips or oughwhere ellis, and the more meke he or sche be, the sooner he or sche schal come into the verry trewe and dew undirstonding of it, which in Holi Scripture he or sche redith and studieth . . .

The third trowing or opinioun is this: Whanne evere a persoon hath founde the undirstonding of Holi Scripture into which he schal come bi the wey now bifore seid of the second opinioun, he or sche oughte bowe away her heering, her reeding, and her undirstonding fro al resonyng and fro al arguyng or provyng which eny clerk can or wole or mai make bi eny maner evydence of resoun or of Scripture, and namelich of resoun into the contrarie, though the mater be such that it passith not the boondis neither the capacite of resoun forto entermete[4] therwith and forto juge and geve kunnyng ther upon . . .

[Pecock says he will state thirteen "principal conclusiouns" against the first opinion.]

[T]he firste is this: It longith not to Holi Scripture, neither it is his office into which God hath him ordeyned, neither it is his part forto grounde eny governaunce or deede or service of God, or eny lawe of God, or eny trouthe which mannis resoun bi nature may fynde, leerne, and knowe.

[He then provides six arguments, a corollary, and proofs for this first conclusion, of which two arguments and a corollary follow.]

The second principal argument into the first bifore sett and spoken conclusioun or trouthe is this: Thilk thing is the ground of a governaunce,

---

3   lie.
4   be concerned.

or vertu, or trouthe, out of which al the sufficient leernyng and knowing of
the same governaunce, trouthe, and vertu cometh, procedith, and growith,
and may be had though al other thing pretendid to be ground ther of be
awey or were not in being, but so it is that al the leernyng and knowing,
which Holi Scripture geveth upon eny bifore seid governaunce, deede, or
trouthe of Goddis moral lawe, mai be had bi doom of natural resoun. Yhe,
though Holi Writt had not spoke ther of or though he schulde nevere fro
hens forthward speke ther of (as anoon aftir schal be proved) and over it al
the forther kunnyng which Holi Writt geveth not upon eny seid governaunce
or deede or treuthe of Goddis lawe and service and is necessarie to be had
upon the same governaunce, trouthe, or vertu, mai be had bi labour in
doom of natural resoun (as anoon aftir schal be proved). Wherfore, doom
of natural resoun (which is clepid "moral lawe of kinde" in the book *Of just
apprising Holi Scripture*)[5] and not Holi Scripture is the ground of alle the
seid governauncis, deedis, vertues, and trouthis . . .

The third principal argument into the same firste and principal conclusioun
is this: Bifore that eny positif lawe of God, that is to seie, eny voluntarie or
wilful assignement of God, was goven to the Jewis fro the long tyme of
Adamys comyng out of Paradis into the tyme of circumcisioun in the daies
of Abraham, and into the positif lawe goven bi Moyses, the peple lyveden
and serviden God, and weren bounde weelnigh bi alle tho moral vertues
and moral governauncis and treuthis whiche bi doom of her natural resoun
thei founden and leerneden and camen to, and so thei weren bounde
weelnygh to alle moral governauncis and moral trouthis into whiche Cristen
men ben bounden now in tyme of the Newe Testament. Aftirward, whanne
tyme of Jewis came and the positif lawe of the cerymonyes, judicialis, and
sacramentalis weren goven to the Jewis, the othere now bifore seid lawis of
resoun weren not revokid, but thei contynueden into charge of the Jewis
with the lawis of cerymonies, judicialis, and sacramentis so that the Jewis
weren chargid with alle the lawis of resoun with whiche the peple fro Adam
thidir to weren chargid and also over that with the positif lawis of God
thanne goven. Forwhi, it is not rad that the lawis of resoun weren thanne
revokid, and also needis alle men musten graunte that summe of hem abode
charging the Jewis, and skile is ther noon whi summe of hem so abode and
not alle; wherfore, it is to be holde that alle tho lawis of resoun with whiche
the peple were chargid bifore the tyme of Jewis aboden, stille charging also
the Jewis into the tyme of Cristis passioun . . .

---

[5] This work and the others below are Pecock's books and treatises.

Of whiche first principal conclusioun thus proved folewith ferther this corelarie, that whanne evere and where evere in Holi Scripture or out of Holi Scripture be writen eny point or eny governaunce of the seide lawe of kinde, it is more verrili writen in the book of mannis soule than in the outward book of parchemyn or of velym, and if eny semyng discorde be bitwixe the wordis writen in the outward book of Holi Scripture and the doom of resoun, write in mannis soule and herte, the wordis so writen withoutforth oughten be expowned and be interpretid and brought forto accorde with the doom of resoun in thilk mater, and the doom of resoun oughte not forto be expowned, glosid, interpretid, and broughte for to accorde with the seid outward writing in Holi Scripture of the Bible or oughwhere ellis out of the Bible. Forwhi, whanne ever eny mater is tretid bi it which is his ground and bi it which is not his ground, it is more to truste to the treting which is mad ther of bi the ground than bi the treting ther of bi it which is not ther of the ground and, if thilke two tretingis oughten not discorde, it folewith that the treting doon bi it which is not the ground oughte to be mad for to accord with the treting which is maad bi the ground. And therfore this corelarie conclusioun muste nedis be trewe . . .

The secunde principal conclusioun and trouthe is this: Though it perteyne not to Holi Scripture forto grounde eny natural or moral governaunce or trouthe into whos fynding, leernyng, and knowing mannis reson may bi him silf and bi natural help come, as it is open now bifore bi proofis of the firste principal conclusioun, yit it mai perteyne weel ynough to Holi Scripture that he reherce suche now seid governauncis and treuthis, and that he witnesse hem as groundid sumwhere ellis in the lawe of kinde or doom of mannis resoun. And so he dooth (as to ech reder ther yn it mai be opene) that bi thilk reherc-ing and witnessyng so doon bi Holi Scripture to men, tho men schulden be bothe remembrid, stirid, provokid, and exortid forto the rather performe and fulfille tho same so rehercid and witnessid governancis and trouthis . . .

The third principal conclusioun is this: The hool office and werk into which God ordeyned Holy Scripture is forto grounde articlis of feith and forto reherce and witnesse moral trouthis of lawe of kinde groundid in moral philsophie, that is to seie in doom of resoun, that the reders be remembrid, stirid, and exortid by so miche the better and the more and the sooner forto fulfille hem . . .

The fourth principal conclusioun is this: It is not the office longing to moral lawe of kinde for to grounde eny article of feith groundid by Holi Scripture. For whi al that the now seid moral lawe of kinde or moral philsophie groundith is groundid bi doom of mannis resoun, and therfore is such a treuthe and a conclusioun that into his fynding, leernyng, and knowing mannis witt mai bi it silf aloone or bi natural helpis withoute revelacioun fro God rise and suffice. But so it is that noon article of feith mai be groundid in doom of resoun sufficientli, neither into his finding, leerning, and knowing mannis resoun bi it silf and bi natural help may rise and suffice withoute therto maad revelacioun or affirmyng fro God . . .

The fifth principal conclusioun is this: Though neither the seide moral lawe of kinde, neither outward bokis therof writen, mowe grounde eny trouthe or conclusioun of verry feith, yit tho outward bokis (as Cristene men hem maken) mowe weel ynow reherce and witnesse trouthis and conclusiouns of feith groundid bifore in Holi Scripture, and so thei doon. Forwhi, it is no more repugnant that bokis of moral philsophie reherce trouthis and conclusiouns propre to the grounding of Holy Scripture than that bokis of Holi Scripture reherce trouthis and conclusiouns propre to the grounding of moral philsophie, and that bokis of grammer reherce treuthis and conclusiouns propre to the grounding of Holi Scripture . . .

The sixth principal conclusioun is this: The hool office and werk into which ben ordeyned the bokis of moral philsophie (writen and mad bi Cristen men in the maner now bifore spoken in the fifth conclusioun) is forto expresse out-wardli bi writing of penne and ynke the treuthis and conclusiouns, whiche the inward book of lawe of kinde, biried in mannis soule and herte, groundith, and forto reherce summe treuthis and conclusiouns of feith longing to the grounding of Holi Scripture that the reders be the more and the oftir remem-brid and stirid and exortid bi thilk rehercing into tho treuthis of feith so rehercid. Of whiche summe ben positif lawis, as ben oonli the treuthis aboute the newe sacramentis of Crist and aboute the usis of hem, and summe ben not lawis, as that thre persoones ben oon God, and that the second of hem was mad man, and that he died and roos fro deeth, and so forth . . .

The seventh principal conclusioun is this: The more deel and party of Goddis hool lawe to man in erthe, and that bi an huge gret quantite over the re-manent parti of the same lawe, is groundid sufficiently out of Holi Scripture in the inward book of lawe of kinde and of moral philsophie, and not in the book of Holi Scripture clepid the Oold Testament and the Newe . . .

The eighth principal conclusioun is this: No man mai leerne and kunne the hool lawe of God to which Cristen men ben bounde but if he can of moral philsophi, and the more that he can in moral philsophie, bi so miche the more he can of Goddis lawe and service . . .

The ninth conclusioun is this: No man schal perfitli, sureli, and sufficienti undirstonde Holi Scripture in alle tho placis where yn he rehercith moral vertures not being positif lawe of feith, but being such as mannys resoun may fynde, leerne, and knowe but if he be bifore weel and perfitli, suerli, and sufficiently leerned in moral philsophie, and the more perfitli, sureli, and sufficientli he is leerned in moral philsophie the more able as bi that he schal be forto perfitli, sureli, and sufficientli undirstonde Holi Scripture in alle tho placis wheryn he spekith of eny moral lawe of God being not positif lawe of feith . . .

The tenth principal conclusioun is this: The leernyng and kunnyng of the seid lawe of kinde and of the seid moral philsophie is so necessarie to Cristen men that it mai not [b]e lackid of hem if thei schulen thriftili serve to God and keepe his lawe bitake to hem in erthe . . .

Out of thes bifore sett seventh, eighth, ninth, and tenth conclusiouns and trouthis cometh forth ful openli and sureli this eleventh conclusioun and trouthe. Ful weel oughten alle persoones of the lay parti not miche leerned in moral philsophi and lawe of kinde forto make miche of clerkis weel leerned in moral philsophi, that tho clekis schulden helpe tho lay persoones forto aright undirstonde Holi Scripture in alle tho placis in which Holi Scripture rehercith the bifore spoken conclusiouns and treuthis of moral philsophi, that is to seie of lawe of kinde. Forwhi, withoute tho clerkis so leerned in moral philsophi and with oute her direccioun, the now seid lay persoones schulen not esili, lightli, and anoon have the dew undirstonding of Holi Scripture in the now seid placis, as is bifore proved in the ninth conclusioun.

Also, out of the same bifore sett seventh, eighth, ninth, and tenth conclusions and trouthis and out of the assay and experience which mai be had in the over reding and studiyng the bokis, anoon aftir to be rehercid folewith this twelfth conclusioun and trouthe. Ful weel oughten alle persoones of the lay parti not leerned oughwhere ellis bi the now seid clerkis or bi othere bokis of moral philsophie, forto make miche of bokis maad to hem in her modiris langage, whiche ben clepid thus: *The donet into Cristen religioun, The folwer to the donet, The book of Cristen religioun* (namelich the first parti fro the bigynnyng of the third treti forthward), *The book filling the four tablis, The book of worschiping,* the book clepid *The just apprising of Holi Scripture,* the book clepid *The provoker of Cristen men, The book of Counceilis,* and othere mo pertenyng to the now seid *Book of Cristen religioun.* Forwhi, in these now spoken bokis thei schulen leerne and kunne (in a ful notable quantite and mesure, and in a fair fourme) the now bifore seid moral philsophie, being so necessari forto be undirstonde and being in it silf the more parti of al her moral lawe and service to God, as it is open bi the seventh conclusioun, and being so necessarie forto expowne or interprete or glose dewli and treuly Holi Scripture in alle placis where he spekith of Goddis lawe and service, except thilk fewe placis where yn he spekith of the

making and using of the fewe newe sacramentis of Crist, as it is open bi the
ninth bifore sett conclusioun. Wherfore, miche oughten lay persoones forto
make and apprise and love the now spoken bokis. And ferthermore, over
this now seid the now spoken bokis techen ful clereli and bihovefulli⁶ the
treuthis and governauncis of Goddis lawe whiche ben groundid in Holi
Scripture and also othere treuthis of feith whiche ben not lawis and ben
groundid in Holi Scripture, and also thei treten ful nobili the positif lawis
of Criste aboute the newe sacramentis, and therefore ful miche good (as y
hope) schal come bi the reeding, leernyng, and using of the now spoken
bokis . . .

[13. To ask of laws and truths affirmed by "lawe of kinde and in moral
philsophi" where they are grounded in scripture, is to be unreasonable. It is
like asking for proofs of grammar in scripture or a truth about masonry in
butchery. Having provided 13 "principal conclusiouns," Pecock turns to
other proofs, including the following.]

If substanciali leerned clerkis in logik and in moral philsophie and in
dyvynyte, and ripeli exercisid ther yn, weren not and schulden not be forto
wiseli and dewli geve trewe undirstondingis and exposiciouns to textis of
Holi Scripture, or ellis, though suche clerkis ben and the lay parti wolen not
attende to the doctrine whiche tho clerkis mowe and wolen (bi proof of
sufficient and open evydence) mynystre to the lay parti, but the lay parti
wolen attende and truste to her owne wittis and wolen lene to textis of the
Bible oonli, y dare weel seie so many dyverse opinions schulde rise in lay
mennys wittis bi occasioun of textis in Holy Scripture aboute mennys moral
conversacioun that al the world schulde be cumbrid therwith, and men
schulden accorde to gidere in keping her service to God as doggis doon in
a market whanne ech of hem terith otheris coot. For whi oon man wolde
understonde a text in this maner and an other man wolde understonde it in
an other dyvers maner, and the third man in the third maner; namelich, for
that weelnigh in ech place where Holi Writ spekith of eny point of moral
lawe of kinde, it is so spoken that it nedith forto have a redressing of it into
accordaunce with lawe of kinde and with doom of reson, and than if no
juge schulde be had forto deeme bitwixe hem so diversely holding, eende
schulde ther nevere be of her strif into tyme that thei schulden falle into
fighting and into werre and bateil, and thanne schulde al thrift and grace

---

⁶ helpfully.

passe awey, and noon of her holdingis schulde in eny point be therbi strengthid or confermed . . .

[Pecock rebukes preachers who interpret for themselves rather than trusting to learned clerks, and he makes special mention of the Hussites in Bohemia and heresy in England. He exhorts England's ruler (Henry VI) to "conquere and reforme" England rather than fight for land in France and Normandy, and he expresses his opinion that university degrees be only given to qualified people and that the people listen more to and pay more money to properly trained preachers. He acknowledges that the people are not at fault if they follow the council of a faulty preacher. He then moves on to his refutation of the second opinion.]

That the second opinioun sett and spoken bifore in the firste chapiter of this present book is untrewe, y mai prove bothe bi experiencis and bi resoun. Bi experience thus: among hem that holden the seid second opinioun many ben whiche han undirstonde certein processis of Holi Scripture in oon certein maner of understonding whanne thei helden hem silf meeke and in good wil forto receyve and have the trewe and dew undirstonding therof, and yit aftirward, whanne thei were not more meke neither more willi to the same, thei han chaungid and varied fro the firste . . . undirstonding into an other maner of undirstonding the same processis, as y here of have had sufficient knowing. Wherfore, thei hem silf, whiche holden the seid second opinioun oughten, bi her owne experience takun upon her owne deedis, prove the same second opinioun to be untrewe . . .

[He continues to reason that equal numbers of people can understand Holy Scripture in opposite ways and that, by both experience and reason, a bad clerk can arrive at a true meaning as much as a virtuous clerk. Finally, he argues that the second opinion is false also because, as reason and experience show, meek people may not gain a better understanding than any others. Pecock then turns to the third opinion.]

The third opinioun put bifore in the first chapiter of this present book muste needis be untrewe, for he is agens Holi Scripture and also agens resoun. [As proof, Pecock quotes and cites the Bible and his own work, *The Folewer to the Donet.*]

Certis, withoute argument can no trouthe be knowe neither learned in the intellect of man and that whether thilk trouthe be of lawe of kinde or of feith, except thilk treuthis in lawe of kinde which ben openest of alle othere treuthis and han noon opener treuthis than thei ben bi whiche thei mowe be proved, as y have openli scheweid in othere places of mi writingis. And therfore ful weel and ful treuli oughte arguyng and disputing be clepid light.

That the third opinioun is also agens reson, y mai schewe thus: even as thilk opinioun or conclusioun of lawe of kinde is not worthi be holde trewe but if he mai be susteyned bi hise propre to him groundis and evidencis, withynne the boundis of lawe of kinde perteynyng to the grounding of suche conclusions and but if sufficient aunswere can be mad to al arguyng, which may ther agens be maad bi skilis in lawe of kinde, right so thilk feith or conclusiouns of bileeve is not worthi to be holde trewe but if he may be susteyned bi hise propre to him groundis and evidencis perteynyng to the grounding of feith and but if sufficient answere can be geve to al arguyng, which mai be mad ther agens. Goddis forbode that eny man schulde so trowe and feele that eny conclusioun of feith oughte be holde for trewe and for feith, and yit couthe be proved bi eny argument to be untrewe and fals, and that eny argument couthe be mad agens eny conclusioun of trewe feith, to which argument it couthe not cleerli at fulle be answerid. For whi ther is no treuthe knowun for a treuthe (whether it be a treuthe of lawe of kinde or of lawe of feith) but that, if he be knowe perfitli and fulli bi hise evydencis and groundis (as it mai bi good labour of arguyng be knowe), he schal be proved trewe agens alle agenseiers whiche evere thei ben, Cristen or hethen, and thei mowe bi strengthe of argument be constreyned in her reson for to consente therto, wole thei nile thei, if thei geve sufficient attendaunce to the arguyng, and also sufficient cleer at fulle answere mai be gevun to al arguyng mad agens the same conclusioun of feith . . . And, ferthermore, the more eny treuthe, whether he be of feith or of no feith, be brought in to examinacioun of arguyng, the more trewe and the more cleerli trewe he schal be seen and, if he be not trewe but seme trewe eer he come into triyng of argumentis, the lenger he abidith the examynacioun of arguyng, the more untrewe and the more cleerli untrewe he schal be seen . . . And therfore Goddis forbod that any Cristen man schulde thinke and trowe to be a trewe and a good governance forto kepe hise feithis and his othere opiniouns privey and lete hem not come into what ever examynacioun of argumentis whiche mowe be mad ther upon, namelich, whanne and where the holder of tho feithis and of hise othere opinions mai be sikir forto come and go and speke and argue and answere withoute eny bodili harme and with out eny losse of his ricches or of his fame . . .

Also that this third opinioun is agens resoun it is evydent herbi: he is lik to the lawe of Macomet and of Sarezenis in thilk point in which her lawe is moost unresonable. Forwhi, the lawe of Macomet biddith, undir greet peyne of horrible deeth suffring, that no man, aftir he hath receyved the feith of thilk lawe, dispute or argue with eny other man upon eny point, article, or conclusioun of thilk lawe and, bi this wrecchid and cursid maundement, the peple of thilk secte ben so miche lockid up undir boond that manie mo of hem myghten be convertid into trewe feith than yit ben if thilk so unresonable maundement of the same lawe ne were. And if any Cristen men wolen locke hem silf so up in her feithis and othere opiniouns of Cristis lawe fro arguyng and disputing ther upon with othere men, as y have knowe bi reporting of ful trewe persoones that thei so doon, certis ther in thei doon foul vilonie to Cristis lawe of feith and of lawe of kinde, making as though Cristis scid lawe were so feble chaffare[7] and so countirfetid and so untrewe that it durst not save his worschip if he were thriftili examyned. And thei doon also ful periloseli to hem silf for to make hem so sikir in a feith eer it be sufficientli tried and proved forto be holde worthi a trewe feith or no. And therfore the thridde bifore sett opinioun in the first chapiter of this book is unresonable.

The English Language

Four principal dialects existed in late medieval England in addition to the western and northern Welsh and Scots. Latin was still the dominant institutional language and French was commonly spoken among the nobility and others. Gradually throughout the fourteenth and fifteenth centuries, however, written English would become the language of many kinds of records, replacing Latin and French. This complex linguistic situation, somewhat exacerbated by Lollardy, caused both anxious and playful reflection on the part of writers (see "Censorship," p. 242).

For information on Ranulf Higden and John Trevisa, see "The English and England," p. 50. The following selection precedes the passage on the English and England, and may be read in relation to that discussion. Here again we see Trevisa glossing Higden's ideas.

Primary documents and further reading

Berndt, R. (1972) "The Period of the Final Decline of French in Medieval England (Fourteenth and Early Fifteenth Centuries)." *Zeitschrift für Anglistik und Amerikanistik* 20: 341–69.

[7] goods.

Blake, N. F. (ed.) (1973) *Caxton's Own Prose*. London: Deutsch.

Clanchy, M. T. (1993) *From Memory to Written Record, England 1066–1307*. Oxford: Blackwell.

Ellis, R. (1994) "Introduction." In R. Ellis and R. Evans (eds.) *The Medieval Translator 4*. Binghamton: State University of New York Press.

Fisher, J. H. (1977) "Chancery and the Emergence of Standard Written English in the Fifteenth Century." *Speculum* 52: 870–99.

Fisher, J. H., M. Richardson, and J. L. Fisher (eds.) (1984) *An Anthology of Chancery English*. Knoxville: University of Tennessee Press.

Orme, N. (1973) *English Schools in the Middle Ages*. London: Methuen.

Somerset, F. (1998) *Clerical Discourse and Lay Audience in Late Medieval England*. Cambridge: Cambridge University Press.

Waldron, R. (1988) "John Trevisa and the Use of English." *Proceedings of the British Academy* 74: 171–202.

Wogan-Browne, J., N. Watson, A. Taylor, and R. Evans (eds.) (1999) *The Idea of the Vernacular: An Anthology of Middle English Literary Theory, 1280–1520*. University Park: Pennsylvania State University Press.

Ranulf Higden. St. John's College, Cambridge, MS 204. In C. Babington and J. R. Lumby (eds.) (1869) *Polychronicon*, vol. 2, trans. J. Trevisa. London, 157–63.
Language: English (Southwestern)
Manuscript date: ca. 1400

De incolarum linguis. Capitulum quinquagesimum nonum.[1]

[Ranulf says:] As it is i-knowe how meny manere peple beeth in this ilond, there beeth also so many dyvers longages and tonges; notheles, Walsche men and Scottes, that beeth nought i-medled with other naciouns, holdeth wel nyh hir firste longage and speche but if the Scottes that were somtyme confederat and wonede with the Pictes drawe[2] somwhat after hir speche, but the Flemmynges that woneth in the weste side of Wales haveth i-left her straunge speche and speketh Saxonliche i-now. Also Englische men, they hadde from the bygynnynge thre manere speche – northerne, sowtherne, and middel speche in the myddel of the lond – as they come of thre manere peple of Germania; notheles, by comyxtioun and mellynge,[3] first with Danes and afterward with Normans, in meny the contray longage is apayred, and som useth straunge wlafferynge, chiterynge, harrynge, and garrynge

---

[1]　Concerning the language of the inhabitants. Chapter Fifty.
[2]　follow.
[3]　mixing.

grisbayting.[4] This apayrynge of the burthe of the tunge is bycause of tweie thinges: oon is for children in scole, agenst the usage and manere of alle othere naciouns, beeth compelled for to leve hire owne langage and for to construe hir lessouns and here thynges in Frensche, and so they haveth seth the Normans come first in to Engelond. Also, gentil men children beeth i-taught to speke Frensche from the tyme that they beeth i-rokked in here cradel, and kunneth speke and playe with a childes broche, and uplondisshe men wil likne hym self to gentil men and fondeth with greet besynesse for to speke Frensce for to be i-tolde of.

Trevisa: This mannere was moche i-used to for firste deth[5] and is siththe sumdel i-chaunged, for John Cornwaile, a maister of grammer,[6] chaunged the lore in gramer scole and construccioun of Frensche in to Englische, and Richard Pencriche lerned the manere techynge of hym and of othere men of Pencrich so that now, the yere of oure Lorde a thowsand, thre hundred, and foure score and fyve, and of the secounde Kyng Richard after the conquest nyne, in alle the gramere scoles of Engelond, children leveth Frensche and construeth and lerneth an Englische, and haveth therby avauntage in oon side and disavauntage in another side: here avauntage is that they lerneth her gramer in lasse tyme than children wer i-woned to doo; disavauntage is that now children of gramer scole conneth na more Frensche than can hir lift heele, and that is harme for hem and they schulle passe the see and travaille in straunge landes and in many other places. Also, gentil men haveth now moche i-left for to teche here childen Frensche.

Ranulf says: Hit semeth a greet wonder how Englische, that is the burthe tonge of Englisshe men and her owne langage and tonge, is so dyverse of sown in this oon ilond, and the langage of Normandie is comlynge[7] of another londe and hath oon manere soun among alle men that speketh hit aright in Engelond.

Trevisa: Nevertheles, there is as many dyvers manere Frensche in the reem of Fraunce as is dyvers manere Englische in the reem of Engelond.

Ranulf says: Also, of the forsaide Saxon tonge that is i-deled athre[8] and is abide scarsliche with fewe yplondisshe men, is greet wonder, for men of the Est with men of the West, as it were undir the same partie of hevene, acordeth more in sownynge of speche than men of the North with men of

---

[4]   stammering, twittering, snarling, gnashing and grinding of teeth.
[5]   the pestilence.
[6]   Fl. 1344–9 in Oxford.
[7]   an import.
[8]   divided in three.

the South; therfore, it is that Mercii, that beeth men of myddel Engelond, as it were parteners of the endes, understondeth bettre the side langages, northerne and southerne, than northerne and southerne understondeth either other. *Willelmus de Pontificibus, libro tertio.*[9] Al the longage of the Northhumbres, and specialliche at York, is so scharp, slitting,[10] and frotynge[11] and unschape, that we southern men may that longage unnethe understonde. I trowe that that is bycause that they beeth nyh to straunge men and naciouns that speketh strongliche, and also bycause that the kynges of Engelond woneth alwey fer from that cuntrey, for they beeth more i-torned to the south contray and, if they gooth to the north contray, they gooth with greet help and strengthe. The cause why they beeth more in the south contrey than in the North is for hit may be better corne[12] londe, more peple, more noble citees, and more profitable havenes.

Plays and Representations

Lollards often objected to any visual representation of religious subjects, including paintings, illuminations, and sculptures (even crosses) (see "Lollardy Trials," p. 59, "Censorship," p. 242, and the "Chaucer portrait: Thomas Hoccleve, *Regiment of Princes*," p. 141). Such a rejection of images was part of a more general late medieval desire for unmediated communication with God and a relationship that was also outside established institutional conventions. Criticisms of devotion to images were frequently coupled with anti-pilgrimage discourse because of a common objection to the veneration of saints (see "Pilgrimage," p. 32). Lollards and orthodox Church authorities began reviving the much older iconoclastic controversies before the 1370s, but debates flourished in the last decades of the fourteenth century and into the fifteenth century.

Written some time before 1425, the *Tretise of Miraclis Pleyinge* offers an analysis of plays that is rare for the Lollards, indeed for any medieval English text, and how much it derives its ideas directly from Wycliffite notions has been debated. The *Tretise*, which falls into two parts (of which the first is included here), appears in an anthology of writings critical of clerical and other religious customs. The first part on the plays is written in a scholastic

---

[9] William of Malmesbury (ca. 1095–1143), *Gesta pontificum Anglorum.*
[10] piercing, shrill.
[11] grating.
[12] grain-growing.

style, with objections raised and then methodically answered (see also "*Enarratio* (Analysis and Exposition of Texts)," p. 249).

Primary documents and further reading

Barnum, P. H. (ed.) (1976, 1980) *Dives and Pauper*, 2 parts. EETS, o.s. 275, 280. Oxford: Oxford University Press.

Hudson, A. (ed.) (1978) *Selections from English Wycliffite Writings*. Cambridge: Cambridge University Press.

—— (1988) *The Premature Reformation: Wycliffite Texts and Lollard History*. Oxford: Clarendon Press.

Nichols, A. E. (1994) *Seeable Signs: The Iconography of the Seven Sacraments, 1350– 1544*. Woodbridge, Suffolk: Boydell Press.

Nissé, R. (1998) "Staged Interpretations: Civic Rhetoric and Lollard Politics in the York Plays." *Journal of Medieval and Early Modern Studies* 28: 427–52.

Pecock, R. (1860) *The Repressor of Overmuch Blaming of the Clergy*, vol. 1, ed. C. Babington. London: Longman, Green, Longman, and Roberts.

Woolf, R. (1972) *The English Mystery Plays*. Berkeley: University of California Press.

British Library MS Additional 24202, fols. 14r–17v. In C. Davidson (ed.) (1993) *A Tretise of Miraclis Pleyinge*. Kalamazoo, MI: Medieval Institute, 93–104.
Language: English (Southeast Midland)
Manuscript date: ca. 1425

Here beginnis a tretise of miraclis pleyinge.

Knowe yee, Cristen men, that as Crist, God and man, is bothe weye, trewth, and lif, as seith the gospel of Jon[1] – weye to the erringe, trewthe to the unknowing and douting, lif to the styinge to hevene and weryinge – so Crist dude no thinge to us but efectuely in weye of mercy, in treuthe of ritwesnes, and in lif of yilding everlastinge joye for oure contunuely morning and sorwinge in the valey of teeres. Miraclis, therfore, that Crist dude heere in erthe, outher in himsilf outher in hise seintis, weren so efectuel and in ernest done that to sinful men that erren they broughten forgivenesse of sinne, settinge hem in the weye of right bileve; to doutouse men not stedefast they broughten in kunning to betere plesen God and verry hope in God to been stedefast in him; and to the wery of the weye of God, for the grette penaunce and suffraunce of the tribulacion that men moten have therinne, they broughten in love of brynninge charite to the whiche alle

[1]   John 14.6.

thing is light, yhe to suffere dethe, the whiche men most dreden, for the everlastinge lif and joye that men most loven and disiren of the whiche thing verry hope puttith awey all werinesse heere in the weye of God.

Thanne, sithen miraclis of Crist and of hise seintis weren thus efectuel, as by oure bileve we ben in certein, no man shulde usen in bourde and pleye the miraclis and werkis that Crist so ernystfully wroughte to oure helthe. For whoevere so doth, he errith in the byleve, reversith Crist, and scornyth God. He errith in the bileve, for in that he takith the most precious werkis of God in pley and bourde, and so takith his name in idil and so misusith oure byleve. A, Lord, sithen an erthely servaunt dar not takun in pley and in bourde that that his erthely lord takith in ernest, myche more we shulden not maken oure pleye and bourde of tho miraclis and werkis that God so ernestfully wrought to us. For sothely whan we so doun, drede to sinne is takun awey, as a servaunt, whan he bourdith with his maister, leesith his drede to offendyn him, namely whanne be bourdith with his maister in that that his maister takith in ernest. And right as a nail smiten in holdith two thingis togidere, so drede smiten to Godward holdith and susteineth oure bileve to him.

Therfore, right as pleyinge and bourdinge of the most ernestful werkis of God takith aweye the drede of God that men shulden han in the same, so it takith awey oure bileve and so oure most helpe of oure savacion. And sith taking awey of oure bileve is more venjaunce taking than sodeyn taking awey of oure bodily lif, and whanne we takun in bourde and pley the most ernestful werkis of God as ben hise miraclis, God takith awey fro us his grace of mekenesse, drede, reverence, and of oure bileve; thanne, whanne we pleyin his miraclis as men don nowe on dayes, God takith more venjaunce on us than a lord that sodaynly sleeth his servaunt for he pleyide to homely with him. And right as that lord thanne in dede seith to his servaunt, "Pley not with me but pley with thy pere," so whanne we takun in pley and in bourde the miraclis of God, he, fro us takinge his grace, seith more ernestfully to us than the forseid lord, "Pley not with me but pley with thy pere."

Therfore, siche miraclis pleyinge reversith Crist. Firste in taking to pley that that he toke into most ernest. The secound in taking to miraclis of oure fleyss, of oure lustis, and of oure five wittis that that God tooc to the bringing in of his bitter deth and to teching of penaunse doinge, and to fleyinge of feding of oure wittis and to mortifying of hem. And therfore it is that seintis myche noten that of Cristis lawghing we reden never in holy writt, but of his myche penaunse, teris, and scheding of blod, doying us to witen therby that alle oure doing heere shulde ben in penaunce, in disciplining of oure fleyssh, and in penaunce of adversite. And therfore alle the werkis that we don that ben out of alle thes thre utturly reversen Cristis werkis. And therfore seith Seint Poul that "Yif yee been out of discipline, of the whiche alle gode men ben maad perceneris,[2] thanne avoutreris yee ben and not sones of God."[3] And sith miraclis pleynge reversen penaunce doying as they in greet liking ben don and to grete liking ben cast biforn, there as penaunce is in gret mourning of hert and to greet mourning is ordeinyd biforne.

It also reversith dissipline, for in verry discipline the verry vois of oure maister Crist is herd as a scoler herith the vois of his maister, and the yerd[4] of God in the hond of Crist is seyn, in the whiche sight alle oure othere thre wittis for drede tremblyn and quaken as a childe tremblith seing the yerde of his maister. And the thridde in verry dissipline is verry turning awey and forgeting of alle tho thingis that Crist hatith and turnyde himsilf awey heere as a childe undir dissipline of his maister turnith him awey fro alle thingis that his maister hath forbedun him and forgetith hem for the greet minde that he hath to doun his maistris wille.

And for thes thre writith Seint Petur, seyinge, "Be yee mekid[5] undur the mighty hond of God that he henhaunce[6] you in the time of visiting, all youre bisinesse throwinge in him."[7] That is, "be yee mekid," that is, to Crist, heringe his voice by verry obeschaunce to his hestis; and "undur the mighty hond of God," seeing evere more his yird to chastisen us in his hond yif we waxen wantown or idil, bethenking us, seith Seint Petre, that "hidous and ferful it is to fallen into the hondis of God on live."[8] For right as most joye it is to steyen up into the hond of the mercy of God, so it is most hidous and ferful to fallen into the hondis of the wrathe of God. Therfore, mekely drede we him heere evere more seing and thenkinge his yerde overe oure hevyd, and thanne he shal enhauncyn us elliswhere in time of his graceous visiting.[9] So that alle oure bisinesse we throwyn in him, that is, that alle othere erthely werkis we don not but to don his gostly werkis more frely and spedely and more plesauntly to him tristing, that to him is cure over us, that is, yif we don to him that that is in oure power, he schal mervelousely don to us that that is in his power bothe in dylivering us fro alle perilis and in giving us graciously al that us nedith or willen axen of him.

[2] partners.
[3] Hebrews 12.8.
[4] rod.
[5] made meek.
[6] comfort.
[7] 1 Peter 5.5–6.
[8] Hebrews 10.31.
[9] I.e., Judgment.

And sithen no man may serven two lordis togydere, as seith Crist in his gospel,[10] no man may heren at onys efectuely the voice of oure maister Crist and of his owne lustis. And sithen miraclis pleyinge is of the lustis of the fleyssh and mirthe of the body, no man may efectuely heeren hem and the voice of Crist at onys, as the voice of Crist and the voice of the fleysh ben of two contrarious lordis. And so miraclis pleying reversith discipline, for as seith Seint Poul, "Eche forsothe discipline in the time that is now is not a joye but a mourninge."[11] Also, sithen it makith to se veine sightis of degyse,[12] aray of men and wymmen by yvil continaunse, either stiring othere to leccherie and debatis as aftir most bodily mirthe comen moste debatis, as siche mirthe more undisposith a man to paciencie and ablith to glotonye and to othere vicis, wherfore it suffrith not a man to beholden enterly the yerde of God over his heved, but makith to thenken on alle siche thingis that Crist by the dedis of his passion badde us to forgeten. Wherfore, siche miraclis pleyinge, bothe in penaunce doying in verry discipline and in pacience, reversyn Cristis hestis and his dedis.

Also, siche miraclis pleying is scorning of God, for right as ernestful leving[13] of that that God biddith is dispising of God, as dide Pharao,[14] so bourdfully taking Goddis biddingis or wordis or werkis is scorning of him, as diden the Jewis that bobbiden[15] Crist, thanne, sithen thes miraclis pleyeris taken in bourde the ernestful werkis of God, no doute that ne they scornen God as diden the Jewis that bobbiden Crist, for they lowen[16] at his passioun as these lowyn and japen of the miraclis of God. Therfore, as they scorneden Crist, so theese scorne God. And right as Pharao, wrooth[17] to do that that God bad him, dispiside God, so these miraclis pleyeris and maintenours, leevinge plesingly to do that God biddith hem, scornen God. He forsothe had beden us alle to halowyn his name, giving drede and reverence in alle minde of his werkis withoute ony pleying or japinge as al holinesse is in ful ernest. Men, thanne, pleyinge the name of Goddis miraclis as plesingly, they leeve to do that God biddith hem so they scornen his name and so scornyn him.

[10]   Matthew 6.24; Luke 16.13.
[11]   Hebrews 12.11.
[12]   disguise.
[13]   serious rejecting.
[14]   Exodus 7–12.
[15]   struck with fists, insulted.
[16]   laugh.
[17]   was unwilling.

[1.] But here agenus they seyen that they pleyen these miraclis in the worschip of God and so diden not thes Jewis that bobbiden Crist.

[2.] Also, ofte sithis by siche miraclis pleyinge ben men commited to gode livinge, as men and wymmen seing in miraclis pleyinge that the devul by ther aray, by the whiche they moven eche on other to leccherie and to pride, makith hem his servauntis to bringen hemsilf and many othere to helle, and to han fer more vilenye herafter by ther proude aray heere than they han worschipe heere, and seeinge ferthermore that al this worldly being heere is but vanite for a while, as is miraclis pleying, wherthoru they leeven ther pride and taken to hem afterward the meke conversacion of Crist and of hise seintis. And so miraclis pleying turneth men to the bileve and not pervertith.

[3.] Also, ofte sithis by siche miraclis pleyinge men and wymmen, seinge the passioun of Crist and of his seintis, ben movyd to compassion and devocion, wepinge bitere teris, thanne they ben not scorninge of God but worschiping.

[4.] Also prophitable to men and to the worschipe of God it is to fulfillun and sechen alle the menes by the whiche men mowen leeve sinne and drawen hem to vertues and, sithen as ther ben men that only by ernestful doinge wilen be convertid to God, so ther been othere men that wilen not be convertid to God but by gamen and pley. And now on dayes men ben not convertid by the ernestful doing of God ne of men, thanne now it is time and skilful to assayen to convertyn the puple by pley and gamen as by miraclis pleyinge and other maner mirthes.

[5.] Also, summe recreacion men moten han, and bettere it is (or lesse yvele) that they han theire recreacion by pleyinge of miraclis than by pleyinge of other japis.

[6.] Also, sithen it is leveful to han the miraclis of God peintid, why is not as wel leveful to han the miraclis of God pleyed, sithen men mowen bettere reden the wille of God and his mervelous werkis in the pleyinge of hem than in the peintinge? And betere they ben holden in mennes minde and oftere rehersid by the pleyinge of hem than by the peintinge, for this is a deed bok, the tother a quick.

[1.] To the first reson we answeryn, seying that siche miraclis pleyinge is not to the worschipe of God, for they ben don more to ben seen of the worlde and to plesyn to the world thanne to ben seen of God or to plesyn to him, as Crist never ensaumplide[18] hem but onely hethene men that evere

---

[18]   set forth as examples.

more dishonouren God, seyinge that to the worschipe of God, that is to the most veleinye of him. Therfore, as the wickidnesse of the misbileve of hethene men lyith to themsilf whanne they seyn that the worshiping of theire maumetrie is to the worschipe of God, so mennus lecherye now on dayes to han ther owne lustus lieth to hemself whanne they seyn that suche miracles pleying is to the worschip of God. For Crist seith that folc of avoutrie sechen siche singnys as a lecchour sechith signes of verrey love but no dedis of verrey love. So sithen thise miraclis pleyinge ben onely singnis, love withoute dedis, they ben not onely contrarious to the worschipe of God – that is, bothe in signe and in dede – but also they ben ginnys of the devvel to cacchen men to byleve of Anticrist, as wordis of love withoute verrey dede ben ginnys of the lecchour to cacchen felawchipe to fulfillinge of his leccherie. Bothe for these miraclis pleyinge been verrey leesing as they ben signis withoute dede and for they been verrey idilnesse as they taken the miraclis of God in idil after theire owne lust. And certis idilnesse and leesing been the most ginnys of the dyvul to drawen men to the byleve of Anticrist. And therfore to pristis it is uttirly forbedyn not onely to been miracle pleyere, but also to heren or to seen miraclis pleyinge lest he that shulde been the ginne of God to cacchen men and to holden men in the bileve of Crist, they ben maad agenward by ypocrisie, the gin of the devel to cacchen men to the bileve of Anticrist. Therfore, right as a man sweringe in idil by the names of God and seyinge that in that he worschipith God and dispisith the devil, verrily lyinge doth the reverse; so miraclis pleyers, as they ben doers of idilnesse, seyinge that they don it to the worschip of God, verreyly liyn. For, as seith the gospel, "Not he that seith 'Lord, Lord' schal come to blisse of hevene, but he that doth the wille of the fadir of hevene schal come to his kindam."[19] So myche more not he that pleyith the wille of God worschipith him, but onely he that doith his wille in deede worschpith him. Right, therfore, as men by feinyd tokenes bygilen and in dede dispisen ther neighboris, so by siche feinyd miraclis men bygilen hemsilf and dispisen God, as the tormentours that bobbiden Crist.

[2.] And, as anentis[20] the secound reson, we seyen that right as a vertuous deede is othere while occasioun of yvel, as was the passioun of Crist to the Jewis, but not occasioun given but taken of hem, so yvele dedis ben occasioun of gode dedis othere while, as was the sinne of Adam occasioun of the coming of Crist, but not occasion given of the sinne but occasion takun of

[19]   Matthew 7.21.
[20]   concerning.

the grete mercy of God. The same wise miraclis pleyinge, albeit that it be sinne, is othere while occasion of converting of men, but as it is sinne it is fer more occasion of perverting of men, not onely of oon singuler persone but of al an hool comynte,[21] as it makith al a puple to ben ocupied in vein agenus this heeste of the Psauter book that seith to alle men and namely to pristis that eche day reden it in ther servise: "Turne awey min eyen that they se not vanitees," and efte, "Lord, thou hatidest alle waitinge[22] vanitees."[23] How thanne may a prist pleyn in entirlodies or give himsilf to the sight of hem sithen it is forbeden him so expresse by the forseide heste of God, namely sithen he cursith eche day in his service alle tho that bowen awey fro the hestis of God. But, alas, more harme is, pristis now on dayes most shrewyn hemsilf and al day as a jay that al day crieth, "Watte shrewe!" shrewinge[24] himsilf. Therfore, miraclis pleyinge, sithen it is agenus the heest of God that biddith that thou shalt not take Goddis name in idil, it is agenus oure bileve and so it may not given occacioun of turninge men to the bileve but of perverting. And therfore many men wenen that ther is no helle of everelastinge peine, but that God doth but thretith us not to do it in dede as ben pleyinge of miraclis in signe and not in dede. Therfore, siche miraclis pleying not onely pervertith oure bileve but oure verry hope in God, by the whiche seintis hopiden that that the more they absteneden hem fro siche pleyes, the more mede they shulden have of God, and therfore the holy Sara, the doughter of Raguel, hopinge heie mede of God, seith, "Lord, thou woost that nevere I coveytide man, and clene I have kept my soule fro all lustis, nevere with pleyeris I mingid me mysilfe persin," and by this trwe confessioun to God, as she hopide, so sche hadde hir preyeris herd and grete mede of God.[25] And sithen a yonge womman of the Olde Testament, for keping of hir bodily vertue of chastite and for to worthily take the sacrament of matrimonye whanne hir time shulde come, abstenyde hir fro al maner idil pleying and fro al cumpany of idil pleyeris, myche more a prist of the Newe Testament, that is passid the time of childehod and that not onely shulde kepe chastite but alle othere vertues, ne onely ministren the sacrament of matrimonye but alle othere sacramentis and namely sithen him owith to ministre to alle the puple the precious body of Crist, awghte to abstene him fro al idil pleying bothe of miraclis and ellis. For certis, sithen

21 community.
22 attending.
23 Psalms 118.37; 30.6.
24 scolding.
25 Tobias 3.14–17.

the quen of Saba, as seith Crist in the gospel, schal dampne the Jewis that wolden not reseive the wisdom of Crist,[26] myche more this holy womman Sara at the day of dom schal dampnen the pristis of the Newe Testament that givis heem to pleyes, reversen hir holy maners aprovyd by God and al holiy chirche; therfore sore aughten pristis to be aschamyd that reversen this gode holy womman and the precious body of Crist that they treytyn in ther hondis, the whiche body never gaf him to pley but to all siche thing as is most contrarious to pley, as is penaunce and suffring of persecution.

And so thes miraclis pleyinge not onely reversith feith and hope but verry charite by the whiche a man shulde weilen for his owne sinne and for his neieburs, and namely pristis, for it withdrawith not onely oon persone but alle the puple fro dedis of charite and of penaunce into dedis of lustis and likingis, and of feding of houre[27] wittis. So thanne thes men that seyen, "Pley we a pley of Anticrist and of the Day of Dome that sum man may be convertid therby," fallen into the herisie of hem that, reversing the aposteyl, seiden, "Do we yvel thingis, that ther comyn gode thingis," of whom, as seith the aposteyl, "dampning is rightwise."[28]

[3.] By this we answeren to the thridde resoun, seying that siche miraclis pleyinge giveth noo occasioun of werrey wepinge and medeful, but the weping that fallith to men and wymmen by the sighte of siche miraclis pleyinge, as they ben not principaly for theire oune sinnes ne of theire gode feith withinneforthe, but more of theire sight withouteforth, is not alowable byfore God but more reprowable. For sithen Crist himsilf reprovyde the wymmen that wepten upon him in his passioun, myche more they ben reprovable that wepen for the pley of Cristis passioun, leevinge to wepen for the sinnes of hemsilf and of theire children, as Crist bad the wymmen that wepten on him.[29]

[4.] And by this we answeren to the furthe resoun, seyinge that no man may be convertid to God but onely by the ernestful doyinge of God and by noon vein pleying, for that that the word of God worchith not ne his sacramentis, how shulde pleyinge worchen that is of no vertue but ful of defaute? Therfore, right as the weping that men wepen ofte in siche pley comunely is fals wittnessenge that they lovyn more the liking of theire body and of properite of the world than likinge in God and prosperite of vertu in the soule, and therfore, having more compassion of peine than of sinne,

[26]   See Matthew 12.42.
[27]   our.
[28]   Romans 3.8.
[29]   See Luke 23.27–8.

they falsly wepyn for lakkinge of bodily prosperite more than for lakking of gostly, as don dampnyd men in helle. Right so, ofte sithis the convertinge that men semen to ben convertid by siche pleyinge is but feinyd holinesse, worse than is othere sinne biforehande. For yif he were werrily convertid, he shulde haten to seen alle siche vanite, as biddith the hestis of God, albeit that of siche pley he take occasion by the grace of God to fle sinne and to folowe vertu. And yif men seyn heere that yif this pleyinge of miraclis were sinne, why wile God converten men by the occasion of siche pleyinge, heereto we seyen that God doith so for to comenden his mersy to us that we thenken enterly hou good God is to us, that whil we ben thenkinge agenus him, doinge idilnesse and withseyinge him, he thenkith upon us good, and sendinge us his grace to fleen alle siche vanite. And for ther shulde no thinge be more swete to us than siche maner mercy of God, the Psauter book clepith that mercy "blessinge of swetnesse" where he seith, "Thou cam bifore him in blessinges of swetnesse" – the whiche swetnesse, albeit that it be likinge to the spirit, it is while we ben here ful travelous[30] to the body whan it is verry as the flesche and the spirit ben contrarious;[31] therfore, this swetnesse in God wil not been verely had while a man is ocuped in seinge of pleyis. Therfore, the pristis that seyn[32] hemsilf holy and bysien hem aboute siche pleyis ben verry ypocritis and lieris.

[5.] And herby we answeren to the fifte resoun, seyinge that verry recreacion is leeveful, ocupyinge in lasse werkis to more ardently worschen grettere werkis. And therfore siche miraclis pleyinge ne the sighte of hem is no verrey recreasion but fals and worldly, as provyn the dedis of the fautours[33] of siche pleyis that yit nevere tastiden verely swetnesse in God, traveilinge so myche therinne that their body wolde not sofisen to beren siche a traveile of the spirite, but as man goith fro vertue into vertue, so they gon fro lust into lust that they more stedefastly dwellen in hem. And therfore as this feinyd recreacioun of pleyinge of miraclis is fals equite, so it is double shrewidnesse, worse than though they pleyiden pure vaniteis. For now the puple giveth credence to many mengid leesingis for othere mengid trewthis and maken wenen to been gode that is ful yvel, and so ofte sithis lasse yvele it were to pleyin rebaudye than to pleyin siche miriclis. And yif men axen what recreacion men shulden have on the haliday after theire holy contemplacion in the chirche, we seyen to hem two thingis – oon, that yif he hadde verily

---

[30]   oppressive, wearisome.
[31]   Psalms 20.4.
[32]   say.
[33]   patrons, persons who encourage.

ocupiede him in contemplacion byforn, neither he wolde aske that question ne han wille to se vanite; another we seyn that his recreacioun shulde ben in the werkis of mercy to his neiebore and in diliting him in alle good comunicacion with his neibore, as biforn he dilitid him in God, and in alle othere nedeful werkis that reson and kinde axen.

[6.] And to the laste reson we seyn that peinture, yif it be verry withoute menging of lesingis and not to curious,[34] to myche fedinge mennis wittis, and not occasion of maumetrie to the puple, they ben but as nakyd lettris to a clerk to riden[35] the treuthe. But so ben not miraclis pleyinge that ben made more to deliten men bodily than to ben bokis to lewid men.[36] And therfore, yif they ben quike bookis, they ben quike bookis to shrewidenesse more than to godenesse. Gode men therfore, seinge ther time to schort to ocupien hem in gode ernest werkis and seinge the day of ther rekeninge neighen faste and unknowing whan they schal go hennys, fleen alle siche idilnessis, hyinge[37] that they weren with her spouse Crist in the blisse of hevene.

---

[34]   elaborate.
[35]   read.
[36]   Gregory I the Great (ca. 540–604), *Registrum epistolarum*.
[37]   hurrying.

Appendix: Currency, Income, Prices; Measures

Currency

farthing = $\frac{1}{4}$ pence
halfpenny = $\frac{1}{2}$ pence
groat = 4 pence
shilling = 12 pence
crown = 5 shillings
mark = $\frac{2}{3}$ pound
pound = 20 shillings or 240 pence

Income

Wages fluctuated according to many factors, including time period, time of year, region, and number of days worked. Workers also often received whole or partial payment in goods such as clothing and food.

1300	unskilled laborer	$1\frac{1}{2}$ pence per day
	skilled building laborer	3 pence per day
1325	Elizabeth de Burgh's income from estates	3,000 pounds (gross) per year
1366–77	Philippa Chaucer, personal maid to Queen Philippa	10 marks per year
1367–77	Geoffrey Chaucer, valet to King Edward III	20 marks per year

1380	Thomas Arundel, bishop of Ely's income	1,000 pounds per year
1387	stationer	70 shillings, 11 pence for illumination and binding of missal
1395	limner	40 shillings for illumination of one manuscript
	John of Gaunt's income from estates	10,000 pounds (net) per year
1390	unskilled laborer	3 pence per day
	skilled building laborer	4 pence per day
1421	scribe	12 pounds, 8 shillings for 12 books on hunting for Henry V
1456	washerwoman	16 pence per year
1464	stationer	3 shillings for writing and limning six ballads for queen's procession
	scribe	8 pence for writing the ballads on display boards
1500	skilled building laborer	5 pence per day

Prices

No simple currency conversion to present day currencies exists. However, the following may give some idea of prices if seasonal and regional fluctuations (some substantial) as well as changes over longer periods of time are kept in mind.

1310	1 quire (12 leaves) of parchment	1 shilling, 11 pence
1343	knight's annual household expenses	60 pounds
1348	squire's annual cash expenditure	7 pounds
1358	average shop rental in Paternoster Row (stationers)	1 pound, 5 shillings, 3 pence
1360	ransom of chaplain	8 pounds
	ransom of servants of countess	10 pounds
	ransom of poultry purveyors	10 pounds
	ransom of king's palfreyman	16 pounds
	ransom of Geoffrey Chaucer	16 pounds

1361	4 books of romance	6 shillings, 4 pence
1376	1 copy "Clensyng Synne"	8 pence
1382	illuminated verse *Romance of King Alexander*	10 pounds
1383	1 illuminated, bound missal	39 pounds, 10 shillings, 10 pence
1385	1 quire (12 leaves) of parchment	1 shilling, 9 pence
1389–1518	1 fine vellum skin	5.4 pence average
1391	work horse	13–15 shillings
1393	lord's annual household expenses	277 pounds
1400–1500	wheat averaged 6 shillings a quarter	
1424	shoes	6 pence
	shirt	8 pence
	gloves	3 pence
	belt	1 penny
1430	psalter	13 shillings, 4 pence
1445	psalter	5 shillings
1456	12 bundles of wood	1 shilling, 6 pence
	12 quarters of coal	3 shillings
	1 lb wax and wicks	10 shillings
1463–1527	1 vellum skin	2.5 pence average
1471	1 missal	20 shillings, 3 pence

Measures

Weight

ounce = 28 grams
pound = 16 ounces = 0.45 kilograms
stone = 14 pounds = 6.4 kilograms

Length

inch = 2.54 centimeters
foot = 12 inches = 30.5 centimeters
yard = 3 feet = 0.9 meters
ell = 45 inches = 1.1 meters

Area

acre = 0.4 sq. hectares
hectare = 2.5 acres

Grain volume

peck = 8.8 liters
bushel = 4 pecks = 35 liters
quarter = 8 bushels = 291 liters

Liquid volume

gill = $\frac{1}{2}$ cup or 5 fluid ounces = 142 milliliters
pint = 4 gills = 0.57 liters
quart = 2 pints = 1.1 liters
gallon = 4 quarts = 4.5 liters
tun = 252 gallons = 1134 liters

Depth

fathom = 6 feet = 1.8 meters

Glossary

Note: i/y, c/k interchangeable

A

abay *see* bay
ac *conj.* but, and
adighten, adyghtyn *v.* adorn
adight, adyth *p.* adorned
advoutri(e) *see* avouteri(e)
after *prep.* according to
agayn *see* ayen
al *conj.* even if, although
alday *adv.* always, all the time
algate(s) *adv.* entirely, continually, nevertheless
Alkaron *n.* Koran
almes(se) *n. pl.* alms (**almes-dede,** good deed)
als, also *adv.* as, also, as well
and *conj.* and, if
anon(e) *adv.* at once, immediately
apeire, apaire *v.* make worse, impair, debase, deteriorate
assoile *v.* absolve
atones *adv.* at once
atte *prep.* at the
avouteri(e), advoutri(e) *n.* adultery

avoutrer, advoutrer *n.* adulterer
ay *adv.* always
ayen, agayn *adv., prep.* again, back, in reply, against
ayenward, agenward *adv.* conversely, on the other hand, back, back again

B

baar, bar *v.* bore, carried
bay, abay *n.* surrounding or cornering an animal (**at abay,** unable to escape)
be *prep.* by
been, ben *v.* be, been
behight *p.* promised
benedicite(e) *interj.* bless you (an oath)
bet *adj., adv.* better
biforn *adv., prep., conj.* in front of, before, superior to, prior
biheste *n., v.* promise
bilyve, blyve *adv.* quickly
binime *v.* take away, deprive, take

blithe *v.* happy, eager
bo *num.* both
bobbiden *p.* struck with fists, insulted
borde *see* bourde
bot *conj.* but
bourde, borde *n., v.* game, story, jest
brenne *v.* burn
but if *conj.* unless, if . . . not

C

can *see* con
carp *v.* talk
catel, cautel *n.* property, wealth, possession
certes *adv.* certainly, indeed
chees(e), chese *v., p.* choose, chose
cherl *n.* churl, low-class person, villain
clepe *v.* call
clerc *n.* learned man, scholar, student, priest
cokewold *n.* cuckold
componed, compouned *p.* mixed
con, conne, cunne *v.* can, know, know how to, understand, have the ability to
conseil *n.* counsel, secret
corage *n.* spirit, heart
crips *adj.* curly

D

dan, daun *n.* sir, master, lord
dangerous, daungerous *adj.* overbearing, disdainful, haughty, aloof
defend *v.* defend, protect, forbid, prohibit
degre(e) *n.* social status

deme *v.* judge
digne *adj.* worthy, honorable
disese *n.* discomfort, distress, disease
disport *n.* pastime, recreation
dom, doom *n.* judgment
Dom, Doom *n.* Judgment, Apocalypse
doute *n.* doubt (**out of doute**, doubtless, without doubt)
drede *n.* doubt
dredeful *adj.* frightening, fearful
dronklew *adj., n.* drunk
dure(n) *v.* continue, remain, extend

E

ech, echon *pron., adj.* each, each one
eek, eke *adv., conj.* also
eer, her *n.* hair
eft(e) *adv.* again
eien, eighen, iyen *n. pl.* eyes
elde *n.* age
elles *adv.* otherwise, else
endite *v.* compose
enjoye, enjoin *v.* enjoin
ensamples *n. pl.* examples, illustrative narratives
ensocied, ensosyyd *ppl.* associated or united (in authority)
erst, erest *adv.* first
everich *pron.* every, each
everichon, overychon *pron.* each one, every one
everydeel *adv.* entirely, throughout
eye, iye, ye *n.* eye
eyen, yen *n. pl.* eyes

F

fain *adv.* gladly
faitour *n.* deceiver, false beggar

fay, fey *n.* faith (**by my fey**, truly)

fele *n., adj.* many

fil(l) *p.* fell

folde *n.* earth

fonge *v.* seize, take, receive

forthy *adv.* therefore

forwhy *adv., conj.* because, wherefore, therefore

fredom *n.* not in servitude, noble, act of generosity

free *adj.* free, noble, generous

freke *n.* man, person

fro *prep.* from

ful *adv.* very

fyn, fyne *n.* end, conclusion

G

gan *p.* began

geere, gere *n.* equipment, utensils

gentil *adj.* of noble birth, courteous, polite, handsome

gin(ne), gryn(ne) *n.* trap, scheme

gome *n.* man

gossib, gossip *n.* close friend, confidant, sponsor at baptism

gost *n.* spirit, soul

gret, greet, grete *n., adj., adv.* great (**gretter, gretteste**)

grote *n.* groat

gryn(ne) *see* gin(ne)

H

han *v.* have

harrow *interj.* help! alas!

hat *v.* has

hathel *n.* man, knight, nobleman

hatte, heet, height, hight(e) *v., p., ppl.* call, called, named

heed *see* hefd

heeng, heng *v.* hung, hanged

hefd, hed, heed, heved *n.* head

heigh *adj.* high

height *see* hatte

hem *pron.* them

hende *adj.* courteous, good-looking, generous

hente *v.* seize, take

her *see* eer

her(e), hir(e) *pron., adj.* their, her

hest(e), heeste *n.* command, commandment, promise

her(e) *see* hir(e)

herberwed, (y-)harberwide *v.* lodged

heved *see* hefd

hyghte *v., p.* wishes, looks forward to; promised; was called

hir(e), her(e), hur *pron, adj.* their, her

hit *pron.* it

ho *pron.* he, she, it, they, who

hom *pron.* them

homely *adj., adv.* simple, familiarly

hote(n), hoteth *v.* command, promise, call, name

hur *see* hir(e)

I

ilk(e) *pron., adj.* same, each, every, very

(i-)now, ynogh, innoughe *n., adj., adv.* enough, abundant, very much

incontynent *adv.* immediately

inwit(t) *n.* mind, reason, spirit, will, conscience

iwysse, ywis *adv.* indeed

iye *see* eye

iyen *see* eien

J

joyne *v.* join, enjoin

K

kan *see* con

keep, kep *n.* heed (**take keep**, pay
  attention)

ken(ne) *see* con

kinde, kende *n.* nature

knave *n.* young man, servant,
  commoner, rogue

kon *see* con

koude *v.* knew how to, could

kouth(e), kowthe *v., adj.* know,
  well known, famous

kunne *see* con

kyndeliche *adj., adv.* natural,
  naturally, innately

L

lache *v.* catch, seize, take, get

lasse *adv.* less

leere, lere *v.* learn

leesith *see* lese

leeve, lef, leve *v.* cease

leeve, leve *adj.* dear

leeveful, leeful *adj.* permitted, legal

lel(e) *adj.* loyal, true, faithful

lemman *n.* sweetheart, lover, mistress

lenger *adv.* longer

lese *n.* falsehood

lese *v.* lose

lesing(e) *ger.* lie

lest *see* list

let, lett(e) *v.* delay, hinder,
  prevent, stop

leve, leeve *adj.* dear, beloved

lever(e), levir *adv.* rather

lewed, lewid *adj.* uneducated,
  ignorant, stupid

lewte *n.* honesty, loyalty,
  adherence to law, justice

liflod(e) *n.* livelihood

liketh *v.* pleases (**him liketh**, it
  pleases him)

list, lest, lust *n.* desire, pleasure,
  lust

list(e), lest(e) *v.* wishes, desires,
  chooses

lite *adj.* little

long(e) *v.* belong, (**hit longeth**, it
  is fitting)

lordynges *n.* gentlemen, sirs

lorel *n.* rogue, beggar, fool

losel *n.* rogue, wastrel

lust *see* list

lyghtly *adv.* effortlessly

M

**Machamete, Machomete,
  Macomet** *n.* Muhammad

make *n.* mate

maugre *prep.* in spite of,
  notwithstanding

maumetri(e) *n.* idolatry

mede *n.* gift, reward

medeful *adj.* meritorious

mengid, mingid *p.* mixed, joined

menging *ger.* mixing, mixture

meschief *n.* misfortune, trouble,
  harm, plight

mete *n.* food, meal

mete *v.* dream

mikel *see* muchel

mingid *see* mengid

mo *n., adj., adv.* more

mochel *see* muchel

moot, moote, mooten *v.* must,
  may

morwe *n.* morning, morrow

moste, mot *v.* must

mowe *v.* may

muchel, mochel, mikel *n., adj.,*
    adv. much, greatly

N

namely *adv.* especially, particularly,
    that is

namo *n., adj., adv.* no more, no
    others

nat, ne, noght, nought *adv.* not

neer *adv.* nearer

neissche, nessche *adj., adv.* soft,
    softly

nice, nyse *adj.* foolish

noght *adv.* not

nolde *p.* would not, did not wish
    to

non, none *n.* noon

nones, nonys *n.* occasion (**for the
    nones**, for the moment, indeed)

noon *pron.* no one, none

noot *v.* know not

nought *adv.* not

ny, nygh(e) *adj.* near

nys *v.* is not

O

o, on, oo *pron.* one

of *adv.* off

ones, onis *adv.* once

or *prep., adv., conj.* before

other, or *conj., adv.* before

other, outher *conj.* or
    (**other . . . other**, either . . . or)

other(e), oother, othir, othre
    pron., adj. other

overal *adv.* everywhere, especially

overychon *see* everichon

owe(n) *adv.* ought

P

parde(e) *interj.* indeed, in truth

pay *n.* satisfaction, liking, pleasure

pay *v.* please

plain *see* pleyn(e)

pleyn *adj., adv.* full, clear, fully,
    clearly

pleyn(e), playne *v.* complain

pleyntis *n. pl.* complaints

preve *v.* test, prove, discover,
    demonstrate

prevy, privee *adj.* secret, private,
    invisible

Q

queynte *adj.* wise, crafty, intricate,
    fashionable, fancy

quit(e) *v.* pay, repay, requite

quod *p.* said

R

recche *v.* care

rede *v.* read, interpret, advise

reed *n.* advice

rehete *v.* show good will towards,
    rebuke

renne *v.* run

rent(e) *n.* income

ribaudes *n. pl.* rascals, foul-mouthed
    speakers

right *adv.* quite, very, completely,
    exactly

roun(e) *v.* whisper, speak

S

sad *adj.* steadfast, serious, sober,
    powerful

sauf *adj.* safe

saugh, say, seigh *p.* saw

schend(e) *see* shende

scho *pron.* she
segge *n.* person
sekyr *see* siker
sekerly *see* sikerliche
sely *adj.* blessed, worthy, simple, helpless
semely *adj.* beautiful, suitable, worthy
semely, semyly *adv.* fittingly, decorously
seth(e) *see* sitth(e)
sethen, sithen *adv.* then, afterwards
seye, seyn *v.* say
sheene, shene *adj.* bright, shiny, beautiful
shende *v.* harm, destroy, corrupt
shrew(e) *n.* rascal, scold
siker, sekyr *adj.* sure, reliable
sikerliche, sekerly *adv.* surely, confidently
sitth(e), sithen *adj., adv., conj.* since, then, after, because
skil(e) *n.* reason, knowledge
smal *adj.* slender
somdel *adv.* partly, somewhat
soth, sooth *adj.* true
soth, sothfastnesse *n.* truth
sothly *adv.* truly
spede(e) *v.* succeed, prosper
stei(e), steygh, sty(e) *v.* rise, ascend
sterve *v.* die, starve
stinte *v.* stop
streyt *adj.* strict
streytly *adv.* strictly, exactly
sweven(e) *n.* dream
swich, swilc *adj.* such, the same
swink(e) *n., v.* physical labor, work
swithe, swithely *adv.* very, very much, quickly

swive *v.* have sex with
sy *p.* saw
syn *conj.* since

T

than(ne) *adv.* then
that *pron.* what
thee, theen *v.* thrive (**so moot I thee**, as I may prosper)
ther as *conj.* in which, where
thilke *adj.* this, that same
this, thise these
tho *adv.* when, then
tho *pron., adj.* those
thoughte *v.* seemed (**me thoughte, it thoughte me**, it seemed to me)
thries *adv.* thrice
thriftili *adv.* properly, suitably
til(l) *prep.* to
to *prep.* until
togidre *adv.* together
touchyng(e) *prep.* concerning
travail(le) *n., v.* work
triste *n., adj.* trust
trowe *v.* trust, think, believe
trowing *ger.* belief, opinion
twey *num.* two

U

uche *adj.* each
unbuxomnes(se) *n.* disobedience
unethe, unneth(e) *adv.* with difficulty, rarely, scarcely, virtually

V

verreili, verreilich(e), verrily *adv.* truly

verrey, verray, verry *adj.* true

vilein *n.* unfree tenant, commoner

vileynye *adv.* rudeness, discourtesy

vitaille *n.* victuals, food

W

weit(e) *see* wit(e)

wend(e) *v.* go

wenden *ppl.* believed

wen(e), weene *v.* believe, anticipate, suppose, think, imagine

wern(e) *v.* deny, refuse

werrey *see* verrey

werrily *see* verreili

whan, whanne *adv., conj.* when

whylom *adv.* once, once upon a time, formerly

wif *n.* woman, wife

wight *n.* person, creature

wisse *v.* instruct, advise, guide, direct

wiste *p.* knew

wit *n.* consciousness, reason, wisdom, intelligence

wit *prep.* with

wit(e), weit(e) *v.* know, find out, understand

withal, withalle *adv.* also, indeed

wol *v.* will

wolde *v.* would, wished, would wish

won(e) *v., p.* live, reside, dwell; accustomed, habituated

wonede *n.* dwelling

wood, wod(e) *adj.* insane

woot, wot *v.* know, knows

worthe *v.* be, become

wost(e) *p.* knew, learned

wrooth, wroth *adj.* angry, apprehensive

wust *ppl.* known

Y

yaf *p.* gave

ye *interj.* yea, indeed

ye *see* eye

yede *p.* went

yen *see* eyen

yerne *adv.* enthusiastically, earnestly

yeve(n), yive *v.* give

yif *conj.* if

yis *adv.* yes, yes indeed

Bibliography

History and art reference sources

Besant, Sir Walter (ed.) (1906) *Mediaeval London*. London: Adam and Charles Black.

Cheney, C. R. (ed.) (2000) *A Handbook of Dates for Students of British History*, revd. M. Jones. Cambridge: Cambridge University Press.

Fritze, D. H. and W. B. Robison (eds.) (2002) *Historical Dictionary of Late Medieval England, 1272–1485*. Westport, CT: Greenwood Press.

Fryde, E. B., et al. (eds.) (1986) *Handbook of British Chronology*, 3rd edn. Cambridge: Cambridge University Press.

Gransden, A. (1982) *Historical Writing in England, vol. 2: c. 1307 to the Early Sixteenth Century*. London: Routledge.

Graves, E. B. (ed.) (1975) *A Bibliography of English History to 1485*. Oxford: Clarendon Press.

Guide to the Contents of the Public Record Office (1963–8) 3 vols. London: Her Majesty's Stationery Office.

Kennedy, E. D. (ed.) (1989) *Chronicles and Other Historical Writings*. In A. E. Hartung (ed.) *A Manual of the Writings in Middle English, 1050–1500*, vol. 8. Hamden: Connecticut Academy of Arts and Sciences.

Previté-Orton, C. W. and Z. N. Brooke (eds.) (1936) *The Cambridge Medieval History*, vol. 8. Cambridge: Cambridge University Press.

Sandler, L. F. (1986) *Gothic Manuscripts, 1285–1385*, 2 vols. A Survey of Manuscripts Illuminated in the British Isles 5. London: Harvey Miller.

Scott, K. L. (1996) *Later Gothic Manuscripts, 1390–1490*, 2 vols. A Survey of Manuscripts Illuminated in the British Isles 6. London: Harvey Miller.

Strayer, J. R. (ed.) (1982–9) *Dictionary of the Middle Ages*, 13 vols. New York: Scribner.

Szarmach, P. E., M. T. Tavormina, and J. T. Rosenthal (eds.) (1998) *Medieval England: An Encyclopedia*. New York: Garland.

Vauchez, A. (ed.), A. Walfrod (trans.) (2000) *Encyclopedia of the Middle Ages*. Chicago, IL: Fitzroy Dearborn.

Selected anthologies of historical and cultural sources

Amt, E. (ed.) (1993) *Women's Lives in Medieval Europe: A Sourcebook*. New York: Routledge.

—— (ed.) (2001) *Medieval England, 1000–1500: A Reader*. Peterborough, Ont.: Broadview Press.

Barratt, A. (ed.) (1992) *Women's Writing in Middle English*. London: Longman.

Benson, L. D. and T. M. Andersson (eds. and trans.) (1971) *The Literary Context of Chaucer's Fabliaux*. Indianapolis, IN: Bobbs-Merrill.

Bentley, S. (ed.) (1833) *Excerpta Historica, or Illustrations of English History*. London: Richard Bentley.

Bryan, W. F. and G. Dempster (eds.) (1941) *Sources and Analogues of Chaucer's Canterbury Tales*. Chicago, IL: University of Chicago Press.

Chambers, R. W. and M. Daunt (eds.) (1967) [1931] *A Book of London English, 1384–1425*. Oxford: Clarendon Press.

Correale, R. M. and M. Hamel (eds.) (2002) *Sources and Analogues of Chaucer's Canterbury Tales*, vol. 1. Cambridge: D. S. Brewer.

Crow, M. M. and C. C. Olson (eds.) (1966) *Chaucer Life-Records*. Oxford: Clarendon Press.

Dobson, R. B. (ed.) (1983) *The Peasants' Revolt of 1381*. London: Macmillan.

Geary, P. J. (ed.) (1989) *Readings in Medieval History*. Peterborough, Ont.: Broadview Press.

Given-Wilson, C. (ed. and trans.) (1993) *Chronicles of the Revolution, 1397–1400: The Reign of Richard II*. Manchester: Manchester University Press.

Goldberg, P. J. P. (ed.) (1995) *Women in England, c. 1275–1525: Documentary Sources*. Manchester: Manchester University Press.

Gray, D. (ed.) (1985) *The Oxford Book of Late Medieval Verse and Prose*. Oxford: Clarendon Press.

Havely, N. R. (ed. and trans.) (1992) *Chaucer's Boccaccio: Sources of Troilus and the Knight's and Franklin's Tales*. Woodbridge, Suffolk: D. S. Brewer.

Hudson, A. (ed.) (1997) *Selections from English Wycliffite Writings*. Toronto: University of Toronto Press.

Miller, R. P. (ed.) (1977) *Chaucer: Sources and Backgrounds*. New York: Oxford University Press.

Minnis, A. J. and A. B. Scott (eds.) (1988) *Medieval Literary Theory and Criticism, c. 1100–c. 1375: The Commentary-Tradition*. Oxford: Clarendon Press.

Myers, A. R. (1969) *English Historical Documents, 1327–1485*. London: Eyre and Spottiswoode.

Oman, C. (ed.) (1969) [1906] *The Great Revolt of 1381*. New York: Greenwood Press.

Rickert, E. (ed.) (1968) [1948] *Chaucer's World*. New York: Columbia University Press.

Riley, H. T. (ed. and trans.) (1868) *Memorials of London and London Life in the XIIIth, XIVth, and XVth Centuries*. London: Longmans, Green.

Sharpe, R. R. (ed.) (1899–1912) *Calendar of Letter-books Preserved among the Archives of the Corporation of the City of London at the Guildhall*, 11 vols. London: J. E. Francis.

Williams, C. H. (ed.) (1967) *English Historical Documents, 1485–1558*. London: Eyre and Spottiswoode.

Windeatt, B. A. (ed.) (1982) *Chaucer's Dream Poetry: Sources and Analogues*. Woodbridge, Suffolk: D. S. Brewer.

Other sources cited in introductions and notes

Al-Qur'an: A Contemporary Translation (1984). Trans. A. Ali. Princeton, NJ: Princeton University Press.

Alexander of Tralles (1963) [1878] *Alexander von Tralles: Original-text und Übersetzung nebst einer einleitenden Abhandlung*, ed. T. Puschmann. Amsterdam: A. M. Hakkert.

Anderson, B. (1991) *Imagined Communities: Reflections on the Origin and Spread of Nationalism*, revd. edn. London: Verso.

Aristotle (1995) *On the Heavens I and II*, ed. and trans. S. Leggatt. Warminster, Wiltshire: Aris and Phillips.

Augustine of Hippo (1987, 1991) [1841] *Sermones*. Patrologia Latina 38, 39, ed. J.-P. Migne. Turnhout: Brepols.

—— (1992) [1841] *Retraciones*. Patrologia Latina 32, ed. J.-P. Migne. Turnhout: Brepols.

Avicenna (1930) *A Treatise on the Canon of Medicine of Avicenna*, ed. and trans. O. C. Gruner. London: Luzac.

Bartholomeus Anglicus (1975–88). *De proprietatibus rerum. On the Properties of Things*, 3 vols., trans. J. Trevisa, ed. M. C. Seymour. Oxford: Clarendon Press.

Bede (1992) *Bede's Ecclesiastical History of the English People*, ed. and trans. B. Colgrave and R. A. B. Mynors. Oxford: Clarendon Press.

Bible (1989) [1899] *The Holy Bible: Translated from the Latin Vulgate*. Douay-Rheims Version. Rockford, IL: Tan.

Boccaccio, Giovanni (1972) *The Decameron*, trans. G. H. McWilliam. Harmondsworth: Penguin Books.

Boethius (1997) [1847] *In librum Aristotelis de interpretatione*. Patrologia Latina 64, ed. J.-P. Migne. Turnhout: Brepols, 293–333.

Clement, V. (1959) [1881] *Corpus juris canonici*, vol. 2, ed. A. L. Richter and E. Friedberg. Graz: Akademische Druck: U Verlagsanstalt.

Constantine the African (1994) *Constantine the African and 'Ali ibn al-'Abbas al-Magusi: The Pantegni and Related Texts*, ed. C. Burnett and D. Jacquart. Leiden: E. I. Brill.

Galen (1997) *Selected Works*, ed. and trans. P. N. Singer. Oxford: Oxford University Press.

Gaston de Foix (Gaston Phoebus) (1971) *Livre de chasse*, ed. G. Tilander. Stockholm: Almqvist och Wiksell.

Geoffrey of Monmouth (1984–95) *The Historia regum Britanniae of Geoffrey of Monmouth*, 5 vols., ed. and trans. N. Wright. Cambridge: D. S. Brewer.

Gerald of Wales (1868) *Itinerarium Cambriae. Giraldi Cambrensis Opera*, vol. 6, ed. J. S. Brewer, J. F. Dimock, and G. F. Warner. London: Longman, Green, Reader, and Dyer.

Gregory the Great (1979) *Moralia in Job*, 3 vols., ed. M. Adriaen. Turnhout: Brepols.

—— (1982) *Registrum epistolarum*, 2 vols., ed. D. Norberg. Turnhout: Brepols.

Henry of Huntingdon (2002) *The History of the English People, 1000–1154*, ed. and trans. D. Greenway. Oxford: Oxford University Press.

Hugh of St. Victor (1854) *De sacramentis Christianae fidei*. Patrologia Latina 176, ed. J. P. Migne. Turnhout: Brepols.

Jacobus de Voragine (1993, 1995) *The Golden Legend: Readings on the Saints*, 2 vols., trans. W. G. Ryan. Princeton, NJ: Princeton University Press.

Jerome, St. (1983) [1845] *Adversus Jovinianum*. Patrologia Latina 23, ed. J.-P. Migne. Turnhout: Brepols.

—— (1986) [1845] *Epistolae*. Patrologia Latina 22, ed. J.-P. Migne. Turnhout: Brepols.

McCann, J. (ed. and trans.) (1952) *The Rule of St. Benedict*. London: Burns and Oates.

Map, Walter (1983) *De nugis curialium: Courtier's Trifles*, ed. M. R. James. Revd. edn. and trans. C. N. L. Brooke and R. A. B. Mynors. Oxford: Clarendon Press.

Prester John (1982) *The Hebrew Letters of Prester John*, ed. and trans. E. Ullendorff and C. F. Beckingham. Oxford: Oxford University Press.

Regnault, L. (ed.) (1999) *Vie des pères. The Day-to-Day Life of the Desert Fathers in Fourth-century Egypt*, trans. E. Poirier, Jr. Petersham, MA: St. Bede's.

Richard of St. Victor (1989) [1855]. *Benjamin major*. Patrologia Latina 196, ed. J.-P. Migne. Turnhout: Brepols.

Strachey, J. (ed.) (1767–77) *Rotuli Parliamentorum*, 6 vols. London.

Vincent of Beauvais (1964) [1624] *Speculum historiale. Speculum quadruplex, sive: speculum maius, naturale, doctrinale, morale, historiale*, vol. 4. Graz: Akademische Druk-U Verlagsanstalt.

Walsingham, Thomas (1863–4) *Thomae Walsingham, quondam monachi S. Albani, historia Anglicana, 1272–1422*, 2 vols., ed. H. T. Riley. London: Longman, Green, Longman, Roberts, and Green.

William of Malmesbury (1870) *De gestis pontificum Anglorum*, ed. N. E. S. A. Hamilton. London: Longman.

Index

Names, titles, and page numbers in bold type are for main entries of excerpts and images.

Smithfield, London, 151, 175, 186, 188–9, 226–9
Sodom and Gomorrah, 117; *see also* sex
sodomy, *see* sex
South English Legendary, 147
Southampton, Suffolk, 172
Spenser, Sir Hugh, *see* Despenser
Stanford-le-Hope, Essex, 177
Statute of Laborers (1351), 163–4, **166–9**, 174
Statutes of the Realm, **164–9**, 215–16, **216–19**
strangers, *see* Others
Strayler, Alan, illuminator, 154, Golden Book of St. Albans, 155
Strohm, Paul, xxxi
Sudbury, Simon, archbishop of Canterbury 1375–81, 175, 180, 181–2, 184–6
Suffolk, 175, 178, 236
Suffolk, earl of, Michael de la Pole (ca. 1330–89), 69, 181
Suffolk, earl of, Robert de Ufford (1298–1369), 171
sumptuary, 4, 7, 41, 44, 54, 55, 98, 116, 123, 127–8, 129, 130, 132, 158–9, 165, 167, 210, 215–24, 228, 266–7; legislation (1336, 1337, 1363, 1463–4, 1477, 1483), 215–19
Surrey, duke of, *see* Kent
Surrey, earl of, *see* Arundel
Suso, Heinrich (ca. 1295–ca. 1366), *Horologium sapientiae (Clock of Wisdom)*, 1
Sustead, Norfolk, 126

Tartary, 170–1
taxation, 21, 79, 163–4, 168–9, 174, 175, 176, 177; *see also* tithes
textual analysis, *see enarratio*
Thalestris, queen of the Amazons, 90, 91–2, 107

Theophrastus (ca. 372–ca. 287 BCE), *Aureolus liber Theophrasti de nuptiis*, 238
Thirning, William, 72, 83, 87
Thomas, Ernest, 236
Thomas of Hereford, St. (ca. 1218–82), 174
Thomas of Woodstock, *see* Gloucester, duke of
Thorpe, William (fl. ca. 1350), 32–3; *Testimony*, 33–7
tithes, 10, 11–12; Lollards on, 33, 67; *see also* taxation
Tobias, husband of Sara, 96, 117
tournaments, 224–31
Tower of London, *see* London
translation, 239, 246
Trefnant, John, bishop of Hereford 1389–1404, 72
Tretise of Miraclis Pleyinge, A, 262–3, 263–72
Trevisa, John (ca. 1342–1402), 8–9; **translation of Bartholomeus Anglicus' *De proprietatibus rerum* (*On the Properties of Things*)**, 9, 14, **15–21**; **translation of Fitzralph's *Defense of the Curates*, 8, 10–13; translation of Higden's *Polychronicon*, 9, 51, 52–5, 259, 260–2**
trivium, 249
Tyler, Wat (d. 1381), 151, 180, 185, 186–9

Ufford, Robert de, *see* Suffolk
unction, Lollards on, 67
universities, 8; *see also* individual institutions and colleges
Urban VI, pope 1378–89, 51
usurpation, xxix, 69–87

Vere, de, *see* Oxford
vernacularity, *see* English language